BROADCASTING BUILDINGS

The MIT Press
Cambridge, Massachusetts
London, England

BROADCASTING BUILDINGS
Architecture on the Wireless, 1927–1945

SHUNDANA YUSAF

© 2014 Shundana Yusaf

All rights reserved. No part of this book may be reproduced in any form by any electronic or mechanical means (including photocopying, recording, or information storage and retrieval) without permission in writing from the publisher.

MIT Press books may be purchased at special quantity discounts for business or sales promotional use. For information, please email special_sales@mitpress.mit.edu.

This book was set in Clarendon and Chaparral by The MIT Press. Printed and bound in the United States of America.

Library of Congress Cataloging-in-Publication Data

Yusaf, Shundana, 1970–
Broadcasting buildings : architecture on the wireless, 1927–1945 / Shundana Yusaf.
    pages   cm
Includes bibliographical references and index.
ISBN 978-0-262-02674-1 (hardcover : alk. paper) 1. Mass media and architecture—Great Britain—History—20th century. 2. Radio broadcasting—Social aspects—Great Britain—History—20th century. 3. British Broadcasting Corporation. I. Title.
NA2543.M37Y87 2014
720.1'08—dc23
                                                            2013023057

10 9 8 7 6 5 4 3 2 1

For tough love and my parents, Fahima and Yusaf
For kind support, Tariq and Cherie

Every established order tends to produce the naturalization of its own arbitrariness.

The most successful ideological effects are those which have no need for words, and ask no more than complicitous silence.

PIERRE BOURDIEU

CONTENTS

List of Illustrations   ix
Preface   xv
Acknowledgments   xvii

Introduction   1

    I Wireless University   1
    II Electric Hearth   9
    III Broadcasting House   19
    IV Organization of the Book   29

1 Figure of Speech: The Place of Radio in the Space of Architecture   35

    I Speech as Action   35
    II Practice without Practice   41
    III Cathedral for the Production of Belief   43

2 The Order of Things: The Place of Architecture in the Space of Radio   83

    I Qualities of Radiophonic Architecture   83
    II The Predicament of Broadcast Culture   91
    III Architecture to the Rescue   95

3 The Politics of Broadcasting and the Broadcasting of Politics   119

    I Art Appreciation   119
    II Good Housekeeping   127
    III Preservation of England   130
    IV The Culture of Listening and the Debate on Flats versus Cottages   139
    V Obstruction to Political Programming   157
    VI The Necessity of Culture   160

4 Speaking of Conservation: The Oral Travelogue and British Historical Imagination   167

    I Oral Travel Guides   167
    II Geoffrey Maxwell Boumphrey: Landscape as Event   185
    III John Betjeman: Town as Scene   194
    IV John Summerson: Stately Heritage as Library   204

5 The Box on the Dresser: The Sacralization of Contemporary Everyday Spaces   217

    I The Street in the Age of Its Radiophonic Diffusion   217
    II The Town in the Age of Its Wireless Dispersion   230
    III The English House in the Age of Its Wireless Dispersion   243

Conclusion: Notes on Method and Other Things   263

Notes   271
Bibliography   305
Index   321

ILLUSTRATIONS

I.1. BBC Radiophonic Workshop at Broadcasting House, producing synthetic sound montages. Courtesy: The BBC.   3
I.2. BBC pamphlet from 1929 accompanying broadcasts created for schools. © Immediate Media Company London Limited.   5
I.3. Illustration accompanying an article by John Summerson in the *Listener*, February 1938. © Immediate Media Company London Limited.   6
I.4. John Reith, BBC's first director general (1927–1938). Courtesy: The BBC. Hilda Matheson, BBC's first director of talks (1926–1931). Courtesy: National Portrait Gallery.   13
I.5. Listening to the radio at home during the 1920s. Courtesy: U.S. Library of Congress.   15
I.6. George Val Myer, west façade of Broadcasting House, London, 1932. Courtesy: Howard Stanbury.   21
I.7. Edward Maufe, studio for religious services at Broadcasting House, London, 1932. Courtesy: *Architectural Review*.   23
I.8. Dorothy Trotter, Studio 3D at Broadcasting House, London, 1932. Courtesy: *Architectural Review*.   24
I.9. Wells Coates, Studio 6E at Broadcasting House, London, 1932. Courtesy: The BBC.   26
I.10. Eric Gill, sculpture of Prospero and Ariel on the front of Broadcasting House, London, 1932. Courtesy: Ben Sutherland.   28
I.11. George Val Myer, Broadcasting House, London, 1932: steel frame construction clad with traditional masonry work and punctured windows. Courtesy: The BBC.   30
I.12. John Nash's All Souls Church, London (1823), with the Langham Hotel (1865) to its left and Broadcasting House (1932) behind. Courtesy: The BBC.   32

1.1. H. S. Goodhart-Rendel, National Lecture on "Architecture in a Changing World," broadcast on October 4, 1938, printed in the *Listener*. © Immediate Media Company London Limited.   36

1.2. Outreach activities of architects: students mounting the Modern Architecture Research Group (MARS) exhibition, London, 1934. Courtesy: John Allan.   45

1.3. Broadcasting House, cover of August 1932 issue of *Architectural Review* devoted to the building. Courtesy: *Architectural Review*.   48

1.4. John Summerson, talk on "Creative Housing," printed in the *Listener* in August 1937, featuring L. H. Keay, St. Andrew's Gardens, Liverpool, of the same year. © Immediate Media Company London Limited.   54

1.5. The pros and cons of public and private spending on social amenities, illustrated by John Summerson in the *Listener*, January 1938. © Immediate Media Company London Limited.   56

1.6. The pleasures of light, air, and space in contemporary schools, illustrated in Anthony Bertram, *Design in Everyday Things*, 1937. © Immediate Media Company London Limited.   57

1.7. A recent view of Fleet Street, showcased in the 1940 *Listener* article by Herbert Read to illustrate the visual confusion of a street born of laissez-faire planning policy. The street since has lost most of its distracting canvas canopies and jarring signage. Courtesy: Ronald James.   60

1.8. Royal Tweed Bridge, Northumberland, England, 1925–1928, constructed by Mouchel & Partners. Courtesy: Barbara Passmore.   63

1.9. Howard Robertson, broadcast on "Structure and Material," published in the *Listener*, May 1930, featuring a steel frame church, Cologne, 1928. © Immediate Media Company London Limited.   64

1.10. The glass walls, white surfaces, and pristine volumes of Joseph Emberton's Royal Corinthian Yacht Club in Essex, 1931, upheld as examples of responsible design. Courtesy: Richard McDonald-Proctor.   69

1.11. Examples provided by Elizabeth Denby of kitchen equipment and layout that would save energy and time, in John Gloag, ed., *Design in Modern Life*, 1934. Courtesy: Taylor & Francis Books (UK).   74

1.12. John Wood the Elder and the Younger, King's Circus, Bath, 1754–1768. Courtesy: Mollie Johanson.   78

2.1. Dreaming of the house of the future. Courtesy: Neenah History.   85

2.2. Challenges of comparing traditional and modern designs: a comparison of chairs designed in wood and fabric by Chippendale and in tubular metal and leather by Serge Chermayeff; Newspaper Printing Office, Abo, Finland, 1929, an example of rational design where the shape of the concrete pillars varies "in thickness according to the strains involved." *Listener*, April 1933. © Immediate Media Company London Limited.   88

2.3. Useful art on the cover of Anthony Bertram, *Design in Everyday Things*, 1937. © Immediate Media Company London Limited.   97

2.4. Design in everyday objects, in Anthony Bertram, *Design in Everyday Things*, 1937. © Immediate Media Company London Limited.   98

2.5. History of the physical environment as history of world, BBC pamphlet, 1937. © Immediate Media Company London Limited.   99

2.6. Hadrian's Wall, begun in AD 122, Northumbria National Park, England. Courtesy: Terry Morgan.   102

2.7. The street in the nineteenth and twentieth centuries, broadcast in March 1930 and published in the BBC pamphlet by J. E. Barton, *Modern Art: The Changing World*, 1930. © Immediate Media Company London Limited.   104

2.8. Eric Newton and H. S. Goodhart-Rendel, interview "Artist and Architect," *Listener*, February 1940. © Immediate Media Company London Limited.   106

2.9. Sir Reginald Blomfield in "Is Modern Architecture on the Right Track?—A Symposium," *Listener*, July 1933, featuring George Checkley, Willow House, Cambridge, 1932. © Immediate Media Company London Limited.   108

2.10. Charles Holden, Sudbury Town Station, London, 1925–1935. Courtesy: Amanda Vincent-Rous.   110

2.11. P. Morton Shand, "The Changing Bridge," broadcast on October 4, 1937, printed in the *Listener*. © Immediate Media Company London Limited.   112

2.12. Anthony Bertram, "What Is a House?," *Listener*, October 1937. © Immediate Media Company London Limited.   114

3.1. Sculpture of Clough Williams-Ellis at the Italianate village of Portmeirion, designed by him in North Wales, 1925–1975. Courtesy: Jude Hall.   120

3.2. Clough Williams-Ellis, Portmeirion in North Wales, 1925–1975. Courtesy: Jude Hall.   122

3.3. Example of a program on good housekeeping by Leslie Menzies, published in one of the earliest issues of the *Listener* in February 1929. © Immediate Media Company London Limited.   129

3.4. Cover of a February 1929 *Listener* containing C. R. Ashbee's broadcast review of an exhibition. © Immediate Media Company London Limited.   132

3.5. Madresfield Court, a quintessential arts and crafts stately home; C. R. Ashbee designed its library. Courtesy: Michael Marrison.   133

3.6. A montage made out of images from the "Ugliness Exhibition," reviewed on air by C. R. Ashbee, *Listener*, February 1929. © Immediate Media Company London Limited.   135

3.7. Locals in the Lion & Lamb, a pub in Hoxton, enjoying a broadcast. Courtesy: The English Heritage.   140

3.8. A winding street in Wythenshawe, Manchester, built in the 1920s, Ernest Simon's image of the better life available in council housing built for suburban living in the gardens. Against it, G. M. Boumphrey places the vertically stacked horizontal lines of flats in Kenner House, Manchester, built in the 1930s as a more prudent approach to housing, *Listener*, October 1935. © Immediate Media Company London Limited   143

3.9. Balcony of a modern flat in Mount Royal, Oxford Street, London; cottages and gardens in Wythenshawe; *Listener*, October 1935. © Immediate Media Company London Limited.   146

3.10. Pamphlet for School Broadcasts, 1933. © Immediate Media Company London Limited.   152

3.11. The *Listener*, November 1934. © Immediate Media Company London Limited.   154

3.12. Pamphlet for School Broadcasts, 1936. © Immediate Media Company London Limited.   155

3.13. Pamphlet for Adult Education, 1932. © Immediate Media Company London Limited.   156

4.1. Ironbridge over the River Severn, Coalbrookdale, 1781. Courtesy: Paul Clarke.   169

4.2. Tram lines in Bristol, 1932. Courtesy: "Collection of Nick Booker, original copyright holder unknown."   171

4.3. Newstead Abbey, originally a twelfth-century monastery and later the seat of the Byron family. Courtesy: Kim Kiddle.   172–173

4.4. Pamphlet, *Travel Talks*, 1937. © Immediate Media Company London Limited.   176

4.5. Bridgnorth Castle's Leaning Tower, Shropshire, twelfth century. Courtesy: Shrewsbury Museums Service, photograph by P. Morris.   187

4.6. Badbury Rings, an Iron Age hill fort in east Dorset, dating from 800 BC. Courtesy: Committee of Aerial Photography, University of Cambridge. Photographed by Dr. J. K. St. Joseph.   190

4.7. John Betjeman broadcasting during the Second World War. Courtesy: simplymediarights.com.   195

4.8. Bedford Street, Plymouth, 1930. Courtesy: Richard and Gill Long.   197

4.9. The rural vernacular captured in John Betjeman's article "The Passing of the Village," *Architectural Review*, September 1932. Courtesy: *Architectural Review*.   199

4.10. Thomas Tresham, Triangular Lodge at Rushton Hall, Northamptonshire, 1593–1597. Courtesy: Kelvin Barber.   205

4.11. John Vanbrugh, Blenheim Palace, Oxfordshire, 1705–1724. Courtesy: Kathy Pearmain.   209

4.12. Compton Wynyates, Warwickshire, dating from at least 1204 AD. Photographer unknown.   212

4.13. Moundfield Road, Stamford Hill, showing the destruction of the English built landscape during the war. Courtesy: Duncan.   214

5.1. Frank Pick on the cover of *Architectural Review*, August 1942. Courtesy: *Architectural Review*.   218

5.2. An early London Underground map, commissioned by Frank Pick and designed by Henry Beck in 1933. Courtesy: Tricia Wang.   222

5.3. Posters commissioned by Frank Pick. Dover Street Underground station, 1930s. Courtesy: London Transport Museum.   222

5.4. Street signs pictured in Frank Pick's article "Design in the Street," in John Gloag, ed., *Design in Modern Life*, 1934. Courtesy: Taylor & Francis Books (UK).   224

5.5. Thinking through consumer goods to explore what the public wants, in Anthony Bertram, *Design in Everyday Things*, 1937. © Immediate Media Company London Limited.   227

5.6. Unit furniture, illustrated in Anthony Bertram, *Design in Everyday Things*, 1937. © Immediate Media Company London Limited.   228

5.7. G. M. Boumphrey, *Your Home and Mine*, BBC pamphlet, 1937. © Immediate Media Company London Limited.   232

5.8. Page from Maxwell Fry's article "Can Belfast Be Reshaped?," *Listener*, November 1936. © Immediate Media Company London Limited.   234

5.9. Scenic setting of Portrush, Northern Ireland, representing town and country as discrete entities. Courtesy: National Library of Ireland.   236

5.10. Ribbon development as an inadequate response to the congestion of cities, causing the destruction of the countryside. Courtesy: Länsmuseet Gävleborg.   239

5.11. Home listening, circa 1935–1940. Courtesy: Bryan Costin.   245

5.12. Modern domestic equipment as great bargains available in the market, illustrated in Anthony Bertram, *Design in Everyday Things*, 1937. © Immediate Media Company London Limited.   246

5.13. Example of type dwelling: Gerrard Gardens, tenement housing, Liverpool. Courtesy: Twentieth Century Images.   249

5.14. A comparison of the cluttered Victorian home to the spacious type dwelling, illustrated in Anthony Bertram, *Design in Everyday Things*, 1937. © Immediate Media Company London Limited.   252

5.15. Frank Lloyd Wright, Robie House, Chicago, 1909. Courtesy: Library of Congress Prints and Photographs Division, Washington, D.C.   255

5.16. Anthony Bertram, illustration showing the evolution of the house starting with the fortified Norman castle and culminating in Le Corbusier's Villa Stein, in "What Is a House?," *Listener*, October 1937. © Immediate Media Company London Limited.   260

PREFACE

This book is a reworking of my doctoral dissertation, "Wireless Sites: Architecture in the Space of British Radio (1927–1945)." The dissertation, 40,000 words longer than what you hold in your hand, was submitted in 2011 to the School of Architecture, Princeton University, for a degree in the history and theory of architecture. This is an interdisciplinary academic book that I hope will be valuable to academic, research, and public librarians; scholars and students in all fields of humanities; and a general audience interested in British history and twentieth-century architecture. Students will find in it new research tools and a model for handling large quantities of data. It should be rewarding for thinkers and practitioners in visual arts, especially those attentive to the changing contours of the history and theory of cultural production.

    I was originally attracted to studying British architecture while exploring the triad of aesthetic modernity, imperialism, and the welfare state. For this, the early BBC's patronage of modern architecture through its hundreds of broadcasts and sound bites by designers, educators, critics, curators, government officials, and public-minded patrons seemed a low-hanging fruit. Not only did the BBC fashion itself as a semiautonomous public service corporation, but the pioneers of its World Service clearly recognized broadcasting as the form empire took in the modern day. They took as their responsibility the protection of traditional imperial institutions and their interests. However, unbeknown to me, the German bombing of Britain during World War II had redesigned the archive. None of the records of cultural programming from the early days of broadcasting—which were also the final days of the British Empire—have survived. The surviving historical documents proposed a different path, and I like a trusting child went exploring. What follows is an account of the BBC's programs on architecture for British and Irish consumption only.

In Britain, "wireless" and "radio" are synonymous terms, and I use them that way in this book. I call the BBC's radio broadcasts on the built environment "wireless sites," for this term sets up the most prominent theme of the book: the oxymoronic relationship between the placelessness of radiophony and the situatedness of architecture. As such, "wireless sites" can be perceived as an interface between the nonhumanistic impulses of technology and the humanist conception of architecture.

ACKNOWLEDGMENTS

Writing and reading are arduous and collective activities. I have taken on many debts with no real possibilities of repayment. First of all, Hélène Lipstadt trusted me, gave me moral and intellectual support, and cultivated a friendship that strengthened as thoughts formed into words and chapters. Christine Boyer read several drafts of this work and gave me directions to different destinations. Our long conversations at her dining table profoundly shaped my goals and ideas. She taught me how to get my hands dirty and dig into data without losing control over it. Mark Jarzombek taught me how to think big while Peter Mandler taught me to how to think small and tread lightly and delicately through evidence. Arindam Dutta read an early version of the book and pushed me to think creatively. Spyridon Papapetros carefully combed through the later version and helped me reorganize the argument forcefully and clearly. This project would have collapsed without their faith and unconditional support.

 A number of grants from Princeton University allowed me to spend time in archives in London and Reading. A grant from the Paul Mellon Institute in London gave me an opportunity to live in London and to befriend the BBC radio staff as well as British architects, architectural critics, and cultural historians.

The wonderful writing environment in Bedford Square at the Institute did much to give me momentum.

No project is possible without librarians. They not only guide us but also research for us. I have benefited from many reference librarians at Princeton's Firestone Library and the New York Public Library, but my most sustained supporters have been the staff at the School of Architecture at Princeton. Ellen Bonin, Christine Shungu, Shabeha Baig-Gyan, and the late Frances Chen kept me updated on publications of potential interest and turned the library into a nurturing home for me. Special thanks go to Erin O'Neill at the BBC Written Archives in Caversham Park, as well as to librarians at Government Document, Lamont, and Widener libraries at Harvard University; Rotch Library at MIT; RIBA Archives at the Victoria and Albert Museum; British Library Sound Archives; and finally Pratt Institute, where the final stages of the manuscript's corrections and proofreading took place.

Audrey Welber and Lori Handleman combed through my South Asian take on the English language. Anjali Aiyappa helped proofread. Teachers and friends who contributed in one way or another include Esther da Costa Meyer, Stephen Kotkin, Rubén Gallo, Anson Rabinbach, Gyan Prakash, Stephen Marglin, Frederique Marglin, Erin Carraher, Elpitha Tsoutsounakis, Leila Ahmed, Dayle Davison, Shafqat Khan, Nudia and Hasan Usmani, Yusaf and the late Lubna Agha. I have had the good fortune of getting advice at different stages of reading and writing from Alan Powers, Jules Lubbock, Andrew Saint, Mario Carpo, Adrian Forty, Mark Crinson, and Tim Benton. Janna Israel, Adnan Morshed, Deborah Kully, Pamela Karimi, Tijana Vujosevic, Sarah Brookes, Sarah Rogers, and Winnie Wong have been my comrades in writing. André Bideau, Steven Thrasher, and Ralph Ghoche stood by me. Luna, Mishka, Kiyan, and Ramis helped me disentangle thoughts just with their comforting presence. Daniel Evangelos Neofitos helped see the manuscript to the press.

I had a child in the first year of my Ph.D. coursework at Princeton. Much more space is required to thank everyone who took care of her so I could write. Scheherezade Banuri, now eleven, has read several transcripts to me to make sure I've quoted correctly. Finally, this book would not have happened without Tariq Banuri, who will always remain my moral and intellectual compass.

INTRODUCTION

I Wireless University

Mass media have transformed the social role of architecture. From film to television, billboards to smart phones, new communication systems have chipped away at the traditional function of buildings as landmarks, markers of identity, and repositories of collective memory. It is now modern signage, not architecture, which organizes public space. The traditional city of experience and memory, the city of mental maps and architectural gestures, has given way to the city of information, advertisement, and consumption. Victor Hugo predicted that "the book will destroy the edifice" by robbing it of its commemorative function. Though this didn't happen with the book, the intrusive growth of advertisement and interactive media has certainly seen to it. Michael Hays calls this condition "architecture's total loss of the real."[1] As Hugo would have it, "this has [finally] killed that."[2]

In this book, I consider the unstudied role played by the medium of radio in architecture's loosening grip on the real. More simply, it is a history of architecture in the space of early British radio. Its technology—the ear and the voice of the interwar and wartime periods—then was under the legislatively protected monopoly of the British Broadcasting Corporation. I begin with the following questions: What happened when the built environment, with its physical and visual mode of knowledge and exercising power, was subjected to the productive, reproductive, and diffusive logic of an electronic medium? What happened when the traditional safeguards of the medium of architecture disappeared? What did radio do to the relationship between art and publicity, British architecture and modernism, and popular culture and built heritage?

Broadcasting in Europe and elsewhere was institutionalized after World War I. It became instantly popular wherever a booster pole went up. Millions of people heard the world through the box on the dresser. From then onward, the dull noises of the house and the mindless tedium of housework had new company at the hearth. The breaths and heartbeats that animated the words of the pre-typographic poet and storyteller returned with a vengeance. Granted infinite reach, disembodied voices channeled democratic change, anticolonial resistance, American popular culture, Mussolini's terror, Hitler's tactics, and Stalin's iron fist through the box on the dresser.

But radio was not a neutral channel for political and cultural change. Like every other technology, it changed the given order of things. It meddled in a number of ways with the traditional mode of creating place, meaning, and identity. Most conspicuously, this nonvisual medium robbed architecture of its defining qualities, like materiality, visuality, spatiality, and locality. Second, unable to convey space and distance visually, the microphone translated these phenomena into temporal events. Third, it destabilized sense perception—our very path to reality—by transporting audition without the witnessing body. Next, it spread the unity of "place" over sites of recording, reception, and transmission. Radio also confounded the relationship between object and spectator by embalming speech as a new sonic object, quite independent from the speaking body. Finally, aerial transmission made a mockery of the logic of physical boundaries and distance. It pierced through walls and overlaid them with the logic of classrooms without walls, immaterial music halls, and aerial museums. Creeping up on us under the cover of silence, all in all, mass listening posed difficult questions about the status of the built environment, object, body, and event.

Undaunted by the challenges of expressing space and place on radio, and undeterred by its obfuscation of buildings and their experience, the British Broadcasting Corporation, from its establishment as a public service corporation in 1927 to the end of its single National Service for the whole nation in 1945, aired

Figure I.1
BBC Radiophonic Workshop at Broadcasting House, producing synthetic sound montages. Courtesy: The BBC.

Figure I.2

BBC pamphlet from 1929 accompanying broadcasts created for schools. © Immediate Media Company London Limited.

more than six hundred programs, published a similar number of articles, and sponsored several traveling exhibitions on the built environment.³ A great number of these projects were integrated with children's and adult education courses in physical classrooms and supported by printed articles, pamphlets, books, exhibitions, symposia, and walking tours.

Designers and critics discussed architecture in the context of culture at large, both past and present, British and foreign. They brought out the aesthetic and novel aspects of the built environment and landscape in conversations on land-use policies and taxation. They talked about the relationship between arts and funding, the role of the architect in the new political economy, the place of their goods in contemporary everyday life, the effects of democratic finance on their section of the luxury market, the myriad challenges that the breakup of large country estates posed for town and country planning, the expansion of local councils' power, and mass tourism.

Over the years, the BBC's work on the built environment involved at least 125 speakers and another 50 writers, including architects, planners, and professional educators. There were municipal architects, public and private patrons of design, government officials, politicians, philanthropists, policy advisors, and several other architectural enthusiasts. Here the established professional voices of Edwin Lutyens, Baillie Scott, and Reginald Blomfield were heard alongside the younger ones of Wells Coates, Amyas Connell, and F. R. S. Yorke. John Summerson argued with his teacher A. E. Richardson over strategies for preservation. John Betjeman and James Richards read manifestos on the virtues of countryside and suburbia. Patrick Abercrombie and Raymond Unwin published their philosophical positions on practical matters of planning. Maxwell Fry condemned both of them and proposed CIAM's ideas as the best solution.

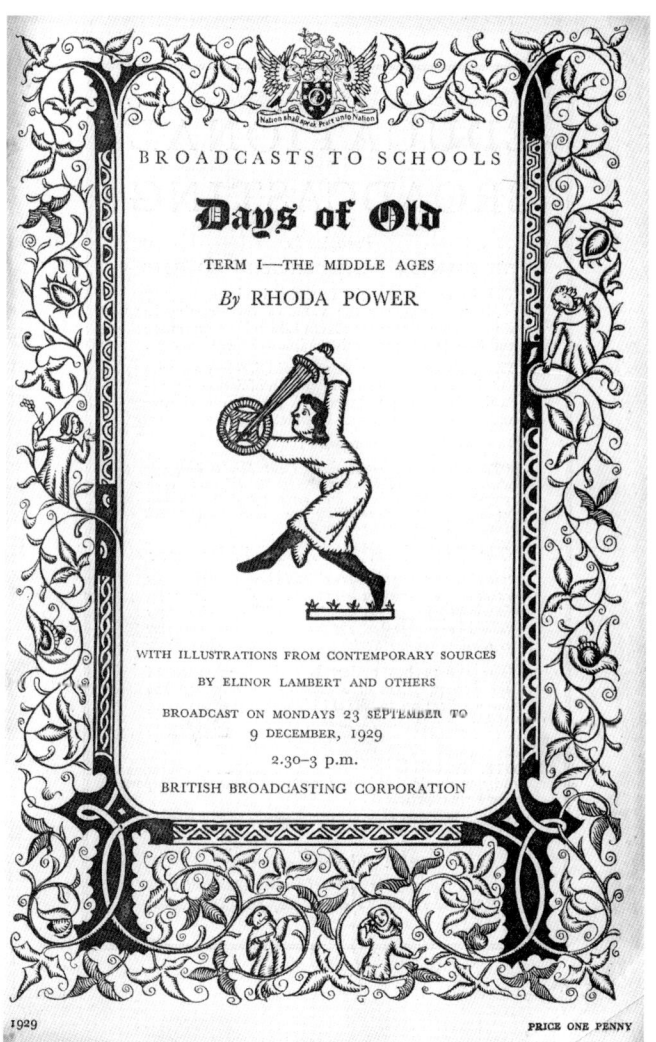

PUBLIC AND PRIVATE BUILDING ENTERPRISE

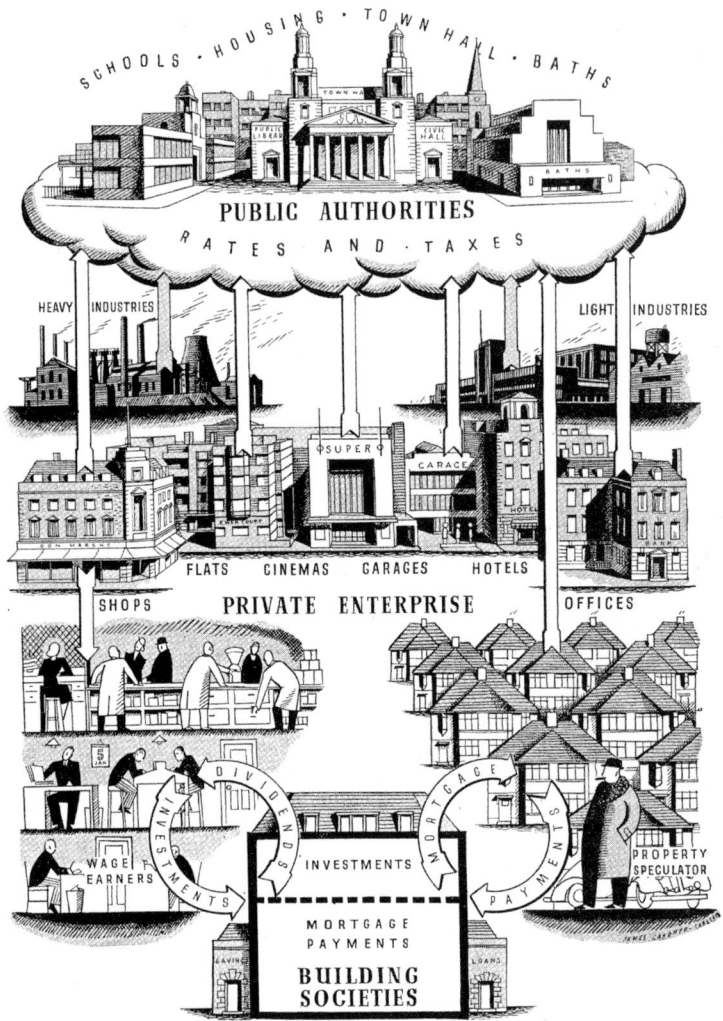

Figure I.3

Illustration accompanying an article by John Summerson in the *Listener*, February 1938. © Immediate Media Company London Limited.

John Gloag and G. M. Boumphrey became household names by giving regular advice on housekeeping, shopping for good design, and building furniture out of wooden crates. This book establishes the amplitude and variety of the BBC's interest in architecture, and dwells on both the collaborative and competitive relationship between the BBC staff and its architectural broadcasters.

This output is no secret, nor is it forgotten. It has provided a steady source of information on architecture for historians of modernism in Britain. Contemporary scholars regularly reference broadcast debates and the discussions generated by them in the architectural press.[4] Some of the most canonical texts in the field were either produced on or reproduced for the BBC; think of some of the most important book-length publications by John Summerson, Nikolaus Pevsner, Herbert Read, and John Betjeman. Yet we have no comprehensive treatise on the role of radio in the history and imagination of the built environment.[5]

In its immediate scope, the BBC's broadcasts on architectural issues were a miniscule part of the broadcast output and had a deceptively simple mandate. Nevertheless, they constituted the BBC's ideological and radiophonic masterstroke. Architectural programming formed the most effective vehicle for realizing British radio as a veritable cathedral of a unifying national culture. These broadcasts fulfilled the BBC's desire to continue into the twentieth century the legacy of Victorian institutions devoted to the cultural education of the public. Conversely, radio was the most effective instrument for asserting the symbolic function of architecture.

Early British radio was thus not just a medium of communication, but a new institution of art—one with an enviable scope and reach in steering power relations. A world connected and separated by radio did not kill architecture, nor did it drain architecture of its aura. It only created it afresh. Radio undermined old forms of artistic expression, but this only strengthened the symbolic status and force of architecture.

The toolbox of concepts I use to deconstruct the collaboration of radio and architecture is left to us by the sociologist Pierre Bourdieu. With Bourdieu, I show that broadcasts about the built environment shaped radio into an art institution only by masking the contradiction of the BBC's desire: the desire to place itself in the lineage of Victorian institutions of art versus radio's impulse to destroy the conditions necessary for the existence of precisely the same nineteenth-century cultural institutions.

Architects and critics, most prominently John Summerson, John Betjeman, James Richards, and after 1945 Nikolaus Pevsner, used radio to erect new mythologies for the production and study of architecture. Radio welded high and low art, and robbed architecture of its age-old functions. It rendered mergers of seemingly incomprehensible objects, images, and even thoughts as culturally dominant, and created new social and institutional mechanisms to perpetuate our faith in architecture—the artist's power to transubstantiate materiality into art. In the twentieth century, it is the mass media that have assumed this role most forcefully, and yet surreptitiously.[6]

The competitive and collaborative relationship between architectural broadcasts and the BBC situates us at a prodigious vantage point. From here, radio appears as a boundless competitive arena for battling out definitions of the architect and architecture. We get a peek at how it regulated architecture's involvement with a geographically diffused and expanded public. We see the changing contours of cultural politics, and hear critics turning their concerns toward a lay population that, for the most part, couldn't be bothered with them.

This collaboration also reveals a cross-section of the field of British architecture: its participants and problems, victories and failures, ideals and illusions, debates and intrigues, commissions and extracurricular activities, and so forth. It displays the involvement of architects—who have traditionally defined themselves and their work by their distance from ordinary building activity (dismissed as vulgar, naïve, philistine)—with a medium of ordinary, everyday consumption. In a global historical context, radio never acquired the prestige that visual mass media like photography, film, and print had come to enjoy rather quickly in architectural communication and imagination, making architects' involvement with the medium even more curious. But some of this interest is explained by the seductive mandate of radio's controllers. For the BBC, attention to the built environment was a "public service"—another Victorian ideal that governed its day-to-day decisions and practices—one that Raymond Williams warns us, in practice, functioned not as service but as government.[7]

II Electric Hearth

Early British radio was an oracle of Gladstone-inspired liberalism. John Reith, the first director general and the most influential figure in the history of British broadcasting, equated radio's ability to overcome the obstacles of physical distance with its ability to overcome mental distance. Its promise to overwrite the entrenched fault lines of class, locality, and ideology emboldened him to envision broadcasting as binding a divided nation culturally.[8] The BBC's corridors were filled with men and women who, like him, were weary of radio's predisposition to create undifferentiated masses. They detested the thought of creating a standardized mind, secured with such success by fascist and communist regimes. The BBC executives instead focused on broadcasting's ability to foster liberal individualism, which had learned its lesson from the excesses of nineteenth-century laissez-faire attitudes. Radio was a magic wand which would realize Reith's ideal community of responsible individualists, bound through intersubjective understanding and common "taste, manners, and knowledge."[9]

The pioneering generation of broadcast producers cherished radio as a domestic medium that replaced the traditional hearth with an electric one. They built upon its capacity to inject intimacy and confidentiality into public communication and to stimulate individualism. Peter Mandler and Susan Pedersen have argued that the home was regarded in the 1920s and 1930s as a training ground for public obligation.[10] Domesticity was intimately woven with moral obligation to society. Only individuals who possessed private decency were deemed capable of exercising public virtue. In his 1924 manifesto on broadcasting, Reith insisted on the suitability of radio to instruct the nation in the responsibilities of citizenship precisely because it was a domestic medium:

> An event, be it speech, or music, or play, or ceremony, is certainly broadcast for any and all to receive; but it seems to be personal to the individual hearer, and is brought to his very room. It is not even left, like the milk, on

the doorstep. ... It is carried to him among all the accustomed and congenial circumstances and surroundings of his own home, and in his leisure hours. It comes in such a way that enjoyment on the one hand, or assimilation on the other, is induced with comparatively little effort ... and great effect.[11]

The conception of broadcasting as an instrument of education in the domestic setting was most valued by people whose Victorian parents raised them to place altruism and cultivation of feelings at the heart of moral action. These liberal moralists were convinced that political liberty would stimulate men and women to think for themselves, initiate independent action, and prefer progressive ideas. John Stuart Mill convinced them that democracy would nourish a free market of ideas.[12] William Gladstone assured them that democracy would create a level playing field, allowing customary and original beliefs to compete so that the best would emerge from reflection rather than unexamined tradition.[13]

The public-minded individuals who filled the executive posts at the BBC, however, found that democracy had not unfolded as projected by their intellectual and political guides, Gladstone and Mill. Democracy had not encouraged the common folk to entertain the benefits of modern planning of their cities. They did not give new art a chance; they didn't value musical innovation; and they didn't put communal good ahead of personal gain. Reason was nowhere in sight. Universal adult franchise, granted in 1918, had brought neither the triumph of duty over inclination, nor of will over appetite. The egoism of populist politics eliminated such generous concepts as altruism from public behavior. Self-governance, the moralists felt, had done nothing to cure the Britons of their philistinism, nothing to spark a desire for moral self-improvement. The young idealists attracted to the BBC had absorbed John Stuart Mill's lesson that self-government was possible only among people who had reached a certain level of moral and intellectual development.[14] Only when they appreciated beauty and imagination could they rise above what Mill called "the littleness of humanity" and make wise and impartial decisions.[15] Men and women who had cultivated a care for the finer things in life, Reith's deputies surmised, would be more inclined to respect tradition, the authority of the state, and national (as opposed to immediate, personal, class-based) interests. Such a public would be partial to consensus, law, and order, thereby improving class relations and strengthening nationalism.

To this pioneering generation of executives, John Reith's ideas glistened as the talisman that would relieve them of their discontents. Radio sparkled as technology's greatest gift, capable of bringing cultural progress up to pace with Britain's advances in self-governance. It would open up people's homes to experts and transform broadcasters into public educators. They would now have the opportunity to rope in "people previously left out from the notion of public." They would be able to influence just as forcefully "the invalids, unadmittables, house wives and spinsters," as they would the "not-so-intelligent and ill informed" and the "intelligent and ill informed."[16] Just when electronic communication was beginning to challenge the superiority of the values associated with artistic culture and educated classes, the BBC gathered all sorts of cultural entrepreneurs and intellectuals to introduce listeners to the higher pleasures of life; all this in order to jump-start the robust participatory democracy envisioned by their forebears.

Reith's staff were not naïve. They certainly had cause to be optimistic about their grand ambitions. In the course of six years, they had transformed from a company, established under a commercial license in 1921, to a quasi-autonomous public service corporation in 1927.[17] They were no longer required to boost the sales of radios for their parent companies. They banned advertising. They had at hand a medium of mass communication over which the Postmaster General had granted them legislative monopoly in Britain. Freedom from market competition and political parties gave them freedom to carve out a mission independent of the exigencies of the public and politicians.[18]

In addition, the BBC staff drew their colleagues not from the pool of journalists trained on Fleet Street, but from elite universities—attracting scholars and civic entrepreneurs with reputations established through innovations in public-sector education. They recruited J. C. Stobart (in the Department of Broadcast Education) and Mary Somerville (in the sub-department of School Broadcasts) from the Board of Education. Stobart, a classical scholar, was a star of the adult education movement, and Somerville was selected for her expertise in youth education and her pioneering work in classroom technologies.[19] Together, they developed a bold broadcast policy for education and its translation into diverse but coherent programming. In addition to these leaders, the BBC hired an astonishing array of accomplished scholars, including the following:

- Hilda Matheson (Department of Talks and News Broadcast), who had studied history at Oxford and served as a secretary for the keeper of the Ashmolean Museum.[20] She was hired from the office of Lady Astor, the first female parliamentarian. Matheson created enduring connections between the BBC and the literary and art world. She paid great attention to the art of broadcast delivery, and established high standards for talks on literature, philosophy, and art.

• Charles Siepmann (Adult Education Broadcasts, later, Talks), who came from a family of educators. His father made a significant contribution to the Waldorf schooling philosophy. He himself had procured teaching and management experience in a borstal reform school for delinquent boys.[21] (After working at the BBC, Siepmann went on to become a world-class expert on broadcast education. He eventually because a professor at the Education School at Harvard, and then was tenured at New York University.)

• Mary Adams (Adult Education), a botanist who left her lectureship at Cambridge to join the BBC. The success of her first series in the 1930s called "Six Talks on Heredity" won her a position as a science producer, which she retained until 1936. She devised formats and styles of presentation appropriate for science broadcasts. When other producers were creating analogous roles in other areas of broadcasting, she took the lead in turning science broadcasting into a specialized genre.[22]

• Richard Lambert, another towering figure in the history of the BBC, the editor of its weekly publication the *Listener* from 1929 to 1940. Son of a Liberal LCC councilor and MP, he came to the Corporation from the Workers Educational Association (WEA), which he had joined to serve the labor movement. At WEA he had succeeded the renowned G. D. H. Cole as staff tutor for classes given under the supervision of the University of London.[23]

• Edward Clark (Music) and Val Gielgud (Drama), who had similarly prominent backgrounds in education and innovation in their respective fields.[24]

Could such a stellar lineup of executives and institutional safeguards make radio as reliable an instrument for liberal idealism as it was for fascism, communism, and laissez-faire consumerism? Totalitarian regimes had exploited it to hammer state-controlled propaganda. The commercial model under which radio was run in America, the English felt, had subjugated the medium to the creation of a mindless desire for commodities and accumulation.[25] But what if it was run as an enlightened, autonomous or semiautonomous "public service" corporation—Reith's greatest invention and historical contribution—whose funding came not from the pool of state funds or commercial interests, but from

Figure I.4

John Reith, BBC's first director general (1927–1938). Courtesy: The BBC. Hilda Matheson, BBC's first director of talks (1926–1931). Courtesy: National Portrait Gallery.

license fees? And what if it was answerable only to a board of governors, drawn from the best civic minds Britain had to offer?[26] Could such an institutional arrangement redeem the technology? Could radio be put to the noble service of rectifying history's failure and realizing Gladstone's and Mill's predictions for democratic culture? Could it nourish the ordinary listener's common sense and faculty of discrimination, and foster a burgeoning culture of democracy? If set up for the purpose, the pioneering generation of British broadcasting convinced themselves, radiophony would most certainly oblige.

That broadcasting was insistent at the hearth instead of at public rallies only bolstered them. That it was received by individual listeners rather than faceless masses, and in a variety of atomized, everyday familial circumstances in place of large theaters, made it suitable for propagating a culture of common sense. Hilda Matheson, echoing others, believed that as an electric hearth, radio was strategically situated to stimulate and exercise an individual's faculties. It submitted its content—the "varied diet including some solid food for the mind"—to the judgment of a listener's specific everyday circumstances, on which there was no better expert than the individual herself.[27]

Under the direction of J. C. Stobart, the BBC turned radio into what Stobart called a "wireless university." It offered courses "aimed at a very broad culture" and at "the equipping of its pupils for good citizenship and cultured home life."[28] Carrying the legacy of nineteenth-century romanticism, Stobart and his peers were concerned that their interventions should not become heavy-handed impositions from above, but wanted them to be natural and organic to each individual and class. Though BBC executives, like most liberals, were suspicious of top-down power structures, when faced with a non-self-starting polity, they accepted intervention as an instrument of education and enlightenment, if well used. They came to see the intrusion of the ruling classes and "well-meaning" public institutions in the most private of affairs as a necessary evil for removing the retarding effects of customs and conventions that kept people from contributing to and assimilating into a unified nation. As such, the wireless university was oriented to initiate a personal and national renaissance in both scale and spirit.[29] The infinite variety of individual expression would coalesce core values and myths into a dynamic but predictable force. It would nurture and develop an organic community of implicitly shared preferences, mindset, ethics, and social certainties that would counter the rising trends of fascist and socialist propaganda across Europe.[30]

Figure I.5

Listening to the radio at home during the 1920s. Courtesy: U.S. Library of Congress.

These overarching ideals directly and indirectly influenced the way architecture was broadcast on radio and the terms by which it was popularized. When broadcasters dealt with contemporary design, the topic was strictly broached through everyday issues such as good housekeeping, gardening, and do-it-yourself projects. Discussion of monumental examples and symbolic form did not figure here except in the presentation of historic architecture. The heritage of the past was considered in terms of its place in the tourist economy and was approached in much the same style as used in advice columns for walking tours or self-improvement in women's magazines. The programs rarely sounded like lectures in the history or philosophy of art. When H. S. Goodhart-Rendel, the president of the Royal Institute of British Architects (1936–1940), gave his first broadcast as a speech instead of a casual conversation over tea, he was afraid he had lost BBC's patronage.[31] Entering the unsuspecting heart of the domestic fortress as a topical issue in twenty-minute packets or even shorter sound bites, architecture proved to be scarcely perceptible yet the most effective crucible of the liberal subject: aesthetically sensitive, socially decorous, and politically deferent to education but resilient to bombastic rhetoric.

Broadcasters presented a variety of viewpoints from which to think about the topic—not with a view to make experts of listeners, but to help them make informed choices, a practice essential to "training for citizenship in its widest sense."[32] Arguments between the architectural establishment and their young challengers were designed to help listeners recognize their own aesthetic and moral preferences, and exercise their faculties of perception, judgment, discriminative feeling, and mental activity. A nation of engaged and alert subjects would certainly triumph over the uncertainties and challenges of mass democracy. Individual freedom, it was estimated, would be reconciled with social stability, and material progress with a fixed moral order.[33]

After World War I, the development of the welfare state made the provision, organization, and surveillance of physical space into hot political and legislative issues.[34] Tories saw all topics pertaining to the physical environment as problems of monetary value and private property, and therefore as needing to be protected from aggressive nationalization. Labour (which in 1922 permanently replaced the Liberal Party as the main party of opposition to the Conservatives) was mainly interested in construction and planning for the material reproduction of "labor power." Consideration of self-development and spiritual growth of the nation did not enter their calculations.[35] The interwar Liberals, in contrast, brought a civilizing framework to bricks and mortar. Composed mainly of the educated and professional classes, their high-minded ideals for redistributive politics were represented neither by Labour's materialist welfare nor by Conservatives' laissez-faire governance.[36] Disillusioned with parliamentary politics as a viable arena for change, the Liberals found that the conversation at the electric hearth on industrial art, architecture, planning, and preservation at once exercised and realized their politics.

In 1931, when the fall of the second Labour government left the country with a government of more conservative character, the BBC came under criticism for "redness" and "pinkness."[37] Satiric cartoons portrayed John Reith as Stalin shoving an artificial proletarian spirit down the throat of a nation. But such criticism was a red herring. The BBC and those who influenced it, while committed to bringing the working classes into public life, had no socialist pretensions and largely accepted the parameters of the Edwardian progressive consensus.[38] They could not fathom the proletarianization of culture.[39] In moments of confrontation between the government and unions, the BBC always sided with the former, with the justification that the government represented not one social group, but a majority of the people.[40] It censored socialist complaints of the establishment, and often rubbed unions the wrong way. When it showcased the voices of the working class, it humiliated participants by coercing them to read prewritten scripts of poetry and statements in the "BBC accent."[41] To protect its monopoly and frail independence, not to mention its very existence—its policies and performance were reviewed by independent commissions for the government every few years—Reith was anxious to present the Corporation as a moderating influence and a bulwark against revolutionism.[42] He and his successors accepted the working classes as an essential part of the public and polity, but they did not promote its class interests, which they dismissed as sectional and narrow. The working classes and the market itself set the direction, for neither really cared to champion working-class culture. The producer of *Men Talking* (1937) conceded that "this question of the working classes is very difficult indeed."[43] Before the outbreak of war, and even after, the BBC was rarely able to give voice to working-class culture. "Culture" was a middle-class preoccupation, as was the notion of collectivist conscience.

An important strand of the argument woven in this book concerns the new form of verbal communication introduced by radio. When broadcast speech breathed life into the inert written word, it changed the organization of expression and thought, and carved a lacuna between the values of the mechanical era (nineteenth-century industrial production) and the electronic era (twentieth-century communication). Radio—reinforced by a horde of follow-up audiovisual media over the century—carried us out of the print-dominated nineteenth century and into a world connected by electronically transmitted verbal expression. Writing and print fixed thought. They preserved memory on a page. With print, we learned to appreciate information that was thought through and presented sequentially. Radio intertwined the formality of written composition with an air of improvisation native to oral communication. More participatory and immediate than writing, it associated authenticity with spontaneity. However, it was now through analytic reflection that the virtues of spontaneity were decided upon. Unlike vision, which is pointed at an object and needs a certain distance between the observer and the observed, sound surrounds us simultaneously from every direction: it places us at the center of our auditory world.[44] In the following chapters, I explore how the unifying and harmonizing sense of hearing meddles with the clarifying and distinguishing sense of sight. I consider how oral expression, and the mode of thought associated with it, surfaces in interwar architectural discourse. Readers will learn about the relationship between the medium of radio and the evaluative criteria put forth by architects and critics for judging not only the built environment, life, art, and heritage, but the more elemental phenomena of reality and truth.

These questions make archives of six hundred or so programs an invaluable resource. However, before 1939 the BBC did not record its broadcasts, but carried them live. The few programs it did tape were lost during World War II to German bombs and their accurate targeting of BBC facilities. As a result, I have heard only five programs recorded before 1945. These are preserved in the Sound Archives at the British Library, and include a book review, a Royal Institute of British Architects (RIBA) speech, two debates—one moderated, one not—and a lecture.[45] Given the faint evidentiary horizon of the spoken word, the claims made in this book are reliant only on the transcripts and the sound of post-1945 recordings. Most of the relevant transcripts are held by the BBC Written Archives in Caversham Park. The rest are scattered in the archives of individuals around the United Kingdom, Canada, and United States. The RIBA Archives in the Victoria and Albert Museum has a good number of them, too. The BBC program producers mandated that speakers write every word in advance and repeat them verbatim. This makes the transcripts faithful records of what was said, though they don't make up for the lack of information on how it was said. As a result, any consideration of the performed text, the participatory and situated utterance, will be mediated by the muteness of the record and theoretical claims. All my subsequent statements on the visceral effect of the ephemeral events—intonation, pace, lift, grace, personality, and so on—are extrapolated and rely on later performances and recordings.

III Broadcasting House

Allen Weiss is one of the most insightful theorists of radiophony today. He diagnoses modern imagination as suffering from a new form of alienation that is founded in broadcasting's annihilation of the body. The externalization and eternalization of voice in a technological mechanism, Weiss notes, has become "the new symbol of the body ruled by technology without divine intervention."[46] Samuel Weber's *Mass Mediauras* probes other ways in which radio and television have alienated, fragmented, and dispersed the self. Weber argues that their "artificial" means to overcome the "natural" deficiencies of the body overcome nothing but the body, or more precisely, the spatial limitations placed by the body upon hearing and seeing.[47]

Though electronic audition is a detached form of hearing, it has a unique quality; it combines this separation with a presentness associated with sense perception. What radio transmits, Weber argues, is not so much representations, as is almost always argued, "but rather the semblance of presentations as such, understood as the power not just to hear but to place before us."[48] Its technology serves as the surrogate for the body in that it allows for a certain sense perception to take place. But it does this in a way that no body can, for its perception takes place in more than one location. The alienation and "abstraction of the self" introduced by the twentieth-century electronic media thus have a persistence and depth that were impossible to imagine in the nineteenth century. If radio dissociates meaning from consciousness and breeds the sundry techno-fantasies that Weiss finds in vanguard literary imagination, the courtship between the BBC and architecture can be understood mainly as a face-off

Figure I.6

George Val Myer, west facade of Broadcasting House, London, 1932. Courtesy: Howard Stanbury.

between the BBC's desire to subjugate broadcasting technology to the perpetuation of humanist and ontological belief, and the medium's impulse to negate precisely that belief.[49]

Nothing demonstrates this conflict more vividly than the design of the purpose-built BBC headquarters (1932).[50] Its interior, designed by a number of modern and not-so-modern designers, was an elegant and glamorous medley of color, luxurious materials, and integrated lighting.[51] This gaiety was a product of two somewhat contradictory design challenges. First were the entirely technical needs of the synthetic sound montages manufactured in a sound factory encased within the building. Since studios had to conform to strict acoustical requirements, the choice of materials was almost entirely determined by their capacities for absorption, resonance, or reverberation; furnishings, equipment, and the layout were calculated in terms of music, singing, and speaking. In the corridors and offices, the sound-deadening materials created such a daunting atmosphere that Howard Robertson thought the "silence at times [could] literally be 'felt.'"[52]

The second design issue concerned the psychological needs of the broadcasters. In 1932, broadcasting was an unforgiving practice. Most transmissions were carried live and did not have the option of second "shots." As a result, John Reith and producers insisted on studio designs that mitigated the psychological obstacles of speaking aloud to imaginary, mute interlocutors. In response, Dorothy Trotter furnished the Talks Studio in the style of a library with a gentle flavor of Empire. A false fireplace, a leather chair, a study table, bookshelves, a wall clock, and a neo-Georgian portrait blurred the boundary between theatrical set and workspace. She created a homey stage set with an older form of artificiality to help broadcasters overcome the new artificiality of radiophonic conversation.

Figure I.7

Edward Maufe, studio for religious services at Broadcasting House, London, 1932. Courtesy: *Architectural Review*.

Edward Maufe gave the religious studio the impression of a chapel. Charming in form and color, with a false window, arches, and steps that led nowhere, the decor created an atmosphere of amplitude in a limited space. An eye-catching sculpture of St. George by Vernon Hill completed the illusion of a solemn, devotional space.

These two cases treated imagination as imitation and remembrance. They denied it as creativity nourished by the medium's infinite overture to vicarious conjecture and visual discord. In both instances, the most self-conscious and contrived environment for speaking and performing was transformed and naturalized. A humanist veneer covered over broadcasting's mechanistic purification of the voice of laughs, hiccups, salivations, and respirations, all the slag that marks the animal, material nature of the production of words by the human body. Robertson captured the avant-gardism of the design problem when he noted, "the designer, with no existing manual to help him, must improvise himself psycho-analyst."[53]

In contrast, Wells Coates's dramatic effects studios embraced radiophony's disquieting grafting of mechanical, electric, and electronic possibilities over orality. Coates connected ten different studios that could be brought together to produce a single play in a control tower. His studios "consist of a loudspeaker for listening to the progress of the production, telephones for communicating to the main control room, and the dramatic control unit itself, in which is incorporated a microphone for giving instructions to the artists during rehearsals."[54] Huge microphones hung conspicuously from the ceiling. Exposed on rubber walls were contraptions to make different noises—thunder, the rattling of chains, a ship's siren—and a tank in which to produce the swish of water and the groaning of oars in the rowlocks. The control of all the circuits was in the hands of the producer who

Introduction

Figure I.8
Dorothy Trotter, Studio 3D at Broadcasting House, London, 1932. Courtesy: *Architectural Review*.

instructed artists and studio officials by means of headphones. These spaces rejoiced in the equipment's transmogrification of bodily limitations. Unlike Maufe's and Trotter's efforts, Coates's tubular seats, insulwood building board, gray rubber strips around the wall, and starkly carpeted floor bespoke the indissociability of our psyche and technology.[55]

This conflicting attitude toward the nature of wireless technology extended to both the plan and exterior of the structure. When the facility opened in 1932, the editor of *Architectural Review* devoted a whole issue to it. He hailed Broadcasting House as the "New Tower of London," without any of the pejorative connotations of the old Tower of London.[56] The building was organized like a fortified castle, protecting the sound factory within. A ring of unassuming, standard office space for six hundred personnel encircled and thus insulated the delicate technology for mummifying sounds, isolating it from the sounds of the city. The mysterious dungeon used for manufacturing synthetic goods jutted above the mass of offices in the form of a stone tower cut short. But the architect and critics explained the design concept and the cushion of offices all along the periphery purely in functional terms of light and views. What this description obscured was the utterly radical nature of the operations within, as well as the appropriation of the BBC's discrete auditory collages as realistic and faithful reproductions of the nation.

Located at the fork of Langham Street and Portland Place, Broadcasting House is situated in one of the most prominent neighborhoods in London's West End.[57] It is flanked on one side by the delicate and sensuous curves of All Souls Church, the only surviving example of John Nash's architectural toils in the area. On the other side it faces the neo-Gothic Langham Hotel, defined by richly detailed punctures of identical arched windows. The severely classical building of the Royal Institute of British Architects (RIBA) stands only a few doors down. Broadcasting House's honorific garb veiled the "phantasmagoric" return of the voice, the disembodied, alienated, repeated, externalized, and temporally malleable body.[58]

The building occupied the entire triangular site, its flanks rising like great stone cliffs, one behind the other. The swing of its south side and roundel windows piercing the core tower gave the building an illusion of parting "the road like a battleship floating towards the observer."[59] The effect was a big clumpy mass of severely and austerely modeled planes rising sheer from the pavement, balanced about major and minor axes. Primitivist reliefs and sculptures carved

Figure I.9

Wells Coates, Studio 6E at Broadcasting House, London, 1932. Courtesy: The BBC.

in stone anachronistically depicted Ariel and Prospero, the lightness of airwaves, flight of birds, and rays of light.[60] These representational and contextual gestures referenced the columns and arches of neighboring buildings, whose weight and grace stood witness to the solidity and stability of the national institutions housed within them. Finally, the membrane of the building's slab and column structure was punctured with symmetrically distributed windows to feign historic continuity with its surrounding institutions.[61] This ensemble masked radio's posthumanist nature and radical break with the past and claimed for it a place in the humanist tradition represented by the buildings around it.

At the same time, these conciliatory gestures were neutralized by Broadcasting House's rejection of the historicism of its neighbors in favor of a watered-down art deco vocabulary. This vocabulary placed Broadcasting House in the conceptual context of buildings that celebrated not historical continuity, but the revolutionary impulse within the fleeting movement of modern aviation, electric lighting, radio, ocean liners, and the urbanity of tall office buildings. Art deco grouped the BBC's headquarters with radio stations around the world, for which it had emerged as the preferred language.[62]

The thin steel lattices and the light electric cables connecting the antennas atop Val Myer's massive building hint of the technological origins of the new institution on the block. Their naked utilitarianism reminded the onlooker that the "New Tower of London" entertained not so much its visitors as the world. The BBC's overtures to cultural and historic continuity did not make it submissive to its neighbors. If the sweep of the bland south facade on which the boosters stood tipped its hat to Nash's picturesque portico on All Souls Church, the brazen artlessness of the booster towers stared wittily down at his elegant spire in a polite reminder that they had robbed church bells of the function of calling the faithful. They had reduced spires to pure visual ornaments and nostalgic

Figure I.10
Eric Gill, sculpture of Prospero and Ariel
on the front of Broadcasting House, London
1932. Courtesy: Ben Sutherland.

---

reminders of a bygone sonic era. The juxtaposition of this weightless infrastructure atop the noble mass below was a faithful statement of the BBC's conflicted self-perception. The poker-faced surface of Broadcasting House, its professed horizontality, its scale and fortress-like plan, its tan sandstone finish, and the subtle projections in the facade plane all performed a critical semantic function. The ensemble put forth British radio as a sophisticated, subtle newcomer. It could not break out of the authority of history and yet it was impenitent about its modernity. It was a force of change, but not uprooting. It was progressive, neighborly, and deferent to tradition and its context, all at the same time.

This Janus-faced quality of the British Broadcasting Corporation penetrates every one of the five chapters of the book.

IV Organization of the Book

In the first chapter, I explore connections between speech on the radio and one of the defining claims of architects: namely, that they infuse the built environment with significance. Sorting through the body of available transcripts and articles based on broadcasts, a picture emerges of the ways in which radio bears upon the production of belief in symbolic goods. As Walter Benjamin noted, before the age of mass production, the aura of art was intimately tied to its uniqueness. Mass production, and in this case radiophonic dispersal, robs art of this uniqueness, but at the same time it frees speakers from buildings' materiality

Figure I.11

George Val Myer, Broadcasting House, London, 1932: steel frame construction clad with traditional masonry work and punctured windows. Courtesy: The BBC.

and the tutelage of clients. It allows them to create symbolic clients afresh. It endows them with the power to assert criteria of judgment that their compromised position in the building industry does not allow them to impose. This chapter demonstrates the specific ways in which the media responsible for the decline of aura reproduced it afresh, for the British Broadcasting Corporation was one of the most enthusiastic publicists of modern architecture. It produced programs on industrial design, Bauhaus ideals, minimal housing, and vertical living even before modern architects had a chance to build much in Britain.

Chapter 2 probes the BBC's interest in new design principles, by comparing the wireless discussions on fine arts with debates on the applied arts. Here I suggest that applied arts were more radiophonic than fine arts. In other words, radio was more amenable to asserting the truth claims made by modern architecture than those made by fine arts. Architecture's claim to link the spiritual with the worldly, and the symbolic with functional needs, translated the BBC's "cultivation" framework into more acceptable, popular, and utilitarian language, resonating with culturally initiated and uninitiated listeners alike. It is now popular mediation that gives meaning to architectural form! Early efforts by the BBC are essential to this phenomenon.

Chapter 3 questions the BBC's interest in new design principles by looking at the themes and politics filtered through architectural shows. It describes the early culture of wireless listening and explains listening conditions—the circulation of study material, supervised listening groups, wireless courses for everyone from schoolchildren to prisoners, and the provision of supporting materials throughout the country from public libraries to village shops. I see these key themes as both a means of English liberals and the realization of their politics.

Figure I.12

John Nash's All Souls Church, London (1823), with the Langham Hotel (1865) to its left and Broadcasting House (1932) behind. Courtesy: The BBC.

In the final two chapters I examine how the public was introduced to contemporary architectural debates by broadcasting. How were listeners taught to recognize desire? What meanings were attributed to form? What patterns of consumption were condoned and condemned? In order to illustrate how popular culture constructs and reproduces ideas about the built environment, these chapters split the broadcasts into two main groups. In chapter 4, I look at oral representation of the historic fabric of towns and countryside, while chapter 5 dissects the discourse on contemporary design production.

Chapter 4 considers the conflicting relationship of the British preservationists with the promotional technology of radio. I compare the oral travelogues of three of the most popular disciplinary storytellers—Geoffrey Boumphrey, John Betjeman, and John Summerson. The genre of travelogue converted all discussions of historic fabric and landscape into compelling storytelling and provided a backdoor avenue for activism on the litigious issue of preservation. These differently situated voices wove conflicting pictures of the built heritage, but they were alike in reconciling the antiquarian canon to a public born of mass culture and welfare politics. They collapsed distance and replaced "cult value" with the ecstasy of the spectacle, and repurposed commonly deemed symbols of aristocratic despotism and historical injustice into monuments of national glory and the inheritance of mass culture. If the railways, photography, and tourism transformed the world into a commodity, these travelogues confirmed their new olde England(s) into its most valued sites. Though modernity undermined differentiation by place, the travelogues reasserted that role of place and locality.

The final chapter presents a survey of the broadcasts on contemporary production. Radio confronted its interlocutors as a reverberating "tribal drum," at once inclusive, pluralistic, and implosive.[63] It favors conversation rather than lectures, examples rather than generalizations, common sense rather than analysis. It considers how this sound-centric space filters the politics of broadcasting. In this chapter I discover that just as radio turned all discourse on historic fabric into oral travelogues, it also transformed the discourse on contemporary architecture into advice literature dotted with assertions and commonplaces. The movement of architectural discourse from the normative space of reading (nineteenth century) to the novel space of wireless listening (twentieth century) transformed the definition of "work" of art. If the individualizing and abstracting written word supported the notion of "work" as "monument," on the radio "work" became synonymous with "design." And "design" was tantamount to large-scale production—mass-produced, mass-consumed, all-encompassing, everyday, and authorless commodity. This profanation of what constituted a work by the likes of Frank Pick, Anthony Bertram, Serge Chermayeff, John Gloag, and Amyas Connell, however, is no avant-gardism. It is the making of a middle-of-the-road, consumer-oriented modernism, invigorating the illusion of egalitarianism so that the underlying hierarchies of culture can operate freely and undetected inside the bodies of cultural consumers, under modern social conditions.

The weight of this evidence forces us to relinquish a vision of British radio as just another medium of diffusion and publicity. It was an institution of art that, like others of its ilk, regulated the distinctions that helped organize the hierarchies of the modern marketplace against its own subversive tendencies at leveling. Whereas the notion of public service places the BBC in the tradition of middle-class voluntary and bureaucratic institutions, the history of its patronage of architecture forms the epilogue of both voluntary and market initiatives such as the women's advice manuals, home improvement magazines, travel guides, William Morris Preservation Societies, municipal museums, and Working Men's Colleges, and their twentieth-century bantlings like the Design and Industries Association (DIA) and Ideal Homes Exhibitions.[64] But unlike these earlier elaborations, radio had a much wider and deeper subliminal effect. Its technology cast a broad net, while its cloak of public service gave it unprecedented license to observe, categorize, and scrutinize its listeners in order to make its message and product desirable to territories yet uncharted by the cultural and building industry.

1 FIGURE OF SPEECH: THE PLACE OF RADIO IN THE SPACE OF ARCHITECTURE

I Speech as Action

What is reactionary and what is progressive in art has no necessary parallelism with what is reactionary and what is progressive in society. ... If my hopes for the happy future of humanity have been first fully aroused by a great architect who builds houses with flat roofs and enormous windows, I ought not to suppose that everybody who builds houses with sloping roofs and moderate windows has lower hopes for humanity than me. ... Unbridled fancy ... may ... be the downfall of modern reformers if they become entangled in stylism or emotionally over-occupied with things outside architecture. The world comes, and will always come, to architects for architecture, and even if it should learn, as I believe it may, to come to architects for advice as to living, it will not accept any social counsel as a substitute for highly specialized skill in the architect's proper profession. Of the two dangers to architectural reform that I can see, sociological impertinence is likely to beset particularly the leaders and stylistic fashionableness the followers. A third danger (which is a rash one for me near the end of a long lecture) is—talk.[1]

Architecture in a Changing World
By H. S. GOODHART-RENDEL

The twenty-second National Lecture, broadcast on October 4 by the President of the Royal Institute of British Architects

WHEN one speaks of a 'changing world' one implies a world that is changing rather more quickly than usual, and that is what people almost always believe of the world they are inhabiting at the moment. Certainly it seems to us now that in this country we are passing bloodlessly through a minor social revolution, and in other countries the difference between what is and what was until lately is even more striking. Science, too, is varying and increasing its applications to our ways of daily life, and the Thought now called modern seems more opposed to the preconceptions of the middle-aged than has been the Thought called modern at other times. Whatever future historians may decide, let us assume that our world today is conspicuously one of change.

Architecture is changing, too, not more rapidly but perhaps more essentially than it has already done in the lifetime of any of us. Like all the other fine arts, it is passing through a succession of experiments, but it seems as though in architecture much more than in painting, say, or in sculpture the experiments are resulting in some common agreement as to desirable lines of development. All the buildings that are praised or abused for being 'in the modern style' seem very much alike. Their similarity may be only the superficial similarity that fashion often imposes upon works of art produced at any one time, but on the other hand it may be a symptom of some real alteration in our architectural outlook. Such an alteration, if it have taken place, may have been the outcome of influences scientific, social, or both ; may have been the reflection of external changes without having been caused by them ; or again may have been the outcome of influences exclusively architectural. The world may be changing architecture, the world's changes may be merely reflected in architecture, or architecture may be changing itself in a way with which the world's changes have little to do.

I do not expect that any of these suppositions will be accepted by everybody, but we must choose one of them before we can form any probable opinion as to what is happening in architecture today. The supposition most likely to my mind is that our world and its changes are reflected in the nature of the buildings we chiefly produce, but have had only an indirect influence upon their architectural character. Thus, I think that although economic causes are driving those who used to inhabit large houses into small houses and flats, that although social causes are obliging us to avoid all undue requirement of domestic labour, that although moral and political causes are inducing us to provide better conditions of living for the poorer among the people, yet the actual buildings resulting from these causes do not necessarily express in architectural terms the world-changes that are bringing them into being. Indeed I should think it marvellous and contrary to experience if they did. There are no words in the language of architecture to express economic pressure or the servant problem or an occupation with the material welfare of others: architecture as an art can speak only of its own affairs, of the

Mediaeval Castle : units grouped but not merged

laws of gravity, of constructional skill, of the primitive associations of certain forms and colours with certain emotions. From the manner rather than from the matter of architectural expression we can often deduce the conditions in which buildings have been produced ; we can remark that the Romans took on trust from their Greek workmen a lot of expensive ornament, that the Arabs were wont to build in a hurry, that mediæval Europeans found difficulty in moving large blocks of material, that Victorian Englishmen seldom understood what their architects were up to. If, however, we go further and believe that the architecture of the Colosseum expresses exactly the Roman mind, or that of the Alhambra the mind of the Arabs ; that the mediæval cathedral was an inevitable outcome of mediæval Christianity, or Victorian confu-

Figure of Speech

Figure 1.1

H. S. Goodhart-Rendel, National Lecture on "Architecture in a Changing World," broadcast on 4 October 1938, printed in the *Listener*. © Immediate Media Company London Limited.

Speech is fundamental to built form, yet architects have often mistrusted it.[2] The Edwardian architect Sir Edwin Landseer Lutyens echoed a commonplace concern when he complained about British architecture's burgeoning culture of the word: "[A]ll this talk brings the ears so far forward that they make blinkers for the eyes."[3] This suspicion stems from a narrow understanding of architecture and how it produces effects. More specifically, it is associated with the belief that the essence of architecture lies in its materiality and materiality alone: it touches our mind and spirit through an automatic, uninterrupted play of space and form. The meaning inscribed in space and materials, according to this view, is governed by logic internal to form and architectural problems, not tutelage, budget, or other nonarchitectural concerns (a romantic ideology underlying architectural pedagogic priorities in many undergraduate programs even today). In this schema of things, language has a secondary role. Its purpose is to represent the symbolic meaning in bricks and mortar that exists prior to and independent of it.

The quotation that opens this chapter is by Henry Stuart Goodhart-Rendel, the president of the Royal Institute of British Architects (RIBA) in 1938. It sheds light on a critical challenge posed to this puritan and charismatic view of architecture by modern architects and mass culture. Mass media changes the balance of power between reality and representation, signified and signifier, model and its image. An architecture belonging to "the masses," rather than to an elite, generated for the people (at all educational and economic levels) rather than the church, the king, or the aristocracy, puts publicity ahead of experience, and words before buildings. Mass culture is also inescapably a product of modern technologies; it arises when visual forms can be widely replicated, broadly distributed, and easily consumed. This again privileges representation over the object and makes the "image" ambassador of the "model."

Goodhart-Rendel recognized that the younger generation did not enjoy the cozy certainties of architectural practice that had existed just twenty years earlier, and therefore had to carve a new market for themselves. But their alliance with the emergent market, he worried, was a heresy: not because it involved courting a culturally uninitiated public, and not even so much because the primacy of representation over experience robbed modern civilization of the pleasure of innocent, unmediated encounters with the physical world. It was a heresy most profoundly because it subjugated the logic of form to the logic of words, thus depriving architecture of its (forever vulnerable) sovereignty. What to him was the "sociological impertinence" of "modern reformers" threatened the self-evidence of beauty. It jeopardized the architect's age-old claim that forms have the power to communicate meaning without help. Architecture had its own laws and standards of judgment. As Goodhart-Rendel put it: "What is reactionary and what is progressive in art has no necessary parallelism with what is reactionary and what is progressive in society." Without its own logic, architecture was nothing but a heap of stones. It is not surprising that Goodhart-Rendel, as president of the RIBA, would voice his concern for "Architecture in a Changing World" on radio, for radio's unprecedented linguistic condition for the production, reproduction, and appropriation of architecture made it a chief culprit of this new problematic.

Better known for his eloquent oratory than for design, Goodhart-Rendel faced a nagging paradox: the modernists' recourse to nonarchitectural means to attract public attention undermined expert authority, turning architecture into a fad. And yet the process of professionalization (over which he himself had presided) and the prestige of the profession (marked by the BBC's invitation) had flourished alongside these subversive tendencies.[4] History too has taken the side of his target, for the aura of a work of art persists, despite the spread of mass culture. Ideologies of talent or competence that attribute the miracles of a true work to a creative artist or a genius architect have never been more secure than in the age of commodification. A cursory glance at the art market and cultural tourism today shows that mass-produced prints have only enhanced the value of Picasso originals or pilgrimages to Le Corbusier's white houses. The media responsible for undermining the distinctions most fundamental to the identity of architecture are also accountable for the conservation of its aura and symbolic capital. Mass media have engendered what Samuel Weber calls media-auratic art, namely aura born of the magical powers and logic of media.[5]

In order to better understand how symbolic systems have mutated to survive under the sign of mass media, in this chapter I dissect the bond between broadcast speech and the age-old claim that architecture is a symbolic system. I consider how the medium through which this news is transmitted to listeners constrains or realizes the autonomy claim. Readers will learn about the confluence of different factors—including the novelty of wireless speech, a predominantly uninitiated audience, mass publicity, interwar liberal idealism, and the BBC's public patronage—and their influence on the social image of architecture. The question at the heart of this chapter is this: What, *in* speaking something and *by* speaking something—i.e., giving a representation—does the speech in radio's specific linguistic structure do *to* and *for* architecture?

My inquiry into these issues proceeds from two fundamental assumptions. First, on the relationship between words and buildings, I side with John Evelyn, the influential English architectural theorist, who in 1664 pronounced "architectus verborum"—the architect of words and interpretation—to be one of the four faces of an architect.[6] Goodhart-Rendel is wrong to subordinate speech to architect's "real vocation," for words and interpretation don't follow building; rather, architecture consists of words.[7]

My second assumption concerns the conditions under which architecture's autonomy claim produces real, objective effects (local identity, books, careers, ticket prices, not to mention wars, museum security systems, and cultural tourism). For this, I part with the RIBA's president again. I turn away from the approaches that explain cultural value by pointing to artistic genius or charisma internal to a work, and follow those that attend to the discipline's social status at a particular time and place. The reality of signifying systems like architecture, I have come to accept, is nothing but a social production. The experiential and psychological effects of disgust at trash and adulation for art (made out of trash) are historically and socially constituted, and speech is integral to this process. The link between speech and the construction of signifying systems should be more obvious today than ever before. For today we prefer "criticality" to "beauty" in the pieces we show in galleries and museums, which demands higher cultural competence from us. Criticality asks for a deeper knowledge of artistic traditions and concerns than do the normative notions of prettiness. It is therefore more dependent on explanation than are internalized preferences.

When orators sat at the microphone to speak of or speak for architecture, their words did not simply stand in for a reality of architecture that could be verified by a visual and spatial object. Speech was publication. It transformed work from a private object into a public one. Words imposed recognition of certain things and spaces as cultural, precious, honorable, and representative and dismissed others as despotic, vulgar, and tedious. Utterance on radio created a market for disciplinary goods as symbolic goods, fostering a belief in their cultural value over and above their material value. It inculcated a distinction between art, counterfeits, and nonart that felt spontaneous. This means that speech was as significant an agent in the fabrication of the physical world as were the impersonal mechanisms of economics, legislature, politics, topography, and climate. It was both statement and *action*.[8] It produced vision, desire, and value. What is this, you may ask, if not (an architectural) practice without (design) practice?

Art historian Roger Hinks has left us a wonderfully syncopated broadcast supporting my thesis, though he accommodates the necessities of the culture of mass listening to the charismatic view of art that we must leave behind.

> The domain of art is contemplative. … [It pertains to the] artist's experience of reality. … But in civilized societies art cannot normally exist in this pure state. The artist and the public are no longer united by the magic communion of a totem-symbol. The artist must make himself intelligible to the public: reflection creeps in; and the imaginative act is communicated in a form which the audience can assimilate. … But imagination cannot communicate directly with imagination: a language is required as a connecting link; and this language is, in the nature of things, more or less arbitrary and distorting. By way of compensation, however, it is language which fixes the intuition in the artist's mind as well as recreating it for the public; and when the relations between the artist and his public are normal and healthy, the language by which they communicate is an agreed convention, causes little trouble. When, on the other hand, these relations are unhealthy, as they are at the present day, there is no agreed convention: the public complains that the artist is unintelligible and the artist complains that the public is unintelligent. Hence these tears.[9]

II Practice without Practice

As you can probably imagine, the creation of a radio program in the years before World War II was a tedious task. It came at a cost and effort to architects and critics that the BBC's monetary reward did not justify. The preparation of a standard twenty-minute program in the simplest format took five months, on average. Programs involving debate or travel were even more time-consuming, as well as more expensive. Preparations involved meetings, written correspondence, and rehearsals. Responsibilities did not end with transmission. Broadcasts were rewritten, abridged, and furnished with pictures for publication in the *Listener*. Speakers responded to audience letters, and some of these responses were also published.

The process was made yet more laborious because the BBC strictly forbade extemporaneous presentations. Even interviews and debates had to be written in advance and approved by the Program Control Board. This was less because of censorship (which was exercised more at the invitation stage) and more because of Reith's discomfort with the openness of the casually spoken word. There were contractual negotiations and the back and forth of editorial comments. After all this effort, the result was usually a one-time twenty-minute broadcast.

Initially the Corporation had difficulty attracting writers and poets. In one of the most brilliant histories of British broadcasting, Paddy Scannell and David Cardiff observe that for literary figures, "reputations were still made elsewhere through established forms and the usual agencies of legitimation."[10] That the monetary rewards were "meager in the extreme" only made things worse. Speakers on architecture also complained about time and compensation. Relying solely on writing for a living, the architectural journalist John Summerson incessantly negotiated fees and travel expenses. His correspondence brims over with complaints about the skewed ratio of preparation time and compensation. Discussing a built environment over a nonvisual medium was riskier than discussing music or literature; a satisfactory transmission of ideas was not guaranteed. Nor did a successful show guarantee further commissions for the speaker. Unlike their approach to music and gardening programs, the production executives were more interested in featuring a variety of points of views and approaches to architecture and the allied arts.

Yet architects, who had to expend far more energy than literary speakers to translate their work and ideas for effective presentation on radio, repeatedly accepted invitations. In fact, they even sought them out. Maxwell Fry, who maintained a busy design practice in the late 1930s, also protested the employment and compensation conditions. The Corporation paid lesser-known architects like him so little money that it forced him to choose between an obligation to his office and an obligation to look beyond his nose.[11] Broadcasting for him was a selfless duty.

Goodhart-Rendel came to the same conclusion soon after his talk. On his watch, the RIBA, an institution established for the protection of architects, advised all its members to pursue the patronage of the BBC.[12] Days after his big broadcast, his home and office were flooded with congratulatory letters and publishing requests that poured in from as far afield as Canada and New Zealand. He was congratulated "on a most convincing and closely argued piece of propaganda for sane architecture."[13] The recently celebrated Lord Reith had personally invited his sixty-minute lecture to observe the passing of the 1938 Architect's Registration Act. Registration gave the Royal Institute of British Architects a monopoly over the selection of members into the ranks of the profession through control over entry exams and college accreditation. It also improved their hold over the standards of architectural production. "Architecture in a Changing World," Goodhart-Rendel's presentation, was given at the most prestigious of the BBC platforms, the biannual National Lecture. Previously, the lecture had featured figures like the Archbishop of Canterbury, the Viceroy of India, the Chancellor of Oxford University, Winston Churchill, John Maynard Keynes, Bertrand Russell, and Cyril Burt. And now it inducted the RIBA's president to the hall of fame.

The lecture symbolically closed the hundred-year-long British architectural battle over "profession vs. art."[14] The winning pro-professionalization wing had hoped that the act would institutionalize professional competence, thereby procuring for architects the respect of experts and distinguishing them from hacks. The pro-art proponents rejected professionalization as the codification of talent. "Architecture in a Changing World" marked the decisive victory of the RIBA and its more pragmatic view of architecture.

Supplementary modes of disseminating disciplinary ideas, Goodhart-Rendel realized, could play a critical role in the perpetuation of architecture in a changing world, and radio could be its unexpected savior. The decline of country home commissions and private patrons (both, before 1914, had sustained a major portion of design practice) on the one hand, and the exponential growth in the number of practitioners who were solely dependent on salaries on the other hand, had forced a conversation on the necessity of expanding patronage. Every general body meeting at the RIBA was preoccupied with the issue.[15] To the institute's president, the BBC began to glisten with the promise of reinvigorating practice by indirect benefaction. After his talk he felt that perhaps his "lecture was less elementary than they would have chosen it to be. I may not have sown a very good seed for future patronage of architecture by the Corporation. It is in my mind therefore that it might be worth while for those who have the popularization of architecture at heart to let the BBC know what they are thinking."[16] If the Corporation could serve modernist propaganda, why couldn't it be roped in to serve the profession?

A little after the National Lecture, the Talks department approached Goodhart-Rendel again. This time, they had in mind a series on something along the lines of "The Civilized Man" or "The Art of Living." He politely objected:

> Your letter conflicts with the resolution I have been making to give the audience a rest from the sound of my voice, seeing that I have a book to write which is only begun and am extraordinarily busy professionally … it takes an extra-ordinary amount of time that I cannot justify at the cost of my practice. Nevertheless, I should very much like to discuss this invitation, seeing that I should like to do what I can at any time towards interesting a large audience in the real values of civilization.[17]

III Cathedral for the Production of Belief

In the 1920s, when radio appeared as a viable outlet for discussing the built environment, British architecture had vibrant traditions of both the spoken and the written word. Its practitioners were involved with various forms of outreach: they participated in preservation societies, spoke at public conferences, organized debates and exhibitions, wrote for popular and quasi-literary presses, led walks and guided tours, and circulated pamphlets, posters, articles, and books on all sorts of issues. Innovation in book publication—for example, Penguin's six-pence pocket-size paperbacks in 1937—as well as changes in the format and content of the architectural press and new exhibition techniques made architecture more accessible to the lay public. This far-reaching effort was carried out by a small segment of designers and connoisseurs to promote causes important to them. Each medium enabled its purveyors to reach different segments of the public, and promoted competing points of view on architecture. The diversification of media and the segmentation of the public impacted the relations between the producers and consumers of architecture, as well as relations among producers.

To the existing modes of raising public and professional interest in the built environment, the BBC added the wireless. Architects were able to access a medium that by 1939 had the ear of 97 percent of the nation.[18] By then, most people at least had access to a set, if they didn't own one. Over the years, technological advances evened out the initial heterogeneous geographical distribution of service.[19] The *BBC Yearbooks* kept the public and policy makers abreast of the steady progress made by the BBC engineers to improve the quality of reception. New and sophisticated boosters went up around the cities and countryside. Crude crystal batteries and homemade sets began to give way to more sophisticated batteries, living room sets, and transistors.[20] Transmission hours steadily expanded,[21] and five regional channels joined the London channel.[22] *Radio Times* published weekly program schedules, human-interest stories about radio broadcasters, program reviews, and trivia. The timing of programs was slowly codified. Until television—still little more than a glimmer in its parents' eyes (who also happened to be the BBC)—established itself as a viable mass medium in the 1950s, radio enjoyed a cultural hegemony unmatched by older modes of architectural publicity.[23]

The culture of listening grew during the Great Depression. While the sales of all luxury items went down, radio purchases increased. Ross McKibbin sees this as an index of the importance of radio, especially as an instrument of consolation.[24] During World War II, radio further took hold as a welcome distraction from the anguish of the prolonged conflict.

Wireless broadcasting followed a tradition of oral media that was already in place to introduce architecture as a cultural pedagogy for the general public. Lectures with lantern slides and guided tours were in use in municipal museums,

Figure 1.2

Outreach activities of architects: students mounting the Modern Architecture Research Group (MARS) exhibition, London, 1934. Courtesy: John Allan.

and were offered by the Workers Educational Association and amenity societies.[25] Radio reproduced these representations in a boundless auditorium with invisible walls and open admission. Thoughts were streamed to a faceless audience, without images, scripted to the word and minute, rehearsed several times in advance, and circulated through a mechanism controlled by the BBC executives. To capture attention, broadcasters had to speak slowly and softly. To provoke action, they required more artistry and intimacy than bombastic prose. Electronic audition made listeners more susceptible to manipulation than to brute force. The speakers who were most effective were those who could give well-organized speech the semblance of impromptu conversation, that is, an air of spontaneity rather than calculation.

If electronic speech followed an established tradition, it also broke with it. Most significantly, it expanded the scale of a classroom's sociability to include the entire nation by fiddling with the spatial boundaries between the sites of utterance and reception. It collapsed periodic educational events like walking tours and museum lectures into the everyday. For the visual arts, radio translated the information encoded in scale, material, space, locality, and vision to audition. Access to the wireless classroom thus came at the cost of properties that differentiated architecture from other visual arts.

While the *loss* of material properties disadvantaged radio relative to other modes of dissemination in certain ways, in other ways this loss heightened radio's power over other media. It is in the intersection of these new conditions of reproduction with the institutional ambitions of the BBC that the particularity of radio's impact on architecture becomes worthy of consideration.

To begin with, broadcasting shares a striking resemblance to periodicals that have served as the principal means of structuring information on architecture since the nineteenth century. Both media possess seriality, regularity, periodicity, and predictable size and length of works. If ideas in a book are analogous to working drawings for a house, thoughts in both the magazine articles and broadcasts are like sketches. Also different from books and similar to one another, articles and broadcasts are ongoing and juxtapose disconnected topics. Both have contemporaneousness, as well as different contributors and the same set of editors and publishers for a given duration. The BBC copied the format of design entries in newspapers and general-interest journals like the *Spectator*, the *Times*, and the *Guardian*. Standard entries—building news, housing and planning discussion, book and exhibition reviews, and correspondence—were found in both the broadcasts and the periodicals. Both were also vigilant about monitoring the emergence of new building types and changes in old ones. This affinity allowed authors venturing into the new space of wireless transmission to capitalize on their existing skill sets and interests. It is therefore only to be expected that the microphone would be frequented by voices that had polished their messages on the space of the periodical page. For example, *Architectural Review*, the most authoritative professional periodical in Britain, and the BBC drew contributors from the same pool of government officials, politicians, industrialists, civic-minded intellectuals, literary and art critics, architects, and architectural historians.[26] The poet and critic John Betjeman and the satirical cartoonist and stage designer Osbert Lancaster secured invitations to Broadcasting House through the *Review*. Conversely, design critic Geoffrey Boumphrey and the archaeologist Stanley Casson found their way to the *Review* via the BBC. When the magazine appointed industrial designer Christian Barman to its editorial team, he was called to address the impact of design on class relations on air, just as he had done on paper. In order to increase artists' voices in literature on art, Stanley Casson conducted interviews of artists for the BBC, which he published as a book called *Artists at Work*.[27] The book was reviewed in the *Review* and found its way into its correspondence and articles. The prolific John Gloag, who gave up a career in the building industry for one in advertisement, was an equal fixture on Russell Street and Queen's Gate. Whether he was reporting on glass products displayed at the Building Centre, identifying first sightings of aesthetic modernity in shop windows, or renouncing the last holdouts of convention in bars, Gloag negotiated these terrains smoothly. Philip Morton Shand was another prominent figure linking radio and the professional press. He wrote and spoke with equal enthusiasm. From him Britons learned about ideas of German architects like Peter Behrens and Walter Gropius, about French works of Le Corbusier, and about the accomplishments of the Finnish architect Alvar Aalto. When civic servants including Lord Gorell, Sir Frederick Sykes, and Sir William Beveridge wrote of the moral responsibility of designers in a welfare economy in the *Review*, they were sure to repeat those words on the microphone. Contributions of eminent artists and literary men (and most of them were men) such as Amédée Ozenfant, W. H. Auden, Eric Gill, and T. S. Eliot could be presented in both media.

During the Second World War, the discussion both on air and on the page turned toward town planning, postwar reconstruction, and the importance of

THE ARCHITECTURAL REVIEW

A Magazine of Architecture & Decoration

BROADCASTING HOUSE

Incorporating
THE
CRAFTSMANSHIP
SUPPLEMENT

Two Shillings and Sixpence Net.

9 Queen Anne's Gate, Westminster, S.W.1.

Vol. LXXII   August 1932   No. 429

Figure 1.3

Broadcasting House, cover of August 1932 issue of *Architectural Review* devoted to the building. Courtesy: *Architectural Review*.

state patronage. The link between the magazine and broadcasting was also strengthened by a correspondence of vision. In 1927, the year the BBC became a corporation, the *Review* was taken over by a new proprietor and editor in chief (1927–1973), Hubert de Cronin Hastings. Hastings transformed the publication to broaden architecture's appeal and stimulated design by situating its discussion within the larger cultural milieu. This orientation was complemented by the BBC's stimulation of the same cultural milieu with architectural experts.

Again, as in the oral tradition, the continuities between broadcasting and professional journalism must not obscure the discontinuities created by the translation of professional debates into entertaining programming. First, when authors went on air, they did not just transform from authors to orators of written text; they moved out of the normative space that favored analytical, distanced, and abstract expression and entered an unfamiliar space where they had to speak in a cumulative, participatory, and specific idiom. They stepped on a platform with an engaging mystique that created communal sense, concentrated on the present moment, and used formulaic organization. There, to get attention, they had to formally employ casualness, artfully sound artless, and consciously take up spontaneity.

In addition, broadcasting took architectural representatives out of the comfort zone of their professional institution. It carried their ideas out of office conversation and planted them into the intimate domain of domestic entertainment bent by the BBC to the instruction of a lay public. Here, contributors brought in from the professional press were not working for just another radio station, but for a unique imperial organ on the world stage and a characteristically gentlemanly institution on the national front. They found themselves on the podium of the most powerful cathedral for the production of belief in professional culture as the ultimate social good. The absence of competing radio stations in Britain gave this podium a national importance that no magazine or newspaper could ever dream of holding.²⁸ On the radio, architects—who had neither been like public servants (such as bureaucrats, politicians, or lawyers) nor like popular celebrities (such as singers and actors)—became public intellectuals.

The BBC also afforded the architectural community the backing of an institution that historians of literature, music, and languages have come to see as a première supporter of high arts. Though writers initially avoided the microphone, it eventually won over the younger generation. Radio served as an alternative publisher of experimental literary works and became a preeminent patron of the atonal music of the Arnold Schoenberg circle.²⁹ In 1951 the Arts Council recognized the BBC as "an exemplary new collective patron" of modern art.³⁰ When the Royal Institute of British Architects had awarded the BBC's first director general, John Reith, an honorary membership a decade earlier, the professional press unanimously applauded the gesture.³¹ The Corporation's senior staff was invited to sit on RIBA committees, the Council for Education in Appreciation of Physical Environment (CEAPE), and the Council for the Preservation of Rural England (CPRE).³² The Arts Council noted that the Corporation granted its support to the arts not by collecting art but by diffusing it, as a sponsor whose "catholicity of programmes, these many years, leaves no doubt that … the BBC could be trusted to practice the new patronage to a common good."³³

Another way in which radio broke with the space of the page was related to the disembodiment suffered on air by all visual arts. It put architects and more autonomous cultural producers (e.g., painters and poets) on the same footing. This equality was particularly purposeful because it came at a period when architects felt especially ostracized.³⁴ There were drastic ups and downs in the market, reaching its lowest ebb in the Great Depression. There were new levies on the aristocracy, the traditional clients of the profession; embargoes on importing steel and raw material for glass; and at times, direct restrictions on construction. The developers' control over commercial markets and engineers' domination of municipal work left very few work opportunities to designers.³⁵ Reality did not support Goodhart-Rendel's belief that "the world comes, and will always come, to architects for architecture."³⁶ Out of the £14 million spent annually on construction between World War I and 1938, only a fraction was used to build in consultation with any of the 13,000 architects registered with the RIBA. The situation was exacerbated by the change in the social composition of designers. For the first time since the establishment of the Institute of British Architects in 1834, most practitioners depended solely on practice for income. Architect Francis Skinner captured the sorry condition of his fellow practitioners in 1935:

> Today, when the need for a skilled solution to housing and town-planning problems is becoming more and more urgent, the architect is finding himself completely unable to assume his proper social responsibilities. Further, while the professional opportunities of the architect are restricted, his economic position is becoming increasingly insecure; employment is more casual, salaried assistance is underpaid, talents are unfairly exploited, the cost of architectural education is out of proportion to the training provided, and there are insufficient opportunities for the students of small means.[37]

At the same time, the large-scale entry of students into design programs was paralleled by the mass exit of practitioners from the profession.[38] Summerson, the architect turned architectural writer and broadcaster, complained that there were so many restrictions on architects that "the practice of architecture might, only with slight exaggeration, be described as illegal."[39]

Weighed down by material conditions, this social group was elevated by aerial conditions. They were now heard in a cathedral of culture, embellished with classical and band music, and scented with poetry and drama.[40] They alternated with lessons in music and film appreciation. They taught history between courses on German and French. They were seated in the company of painters, sculptors, and gardeners. They were featured on the covers of the *Listener* and *Radio Times*. To improve reception, their hosts invested in group listening, circulated etiquette manuals, and devoted broadcasts to emphasizing the advantage of selective listening.[41]

The BBC gave architectural producers the backing of an institution that had secured a reputation for objectivity and dignity, much missed in the lay daily press.[42] Alternately praised as a forum for talent and condemned as a biased patron of "ultra-modern" doctrines, the BBC continued to exercise a compelling fascination, even for its most eloquent detractors like Eric Gill.[43] Summerson remembered broadcasting as an institution "from whose allure few academics are immune."[44] By 1939, the microphone had come to possess such authority that architects on air felt both comfortable and proud. Worried that "the technical press was too afraid to tackle and the lay press too ignorant to care about" architectural criticism, observers had at hand a publisher widely recognized as enlightened and bold.[45]

This publishing venue gave words their efficacy and distinguished the consumption of utterances as "aesthetic" and "powerful."[46] *It is not just what was said but that it was said on radio that empowered speech.* Broadcast speech not only fed vanity, not only indulged the seduction of fame, and not only satisfied the desire for recognition; it also contributed to professional development. One of the most important architectural historians of the twentieth century, Summerson, noted that broadcasting was integral to the consolidation of his expertise.[47] Access to the space of British radio often seemed—to both observers and participants—like being part of history in the making. Patronage now became a public event. The BBC's benefaction offered architects a long-term symbolic interest in key ideals of "nationality," "inclusivity," and "extendibility" as a principle of legitimacy that competed with their clients' immediate material interest. It supported architects who wanted to root out "the seeking of the interests of the private client as opposed to the community, and a consequent unwillingness to face up to those social responsibilities for the assumption of which many contemporary architects are—by training and experience—essentially qualified."[48]

Broadcasting supported the discipline's turn toward the community. It promoted J. E. Barton's book, which placed art and architecture squarely within the Victorian notion of social service:

> The ideal of social service, converting men from sordid aims to an unselfish passion for general betterment, is today one of the most widely recognized of spiritual forces. Art … is the natural ally of this growing social ideal. If the true spirit of art inhabits the manners and purposes, the works and the recreations, of a whole society, it enriches public life with new and qualitative standards. Men in their mutual relations become more discriminating and larger-minded. What used to be mere businesses are raised to the level of professions, and people live more happily together because they have learned to enjoy and share a finest savor of life.[49]

Radio also distinguished itself from the professional press by helping British architects create clients for their skill sets and value systems. This group could not claim a monopoly over designing, building, conception, or realization.

On radio they discredited their rivals for professional services (as the medical profession did the charlatan).[50] "Look at many of the houses that have sprung up along our new arterial roads—'bungaloid growths.' Anti-civilized is a mild word for these contraptions," charged Barton. And what was their crime? "To begin with, they are not designed by architects."[51] British radio gave architects a privileged status among other claimants for the title and services of an architect. "Look at the street," moaned an aggravated John Summerson. "The street is not the *sine qua non* of a town. It has come to exist as a result of a way of living and a system of property-holding. ... And the alternative? The alternative is to take an area defined by three or four important traffic routes, wipe out all the streets, and rearrange the dwellings in a pattern which allows for a greater degree of pleasantness—for more and better gardens, for freer circulation of air, for an escape from the menace of dust and noise."[52] An exemplary solution could be found in Liverpool where the city's director of housing was an architect, L. H. Keay. Only an alert architect of Keay's caliber, Summerson stressed, could have had the foresight to bring the lessons of the vast and comprehensive schemes carried out under welfare governments in Germany, Austria, and Holland to bear appropriately on English soil.[53]

Architects and critics used radio to create a need for themselves. They identified needs they could fulfill and pointed to problems that had arisen by keeping architects out. Speakers showed the import of designers' imagination. Robert Atkinson highlighted the contribution they could make to schools that had been subject to fixed budgets by the depression: "Only really good designers [could] work with an arbitrary figure like this and produce admirable designs cheaply."[54] John Gloag insisted that only "the trained and disciplined imagination of the architect" could elevate the standards of mass production, and only "*his* knowledge and judgment" could ensure the competitiveness of British exports. Clough Williams-Ellis confidently asserted, "It is in the interest of the state when [the architect's] prestige and authority are increased, and bad for the state when they are diminished."[55] Modern building expresses modern industry, said Frederic Towndrow, but this "does not mean that the functions of the architect do not matter. On the contrary they matter all the more. It was easy enough to trick people into thinking that a building looked beautiful when you plastered it with classic or Gothic features, but when you have to get your architectural beauty by pure planning, good composition, and harmonious proportions, then you have to think hard."[56]

Creative Housing

By JOHN SUMMERSON

THE Minister of Health is, no doubt, justified in pointing with pride (as he constantly does) to the sum total of over three million dwellings which represents the nation's housing achievement in the post-War period. As an economic achievement it is certainly pretty formidable. It reflects a high level of prosperity about which you may be complacent or cynical according to the colour of your politics. But once you look at this achievement as a concrete affair of structures and lay-outs the inglorious truth emerges that it has been possible to construct three million tolerably substantial dwellings and yet create absolutely nothing. Our towns remain much what they were, the only change being that their girth has bulged, or straggled into the country, as one estate after another has become ripe for profit-making.

It is only with the official slum-clearance and rehousing drive of the past few years that people have begun to realise that 'housing' is not the same thing as 'houses', and that in the redevelopment of the central areas of our towns we are introducing a concept which has very definite architectural implications. To indicate what these implications are and how they are being demonstrated in some recent buildings is my present purpose.

Look at the street. The street is not the *sine qua non* of a town. It has come to exist as the result of a way of living and a system of property-holding. It has certain disadvantages. Those successive strips of property with narrow frontages, narrow yards and narrow gardens behind, use up the ground blindly. The front of each house is invaded by dust and noise; the back is marred with the requisites of drainage. Between one street and the next you have a criss-cross of garden walls enclosing patches of ground, some of which may be nicely kept, others neglected and squalid. As the houses become split up horizontally into flats, the backs are laden with more pipes, the gardens suffer from the indifference of divided ownership and landlords who don't care. For townsfolk who are getting used to living horizontally, in great centres of habitation, the street is already an anachronism.

And the alternative? The alternative is to take an area defined by three or four important traffic routes, wipe out all the streets, and rearrange the dwellings in a pattern which allows for a greater degree of pleasantness—for more and better gardens, for freer circulation of air, for an escape from the menace of dust and noise. Can it be done, or is it just a town-planner's theory? Yes; it can be done where a single owner possesses a sufficiently large area of ground, and where there are good reasons and economic means for pulling down the existing houses and rebuilding. In fact it is being done in towns which have acquired great areas of slum property for redevelopment. It is not always being done in the best way. Sometimes a system of closed, or nearly closed, courtyards kills every possibility of real improvement. More often the smallness of the site leaves no alternative but to repeat the old formation in the new structures.

But for my present purpose, which is to show where and how the best direction is being taken in this country, I have

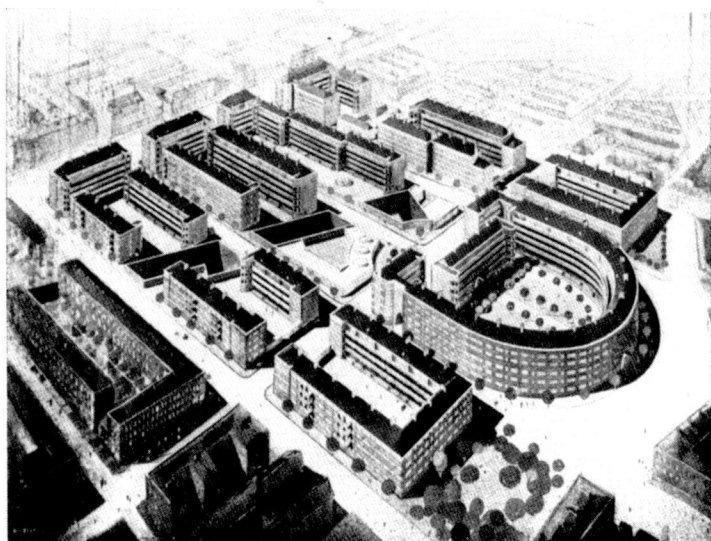

St. Andrew's Gardens, Liverpool, a recent slum-clearance scheme, now practically complete. The architect was Mr. L. H. Keay, the Director of Housing

Figure 1.4

John Summerson, talk on "Creative Housing," printed in the *Listener* in August 1937, featuring L. H. Keay, St. Andrew's Gardens, Liverpool, of the same year. © Immediate Media Company London Limited.

Broadcasters attended to a wide range of activities in which architects, given a chance, could be involved. J. Dower brought up the relationship between "Architecture and Aerodromes" (1930), while Sydney N. Bushell enumerated the challenges of "The Maidless House."[57] Others addressed the needs of listeners who would never be able to afford the services of an architect—they talked about things to watch out for in self-built homes.[58] They gave tips on "Garden Design" (1930), enumerated ways of dealing with "Damp in the House" (1932), and introduced provisions for "Housing the Working Classes" (1936) in the 1935 Housing Act. A garden, Doreen Joad emphasized, "must be conceived and developed as a whole. ... Additions and excrescences that cannot be fitted [in] the original plan must be foresworn."[59] She laid out a set of precepts by which gardeners could design their planting in relation to the house and size of the lawn. Geoffrey M. Boumphrey assured audiences that "widening the crack a little, and then filling it in with bitumastic" could easily fix "damp near windows and doors."[60] Anthony Bertram connected the design of schools to the production of liberal notions of civic identity, while Ivor Thomas explained that "the new [Housing] Act makes illegal overcrowding above a certain standard—roughly that of two persons to a room. In order that the standard may be enforced, the Act provides where necessary for financial aid for ... blocks of flats of not less than three storeys on expensive sites."[61]

Radio programs showed that design was not just about mastery of historic styles, but touched upon extraformal issues of paramount importance—health, safety, recreation, amenities, and privacy. These, the speakers contended, did not undermine the architect's specialized authority but were the very substance of it; it was giving form to these ordinary needs that made architects a different kind

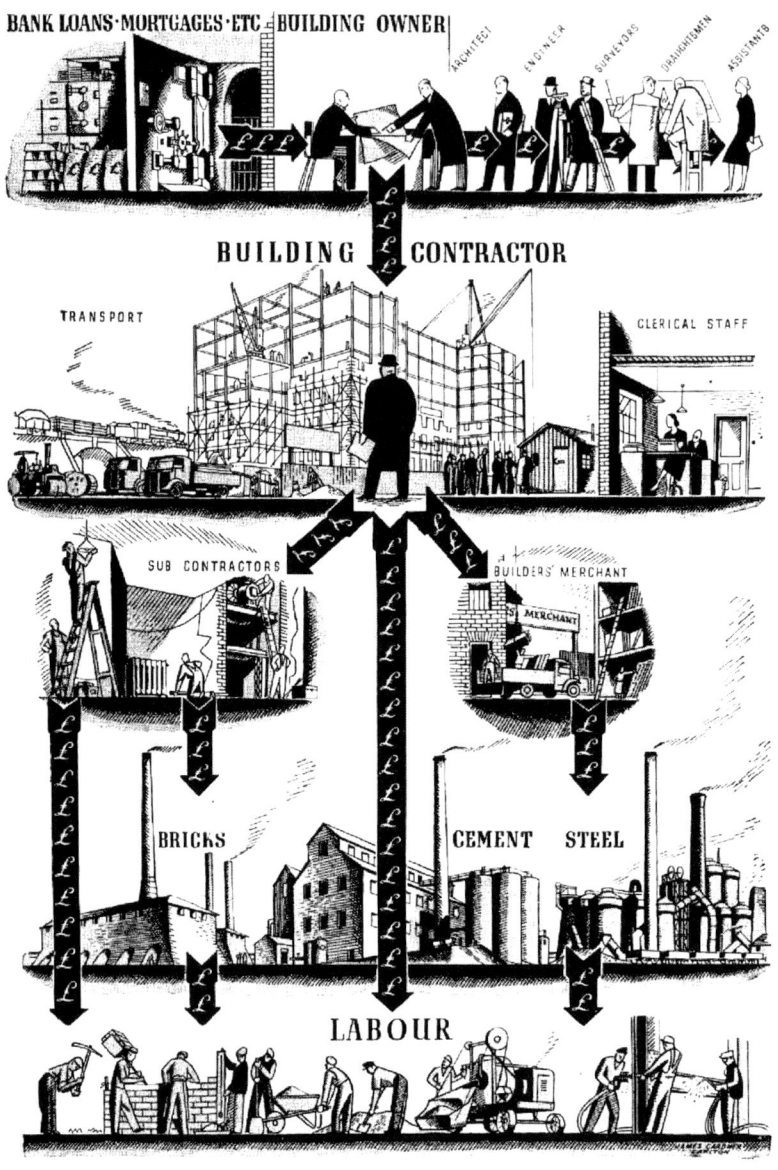

Figure 1.5

The pros and cons of public and private spending on social amenities, illustrated by John Summerson in the *Listener*, January 1938. © Immediate Media Company London Limited.

Figure 1.6

The pleasures of light, air, and space in contemporary schools, illustrated in Anthony Bertram, *Design in Everyday Things*, 1937. © Immediate Media Company London Limited.

of artist from painters, sculptors, musicians, poets, and actors. They touched upon the role of government in their domain and their role in government, thus positioning themselves as critical players in the arena of politics.

The presentations featured prominent public personalities—MPs, social scientists, health officials, urban psychologists, and anthropologists—showing that modern architects incorporated the considerations of external experts in their design. For example, in 1933 John Gloag hosted the series *Design in Modern Life* for which he invited Frank Pick from London Transport to discuss the virtues of simplicity in the design of everything from household objects, to the street, to the city and beyond.

To the aforementioned topics, the war introduced issues such as "An Archive for Architecture" (1944) and "Reconstruction: Plymouth Rebuilding Plans" (1944).[62] Speaking as the deputy director of National Building Records, John Summerson argued that such an archive would at once open up "all sorts of deeply relevant issues of social history" and aesthetic heritage. "An archive" as an instrument of preserving records "will do for architecture what the great libraries do for … literature and music." Photographic records of lost buildings would "reveal extraordinarily clearly the roots of so many of our present-day problems and our traditional attempts at solving them."[63] Summerson framed knowledge of architectural history as indispensable for solving contemporary problems. The bombing of London and other cities in 1940 turned the radio discussions to the urgency of town planning, rebuilding, historic preservation, and documentation of built artifacts. Herbert Read made a public case to the Ministry of Works for hiring those architects who saw man as an "organic being" and who had realized that a city must "include variety within its seeming uniformity" and "individual idiom within the universal style." The phantasmagoric scene of Fleet Street in London was cited as a cautionary tale. He concluded on a high note:

> There are modern architects who have realized these truths and, who have begun to create a tradition where no tradition now exists. It would be a supreme national tragedy—indeed, a proof that we have not yet cast off the spirit of defeatism—if the opportunity is not now given to those architects to rebuild our devastated cities. The country is in a mood for such enterprise, and the architects are ready, pencils in hand. If anyone stands in the way, it is only a sinister figure surviving from a world that has gone down in flame and fury.[64]

This new criticism, feeling the need to formulate peremptory verdicts, placed itself unconditionally at the service of the new architect. All in all, from aerodromes to archives, from evacuation to returning home, such broadcast initiatives intimately bound historic architecture to self-preservation.

Speakers like C. R. Ashbee, G. M. Boumphrey, and Maxwell Fry used the wireless to create new projects. In 1929, Hilda Matheson invited Charles Ashbee on two separate occasions to represent the Council for the Preservation of Rural England (CPRE). Ashbee seized the occasion to make a design proposal. He posed a problem: the visual destruction of the countryside, namely England herself. He positioned himself: "I address you as an architect, a town planner, and one who has studied this question practically in all its detail not only in England, but in Europe, the East, and America." Then came the strategic intervention: the modernization of the countryside was an aesthetic issue. Next unfolded the goal: to make sure "all this [development was done] in the public interest." Stakeholders were identified: "local community and tourists," and the client: "the local municipal councils." The government employees had to be pressured into this role by the community. Having set up the scenario, Ashbee made a three-step design proposal, discussed the policy change required to implement it, and gave the listeners a clear role in the proposed course of action. Widely dismissed as an antidevelopment nuisance, the CPRE had little popular support at the time.[65] Yet Matheson created an opening for Ashbee to explain his position to a hostile audience and to persuade it to add "beauty" to the list of considerations in development programs.

Ashbee's case stands for several others in which speakers turned the wireless classroom into a studio-like environment—a place where architects rather than clients defined the building program, and peers, not an indifferent public, judged the design proposals. The wireless classroom both complied with and transcended the limits of an architect's studio. First, it laid out the stakes involved in matters important to architects. Second, it expanded the horizons of professional practice. Finally, it involved the members of its community in new design tasks that could only have been created through nondesign, extracurricular practices.

Broadcasts furnished listeners with competing principles of architectural appreciation. In 1927, the literary critic Amabel Strachey and the neoclassical architect Clough Williams-Ellis critiqued the modernist doctrine of "form follows function" for its failure to satisfy architecture's most vital social purpose:

Figure 1.7

A recent view of Fleet Street, showcased in the 1940 *Listener* article by Herbert Read to illustrate the visual confusion of a street born of laissez-faire planning policy. The street has since lost most of its distracting canvas canopies and jarring signage. Courtesy: Ronald James.

its aesthetic function.[66] The pleasure of architecture, for both occupant and visitor, they argued, was grounded in visual appeal alone—its shape, harmony with the street, setbacks, and visual dynamism. This effect demanded no prior knowledge, only curiosity. As such, its delights were available to all.[67]

The modernists were not much behind the neoclassicists and neo-Gothicists in putting forth their case for the myth of universal accessibility and the role of spectatorship. Frederic Towndrow was one of the many figures to align architectural appreciation to modernist principles of design. Speaking on *Adventures in Architecture*, a program targeted at schoolchildren, he condemned the separation of visual pleasure from the "story of the building." "Beauty" in that case was frivolous, he argued; it became skin deep and a lie that "muddled our minds." The detachment of appearance from the purpose of the building was a social menace, responsible for "lack of town planning and our vulgarity in our showy little suburban houses." "When you look at a building it should be able to tell a story." It is this story that should give pleasure. A building "should be able to say to you, 'I was created for such and such a purpose by such and such a people, and the man who designed me was either a fine and intelligent sort of fellow, or a liar and thief.'"[68] A building delivered by the impersonal logic of the machine, Towndrow took pains to imprint upon the children's minds, must not be misrecognized for an automatically generated architecture. Achieving a quiet beauty was a tougher feat, requiring artistic genius. The modernists kept the charismatic ideology intact, and affirmed the irreducibility of work to the status of simple merchandise.

Other noteworthy programs on this theme included a talk by Banister Fletcher based on his book *Romance in Architecture* (1929), and a travel series

Figure 1.8
Royal Tweed Bridge, Northumberland, 1925–1928, constructed by Mouchel & Partners. Courtesy: Barbara Passmore.

by Stanley Casson called *Travelers' Tales from Plymouth* in autumn 1930. W. E. Williams, editor-in-chief of Penguin Books, spoke of architectural appreciation on "Art for the People," in a series called *Far and Near* in 1937. In all these cases, the pleasure of visuality and the theme of its popular appeal did not rely on the natural mechanisms of vision; they all counted on language.

Yet, I must stress again, Towndrow's dependence on words was much greater than that of Williams-Ellis and Strachey. He rejected the huge bag of historically accumulated shapes cherished by a historicist like Williams-Ellis, in favor of modern experimentation. He needed words to do what innovations like roof gardens and open plans could not do by themselves. Words helped innovators offer the audience a system appropriate for deciphering their advances. Flat roofs and horizontal windows, we must recognize, held current codes for interpretation in abeyance. Their designers were not satisfied with stylistic innovations for their own sake, but wanted them to be judged as socially responsible. Speech ensured that their contributions would not be decoded according to criteria used to make sense of pitched roofs and punctured windows. In other words, language adjusted the frequency of emission and reception of meaning. It provided explanations, elaborated principles, and articulated aims. It posed problems and devised strategies. It elevated the audience's ability to comprehend complicated messages. Words made design visible. Speech created audience.

In this paradigm, the 1930 series *To-day and To-morrow in Architecture* offered explanations of how to think about architecture. It featured five prominent educators from Britain's prestigious architectural school, the Architectural Association. Professor Humphrey Pakington opened the talks; his task was to discredit the much-beloved Edwardian architecture for its imitation of past styles. "The great tradition is to experiment," he told listeners. We do not follow the Roman tradition, he argued, "when we build a miniature triumphal arch and move it about

To-day and To-morrow in Architecture
II—Structure and Material
By HOWARD ROBERTSON

EVERYBODY interested in architecture to-day is talking about the new movement, the modern spirit which all over Europe and America is bringing about a renaissance—some call it a revolution—in architectural design.

How is it that such a movement comes about? Is it due to discontent with old forms, a sort of fatigue, the desire for something fresh? Is it the result of a realisation that the old architecture no longer properly serves our present day needs? Or does it spring from the fact that science has given us a great number of new materials with which to build, and we are feeling the urge to use them?

Are these largely responsible for the striking of a new note in architecture? The answer is 'yes', but only up to a point. For when we glance over the list of materials most widely used in buildings to-day, we find that many of them have been employed for centuries. Brick, stone, concrete, terra-cotta are the chief materials for walling; and there is nothing new about these. The Romans used concrete and terra-cotta extensively, and the mediæval masons knew quite as much about stone cutting—technically known as 'stereotomy'—as we do. So there is nothing very novel here, nor in the multifarious uses of wood. So while we have a good many new materials, they are not dominating present day architecture to the extent of causing a renaissance through materials alone.

There must be, therefore, some other factor contributing to modern development. This factor is *structural design*, the method of constructing buildings and using materials both old and new.

If we look back through architectural history, we find a great number of so-called 'styles' or 'periods'. Now these forms are the outcome of the social and cultural influences of their day, and of what may be called the 'building programme' of the day, that is to say typical building problems such as the Temples of Greece, the baths and public buildings of Rome, the mediæval cathedrals. But, above all, they are the outcome of the structural methods used in solving and realising these problems of building, the technical knowledge which the builders had, and the materials which were available.

The Romans discovered how to use a new material, concrete, which set into a solid homogeneous mass, more or less in the form of a huge casting. By discovering the possibilities of concrete, the Romans were able to bridge huge spaces, and construct great domes like that of the Pantheon, over 140 feet in diameter, without any intermediate supports.

An All-Steel Church at Presse, near Cologne (1928)
By courtesy of 'The Studio', Ltd.

The mediæval designers, in tackling the same problem of covering space, hit upon an entirely different structural solution. Instead of solid inert masses of concrete, they imagined a roofing of stone vaulting, consisting of small stones which exerted thrust one upon another, and finally upon stone ribs, in the principle of the arch. The thrust of these ribs was taken down to the ground *via* stone piers, and the outward thrust on these slender supports was counterbalanced by a system of buttresses. The Renaissance period did not make such a vital contribution to structure; but it did witness an advance in engineering science, with great structural feats like Brunelleschi's dome in Florence Cathedral and Michelangelo's dome of St. Peter's. The Renaissance attitude of mind was that of exploring and improving upon past performances as regards structure, without contributing any distinctly new system.

The fact that structural development, after the early outbursts of daring in Florence and Rome, remained more or less stationary, in part accounts for the gradual decay of architecture up to the nineteenth century. Architects concentrated upon externals, on styles, manners, and fashions, because there was not much else to do. And they turned over the old ground of the past in the form of Revivals, Gothic and Greek, in the effort to keep moving within the structural limitations which seemed to have been reached.

However, as always happens, a new development was lurking round the corner. It was the biggest, perhaps, that had happened in all the history of architecture, more far reaching than the Roman domes or the Gothic vaults. That great structural development was the invention of the steel frame building. The steel frame is the great contribution to architecture of our own age, the magic ladder up which our own modern architecture may climb to great heights. With the steel frame enters into the field a new factor which is supremely important, and lies at the very basis of the modern movement.

That is the scientific attitude towards architecture. This scientific attitude is born of the absolute necessity, in utilising steel, for an exact science of calculation. The great difference between structure to-day and that of previous ages, is the substitution of scientific calculation for guess work and rule of thumb. That difference has come about through science and engineering. Exact knowledge is the governing factor in the design of modern building structure, and from this attitude of precision towards structure has come about a new attitude towards architecture generally, the application to its problem of processes of reasoning and logic.

Figure 1.9

Howard Robertson, broadcast on "Structure and Material," published in the *Listener*, May 1930, featuring a steel frame church, Cologne, 1928. © Immediate Media Company London Limited.

London, and finally deposit it at the juncture of Park Lane and the Bayswater Road. ... Poor little Marble Arch, leading to nowhere, at least you have the satisfaction of getting in the way of the traffic!" The plagiarism of Marble Arch belittled the Roman tradition, Pakington said. In contrast, "when we set ourselves, armed with new knowledge, to experiment in the solution of greater structural problems than the Romans ever had to face; to burrow a building a hundred feet into the earth and to throw it a thousand feet into the sky, or to fling a bridge across a mile of water into a single span," we glorify the Roman epic of art. He pointed to the Royal Tweed Bridge at Berwick-on-Tweed to prove that "modern architecture [could] be as beautiful and striking as traditional architecture."[69]

The following Tuesday, Howard Robertson made the point more boldly. Architectural history, he told listeners, turned neither on changes in needs, nor fatigue from arches, nor even the invention of new materials, but on something utterly more architectural: *structural design*." It was structural daring that offered a key to "the modern spirit." "The steel frame" replaced "guess work and rule of thumb" with an "attitude of precision towards structure." Precision introduced "a new attitude towards architecture generally, the application to its problem of processes of reasoning and logic."[70] Finally, reasoning and logic prioritized social relevance over visual composition. The listener to the program was now told to judge artistry by the level of mastery of science and engineering, not according to rules of classical proportions. The following week, Maurice Webb spent his time on the air supporting the same evaluative criteria with examples of steel-frame skyscrapers in America.[71] In the fourth show in the series, Harold Tomlinson tied structural originality to economic efficiency. His audience heard that budget constraints, with the best architects, produced new structural solutions. It was financial necessity that had led to the discovery of concrete in Germany and Austria. Concrete allowed larger openings; larger windows introduced air and light; and air and light created healthier living spaces![72]

R. A. Duncan concluded the series *To-day and To-morrow in Architecture* with a recapitulation of all the benefits to the everyday life of ordinary citizens brought about by the recent shifts in architectural thinking. In 1928, he had exhibited a "home-grown manifestation of modernism" at the 1928 Ideal Home exhibition.[73] Backed by its example, his listeners learned that architect-designed houses could be as economical as conventional spec-built designs.[74] Incessant redefinition of the foundations of modern architecture rescued unadorned, white cubic houses from normative judgments.

This rather lengthy explication should foreground the role critics played in producing architecture in the age of radiophonic connectivity. Mediating between the built environment and its intelligibility, critics' words were as vital to transforming a building into a work of architecture as were the skill, intellect, and education of the designer. This look at the role of broadcast utterance in the space of architecture should encourage us to break with the old-fashioned ideology of designers as the sole producers of architecture.

Broadcasting favored the modernists more than the traditionalists who dominated contemporary design practice. Since it relieved speakers from the need to support their ideas with material proof, technologically mediated speech made newcomers the "equals" of practitioners, with greater opportunity to build. A 1934 broadcast debate between Amyas Connell (1901–1980) and Sir Reginald Blomfield (1856–1942) exemplifies radiophonic "leveling." Blomfield was the knighted remodeler of Regent Street, a former president of the RIBA and honored by that institute with a gold medal, and a recognized scholar, toward the tail end of his career. Connell, on the other hand, was a young New Zealander, five years out of school with two small houses to his credit. The space of radio sublimated Blomfield's field advantage over his interlocutor as they debated the virtues and vices of the modern movement.[75] One could thus claim that early British radio changed things for modernists in more ways than merely by endorsing their self-representation.

While the technology was partial to youth, the BBC aired propositions of practitioners and critics with competing philosophies. Broadcasting was like a sporting arena, a comparison realized most vividly in an architectural symposium held by the BBC on modern architecture in 1934. The show was quite literally set up as a competition between two teams, called the functionalists and the traditionalists. Each participant was given six questions, and each team alternated turns to present their positions. The questions dealt with the suitability of modern architecture to England. For example, "Has functionalism in building gone too far? Can the English town and city ever properly assimilate the new architecture?" Identifying modern architecture only with functionalism, on account of the second question, Sir Reginald Blomfield, Professor A. E. Richardson, and M. H. Baillie Scott thought not. Blomfield declared that "the surest test of architectural effect is the viewpoint of the man-in-the-street," and this man "has grown accustomed to reverence ancient buildings." As a result, "it is doubtful whether undue disturbance of the pictorial values by cubist designs will find favor." For Richardson, new architecture's indifference to the authority of history resulted in its lack of deference to "maintain[ing] artistic harmony."[76] Baillie Scott likewise dismissed the "new architecture" as "violently at variance with the spirit of the old town":

> The particular charm of an English town derives from its expression of national and local character, influenced no doubt originally by climate, habit, and the special technique of the material available. The new style apparently owns no such allegiance; it has neither ancestry nor kindred; it cannot be on speaking terms with its neighbors, for it does not know their language.[77]

Maxwell Fry, Charles Holden, W. Curtis Green, Wells Coates, Frederic Towndrow, and Joseph Emberton, representing the modernist faction, took exception to the idyllic portrayal of English towns. "As to the jumbled, fused, maltreated English town," Fry retorted, "is there anything it cannot assimilate?"[78] Wells Coates, irritated at the entire premise of the symposium, snapped, "In case no one has noticed, England went off the gold standard in architecture about a hundred years ago." Breaking with the "banker-architects" and their policy to "Pay Bearer on Demand," Coates argued, modern architects were not being imprudent, but were finally getting responsible.[79] Fry disagreed with the charges against modern architecture and its antagonism to the existing built fabric: "The purity of modern architecture at its best can only bring repose to the confusion of fruitless nineteenth century ornamentation, order into unplanned chaos, and standards of excellence where none exist. ... Our job as architects is to serve society completely—and to raise its standards."[80]

The final word went to Wells Coates. He asserted that his opponents complained about functionalism because its standard of beauty did not comply with their rearguard notion of beauty:

> The new architecture is traveling on two parallel permanent ways: one is the way of Science—the science of the *inside* of things, science the *identifier*, measurer, and calculator; the other is the way of Art—which is the science of the *outside* of things: art the *differentiator*, selector, and maker. For Architecture—the surest and completest art—is both science and art, moving on parallel lines.[81]

Alternating views, like a tennis ball going from one side of the court to another and then back again, were judged not by the audience but by an architect—another past RIBA president. Sir Raymond Unwin said that "to sum up [the debate] with fairness is difficult because those who have spoken for tradition have been so ready to admit that 'the modernists [had brought] architecture to its essentials,' while some advocates of modernism have relied on very doubtful assumptions." He explained, "Let every dwelling be convenient and well equipped with efficient apparatus, certainly, but that is the beginning, not the end of design." Unconvinced by the functionalist definition of beauty, he went on, "It is the special function of the architect to transform the sanitary family stables or economical man's warehouse into homes, with all the content of comfort and beauty which that old English word implies."[82] The participating architects had presented their positions in anticipation of their judgment by an architect and thus had spoken to architectural takes on formal approaches. The presence of a disciplinary referee on the playing court organized by diverse institutional interests of the BBC distinguished this competition from normal free-market conditions. In this arena, the success of a player and his team was measured by strokes of artistic originality in responding to the public responsibility of architects. The prize was the monopoly over public opinion and the definition of architecture.

In airing competing viewpoints, radio did for architecture what the professional press could not do and the lay press did not do. J. M. Richards, an editor at the Architectural Press, had tried "without much effect" to persuade the

Figure 1.10

The glass walls, white surfaces, and pristine volumes of Joseph Emberton's Royal Corinthian Yacht Club in Essex, 1931, upheld as examples of responsible design. Courtesy: Richard McDonald-Proctor.

New Statesman to take up the discussion of modern architecture.[83] The popular press, he believed, would provide modernist trends a neutral venue that polarization in the professional press deprived them of. But *New Statesman* didn't cover the topic well. The BBC, in comparison, met Richards's expectations and even exceeded his standards. It served as an arena where competitors tried to score against one another with their personal best, and team efforts forged camaraderie among participants.

The BBC's sponsorship enhanced the modernist position both within architectural circles and in society at large. But it also brought gains to those in the discipline who did not appear on the airwaves. Different occasions for programs—publications, exhibitions, presidential speeches at the RIBA, sales of historic properties, college graduation—portrayed architecture not just as technical but as a literate occupation. In this, radio serviced architects as a social group, those who spoke on the radio and those didn't alike.

Prohibited by the RIBA from directly advertising their services, architects found in radio a way to build a market for their goods, without resorting to commercials. In fact, John Reith banned direct advertisement on radio. The departments of Broadcast Talks and Broadcast Education took pains to ensure that none of their works brought complaints of free advertisement for any particular company or group, artists, or art institutions. Architects were almost never allowed to discuss their own professional accomplishments or works in progress.[84] This information was separated from the design methods that informed their practice. Reith foreclosed the use of radio to raise business for oneself, presupposing participation by only those who could rise above business as usual.

The difference between hard and soft sell, propaganda and education, shop and museum, was a critical distinction for designers, who like the RIBA's president thought of their kind as superior to developers. Take, for instance, the line drawn by the architect Charles Reilly in a peer address at the institute a few years before the establishment of the BBC: "The commercial gentlemen who plaster our walls and flood the press with the virtues of their wares really inhabit a different planet from ourselves."[85] Operating as tradespeople, builders freely used commercial maneuvers. But, aspiring to cultural production, architects dismissed such maneuvers as depraved. "Imagine," asked Reilly of his audience, "what would happen to you personally if the Institute took to advertising the advantages of employing its members by publishing pictures of its President. You would become standardized!!!! ... We cannot proclaim virtues of ourselves or our buildings in the mass. *Propaganda* we must leave to the market-place and those who work there. But that does not mean that we cannot do anything to *educate* the public as to what is good architecture."⁸⁶ The microphone provided Reilly's peers with a discreet source of advertising as public relations. And, more than that, broadcasting itself became a line of demarcation between the invitees, who refused to be assessed by the market—on which they relied and within which they operated—and commercial architects who embraced and dominated the market.

Wireless words were similar to written words, in that they both produced effects according to specific rules. While the printed page dictated a posture through fixed type and vision, broadcasting obliged the listener through an auditory, verbal, and ephemeral resource (especially prior to cheap recording equipment).⁸⁷ The first preserved memory on page. The second was dependent on human memory. The first usually connected a solitary and isolated writer to a solitary reader; the second connected a similarly isolated speaker (cut off from the context of his audience) to multiple listeners.⁸⁸ Reading forced readers to abandon themselves to the text. Distant listening could not command this undivided attention—*listening in* was passive; it took less effort than reading. While a reader could choose what, when, and at what pace she took in a message, a listener had no such luxury. She, like the broadcast itself, was bound to the constraints of time. Broadcasting was apprehended in a state of distraction. It exalted the role of voice in reframing social relations. The printed word gave the reader a relatively remote consciousness of community, whereas the wireless word created both a vast and immediate social unity. Walter Ong observed that orality favors thought that is often uncongenial to the literate mind. Verbal thought is "formulaic, structured in proverbs and other set expressions." It favors ideas that are "aggregative rather than analytic, participatory rather than distanced, situational rather than abstract."⁸⁹ Radio creates an illusion of honest response and a peep into character. Elizabeth Eisenstein points out that print allows writers to juxtapose large amounts of disparate material, add multiple layers, and weave them together intricately. The reader can then go back and forth to clarify ideas. Wireless presentation, however, must be cyclically organized, and so the listener cannot return to evidence. Therefore, a broadcaster must keep specialized discourse on an informal plane, provide simple diagnoses, and handle a limited amount of evidence. Repetition, an anathema in writing, is essential to oratory. It secures the thread of the argument. Hadley Cantril and

Gordon W. Allport, two of radio's earliest theorists, realized that salvation for specialized discourse on radio was available only in the form of slogans.[90]

As products of a literate tradition, architects and critics worked with drawings, models, and photographs in logical terms (with concepts, variables, axioms, propositions). Their ideas proceeded from particular logical properties (generality, abstractness, precision). Their thoughts stood in specific logical relations with one another (consistency, contradiction, implication). They performed certain logical operations on concepts (deduction, generalization, specification, codification). Radio combined literate expression with oral idiom; it relied not on sound argument made in the way stated above, but on a talent for making words *sound* like a sound argument. Arresting messages required self-assured speakers. Such a lively impression of universality created a wireless crowd. The medium favored voices that gave listeners a sense of participation in decision making. "By the trick of verbal juxtaposition," observed Cantril and Allport, in this space "the glory that is God's, Christ's, Bacon, Milton (and to which the speaker has allied himself) is made to shine upon the speaker."[91] Those who were good at it exploited explanation and defense, humor, and sharp wit, and cultivated informality and studied spontaneity. Berthold Lubetkin and Wells Coates reinvented themselves from mere cogs in the machine to thinkers of social housing and town planning. Clear pronunciation and the lighthearted styles of John Gloag and Frank Pick created a sense of social contract between the audience and the performer. Authoritative accent and strong voice partook in the persuasiveness of their ideas. Listening reduced criticality. A radio audience was more easily persuaded than were readers.[92] The medium's blunting of the analytical faculty was invaluable to the development of the impersonal market for architects. It projected them not only as experts and rightful designers, but also as caretakers of their symbolic clients. Beyond promoting the spokespeople, radiophonic speech advantaged the whole group for whom they spoke; it put them across as men and women of wide culture and confidence, worthy of emulation.

Howard Robertson in 1930 counseled potential clients on what (and what not) to demand from an architect. "Do not bring up a picture of a tudoresque window with you."[93] John Gloag spent weeks furnishing builders with detailed specs in front of potential buyers of the "house we ought to live in": "In plan the small house should be compact. Floor adjoining the range, draining boards and sink must certainly be tiled. The door should be simply paneled, and if constructed of hard wood may be stained and polished, or if soft wood is used then it may be painted and finished in enamel, or better still a clear varnish."[94] Maxwell Fry filled airtime, guiding women to treat the kitchen as "a machine room, a room of kindly, helpful machines, designed to simplify and make work enjoyable."[95] Elizabeth Denby was even more specific: "Pots and pans should be chosen because they are easy to clean, economical in use and in addition good-looking."[96] Geoffrey Boumphrey proceeded as a consumer protector, tipping off buyers against the tricks of jerry-builders: "As a rule you will be given very little information about the structure itself, unless you insist on it."[97] He systematically went through a working section of a prototype house—from the foundation up to the drains, floors, skirting, all the way to the roof proofing—explaining what buyers must inquire after. He encouraged his audience to shop for "clean lines" and "healthful living," saying they must look for "purposeful" design.[98] Architects and critics thus assumed the role of modern day sages, imparting both wisdom and advice on how to shop!

The growing demographic of first-time homebuyers heard:

> How to get honestly-built houses that look as they should look is the question. Houses that are not faked, that are well built, and may even be good architecture. I do not myself think that it is really possible under the normal system of speculative building. The risks are too great for the little man and the building societies are not interested in the qualities which produce good architecture: they are merely lending money on building security. What people *can* do, to cure this state of things, is to learn what are the things to look out for in buying a house. In this way they can gradually raise the level, even of speculative building. The builders will follow the demand quickly enough.[99]

These programs brought about an inversion of outlook; for example, the assessment of materials was gauged by an emphasis on durability, affordability, structural flexibility, strength, shrinkage, and fire resistance. Timber was promoted—not for sentimental reasons, but for economic ones.[100]

What came across in print as opinion sounded like advice on the radio. Aesthetic ideals metamorphosed into aphorisms and rules. As sentences shortened and language simplified, details vanished and caveats subsided. The linearity of written argument gave way to nonlinear, repetitive, and intuitive suggestions. Propositions proceeded by analogy instead of sequential development; recondite

Figure 1.11

Examples provided by Elizabeth Denby of kitchen equipment and layout that would save energy and time, in John Gloag, ed., *Design in Modern Life*, 1934. Courtesy: Taylor & Francis Books (UK).

---

philosophical underpinnings faded behind assertions. What was spelled out in writing became quick and implicit in speech.

The persuasive power of the medium allowed the BBC to surreptitiously advocate for the controversial issue of historic preservation. As preservation was wound up with death duties, the rural electrification bill, planning laws, corn subsidies, and so on, the BBC had initially resisted touching the litigious issue. Talented broadcasters like G. M. Boumphrey, John Betjeman, and John Summerson put their conservationist opinions on the map by slipping them into oral travelogues. Using storytelling—a genre proper to radio—they changed the limits of what was possible to say in public. These men realized that radio favored the active voice; it relayed ideas most effectively in the form of personal experience and practical counsel. Boumphrey and Betjeman didn't provide precise information or exact directives. Instead, they impressed their messages upon the mind subliminally and imperceptibly. Their stories knitted myth and experience with fantasy and provocation, for they understood well that the more miraculous the narrative got, the more stimulating and intriguing it became. The more intriguing it turned, the greater its chance to be repeated by word of mouth. In turn, the more often their ideas got repeated, the more forcefully they would integrate into public know-how.

During the Second World War, when the British economy transitioned from an empire to a welfare state, the BBC asked architect F. S. Yerbury to report on "Housing and Social Conditions in Sweden," and give an overview of prefabricated housing. "In summer time," Yerbury explained, "you'll see whole families getting to work on one of these sites, excavating and building up the cellar walls, and when sections of the house arrive, mother, father, children and friends help to place them together." The completed houses are "warm, spacious, cozy and well-furnished."[101] An excellent example of partnership between government and architects, the project showcased public housing not as one challenge among many, but as the most urgent one confronting contemporary practice. The broadcast suggested, without saying so, that only modernists (attentive to prefabrication) addressed it head on.

While the survivors of the arts and crafts tradition, whose clients had both wealth and artistic taste, could find nothing in the machine, design for the people embraced prefabricated industrial products and made architecture affordable. "Anyone looking for ideas on how to live in a democracy and making life pleasant and beautiful for the people," said Yerbury, will find Sweden "a very fertile hunting ground."[102]

Such functionalist and materialist interpretations created the illusion that modernists in Britain simply submitted themselves to the preexisting demands of the expanded market. Their grandiose claims, however, did not give users any say in the evaluative criteria of architecture. For example, on the question of reconstruction after the war, John Summerson drew a line between architectural and emotional value, making only the former worthy of saving: "I do believe in putting back those destroyed buildings—and only those—whose merit is not merely in age or sentiment but whose lines embody an expression of genius which will shine as clearly from the sharp-cut stone of the twentieth century as it did from the worn masonry of the seventeenth and eighteenth."[103] This position, when taken on as policy, gave not the public but experts command over the definition of architectural heritage.

For Goodhart-Rendel, rebuilding was an irreverent act. It was analogous to reproducing a lost painting in such exactitude that no one recognized the difference. Why should architecture be held to lesser standards than the masterpieces in national galleries? When it's gone, it's gone. "We ought to shed a tear for what is gone, and then put something frankly new in its place," he argued.[104] Rebuilding desecrated the original no less than bombing. "I hold that to make a sham antique building can be not only inartistic but unpatriotic. ... We must not let our idealists to continue the dreadful work of the enemies."[105] Here patriotic sentiment was stirred against sentimentalism.

Architectural discourse maintained the architect's pride by upholding his self-perception as a charismatic creator of urban and rural life. John Summerson's social history of architecture also failed to escape the illusion. Take his discussion of the city of Bath:

> Today, Bath is quoted over and over again as almost the one city in Britain, which in its origin, was planned. It is curious to remember how that plan originated. No ministries, no committees, no well-known experts. Only the young engineer up in Yorkshire, drawing in his spare time, inspired far less by the logic of contemporary needs than his private notion of a kind of magnificence, which had existed in the world eighteen hundred years before he was born.[106]

In addition, John Betjeman made a career on radio by elaborating the specifically artistic manner in which buildings expressed the world. Wells Coates and Frederic Towndrow committed themselves to elucidating the meaning objectively inscribed in works by their authors.[107] Morton Shand and John Gloag focused on the artistry of Mies van der Rohe, Erich Mendelsohn, Marcel Breuer, and Le Corbusier to explicate the efforts of these men to break with conventions of artistic thought. Finally, radio mediated the perception of buildings not just by the public but by their authors as well. The BBC made review integral to architect's self-recognition.

This is a rather long inventory of the media-specific powers of speech, but it has an important effect: it gives radio an uncanny resemblance to the modern invention called the museum. The BBC reinforced the modernists' claim that a building's function could be aesthetically expressed, and it acknowledged the contention that the artistic innovations of the period were valuable to the communal needs of an evolving democracy. By giving these ideologies a platform that claimed to be a public service, the BBC implicitly agreed to the capacity of these ideas to "update" the social image of elite artistic culture. Engagement with the mechanisms of mass marketing on the one hand, and manifestation of the political maneuvers of interwar liberals on the other—"the sociological impertinence" and "propensity to talk" that so offended Goodhart-Rendel—are all at play here. But, far from undermining the specialized authority of the title "architect," far from flattening him into one worldly producer among others, *speech in the particular linguistic condition of radio reinstated all the hierarchies upon which the identity of architect relied*. The adaptation of the principle of legitimation to a world connected by radio confirmed the architect's special status outside

Figure 1.12

John Wood the Elder and the Younger, King's Circus, Bath, 1754–1768. Courtesy: Mollie Johanson.

the building process, just as the Registration Act assured a continued presence within it.

Architects and critics did not passively submit to tight controls on what and how things could be said. The *supply* of their goods (discourse and its proof in design works) fit between Reith's *demands*. As a group, representatives of architecture were just as eager as Reith to expand the public for cultural production, just as willing to foster civilized and enlightened debate, and just as ready to blunt social, political, *and* cultural radicalism.

The correspondence of vision and mission of the BBC and the architects gave speakers unusual leeway in setting the tone of debates. They brought topics, agendas, and colleagues important to them. The role of designers in the building sector seldom allowed buildings to function as faithful representations of what their authors wanted them to communicate. But on air, architects found themselves in charge of their own affairs. Between 1927 and 1945, British radio constituted an alternative site of practice in which the invited architects enjoyed greater than usual control over the reception of their work. Radio increased the architects' power over the circulation of a belief in the value of their works— that is to say, the power to manufacture an image of work as a cultural product, as opposed to merely an economic good. Every sigh, exclamation, agitation, and silence, every adjustment of volume and pace, measure of word and mistake, presentation genre, mastery of monologues and scripted debate, every sound effect, interpretation, and privileging of "creator's" intention, was geared toward the reproduction and expansion of a *market,* without concessions to the existing market, in which a new conception of professional practice had an *exchange value*.

In short, mass diffusion did not collapse the logic of high art into low, but created fresh differentiations. Spokesmen accepted public service and they admitted ordinary determinations to decipher works. But these external determinations were translated in conformity with architectural discourse's own principles of functioning. Architects' engagement with mass culture refracted external forces through their prism, distinguishing cultural production from its surroundings.

While British radio itself was not set up as a "market," broadcasting developed an "impersonal market" for architecture. Most importantly, it was not this or that statement that created the public meaning of work. This meaning was attended upon by the entire network of relations surrounding it; between architects and critics, critics and publishers, educators and legislators, established and new entrants into practice, and so on. The history of architecture in the space of early British radio is the history of conversion of the social identity of architecture from a personal possession to a public symbol. This history turned not on a single creator, a Michelangelo or a Leonardo da Vinci, with the quasi-magical power capable of transubstantiating objects and actions into symbolic goods. Rather, it was a collective enterprise. It was in the disciplinary rivalry between Goodhart-Rendel and Summerson (otherwise good friends) that meaning was elucidated and things were objectified as art. Through their disagreement over modernist fusion of form and responsibility—the identity of flat roof and conscientious conduct—disciplinary relations and positions in British architecture were consolidated. The fleeting readings that speakers and program producers gave to things did not stand on their own. Their public meaning was created in light of the importance speakers publicly attached to them: the fact that they considered these things worthy of devoting their lives to (even when they critiqued and ridiculed their past importance) and that they drew the meaning of their lives from debating, representing, elucidating, making, and re-making architecture.

    The reality of symbolic structures, I reiterate, is socially constituted. Human beings make meaningful the world that makes them. Nothing demonstrates this claim more lucidly than a symbolic system and the analysis of the denials and recognitions, beliefs and illusions on which it is founded. We assimilate the entire ensemble of critics, art historians, and educators with the direct makers of material works, making them all participants in the production of works by conditioning their perception. The same must be done for radio and the administrative authorities of the BBC; competent in matters of art (though nothing like speakers), they and the institution they monopolized must also be absorbed into the list of agents and institutions that contributed to the production of cultural goods. British radio acted on the art market by verdicts of consecration (showings and awards). It produced consumers capable of recognizing works of arts and endorsed analytical categories of heritage, identity, memory, psychology, sociology, and excellence. Among the makers of work of art we must finally include the public, which helped to create its value by appropriating it materially (collectors) or symbolically (audience, readers), and by objectively or subjectively identifying part of its own value with these appropriations.

    In the space of radio, architecture and architects gained relative authority with regard to other fields of cultural production (art, literature, music, philosophy) that they did not otherwise enjoy at that historical moment. Architects gained this cultural authority not just by being able to act as artists—and this is critical—but by underscoring the *difference* of their artistry from that of other producers of culture. This momentary and limited authority did not exempt architecture from commendable or lamentable external influences. Art historian Ernst Gombrich, radio monitor for the BBC during World War II, put it eloquently: "While power *can* succeed in making art its spokesman, art in itself, art pure and simple, allowed to foster without interference, becomes the most powerful, the most lasting propaganda."[108]

This authority was greatly indebted to verbal presentation. As Walter Ong writes, "Listening to spoken words forms hearers into a group, a true audience, just as reading written or printed texts turns individuals in on themselves."[109] The oldest function of pre-typographic orality, this authority was carried out by radio at a scale impossible in preliterate societies. Ong specifies:

> Before writing, oral folk were group-minded because no feasible alternative had presented itself. In our age of secondary orality, we are group-minded self-consciously and programmatically. The individual feels that he or she, as an individual, must be socially sensitive. Unlike members of a primary oral culture, who are turned outward because they have had little occasion to turn inward, we are turned outward because we have turned inward.[110]

This power of the spoken word was reinforced by radio's virtuality. Radio changed the manner in which buildings exerted force. If previously buildings had exerted power through the theatricality of their materials, they now asserted it through the theatricality of words. If previously the meaning of the physical environment was subservient to the logic of economic production, it now became subservient to the logic of virtual production.

2 THE ORDER OF THINGS: THE PLACE OF ARCHITECTURE IN THE SPACE OF RADIO

I Qualities of Radiophonic Architecture

Radio dealt a decisive blow to the edifice of nineteenth-century art institutions. Older institutions, such as periodicals, museums, exhibitions, and touring, were united by a unique quality: they gathered disparate works of art in one place. Such assemblage had the critical effect of neutralizing the diversity of functions (religious, political, archival, or personal) to which art (whether built, painted, written, or performed) was originally subordinated. It privileged form over function, technique over theme, and format over content. It promoted a belief in the symbolic value of works as a value in itself. Visitors to specialized environments of culture checked their daily concerns with their coats and bags at the door, freeing themselves, both physically and mentally, for "pure gazing." These nineteenth-century institutions fostered in artists and the public an unquestioned belief in the primacy of the mode of representation over the object of representation.

The self-evidence of art thus constructed came under attack from all directions with the emergence of radio. First, radio settled in our lives in the guise of an innocuous household item, akin to a piece of furniture or a potted plant.

But unlike those objects, it pierced through walls and delivered art, music, and drama at home as a utility. Its listeners were free from the conventions of seeing and being seen. One could enjoy a concert of Lorenzo Da Ponte's music or a lecture by Sir Edwin Lutyens while in one's slippers and drinking a beer. Bypassing the decorum of traditional cultural institutions, radio facilitated the immediate absorption of culture. It pulled art out of institutional shelters committed to the veneration of artists and delivered it and its discourse to sites devoted to the pleasures and vital necessities of life. Radio's location in the home was a setting for contingencies, practicalities, mixed use, and distractions. The rituals and relations in the domestic environs were born not of the freedom and leisure of the museum, but of necessity.

Second, the public nature of broadcasting presented artists with new tasks and challenges. The modern artist was no longer a private person, her work no more a private commission. She was not responsible to an individual or the paying client alone, but was instead required to court the multitude. She "published"! What she brought out she delivered into the hands of all. She had to take into account the formlessness, and the breathtaking scale and reach of the wireless audience.[1] "There was a courtly art for the court, the poetry of master singers for the rich artisan of the cities, a bourgeois art for the bourgeoisie—now there will have to be an art for nine million," predicted Arno Schirokauer.[2] Radio was hardwired with populist impulses and therefore intolerant of eccentricities. "Not a word can be spoken on the radio," exclaimed one frustrated critic, "that has not been understood and approved by a host of uncontrollable, irresponsible, and nearly surreptitious bureaucrats and independent reactions, average citizens, and obedient little shopkeepers."[3] The impracticality of production for a niche audience led the sculptor and typographer Eric Gill to sentence radio to mediocrity.[4]

Third, the pedagogic scenario of the home was diverse, dispersed, and undemanding. The unity of an aesthetically disposed public was disrupted, and social interaction was changed from the public to the domestic scale. With this shift, broadcasters lost the benefit of established strategies for commanding attention that a trip to an actual museum, a walking tour, or a classroom lecture imparted in and of themselves. Listeners did not enjoy the unique experience or the memorability that were part of physical visits. A vicarious trip to a town or a RIBA show through listening to a radio program was an ordinary event. It was a less demanding event even when one paid attention to what broadcasters were saying. This

Figure 2.1

Dreaming of the house of the future.
Courtesy: Neenah History.

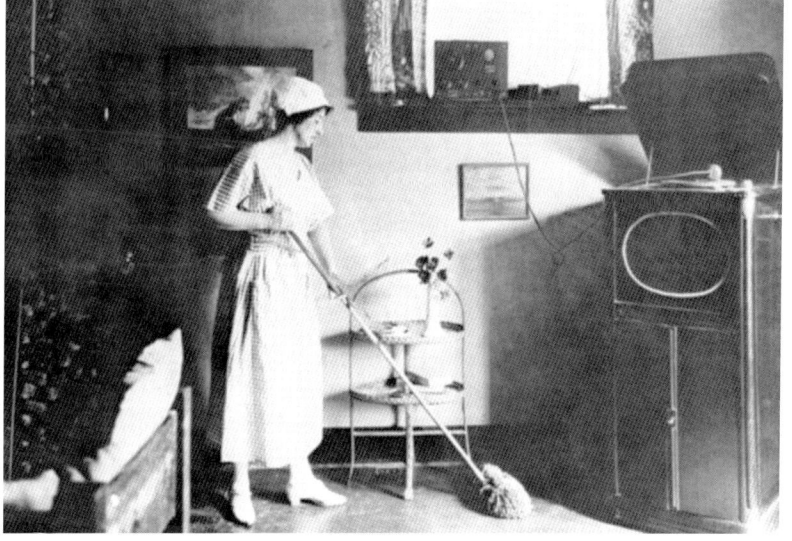

mode of communication compelled guides to compete for the consideration of listeners for whom, unlike museum-goers, listening was potentially one task among many. Orators had to struggle against the tyranny of the listener's power, so celebrated by Walter Benjamin, to shut a speaker off in midsentence.[5]

Fourth, as Frank Warschauer wrote of broadcasting opera, radio was "the most powerful disintegrator of the old opera public that had a mind set, or at least the preconditions for one, produced by definite educational and temperamental prerequisites."[6] A renowned composer and an astute contemporary of Benjamin, Warschauer anticipated that the culture of wireless listening threatened to "undermine the aristocratic prerequisites of the opera and thereby pose the question of its fate, a question that has so far received no better answer than the problems of this age of denial and of the transcendence of existing relations."[7] Others thought this new venue brought a definitive end to the attempts to use traditional artworks to unify people. When conveyed on radio, issues and thoughts were too dispersed, too displaced, and too deprived of their material properties to arouse any contemporary's confidence in their ability to shape and consolidate a public in any recognizable way.

Finally, radio set up a confrontation between the aesthetic and the ordinary modes of seeing. It did so by creating a public whose eye and etiquettes of appreciation were formed and informed without familiarity with art. As a medium of mass communication, radio objectified demands of the ordinary perception, the passions, emotions, and feelings which ordinary people put into their everyday existence. It subordinated form to function. It prioritized the demand for the immediately accessible, the obvious, generic, and common. This included everything that reduced the aesthetic animal to pure and simple animality, to palpable pleasure and to sensual desire.

Charles Siepmann, the director of the Talks department, required artists and critics to articulate the value of art in terms "that could be traced within the life-time of an ordinary man."[8] Broadcasting demanded nothing less than the translation of the beliefs of one world (aesthetic) in terms of the mutually exclusive belief system of another (ordinary). Nothing concerning art was a given anymore, "not its inner life, not its relation to the world, not even its right to exist." It undermined the notion of art as something pregiven, immediately recognizable, and whose virtues were only awaiting discovery by the spectator. The BBC, in inviting art producers to interest and transform the greater public into an art-consuming public, put speakers on the defensive, on trial as it were. The title of a 1940s series of interviews, *Artist in the Witness Box*, vividly captures this quandary. "It is not easy," confessed a frustrated Doreen Joad, "to argue what is almost an article of faith."[9] (She was attempting to enumerate the rules of garden design on air.)

The scripted conversation between architectural critic John Gloag and artist Edward Halliday highlights this deadlock:

J.G.: And that brings us back to the point again: how are people to know what is good design and what isn't? … For example, Halliday, how does one know what is bad pattern on a piece of cretonne? We all believe that we know good from bad, but can we give reasons?

E.H.: That's a very deep subject, Gloag. …

J.G.: The question of taste's too big a subject to be talked out tonight. …[10]

The objectification of aesthetic perception in terms of ordinary perception was a death sentence for broadcast culture, since these two modes of making sense of the world have been historically defined against each other. For example, aesthetic perception is self-consciously distant, exceptional, and isolating, while ordinary perception is immediate, formulaic, and associative. The first is a pure aesthetic that brackets off practical ends and makes viewing an end in itself, while the second is an involved aesthetic that legitimizes works of art by reducing them to the things of life. If the first holds associative thought and the world in abeyance, the second insists on applying to art the schema of the ethos that pertains in ordinary circumstances of life.

The broadcasters were aware of this predicament. They were at pains to point out the differences between aesthetic and ordinary perception. If Herbert Read, a regular contributor to "Weekly Art Notes" in the *Listener*, talked up the artistic eye as a function of the free mind plus the sensibility and feeling that transcends communicability, Charles Holmes, curator of the National Gallery, pulled down common disposition as a function of the simpler instincts of a savage.[11] If the first "sensibility comes in where communicability is blocked," the second is stuck in the rudders of utilitarian association.[12] For the (later infamous) psychologist Cyril Burt, aesthetic judgment was objective while ordinary perception was personal and whimsical.[13] One of England's most influential artists and well (and so saving wasted material), and it *does* become beautiful.

J. G.: I don't think that beauty derived from fitness is accidental. Norman Douglas has said, 'There is a beauty in fitness no art can enhance'. I think you and Boumphrey are both getting at the same thing, but from different angles. But there's one matter on which we all agree: there's far too much bad design about; and we're all profoundly dissatisfied about it—you, Halliday, as an artist, you, Boumphrey, as an engineer, and I as a minor critic of architecture and industrial art. Our dissatisfaction isn't just a personal peculiarity—it must come to anybody who looks about him and begins to criticise the buildings he passes in the street, and the shape, convenience and colour of everyday things he lives with. But let's come back first of all to this business of definitions: what exactly do we mean by good design?

G. B.: I take it there are two obvious meanings to the word: design in the artistic sense, and design meaning purpose.

J. G.: Well, I always hold design to mean planning what you want to do in the most direct way.

E. H.: I believe you can't dissociate good design from beauty—or, rather, what I mean by beauty.

G. B.: Exactly. If a thing is designed to do its job really well—honestly designed without any frills on—you do get, whatever you like to call it, beauty or satisfaction or anything else. And that, I take it, is exactly the feeling we all agree we don't get nearly often enough from the things we use in everyday life.

J. G.: We're certainly all agreed about that.

E. H.: What about wireless cabinets in the style of a Charles II chest, or ye olde flickering yule-logge electric radiator?

J. G.: What about a carpet factory dolled up to look like a Venetian palace, or a filling station pretending to be a Tudor gate house?

G. B.: What about a gas fire with a box under it to catch the cinders?

J. G.: Of course, we could go on all night. We're all surrounded by examples of things that are fundamentally bad, because they haven't been designed at all, things that are just romantic adaptations lifted from the past and used for an exclusively modern purpose.

E. H.: Or things that are badly designed in themselves.

G. B.: Now that's a very important distinction to make. Your complaint, Gloag, is of things badly designed because they're dishonest, even if they're romantically dishonest; and yours, Halliday, is that things are just badly designed. And the reason why the level of design is so deplorably bad in this country is because it has been debased by this absurd worship of the past.

J. G.: Why shouldn't we have an affection for the past, if we want to? Some things have been invented and perfected in the past, and to discard them would mean throwing overboard all sorts of civilised legacies. For example, I think that the solution to chair design was made for all time in the early eighteenth century, when we produced something that was perfectly adapted for the lines of the human body, something that was unforgettably gracious and extraordinarily comfortable.

G. B.: You talk as though conditions today were the same as those in the eighteenth century!

E. H.: Surely the human frame hasn't altered so much in that time, has it? A comfortable chair is still a comfortable chair.

G. B.: Yes, but the conditions under which it was made and the people for whom it was made have altered profoundly. Chippendale and the earlier craftsmen made chairs for a comparatively few rich people. They were hand-made. They couldn't be anything else but hand-made. They suited the dress and manners of the eighteenth century. But now hundreds and thousands of people want chairs, and most of them aren't rich. And because they've been told that Chippendale chairs are beautiful they buy the nearest thing they can to them—beastly machine-made copies with none of the beauty of the original left.

J. G.: Chippendale only made things by hand because woodworking machinery which is used in mass production today was not invented in his time—but he organised production by hand so that men took the place of repetitive machines. The same man would be concentrated, perhaps all the time, on shaping the front legs of chairs, another would turn out the arms or the carved cresting on the top rail of the chair back.

Contrasts of design—chairs designed by Chippendale (right) and Chermayeff (left)
Photograph, Country Life

Newspaper printing offices at Abo, Finland, showing concrete pillars 'varied in thickness according to the strains involved'
By courtesy of Mr. P. Morton Shand

It was slow and expensive, this hand-power factory, so he could only work for rich people. If by mass production you mean making a number of things of the same design in a factory, then Chippendale and other eighteenth-century furniture

Figure 2.2

Challenges of comparing traditional and modern designs: a comparison of chairs designed in wood and fabric by Chippendale and in tubular metal and leather by Serge Chermayeff (above, right and left); Newspaper Printing Office, Abo, Finland, 1929 (below), an example of rational design where the shape of the concrete pillars varies "in thickness according to the strains involved." *Listener*, April 1933. © Immediate Media Company London Limited.

---

critics, Roger Fry, in turn highlighted that the ways the ordinary man and the artist look at things are mutually exclusive: "For most of us sight is used for some other purposes than the mere enjoyment of visual sensations. ... We look in order to recognize our friends or to distinguish one object from another, while the artist ... looks for the sake of looking."[14] Art educator J. E. Barton called the first a focused form of observation while the second was the habit of scanning.[15] For Robert Lyon, a painting instructor for coal miners in Bristol, "aesthetic appreciation" "come[s] from within" while ordinary appreciation "is the reach-me-down opinions of others. "Aestheticization of sensibilities" is a result of the awakening of our "sophisticated and subtle instinct [and] the insatiable curiosity" of an artist about the ever-shifting shapes and patterns that nature puts before him.[16]

These definitions asserted the hierarchies of cultural legitimacy and unconsciously deciphered the countless signs which at every moment say what is to be loved and what is not, what is to be seen and what is to be discounted. The aestheticized eye, Fry said, takes a distant view of things; it "looks not for what distinguishes one thing from another so much as for what unites everything into a coherent system; ... some underlying and pervading quality in shapes," the "tune which the sights of nature arouse in his mind."[17] Barton argued that only an art lover who regularly visits galleries and museums and who is familiar with the latest in art and architecture is capable of deriving true pleasure from modern, abstract, and seemingly strange developments. A person whose choices are informed by associative cognition is content with just "a quiet, gentle, easy, lukewarm feeling about the works he admires." But associative taste is not real taste: "This pleasure in reminders of agreeable things has nothing whatever to do with taste. ... What 'stirs' an 'art lover' is the magical inner life with which things are filled in the picture—or rather, it would be better to say, the magic with which the whole arrangement ... is filled. Colour that moves him like stained glass he has seen in very old churches ... the life that comes across to him, and fills him with deep satisfaction, is a life that only existed in the vision and in the touch of" the architect, the sculptor, and the painter.[18] Since these oral investments pursue profits that do not need to be pursued as profits, they present professional producers of culture as entirely disinterested. They assert the superiority of artistic culture over popular culture and the professional producers of the first as the leaders of high culture.

At the same time, radio required these men who have legitimate culture as their second nature to define the aesthetic taste's demand for originality in terms of what they considered the conservatism of popular taste. Eric Newton, the Manchester *Guardian* art critic, was confronted on the microphone with the predicament of translating art that demands contemplation into most people's demand for immediate gratification. Newton told listeners that derivative art makes consumption easy, while originality *demands* thought before *giving*.[19] But how was one to represent the obscurity of original art in terms of the derivative nature of popular art? Housing critic Geoffrey Boumphrey had noticed that unsophisticated people who "prided themselves on being practical men" were "ready to adopt an antagonistic attitude whenever any question of aesthetics crops up."[20] "To the town-dweller today," Frederick Etchells commented, "Nature has given a kind of eye which makes him blind to the blatant ugliness by which he is surrounded. She has affected his critical reasoning and his eyesight."[21] How was one to translate the logic of thoughtfulness, expansiveness, and long-sightedness into the logic of thoughtlessness, myopia, and short-sightedness?

Inside the BBC, the "broadcasting service [was] looked to as" merely extending and "giving the best there [was]."[22] It would educate those who did not know how to tell culture from nonculture by simply exposing them to it. "It should be remembered," warned John Reith, "that for acquiring of knowledge, building of experience and the formation of taste, there are two distinct and fundamental requirements. Inclination is one; opportunity is the other. ... Given some degree of inclination, and no opportunity, broadcasting carries sufficient of the latter to encourage the former."[23] Culture, in this context, meant the development of literary and artistic culture as well as all sides of humanity. This formulation had its source in the nineteenth-century cultural theories of Mathew Arnold.[24] Culture was "the pursuit of our total perfection," "the best which has been thought and said in the world."[25] It did not include the symbolic expressions of different social factions. Cultural diffusion, in the hands of the early BBC, meant culture for the people, not of the people.

Hilda Matheson (director) and Christopher Salmon (assistant director) of the Talks department were confident that transmitting the point of view of musicians, authors, actors, filmmakers, artists, and architects to the public's sitting rooms was mainly a matter of preparing preestablished content for oral delivery.[26] They courted musicians like Sir Adrian Boult and Percy Pitt and established the department's own orchestra; hired staff members who could attract the loose consortium of artists, architects, and scholars affiliated with Bloomsbury, Unit One, and the Modern Architectural Research Group;[27] and sought the cooperation of literary figures such as Rebecca West, E. M. Forster, and Geoffrey Grigson.[28] But broadcasting was not a frictionless path to spreading culture.

The five challenges to representing art on the radio made attempts to relate, for instance, a Picasso or a Gainsborough to the everyday concerns of listeners a self-defeating premise. While the medium did not take well to abstract issues, the demand for linking the applied arts to life was perfectly appropriate. These arts bridged the utilitarian taste of the new public and the aesthetic perception demanded by sincere works. Their combination of artistry and use, the esoteric and the mundane, the visible and functional, addressed the challenge of broadcast culture. The physical environment, therefore, made far more robust topics of conversation than fine arts, and resolved the problem of broadcast culture.

II The Predicament of Broadcast Culture

Seated behind his Sheesham desk in his Oxford study in late November 1931, Stanley Casson read over the latest proposal he had drafted for his former student, the current director of BBC Talks, Charles Siepmann.²⁹ Siepmann had secured an influential position in Adult Education Broadcasts just three years after graduation and needed Casson's advice on art shows. They had met in London to brainstorm ideas for a series on art, and were now in correspondence to refine those ideas. Casson glanced at the program proposal and the letter from Siepmann, which stressed: "We must at all costs avoid highbrow presentation and if you can think out any scheme of talks with subject headings that would in themselves be attractive and a stimulus to thought, I should be very grateful."³⁰

Casson thought of topics appropriate for an occasion without the direct give-and-take he enjoyed with his Oxford students. Scanning the covers of the books lining the walls of his study, he decided upon interviews of artists. His shelves were filled with books on classical archaeology, Greek architecture and sculpture, Byzantine use of color, and material for courses he taught at New College and the Ashmolean Museum. Across from his desk hung the medal he had won for service in World War I. It reminded him of the ease with which he had combined knowledge of all things Greek with the urgencies of military affairs. He had linked his talents for contemplation and action in order to come up with a winning war strategy. His attention turned to a pile of books and magazines on contemporary artists and sculptors. He jotted down the names and addresses of some of the most articulate artists in the nation and made the following proposal for weekly topics.

> **1.** How am I to learn to appreciate works of art?—Self and group leader
> or
> Producers and Consumers—Self and any artist
> **2.** How a sculptor works—Eric Gill and self
> or
> Stone Carving and modeling—Pilkington-Jackson (a Scottish sculptor)
> **3.** What arts can be combined with architecture? Morley-Horder or Frank Dobson
> or
> **4.** What is applied art?—Any architect (suggestions to be got from secretary of Architectural Association, Bedford Square).
> **5.** Why and how I paint?—(Augustus John, if possible)
> or
> Landscape and figure painting. How the painter paints—Paul Nash, Ed Halliday and self in discussion.³¹

Interviewing capitalized on the testimonial character of the medium and recorded debates ordinarily carried out in paint and stone. Without the prohibitively laborious demands of writing, it filled a glaring gap in the archive and scholarship of contemporary art history.

The series Siepmann and Casson designed was kicked off with an imaginary discussion called "Why Bother about Art? A Discussion between Stanley Casson and a Philistine." Casson acted as himself—a "professional visual observer." The philistine, played by his friend Dorothy Donald, portrayed a stereotypical listener by whom Casson imagined himself confronted: the "proud possessor of two excellent eyes that hardly function at all." She was "the untrusting philistine, the unreliable steward of public taste who says 'I can see all right.'"

> **Casson:** I had this curious defect in the English education—the neglect of teaching how to see—most forcibly brought before me during the War. Young observers in the Air Force … at first [used] to fly over the enemy lines, and on returning draw up a report on what they had seen … it was obviously most urgent that their reports should be full, accurate and careful. In fact … [they were] entirely unable to observe at all. If a report … contained three lines we were lucky. But after a time we persuaded them that it was more likely to help us to win the War if they would watch most carefully for railway trains, marching troops, increased supply dumps, guns, traffic, and hidden supplies, than to risk their lives in unnecessary fighting. What they found out might save thousands of British lives. After a time they saw what was wanted, but they were taught what to look for by a most methodical system of training by means of photographs. Experienced observers were told to take photos of the sort of things the inexperienced observers had to find. So gradually their reports became full and instinctive and led in the end to giving us information upon which the bulk of our successful strategy was based.
>
> …
>
> **Philistine:** I admit your example of the young observer is of some importance. Besides it is a reasonable argument based in fact. But what do you propose to do with me?
>
> …

Casson: I should simply start by going to as many picture galleries and exhibitions of art as you can.[32]

There it was, the predicament of broadcast culture at the heart of Casson's worldly endeavor. To explain to a philistine why art mattered, Casson was forced to turn to nonaesthetic parables. The beliefs of one world (aesthetic) had to be explained in terms of the mutually exclusive belief system of another (ordinary). Nothing short of it would sustain the attention of the steward of public taste created by mass media: "untrusting, self-satisfied, and unreliable."

"Why Bother about Art?" spearheaded the broadcasts that expanded the definition of art to include the useful, mundane, and functional. As Casson said, "When I say works of art, I don't mean merely pictures in galleries or statues in market places, tombstones or memorials, but I mean almost every object that is round you which is capable of being made more beautiful or less ugly."[33] Other art historians, such as Herbert Read, called for the reinvention of artists as designers,[34] while Eric Newton of the *Guardian* asked for an accessible and enjoyable public art.[35] Anthony Blunt, an art historian at Cambridge University (and, as later discovered, a Soviet spy), yearned for earlier times when an "artist was a practical servant of the day," and his work "related to serious things in life." "Today art is only a work of art," he complained. "The demand for independence is only narcissism," and damned artists to irrelevance.[36] Blunt's hero was Diego Rivera, whose realist representation technique had drawn working people to the museum in Detroit and opened for them a new door to self-reflection and self-understanding.

Radio confronted the gatekeepers of culture with a predicament. Their ambition was to reconcile the protocols of the mass listening space with the concept of art as unique, bounded objects, created by supreme individuals, and intellectually or sensually experienced by independent spectators. In venturing out with tips on how to look at pictures, Casson was bound by a "creator-centered" approach of genius at work, as shown by his suggestion, "Before you make any judgment of a work of art, look very closely at it indeed, and ask yourself what was the intention of the artist, what did he think and want when he did it."[37] In "The Artist and His Public," Eric Newton's notion of pleasure in art remained subservient to the idea of higher pleasure: "The primary condition of all art is to be contemplated." A great enthusiast of revolutionary artists such as Cézanne and Picasso, Newton rejected the growing popularity of functionalist positions among architects. He denounced functionalism on the basis that use was a distracted mode of appropriation; it involved action and not contemplation.[38]

Margaret H. Bulley, a student of the German art historian Heinrich Wölfflin, came to a similar conclusion when she was invited by the *Listener* to carry out a quasi-scientific statistical survey and analysis of the nation's taste. She blamed functionalism for interfering with art appreciation. People preferred realist art to abstract art, she argued, because they associated with the former.[39] Herbert Read in turn believed that an artist "must be left to proceed alone, as an individual." A true artist remained untouched by the process of production, marketing, and "all the restrictions and conventions of the compromise we call civilization," he said. Only then could an artist "cross the threshold" and reach the "subliminal self … a self which is another order of reality, profounder and more extensive than any known to our daily perceptions" and push the civilization along.[40] When it came to the concrete value of art, broadcasters thus inevitably turned to spiritual or psychological explanations.

III Architecture to the Rescue

Resorting to abstract ideals to define art was not a problem for broadcasters discussing architecture; they never let architecture's synthetic attributes go by without mention. Historically the most prestigious of the applied arts, architecture was discussed as an "object man makes for use in which he has some freedom of choosing shapes, colors, textures, and so on, *for their own sakes*."[41] Frank Pick, head of London Transport, assured listeners that he could talk about all art through "homely" and "familiar" examples, saying: "The illustrations I have chosen have nothing to do with art or aesthetics, or beauty in itself and yet they may be artistic or beautiful."[42]

Broadcasts presented the built environment as an artist's gesture made not in the museum but in the street. Architecture was an endeavor that could be discussed through "its business as well as its aesthetic side."[43] It was both of this world and of another world. In a world that seemed to be hell-bent against public discourse on art, that resented cultural conversations on radio, architecture

Figure 2.3

Useful art on the cover of Anthony Bertram, *Design in Everyday Things*, 1937. © Immediate Media Company London Limited.

performed a special duty: "Architecture is not a mere plaything, a toy: [but] the very trappings of our life."⁴⁴ As such it gave debate on art an urgency and immediacy. Architecture gave broadcasting a genre of artistic expression possessing a greater familiarity factor than any other. Frederick Etchells, translator of Le Corbusier, commented that "whether the 'average man' knows anything about architecture or not, he certainly must in the nature of things know a very great deal about the tangible results provided by the particular constructions in which he has to live or work."⁴⁵ John Summerson was sure to remind his listeners that, "next to literature, architecture is the most social of the arts, the one most mixed up with our daily life."⁴⁶ That it was perceived inattentively by users and passersby was all to the good. Unlike with painting, the listener has no escape from the physical environment. This gave architecture the power to work on the unconscious without being ambushed by conscious thought.

The BBC program producers accepted that great buildings that rose above their worldly entanglements had as much cultural worth as art and literature. The public existence of buildings complemented the public nature of broadcasting. Programs on the physical environment gave them greater powers of cultural education and enlightenment than other arts. Broadcasters valued this virtue of public buildings. "Each person who has the cause of education at heart," emphasized Professor A. E. Richardson, "will realize the enormous influence a really good [railway] station [or any public building] could exercise on the mass mind."⁴⁷ The direct experience of domestic, work, and public places (churches, schools, hospitals, shops) gave listeners, who did not have regular contact with works of art, the necessary preparation to be interested in the topic. Their involvement in questions of shelter, safety, and health made these issues topical and of general interest. All in all, the duality of architecture made it a better fit

Figure 2.4

Design in everyday objects, in Anthony Bertram, *Design in Everyday Things*, 1937. © Immediate Media Company London Limited.

Figure 2.5

History of the physical environment as history of the world, BBC pamphlet, 1937. © Immediate Media Company London Limited.

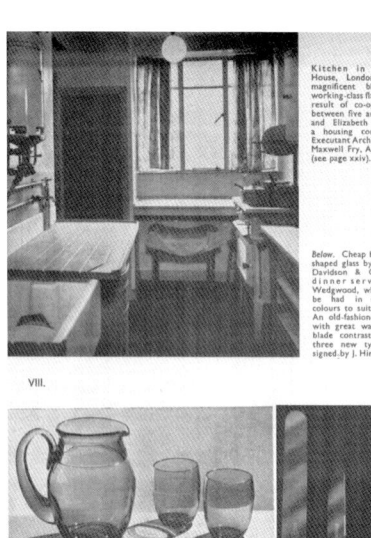
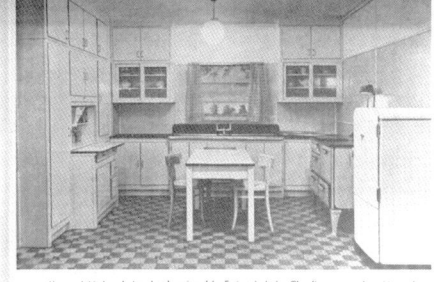

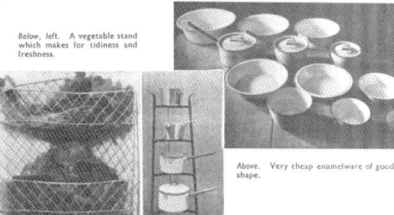

for radiophony than fine arts. It best fulfilled the BBC's demand for topics that promised outreach without sacrificing the mandate of improvement.

"Topicality" was the operative word in the halls of Broadcasting House. The BBC favored social topics. Field researchers for the Council of Broadcast Adult Education endorsed social topics as the most vibrant for listener study groups. Social issues involved the immediate quality of life, on which everyone had an opinion, and thus encouraged audience participation. They put architecture on the radar of the BBC producers. Field surveys led administrators to the view that if abstract topics like art and philosophy could be tied to concrete social concerns of listeners, they could continue to give them advanced (as opposed to more popular) treatment and still expect to spark broad interest and discussion.[48] They asked for presentations that contributed to the "improvement of taste, understanding, extend[ing] privilege and influence on the unfolding mind of a child,"[49] as well as that of an adult. Applied arts popped up in proposals for topics all the time.

Architecture-related topics were presented four and a half times more often than visual arts (painting and sculpture combined), and almost twice as often as literature.[50] They were second only to poetry; for every nine programs on architecture, one heard twelve poetry recitations. Every department at the BBC produced architectural broadcasts in all sorts of forms. They addressed every segment of their audience: schoolchildren of different ages, women of various backgrounds, and men in diverse occupations. Critic John Gloag narrated a clip on the removal of fences around public parks and Buckingham Palace on the six o'clock news bulletin. He made an occasion out of it, stressing that the royal fence removal signaled the importance of urban beautification and the inauguration of a reformed relationship between the royalty, private property, gardens, and the city. In 1935, *Women's Hour* brought architect Maxwell E. Fry to give tips on how to combine labor-saving techniques and good taste in the decoration of a home. John Summerson appeared on a variety show to criticize the shortsightedness of the Health Ministry for revealing the "inglorious truth that it has been possible to construct three million tolerably substantial dwellings and yet create absolutely nothing."[51] Howard Marshall, a regular sports commentator, produced a heart-wrenching documentary called *Other People's Houses* (1933). His eyewitness accounts of life in the slums of Tyneside, London, Manchester, and Glasgow highlighted the relationship between built environment, health, and mental development. *Children's Hour* gave modernist readings of the "Castles of Scotland," "Adventures in Architecture," and "The Roman Roads." In addition, the Corporation published multiple books and pamphlets, organized a symposium, and sponsored several exhibitions on architecture and the allied arts. In 1937, together with the Victoria and Albert Museum, it supported a number of traveling exhibitions to every nook and corner of England and tastefully displayed them in village shops. The exhibits featured a selection of prints of paintings, replicas of sculptures, photographs of buildings, and reproductions of household goods (lamps, chairs, china) from eighteenth- to twentieth-century Britain. When the BBC established the weekly *Listener* in 1929, most of the architectural broadcasts also began to circulate as articles. Its editor added supplemental articles as accompaniments to broadcasts.

This sustained effort aired a wide spectrum of opinions, including those of established authorities, the Who's Who in practice (Sir Raymond Unwin, Sir Giles Gilbert Scott, H. S. Goodhart-Rendel); the unknown, recent entrants (Amyas Connell, Serge Chermayeff, Raymond McGrath); professional educators (Howard Robertson, A. E. Richardson); historians (Sir Banister Fletcher, John Summerson); critics (John Betjeman, Noel Carrington); municipal architects (Frederic Towndrow); and journalists (James Richards). Public and private patrons of design, government officials, politicians, philanthropists, policy advisors, and other architectural enthusiasts accompanied them (Frank Pick, Sir Frederick Sykes, and Herbert Morrison).

Traditional architectural legacies also got their due. On the tercentenary of Sir Christopher Wren's birth, the Drama department produced a play on his life. Schoolchildren heard about the travels of Renaissance architect Inigo Jones. They learned that in order to demonstrate the hygiene of the sanitary system for disposing of toilet waste, Norman Shaw displayed the whole system in his living room. During Lent, the Department of Religious Broadcasts called upon H. S. Goodhart-Rendel to talk about "Christian Tradition in Architecture." The regional channel from Scotland had Ian Gordon Lindsay speak of the quiet dignity and beauty of Scottish traditions in architecture before the nineteenth-century outbreak of "mock Gothic" and "sham baronial." Travelogues raised the difficult question of preservation of stately homes, and regional channels hired architects to boast about their worthy churches, chapels, inns, gardens, and country and town houses.

Speakers tailored issues to the known and imagined interests of every segment of their audience. Architects and critics provided the BBC producers with

Figure 2.6

Hadrian's Wall, begun in AD 122, Northumbria National Park, England. Courtesy: Terry Morgan.

a good pool of eager participants, and what Matheson of the Talks and News called "ready-made speakers."[52] J. E. Barton, one of the BBC's most successful broadcasters on art, made a succinct case for the educational value of architectural appreciation. He was the principal of the famous Bristol School where he had introduced Allen Lane of Penguin Books to Le Corbusier and other modernists. Barton spoke of architecture as the mother art. His teaching experience had shown him that the most effective way to study art was to begin with an introduction to crafts that served some daily purpose and were pursued without too much in the way of artistic intention. In *Purpose and Admiration* (1932), where he made a case for modern art, he argued that the keystone of initiation into art was architecture:

> It is true that before men could build temples and cities, they achieved art unknowingly, as potters or weavers or thatchers. But civilization only begins when the crafts instincts of men are regulated and coordinated in a scheme that makes for permanence, and enshrines the stable beliefs of a settled community. From architecture proceeds sculpture, the monumental art and the least transient expression of individual genius.[53]

The BBC Council for Adult Education generously and enthusiastically promoted Barton's book. It appeared in the bibliographies of the Talks' art pamphlets, was referenced in speeches, and got Barton invited to the microphone for the six-part series *Art in a Changing World*. The pamphlet based on the series made broadcast history by becoming the BBC's bestseller.

Eric Newton, in an interview with the architect Goodhart-Rendel, gave voice to the strategic advantage of architecture in the following words:

> In one or two of my recent broadcasts, I made the point that the artist of today, unlike the artist of the past, has been forced to retire, as it were, from the world and take refuge in his studio … since nobody but the advertiser and the man who wants his portrait painted seems to need his services, he is in the position of an unemployed workman who is so keen on his work that he goes on doing it even after the demand for it has ceased. It seems to me that perhaps the architect can find a remedy. Architecture is supposed to be the Mother of the Arts, though of late years many architects seem to have been deliberately avoiding the responsibilities of motherhood. Can't

Figure 2.7

The street in the nineteenth and twentieth centuries, broadcast in March 1930 and published in the BBC pamphlet by J. E. Barton, *Modern Art: The Changing World*, 1930. © Immediate Media Company London Limited.

the architect step in and give the artist a sense that he is really needed? ... I should be interested to hear how you as an architect think that architecture ought to play the mother to the painter of pictures?[54]

The BBC drew out the socially relevant elements in contemporary architectural movements of all stripes, including arts and crafts vernacularists, Edwardians, and proto-Continental modernists. But the modernists were most successful in relating the revolution in representational conventions ushered by Le Corbusier, Walter Gropius, and Alvar Aalto to the possibilities of "architecture for everyone." Talks by Humphrey Pakington, a professor at the Architectural Association School of Architecture in London, demonstrated that the history of architecture was not just the history of art but the history of the world. It was a past belonging to everyone, not something insular reserved merely for the enjoyment of aesthetes.[55] John Summerson broadcast on architectural history in reflection of this assumption; he framed it both as a social history of the building and as artistic expression. The quest Maxwell Fry set for his generation of practitioners was not the development of an individualistic, romantic, and oversensuous work of art but a "contemporary vernacular," in which "the economics of living dictate[s] the form of architecture" and in which "that form ... ha[s] nearly universal validity."[56] Industrial exhibitions enabled architects like Serge Chermayeff, F. R. S. Yorke, and Wells Coates to show that modern design could bring the artist's work out of its previous seclusion and take it to every shop, if not every home in England. John Gloag and Anthony Bertram stressed how contemporary industrial design could infuse everyday things from a toilet seat to a radio set to white walls with the psychic energy of a designer.[57]

Architects trained in the academic tradition found such initiatives heretic, philistine, and uneducated. "They are killing the art of architecture," bemoaned Reginald Blomfield.[58] An architect was first and foremost "a designer of beautiful things, limited like a sculptor, by his subject and materials, ... not efficient things," exclaimed the famous archaeologist Professor Bernard Ashmole. Efficiency and structural integrity, which anyone could achieve, were of secondary importance. This generation evaluated architecture according to criteria of more independent fine arts. "It has always seemed to me odd," regretted H. S. Goodhart-Rendel,

8 FEBRUARY 1940 THE LISTENER

The Artist in the Witness Box

Artist and Architect

Discussion between H. S. GOODHART-RENDEL, Past President of the R.I.B.A., and ERIC NEWTON

NEWTON: In one or two of my recent broadcasts, I made the point that the artist of today, unlike the artist of the past, has been forced to retire, as it were, from the world and take refuge in his studio; and that once there he tends to experiment in methods of expression instead of regarding painting as a way of supplying a human demand. In other words, since nobody, except the advertiser and the man who wants his portrait painted, seems to need his services, he is in the position of an unemployed workman who is so keen on his work that he goes on doing it even after the demand for it has ceased. It seems to me that here perhaps the architect can find a remedy. Architecture is supposed to be the Mother of the Arts, though of late years many architects seem to have been deliberately avoiding the responsibilities of motherhood. Can't the architect step in and give the artist a sense that he is really needed? Easel pictures will always be painted, I suppose; but do you think that the solution of the problem lies in more and more easel pictures? I should be interested to hear how you as an architect think that architecture ought to play the mother to the painter of pictures?

Goodhart-Rendel: By seeing that painters get more and more walls to paint on, so that they don't have to use easels so much. Paintings come to the wall in the end, so why shouldn't they start there? The easel picture with no fixed destination is a homeless child at best, more often out of its proper place than in it. People kidnap it and pamper it and make money out of it, and shut it up in horrible institutions where it looks aimless and unhappy. Whereas a painting on a wall can live a useful life, doing all the time what it was intended to do. I admit that you must have portable paintings as well as fixed ones; family portraits, for example, and small devotional pictures perhaps (like ikons), and ornamental pictures that you can move with the china, linen and glass from one house to another. But all these would be only a sideline if painting really meant anything in the daily life of ordinary people. The main body of painting would be on the walls of the buildings in which that life was led.

Newton: I quite agree with you that art no longer means anything in the daily life of ordinary people. But suppose there were a general demand for it. Suppose every wall of every house had its painting. Surely nine-tenths of it would be pretty mediocre stuff?

Goodhart-Rendel: Certainly, if painting were universal, a good deal of it would be bad—but it's that anyway. Very likely a sort of universal painting, all over the place, would mean a downward step in quality. You'd get stuff like that on the outside of South German houses or on the ceilings of old-fashioned Riviera villas. But I don't think that would matter any more than it did during the Italian Renaissance, when there was quite as much bad painting as good. If you got the bad with the good, you'd also get the good with the bad and some of the bad might be quite enjoyable!

Newton: Yes, but if an easel picture is bad you can just scrap it or refuse to buy it, whereas there's something horribly permanent about mural painting. If it's bad you can't easily get rid of it; if it's good you can't take it with you when you move into another house.

Goodhart-Rendel: Of course, the kind of painting that you do in a house which you may leave or let must be a very sketchy affair. The Italians understand that very well, and, to a certain extent, so do the Japanese. What we need today are young men who will paint people's walls on the understanding that they will

'The Empty Tomb'. Mural painting by Colin Gill : All Saints' Church, Valescure

paint them over again at a very low cost if the people get bored with them.

Newton: All the same I have grave doubts about the suitability of mural decorations in private houses, though I'm willing to be convinced. Public buildings are different; you only pass through a public building.

Goodhart-Rendel: Obviously the painting of public buildings must aim at some degree of permanence and importance. That's a different problem from the private house problem. In private houses I think you have two alternatives: you can either have the wall-painting on canvas that looks fixed but really is movable, or you can have the painting not worth moving—the temporary painting that is a decoration the artist must be prepared to do cheaply and quickly. It's this sort of temporary painting that I most hope for in houses. Whether we get it or not will depend, of course, on the demand. After the extraordinary

Figure 2.8
Eric Newton and H. S. Goodhart-Rendel, interview "Artist and Architect," *Listener*, February 1940. © Immediate Media Company London Limited.

that the least interesting of all these dead and bottled ideas, the one labeled "functionalism," should have arisen and spread in the years when ordinary people first began to be interested in the sub-conscious mind. You would have supposed that anybody who realized how much hidden wisdom and how much forgotten but still influential experience may lie behind the apparently unreasoning choice made by an artist—you would have supposed that anybody realizing this would be especially wary when measuring art by the yard-stick of conscious thought. ... No reasoning can determine the entasis of a column.[59]

Charles Holden, the designer and planner of the first modern-*cum*-arts-and-crafts underground stations, disagreed with this assessment. Functionalism did not imply the elimination of art, he asserted, but the inversion of the existing criterion: "Architecture is not embroidery. It fulfills a fundamental human need, and it is in the fulfilling of this need with pride and pleasure in the truthfulness of expression of its various functions that we convert building into a fine art."[60] John Summerson argued that architecture was not like painting, which was "used" by hanging and seeing and which possessed a priori legitimacy. Architecture and the city became works of art by being used, desanitized, and depurified.[61] In Herbert Read's words, "The New Architecture rests on a fundamental distinction between art and utility. It does not deny architecture, or even seek to reform it. It only asks it to keep in its place."[62]

Modernists argued that their exaltation of "fitness for purpose" against the existing traces of Victoriana—which considered decoration, the least essential element of building, as the most sacred—made works more open to the new public. By the same token, some critics and architects believed that the philistine

IS MODERN ARCHITECTURE ON THE RIGHT TRACK?

Architecture, which of all the arts lends itself most easily to public criticism, has undergone an admittedly remarkable transformation in the last twenty years. The question which springs uppermost in the minds of those who see great new buildings rising in their midst must be: Are we entering on a new era of great architecture; or, on the other hand, is architecture disappearing as an art, as a result of new constructional methods? We have accordingly asked a number of architectural experts to answer this broad question, which we have tried to translate into the following specific queries:

(1) *Is the engineer making the architect unnecessary today?*
(2) *Has functionalism in building gone too far?*
(3) *Can the English town and city ever properly assimilate the new architecture?*
(4) *Is the new architecture ugly?*
(5) *What will the next generation think of the ultra-modern style of present-day buildings, including the ultra-modern home?*
(6) *Are we likely to evolve in the near future a new style of architectural ornament?*

SIR REGINALD BLOMFIELD

SOME of us had hoped that Modern Architecture, having gone off the deep end, might come to the surface again with a clearer vision of what architecture really means, and has always meant hitherto. We realised that the modernists had got rid of a lot of unnecessary trappings, and were making a laudable effort to bring architecture back to its essentials. Unfortunately, they appeared to have an inadequate perception of what those essentials are, and in their zeal for 'functionalism' or whatever they call it, they are simply killing the art of architecture. The art critic of one of our daily papers recently assured its readers that in future professional painters will confine themselves to making patterns, and, following the same line of thought, our modernist architects would seem to limit architecture to factory design.

They are handing over the art to engineers, and greatly as I admire the ability of engineers within their own province, their incapacity in matters of æsthetics is notorious, and indeed is recognised by themselves. The modernists are selling the fort of architecture.

Yet, after all, architecture is an art and from time immemorial it has been regarded as one of the greatest. Beautiful buildings, the Parthenon for instance, the Pantheon, Chartres, or St. Paul's have moved men and women more profoundly than any but the very greatest masterpieces of painting and sculpture; but who is going to be moved, except to resentment, by buildings such as Herr Mendelsohn produces in Germany or M. Corbusier in France, or by buildings of steel and brick that purport to be made of concrete, buildings

Thurso House, Cambridge   Architect: George Checkley
By courtesy of 'The Architect and Building News'

Figure 2.9

Sir Reginald Blomfield in "Is Modern Architecture on the Right Track?—A Symposium," *Listener*, July 1933, featuring George Checkley, Willow House, Cambridge, 1932. © Immediate Media Company London Limited.

populace was more open to modernist principles than the cultivated public. Modernists made concessions to naïve reaction and its affirmation of the continuity between art and life. G. M. Boumphrey held that the masses were indifferent to architecture as it had stood until then. Lacking the knowledge necessary for the perception and appreciation of modernism and comparison with other styles, they felt themselves ignorant and left out. Traditional design was the product of a culture of injustice. Why should the masses emulate glories of a past they'd rather forget? "They are more interested in to-day and to-morrow than in yesterday."[63] Their judgment was alive, immediate, and based in common sense. It was therefore a potential corrective for the art of architecture. An uncultured person found beauty in something he spontaneously delighted in. His taste made no recourse to outworn traditions.[64] Maxwell Fry argued that functionalism was a "well spirited attack upon some of our Dictators of Taste. ... Whether it is ugly or beautiful, is not within the competence of men whose taste has been maimed by the last century to judge."[65] It must be left to the future patrons whose condition, "with all their crudities of taste," was "healthier" and more prepared for the reception of "the new architecture [that] had found its finest expression up to the present, not in houses or public buildings where beauty had been the primary object but in factories and the like, designed mainly for utilitarian ends." The job of a modern critic was to let the man in the street "realize that he should judge the design of his house, its environment, and furniture in precisely the same way" he selected "his car or his wireless."[66]

While for modern *art* critics, functionalism was an impediment to the transformation of popular taste, modern architectural critics could celebrate the fact that it demanded nothing of its users and spectators. Morton Shand,

Figure 2.10

Charles Holden, Sudbury Town Station, London, 1925–1935. Courtesy: Amanda Vincent-Rous.

editor and contributor to the *Architectural Review*, spoke of the symbolic revolution ushered in by the nineteenth-century British bridge engineers. They had introduced structural innovation as a design criterion amid the battle of styles between architects. The engineers' contribution to architectural developments lay precisely in the "knock-out blow" it dealt "those who believed that art meant borrowing the eyes of Alma Tadema and Lord Leighton."[67] This was no longer the case. An inclusive idiom was born that, he insisted, had prepared potentially everyone to be competent judges!

While traditional architects like Reginald Blomfield alleged that modernism was cosmopolitan (that is, rootless) and internationalist (the imposition of foreign communists), the Continent-inspired architects held that modernism was utterly English. They saw the style as only reestablishing a building tradition disrupted by "the chaos of a hundred years" of industrialization.[68] In a 1934 radio show, Blomfield accused the "flat-roof club" (a derogatory term for the modernists) of a self-imposed deliberate ignorance of the past.[69] The young architects had cut themselves adrift from the preferences Englishmen had developed over generations. His interlocutor, the young Amyas Connell, lashed back: "Modern architecture is in the highest sense traditional." The liberation of architectural idiom from the authority of antiquity, Connell contended, was not a repudiation of national history, but its affirmation. "From its understanding of the spirit of the past it is able to create, not superficial imitations in this or that style, but living successors in the true line of descent."[70]

Architect F. R. S. Yorke and others also insisted on modernity's Englishness and historical continuity. "It is traditional to look forward."[71] Modernists did not mimic but innovate, and innovation was a quintessential trope of English architecture. "The abominable Tudoristic villa by the By-pass road ... this crude imitation of the forms of the past ... is entirely contrary to tradition," said an irritated Anthony Bertram; "Those of us who advocate twentieth century houses for twentieth century people are the real traditionalists."[72] John Summerson made a career out of his search for British precedence for the modern movement. For J. M. Richards and G. M. Boumphrey, modernism had made the English house English again by turning it into a strict formulation of function and economics. They revisited architectural history, making function, structural economy, and building techniques the defining determinants of the English house, and showed the consistency of these principles through time and across classes. In its modernist rendition, "the history and pre-history of the

6 OCTOBER 1937 THE LISTENER 723

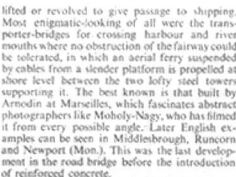

lifted or revolved to give passage to shipping. Most enigmatic-looking of all were the transporter-bridges for crossing harbour and river mouths where no obstruction of the fairway could be tolerated, in which an aerial ferry suspended by cables from a slender platform is propelled at shore level between the two lofty steel towers supporting it. The best known is that built by Arnodin at Marseilles, which fascinates abstract photographers like Moholy-Nagy, who has filmed it from every possible angle. Later English examples can be seen in Middlesbrough, Runcorn and Newport (Mon.). This was the last development in the road bridge before the introduction of reinforced concrete.

We are only just beginning to realise that the great engineers of the last century were not only among its master minds but the unconscious pioneers of our new mechanistic æsthetic. True, as the horny-handed captains of a *laissez-faire* society, they had unique opportunities to dare and achieve; and that may be why we have not since seen the like of them. Perhaps the greatest was Gustave Eiffel, who discovered the principle of parabolic arched support, which by greatly economising weight and bulk enabled much longer spans to be used. Its most famous and spectacular embodiment is his amazingly attenuated Pont de Garabit (1879), which looks like a delicately metal-rimmed rainbow. A few years later Baker's Forth Bridge was finished, and the fantastic lattice-work of its huge cantilevered hexagons must have been the knock-out blow for those who believed that art meant borrowing the eyes of Alma Tadema and Lord Leighton.

The next development was the indirect result of great technical advances in the binding and

A new suspension bridge of the old type crossing the River Durance at Cavaillon, Provence. A cautionary example of what 'collaboration with an architect' often results in

work ' constructed by the State, not ' a triumph of private enterprise ' establishing a vested interest and built to earn dividends.

Suspension bridges went out because they were impracticable for railways. In America, however—owing to the peculiar geographical configuration of New York—there has been an uninterrupted evolution of the suspension principle leading to ever wider spans from Brooklyn Bridge to the new Washington Bridge, to say nothing of the two gigantic bridges across San Francisco Harbour and the Golden Gate finished this year. In 1929 the suspension bridge made a belated reappearance in Europe in the robuster guise of what is called the ' stiffened-girder ' type (meaning one with a completely rigid platform), the prototype of which, the 1,033-foot span Mülheim Bridge at Cologne, served as the model for our new Chelsea Bridge.

Thanks to the rigidity of iron girders, it became possible about 1850 to make the arches of railway bridges rectangular instead of semi-circular in section, which resulted in mathematical shapes shunned as ' positively brutal '. The next form to emerge was the ' bowstring '. It was not till the Bessemer process had been industrialised that steel could replace wrought and cast iron. A great gain in tensile strength was the result, followed by the development of new and specialised types of bridge—bridges with cantilevered and suspended spans, even bridges with reversed bowstrings suspended beneath their platforms, bascule bridges that opened like portcullises, bridges with spans that

A new bridge doubles an old. A fine example of an iron nineteenth-century railway bridge which crosses the River Aare at Berne, with the new Lorraine road bridge, built of interlocking concrete blocks, under construction beside it

Figure 2.11

P. Morton Shand, "The Changing Bridge," broadcast on 4 October 1937, printed in the *Listener*. © Immediate Media Company London Limited.

[English] house has been shaped to suit the needs and habits of its owners by using to the best possible advantage all the knowledge and materials at the disposal of its builders. Only when this principle has been followed—never when it has been neglected, has true beauty been achieved."[73] Broadcasters claimed that functional efficiency together with the objectivity and neutrality of techniques of mechanical reproducibility liberated architecture from the artificial gestures of beautification prevalent in housing estates. They reinstated the English tradition of unselfconscious art, founded in the immediacy of needs rather than fashion or professional decorum. Architecture on air supported the consequent honesty, purity, and unadulterated state of the resultant art, tempered by the "unegotistical" hand of the modern designer.[74] It was oriented to draw healthy support from the unselfconscious taste and immediate mode of appreciation of mass consumers.

After 1945, when pale-looking modernist municipal housing and commercial buildings mushroomed throughout England beside the much maligned Tudoresque villas, many critics who had supported the modern movement in the 1930s now turned against it. Some remembered the critique of the late Reginald Blomfield (d. 1942). Others joined the theorists at the *Architectural Review* who envisioned "picturesque modernity"—with winding streets, picket fences, suburban villas, and bay windows. Modernism, it was then stated, needed correction.

But the 1930s was a period of optimism and experimentation. Architectural education took up scientific research promoted by the Modern Architecture Research Group (MARS Group) and the Architects and Technicians Organization (ATO) established by Berthold Lubetkin and his architectural practice, Tecton. This was an age when architects claimed that "Architecture mirrors our life or it is nothing."[75] And because life evolves constantly, so must the envelope. This was a moment when the new entrants into architecture elevated the building

Design in Everyday Things

What is a House?

By ANTHONY BERTRAM

I BELIEVE that if everybody really knew what a house is and insisted on getting it, we should not have to put up with all the bad imitations that most of us occupy. But what is a house? My dictionary says it is 'a building for human habitation'. There has been a modern variation on that—a phrase invented by the great French architect, le Corbusier, in about 1923, 'a machine for living in'. That phrase has upset quite a number of people, and it does sound at first rather uninviting. You may

'I have never yet seen a thatched car', says Mr. Bertram. But here is one that may be seen any day on the outskirts of London

imagine that it means living among cogs and levers and oil-gauges, like Charlie Chaplin at the beginning of 'Modern Times', without any home comforts, so to speak. But that was not what le Corbusier meant. He simply meant a machine suitable for living in. After all, a car is fairly comfortable though it is a machine—a machine for getting about in—and we take care that our car is as good a machine as we can get for our money. Supposing you were looking through advertisements of second-hand cars, would you be attracted to one that read something like this: 'Really choice genuine old 1903 So-and-So. Original upholstery throughout. Many quaint features. Delightfully situated on romantic solid tyres', and so on. I suppose you might if you thought of going in for the old crocks' annual race to Brighton, or because you just collected old cars as other people collect old books or old china. But is there anybody in the world who would fall for this sort of advertisement: 'As in the days of Edward the Peacemaker. Pre-War England. That's what we think of when we look at So-and-So's new crooked eight. 1903 exterior with 1937 engine'. Yet that is just the sort of way people advertise houses. As in the days of bluff King Hal. . . I wonder how many people have asked themselves why it should be a merit in a house to be old or imitation-old and not in a car? If you have a house with a hot water system and electric light and gas cooker and perhaps a radio and a refrigerator, why should you want it to look outside as if it were built three hundred years ago with beams and gables and leaded panes? I have never yet seen a thatched car, but I have seen a trailer caravan with leaded panes and imitation beams.

You may object that the car is entirely a modern thing, but I don't see the force of that argument. 'House design has grown', you may say. 'It's got roots in the past. It's got a tradition'. Well, so have you and I. We have grown; But we don't go about in crawlers and take rattles to the office, It seems to be only with houses that people want this constant reminder of a tradition, these disused characteristics stuck on their modern grown-up houses. I wonder if that is simply because people don't know what a house is. They knew perfectly well in the past. There was none of this nonsense then. It seems as if the human race—or at least our part of it—had forgotten something. You may be a little surprised if I say now that what I think people have forgotten is tradition, and that though I am going to spend all my time advocating new architecture and new design in everything, I am going to make a claim right away that we so-called modernists are the real traditionalists. Because, after all, the tradition of design is to make new things for new purposes, new things for new kinds of people, to use new materials and new methods of manufacture in new ways. And as there always has been a continual change of purposes and social habits and material and so on, there has been a continual stream of new things. People in the past did not imitate what had gone before. They moved from mud and wattle huts, through timber-frame cottages to the civilised brick buildings of the eighteenth century. The dark, insanitary Norman castles, which were purely military, of course, gave way as soon as it was safe to domestic manor houses with large windows and all sorts of comforts, and these in turn gave way to the stately planned homes of the eighteenth century. Why did the tradition stop then? Why, at the end of that century, did people begin to build imitation Gothic, imitation castles, and why did they get worse until we have the by-pass villa style of today?

If we twentieth-century people were logical and traditional we should want a house that gives us the greatest efficiency and comfort possible for our money and one that looks like what it is, an honest piece of work, not wearing some fancy dress of dead ways of life and dead technique. I will not say much about technique because so few people seem to take any interest in it. It will, however, be readily appreciated that different methods of construction produce different kinds of houses,—different in plan and different in appearance—unless there is deliberate hanky-panky. A timber-frame house is and looks different from a brick house, so when people stick on the outside of a brick building the stained deal laths that pass as beams and permit a house to be labelled Tudor-style, they are trying

1066—and all flats

Figure 2.12

Anthony Bertram, "What Is a House?," *Listener*, October 1937. © Immediate Media Company London Limited.

program to the same importance as the stylistic preference for flat roofs and horizontal windows. Its practitioners tried their hand at industrial design, public housing, small dwellings, urban renewal, and rural protection. Clearly, this group did not have a monopoly on any of these issues; Edwardians had made great strides in reconciling reason and design. The arts and crafts movement had already championed artistic collaboration, attention to the honesty of materials, and simplicity. These established approaches were also vigilant to town planning and housing. The uniqueness of moderns lay in drawing upon technological advances for cultural advancement, linking formal solutions to political conditions, and thinking of preservation within the paradigm of social change.

This conceptual packaging of architecture by modernists was singularly attractive to the BBC decision makers, because it promoted modernism as the aesthetic of a fiscally responsible people.[76] Supporters coupled design informed by an industrial mode of production, rather than handicrafts, with an egalitarian impulse. In this, modern architecture reinstated the grand narrative of English public history. It promised to align Britain's progress in democracy, "liberty, justice, and enlightenment" with "all things decent." The younger generation's desire for honest use of materials and truth to function became coupled with an enlightened mass democracy. This idiom relieved the BBC from the constant stream of outside complaints about the difficulty and pointlessness of its cultural productions. Modernism's insistence on approaching architecture as an applied art bridged the gap between the cultivated and uncultivated eye. It gave hope to the desire of converting the unconverted, and clarified the postulates of formal appreciation in ways that gave the audience an opportunity for participation. Discussing modern architecture on radio promised a spontaneous affinity between beauty and the eye of the expanded public. It rationalized work's importance and autonomy. It allowed artists and critics to spell out the virtues of their activities without resorting to the esoteric arguments and aestheticist assumptions that had hitherto assured their raison d'être. And just like this, in a brilliant turn of events, the space of radiophony encouraged architects and critics to promote the abstract forms and modifications of architectural traditions as populist, democratic, and economical.

The insistence on architecture as an applied art rather than a fine art maximized outreach without losing sight of the mandate of cultivation. It enabled broadcasting to "blow out of the water" what the BBC's Richard Lambert called "the hierophantic notion of culture and knowledge as the secret of few, to be imparted judiciously and by degrees to the many, but not in such a way [as] to impair the veneration for those who impart."[77] Architectural broadcasting realized the BBC as a patron of art. It made the Corporation a player with stakes in the game of culture and endowed it with the kind of capital with which it could produce real effects in the world of the self-indulgent creativity of high arts and the crudities of popular arts. In fact, the BBC was the interface between them; it objectified the definition of "progressive" and "regressive" culture. Radio's involvement with modern architecture set the standards for democratic culture; radiophonic space institutionalized the terms on which democracy was extended to the younger generation of Britons. Modern architecture, like nothing else, realized radio as a legitimate medium of communication—the primary struggle of the Reithian and immediate post-Reithian administration—and a legitimate mode of cultural pedagogy for the layman. The professed attributes of modern architecture expressed the cultural modernity the BBC wanted to generate: namely, one that was accessible to everyone. Modern architecture crystallized the terms by which aesthetic production could be democratized, and defined the gap between legitimate and popular cultures negotiated in the age of wireless listening.

The fresh definition of the architect and architecture's function, signaled by the modernists, made architectural appreciation the gateway to the appreciation of more esoteric cultural enterprises. The space of radio thus ushered us into a new order of things. A different constellation of symbolic system appeared. There, the built environment—the most worldly, the most compromised, the art most subjugated to the aesthetic and ethical demands of patrons and users, and therefore one of the most marginal forms of artistic expression—emerged as the representative of more independent cultural production. "Why," asked J. E. Barton, "are we all so very earnest in drawing the line between art that is applied and art that is pure, art that is decorative and art that is creative? What is wrong in thinking of all art as a continuous chain of many links, sincere in every link, and ascending steadily from the humblest piece of really good practical work to the highest achievement of the most original imagination?" In this upside-down space, or rather right-side-up world, the material value of things became the plea for the consideration of their immaterial worth. In other words, *interest* rose as an ambassador of *disinterest*! "It is true that in these days," Barton went on,

> our sculptors and painters ... are forced to work independently of architecture or of immediate social purpose. Yet in spite of this independence and isolation, which many of us deplore, we recognize that the most important artists are architectural artists. They no longer have cathedrals to build or to work in, but our progressive civilization is in itself an invisible cathedral and the function of living art is to embody those ideals from which our civilization draws its life-blood, its faith, and its hope.[78]

The institution of art structured by radio—the most surreptitious, if not the most serpentine, of household items—did not offer its monopolists a frictionless path into the domestic realm. It was an obstacle course, full of detours that demanded new strategies of maneuver. Architectural programming offered the liberal idealists at the BBC a channel to glide through this obstacle course. Broadcast architecture sustained the interwar period's enlightenment and liberal confidence in the universality of artistic communication. It sustained the construct that broadcasting was really nothing more than a means of transportation of influence "which shall be permanent and good and widespread."[79] It nourished the belief that the unsettling effect of broadcasting culture was little more than a "reformed resettling."[80] In other words, broadcasting buildings ensured that culture remained a site, par excellence, of misrecognition.

3 THE POLITICS OF BROADCASTING AND THE BROADCASTING OF POLITICS

I Art Appreciation

On day six of public service broadcasting in Britain: Imagine the forty-four-year-old architect Clough Williams-Ellis dressed in his smartest suit going nervously over the script for a radio show about to air. Savoy Hill was a magnet for preppy Cambridge and Oxford men (and some women) like him. Its corridors and smoking areas echoed with references to Kant and Locke in small talk. It was not a place for the casually dressed, and so the architect put on his lucky tie and tried out matching scarves.[1] Across the hall, his wife Amabel Strachey, a novelist, editor, and publisher, got ready for the same event in her dressing room. She was a literary critic for the general-interest magazine *Spectator*, which was owned by her family and run by her father. More accustomed to formal events than her husband, she was unruffled. The couple was giving a dinnertime joint broadcast on architectural appreciation and what it could do for government school education. We have indications about their state of mind from the letters in Williams-Ellis's BBC records and autobiography.

The broadcast was based on their popularly acclaimed 1924 book, *The Pleasures of Architecture*. When the Post Office gave John Reith complete monopoly

Figure 3.1

Sculpture of Clough Williams-Ellis at the Italianate village of Portmeirion, designed by him in North Wales, 1925–1975. Courtesy: Jude Hall.

over the airwaves, he had wanted radio to raise the standards of political journalism. But the charter and license that ensured the monopoly and relative freedom from government interference banned him from editorial comment on public policy and programming on political, religious, or economic controversies. Disguised as "soft" programming, benign shows like *Pleasures* showcased public service transmission and served as proxy for political journalism.

Clough Williams-Ellis was one of England's most fashionable country house and estate architects. He dabbled in planning for village centers, and was consulted on development schemes that were breaking up large estates into affordable-sized holdings at a breathtaking speed. Self-trained in neoclassical vocabulary, he was on air to critique modernist design principles. His command of the Beaux-Arts tradition literally made him the official architect of the Conservative party, though he swore that the affiliation was only aesthetic and not in the least political.[2] Indeed, his membership in the radical Independent wing of the Labour Party testifies for him. Williams-Ellis was an energetic writer and an experienced speaker who regularly spoke at J. C. Squire's Architecture Club and the RIBA-connected Council for the Preservation of Rural England. He frequently wrote for the technical press, including the *RIBA Journal*, the *Builder*, and the *Architectural Review*, and religiously contributed to the *Times* of London and the *Spectator* on architectural causes dear to him. Though coauthored with Strachey, *The Pleasures of Architecture* was the result of his professional interests.

Williams-Ellis and Strachey were the guests of the Talks and News department. They had been asked to prepare a casual dinner talk on architectural appreciation; it was not a long talk, about 20 minutes in length. The topic was one he had thought about extensively. They had gone over dozens of rehearsals. The script was set in stone; their producers would not allow them to deviate from it by even one word. Yet Williams-Ellis had butterflies in his stomach, for he was painfully aware that broadcasting was nothing like the venues he knew. It was an eerie territory, uncharted and untested. He was required to speak, looking not into someone's eyes, but at a piece of equipment. He sat in a windowless room with padded walls so he could neither hear nor be heard through them. He couldn't be sure how he sounded. He had no idea who was listening, and yet he had to assume that everyone was. Plus, it felt as if his entire reputation—in fact, that of the whole architectural profession he represented—hung in the balance.

They arrived at Savoy Hill earlier than required. When the time came, their assistant producer, Christopher Salmon, ushered them into a makeshift studio.

Figure 3.2

Clough Williams-Ellis, Portmeirion in North Wales, 1925–1975. Courtesy: Jude Hall.

Williams-Ellis and Strachey organized themselves and waited for the light above the door to turn green. They had to get into their take on school curricula, instantly.

> It is fair to demand that any subject that is taught must fulfill certain conditions of convenience, and be, moreover, something more than an end in itself. To begin with, it must be a subject in which the learners can be easily interested. Then in the case of an art, it must either be executively easy and convenient, or else it must be one in which examples are either ready at hand or can be agreeably searched for. It must further be a subject, which will be illuminating and in the broadest sense humane. That is to say, its history must work within and help the panorama of ordinary political history, and if it can help also to define and make actual foreign places and habits, so much the better. But this usefulness is not enough. These are conditions which are fulfilled by glass-blowing, costume, or furniture. To be worth a place in a general curriculum, an art must also be a fine art. It must, like music or poetry, ultimately suggest the existence of an aloof and abstract perfection.[3]

They go right on:

> To the boy or girl with natural taste it obviously does not matter so very much which art you teach in school, for one art to naturally initiate is the gateway to all the others. But to the learner who has the power of going directly to the stream of life, and whose thirst for the distilled waters of the arts is not therefore in the least pressing, it matters very much indeed. In the first place, he must probably at first be interested in the art by the help of some outside agency, an already existing one perhaps. In the second place, as he will probably not pass on beyond what he has been taught to enjoy, an art must be chosen that will, so to say, be "useful" to him in later life, one which he can enjoy from China to Peru, or one which will come into, and illuminate and refine, his practical interests. The art to be taught must provide, in the expressive phase, "a nice hobby" for the student. The art of architecture seems to us second only to the literary arts in ultimate "usefulness" and to exceed them in ease of approach.[4]

This was a proposal for building not a nation of talented architects or historians, but rather a nation of sensitized spectators. Architecture, listeners heard, offered pleasure to anyone who cared to look. It was not a matter of structural acrobatics or fulfillment of functions. Those who elevated these elements to the status of generative principles for design did so unduly, for these were only the preliminary principles of construction. Architecture was a visual art. Its raison d'être lay in its visual appeal, and to be truly universal, this appeal had to be guided by man's natural preferences. To enjoy architecture, a spectator did not need a command of the laws of visual composition (proportions, symmetry, light and shade, and so on). All he or she needed, Williams-Ellis and Strachey said, was curiosity and five simple questions. These included: "Do you seem beautiful to me, or … seem beautiful—not merely correct and expensive—to those who built you?" and "Are you a good neighbor so that any buildings … near you gain rather than lose in beauty or seemliness by your existence?"[5] The foregrounding of visual pleasure, Williams-Ellis and Strachey hoped, would justify the endurance of neoclassicist formal practices. They hoped that this most intellectual, geometrically contrived, and archaeologically learned of architectural styles would emerge as commensurate with inborn and natural taste. Confident of its "natural truth," they called upon listeners to reject "the commoner clichés … of correctness, of simplicity, of expressiveness, of truth of construction—all notions that imply some outside standard independent of an onlooker's enjoyment." "It is not an essential for our pleasure," they assured new listeners, "that the columns we see should, in fact, bear the load. It is enough for the eye if they seem to bear it."[6]

Ironically, this defense of a traditional style was entirely avant-garde as it handed the yardstick of beauty to the spontaneous pleasure of the ordinary spectator. Architectural appreciation and the elementary curriculum of grammar schools were accommodated to one another by freeing the former from belabored disciplinary protocols; this reception of art dismissed knowledge of history of styles, structures, and materials as an obstruction to authentic experience. The "mechanical fallacy," i.e., the reduction of architecture to mechanical components, fell by the wayside. With knowledge and pleasure disentangled, *The Pleasures of Architecture* made architectural appreciation populist! Yet, by prioritizing appearance over the applied aspect of architecture in their broadcast, Williams-Ellis and Strachey kept alive the idea of architecture as an applied art. Their case for the importance of architectural appreciation was predicated precisely on architecture's exceptional ability to fuse artistic freedom and material necessity: "Architectural history could build on the pomp, scale, glory and drama that makes history attractive to children."[7] Appreciation of architecture, as they conceived it, was more than one route to art appreciation—it was the most forceful route. Its effectiveness was second only (if that) to literature:

> The value of architectural enjoyment once it is learnt seems to us to be based upon two sets of considerations, practical and psychological. From the practical point of view we may think of it as an art with which three quarters of the English race who live or work in towns are bound to come into everyday contact. An understanding of its principles makes the dullest town come alive, and indeed to the townsman the architectural sense fills very much the place of a countryman's knowledge of natural history and of agriculture.[8]

In demanding the inclusion of architectural appreciation in the general curriculum, Williams-Ellis and Strachey were not fighting a single proposal but the whole spirit and tone of British education. Everyone could agree that the purpose of education was to secure, as far as it was possible, man's advance toward good living. But our two broadcasters could not accept the privilege enjoyed by utilitarian training in government-funded education for almost a hundred years. They were of the mind that utilitarianism had stunted the development of man's full humanity by freeing material improvement from his holistic growth.

Others, in coming years, stressed that the appreciation of art was the most expedient form of creating a participatory democracy. Art appreciation taught people to look at their surroundings as man's struggle (rarely won and mostly lost) to rise above worldly constraints. It created an electorate that demanded not the provision of space, but the provision of noble space. It made a house something more than property and a plaza something more than a gathering place. Art appreciation was the easiest mode of education to impart, and the surest way of gentrifying collective behavior.

Geoffrey Boumphrey, an advocate of functional urban planning, assured "the man-in-the-street" that he need not be bogged down by abstract standards of beauty: "He should judge the design of his house, its environment and furniture in the same way" that he considered the "good looks of his car or wireless."[9] "You don't read books about games, but begin by practicing them," Sir William

Rothenstein, president of the Royal Academy of Art, said in a broadcast to schoolchildren.[10] In the same stride, Sir Charles Holmes, landscape painter, art critic, and the retired director of the National Portrait Gallery, pointed out that "a trip to the National Gallery was worth more than reading a hundred books."[11] George Furlong, director of the National Gallery of Ireland, emphasized that a visitor to an art gallery "will soon find himself deeply influenced whether consciously or unconsciously by the ideals inherent in all great works of pictorial art."[12] The renowned English educationalist Michael Sadler seconded Furlong by suggesting that both art and architecture affected observers by communicating a priori universal virtues.[13] An artistic encounter had nothing to do with the acquisition of knowledge in the traditional sense; it was a matter of *experience*, affirmed every architect and artist who found in this romanticist position a valuable critique of academic erudition and its accompanying preference for an impersonal, mechanical expression. One need not be weighed down by the irrelevances of the content or context of a painting or buildings. An aesthetic encounter was an "unconscious intercourse with beauty."[14]

Clough Williams-Ellis and Amabel Strachey were the pioneers of these positions on the radio. They declared that architectural appreciation required no technical or historical knowledge: "It was perfectly proper for the layman—the citizen, the voter—to have an opinion about any piece of architecture."[15] Architect Halsey Ricardo also insisted on air, "There is no need to encumber yourself with second-hand opinions as to 'style' and 'beauty.'" One's "duty is to deal honestly and conscientiously with oneself, and then to apply what one's knowledge and experience may supply."[16]

Equipped with such assurances, the BBC set out to create a modern viewer of art. He or she was to be illuminated without technical, historical, or theoretical knowledge. In his 1939 contribution to the series *Art in Education*, critic Herbert Read asked school officials "to see every school itself as a work of art and all its fittings work of art. These should work on the child's unconscious—should be an ambiance as wide and as accepted as nature itself."[17] The message of the economy of effort and the surplus of effect promised to realize Reith's newfound power to command from a distance and build a community of shared taste. All that was required was his institution's resolve to make known the highest cultural achievements of British artists. Under Reith's discerning control, the culture of listening would restore to the common man his natural capacity for experience, discrimination, and judgment on the basis of that experience.

Pleasures of Architecture was part of the political maneuver of men and women who wanted to change the direction of parliamentary politics via cultural change. Various types of cultural politics were practiced by interwar liberals who were unrepresented by the current political parties. Staunchly nationalistic in their outlook, they were alienated by Labour's working-class politics, and the Labour party likewise dismissed their nationalism as a form of classism and ridiculed their high-minded "educational" efforts as snobbishness. The Fourth Reform Act of 1918 had widened suffrage by abolishing almost all property qualifications for men and reducing them for women over thirty; the result was an overnight tripling of the size of electorate from 7.7 million to 21.4 million. The election of numerous working men to the House of Commons in 1922 and the first Labour-led government in 1924 had done little to substantiate the liberal theory that the distribution of liberty created a more culturally evolved, more interdependent, and more powerful United Kingdom. Molded by the ideals of mid-nineteenth-century social reform movements, they idealized a society that sought the redistribution of material and political advantages while avoiding the confrontation of classes and social unrest. The purpose of social and economic freedoms, liberals believed, was to revive the human capacity for self-motivation and self-inquiry.[18] *Pleasures of Architecture* and other books of its kind played catch-up with the progress of democracy by provoking the curious among the people to expand their horizons, engage in public life with acumen, and qualify themselves as citizens and governors. They shifted the inspiration to self-management as a larger inspiration than that of voting. Only when people responded to this call would the nation fulfill the recurring liberal dream of a united people, propelled forward by dazzling visions of national greatness.

II Good Housekeeping

In 1929, two years after Williams-Ellis and Strachey's broadcast conversation, the BBC launched its general-interest magazine, the *Listener*. It was printed weekly in an approximately 60-page issue. Its editor Richard Lambert had joined the post after serving in the Talks department. He followed the department's

Figure 3.3

Example of a program on good housekeeping by Leslie Menzies, published in one of the earliest issues of the *Listener* in February 1929. © Immediate Media Company London Limited.

example and circulated the first set of issues with a printed record of a program on the built environment. It included clever ideas on home improvement that daytime home listeners had heard that week:

> Glass painting is a most effective form of decoration. For it you will need some pots of good enamel, and some bowls to paint. ... Having first chosen a design bold in outline and scanty in detail (oranges, butterflies and flowers of almost every description are easily reproduced) you can proceed to work; either as a skilled artist, who is not afraid to take his brush and paint straight on to the outside surface of the bowl; or as the careful amateur who can place his design on the inside of the bowl and trace over it.[19]

With tips and technical advice so freely at hand, no woman could complain that she didn't know how to create cheerful surroundings on a budget. Over the years, a steady stream of programs translated into articles on the beautification of home and garden conveyed to readers that a humble home did not have to be merely an endless cycle of unpaid and backbreaking work. A prudent and perceptive woman could take the opportunity to convert her rental from a picture of scarcity and apathy (the consequences of poverty) to a canvas of imagination and industry (the results of a refined upbringing). All that was required was the right advice. Here radio was stepping in and following the lead of advice columns and women's weeklies. The right information, followed by a little imagination and industry, could go a long way to transform the most meager of environs for the benefit of a happy and healthy family, and prove to all living in and near it the power of thrift, enterprise, and fortitude.

About the Household

Painted Furniture

By Mrs. LESLIE MENZIES

THE present vogue of painted furniture is very kind, both to our homes and our pockets. There are probably few of us who have not in our houses one or two very shabby, apparently hopeless pieces of once-polished furniture. These pieces are often in perfectly good condition as to structure. It is merely the surface which becomes depressingly tired-looking after some years of use, and yet with the aid of a paint-brush and a few other equally cheap and simple accessories, it is possible to transform these "has-beens" into up-to-the-minute specimens of the most fashionable type.

First of all, of course, the structure and general condition must be well overlooked. Rusty hinges should be unscrewed, soaked in vinegar and then rubbed down with emery paper before being replaced. Loosened hinges, handles or other fittings may be made firm and taut again by filling the screw holes with that most useful new discovery—plastic wood.

This material may also be used to make up broken detail in small mouldings, to fill up knot or screw-holes, and for a hundred other small repairs. Then you must see that all fittings are intact.

Having made sure of these details, the next thing is the removal of the old paint or varnish. There are many paint-solvents sold, which serve admirably for this purpose. They are applied with a brush, left for a few minutes to do their work of softening the paint, which can then be removed with a paint stripper, or the back of an old, flexible knife. When the surface is clear of old paint and varnish, it should be rubbed with sand-paper, when it will be ready for painting.

An Example of Home Painted Furniture

Here, an enormous field of choice opens up. That is one of the most delightful things about painted furniture. You can do just anything with it. Whether the furniture under treatment is scarred with one's own wear and tear, or whether it has been rescued at the cost of a few shillings, there is practically no limit to the possibilities of its redecoration.

The choice of colour is, of course, immensely important, but it must, naturally, be guided by the type of room in which the furniture is to be placed. White is rather out-moded at present, except for nursery suites, of which I have seen some delightful specimens, stencilled, either in black or natural colours, with animals, flowers, or fairy-tale figures. A deep ivory cream—almost a tint of real old ivory, produces a delightful effect in the right room; but it needs careful placing.

A room in soft browns and fawns gives it the best possible background, and if a touch of colour is desired, any mouldings may be touched in, while the ivory tint is still wet, with a tone that darkens almost to a brown. The application of one paint while the first is still wet will give soft edges and a mellow effect, which is very pleasing. Pastel colours also lend themselves very effectively for applied design.

A vogue of the moment is for lacquered furniture, and a most appealing vogue it is, but, unfortunately, far beyond the reach of most of us. There is, however, no need to despair. Although actual lacquering is a difficult and patience-straining business, almost equally pleasing effects may be obtained by the judicious use of paint and stencils. Japanese hand-cut stencils in most exquisite designs are imported into this country and sold at prices ranging from about twopence each, for small designs. It is quite simple, after a little practice, to fill in the trio of a stencil plate, and so obtain the effect of a solid design. Where it is desired to raise the design slightly, the stencil should first be rubbed on with foundation white stencil paint, and the raising done by putting on thin gesso-paste with a paint-brush till the desired relief has been obtained. The whole design can then be painted in with colours or gold, according to personal preference.

In using a stencil, it is better to use the paints specially prepared for this purpose. Ordinary paints are often too liquid, and they are inclined to run under the edges of the design, which is completely ruined if the details are blurred. English stencils of a much heavier type are also available both in hand-cut and machine-cut varieties. The latter, which, of course, are much cheaper, need careful watching, as the inner edges of the design are apt to be blurred, and sometimes need smoothing off before the plate is used.

Another source of useful designs from which I have obtained many borders, floral, fruit and conventional motifs, is the ordinary embroidery transfer. These transfers can be obtained in a wide range of designs with clear, bold outlines and are applied by tracing them through white carbon-paper, with a hard, sharp-pointed pencil. The body-colour paint, of course, must be perfectly dry and hard before this is attempted.

(*From a talk on January* 28)

More "Balanced Ration" Menus

By Miss JESSIE LINDSAY and Professor V. H. MOTTRAM

THIS first set of meals is upon a much more economical basis than those given last week. They are judged suitable for a household of husband, wife and three children, the wife doing all the cooking with a gas or a modern oil stove.

Breakfast. Porridge and syrup; fresh herrings; bread; butter; tea. Quantities: (For porridge) $2\frac{1}{2}$ ozs. Rolled oats, $\frac{1}{2}$ pt. milk; 3 ozs. golden syrup; $1\frac{1}{4}$ lbs. herrings; 1 lb. 6 ozs. bread; 2 ozs. butter; tea; $2\frac{1}{2}$ ozs. sugar; $\frac{3}{4}$ pt. milk.

Midday Meal. Steamed steak and vegetables; potatoes; steamed fig pudding and custard sauce; bread. Quantities: 1 lb. skirt of beef; 3 ozs. each carrots, onions, and turnips; 1 cube of meat extract; potatoes, $2\frac{1}{2}$ lbs.; steamed fig pudding—6 ozs. flour, 3 ozs. sugar, 2 ozs. suet, 4 ozs. figs, $\frac{1}{2}$ teaspoonful bi-carbonate, $\frac{1}{4}$ teaspoonful baking powder, $\frac{1}{8}$ pt. milk; custard sauce—$\frac{1}{2}$ oz. custard powder, $\frac{1}{4}$ pt. water, $\frac{1}{4}$ pt milk, $1\frac{1}{2}$ ozs. sugar; 12 ozs. bread.

Evening Meal. Tripe and onions; jam tart; bread; tea. Quantities: Tripe and onions—$1\frac{1}{4}$ lb. dressed tripe, 2 large onions (13 ozs.), $\frac{1}{4}$ pt. milk, 1 oz. flour; jam tart—6 ozs. flour, $1\frac{1}{2}$ ozs. margarine, 1 oz. lard, $\frac{1}{2}$ teaspoonful baking powder, 8 ozs. jam; tea—$\frac{1}{4}$ pt. milk, 2 ozs. sugar; bread, 8 ozs.

The total cost of the meals is 5s. 7d., or 1s. $4\frac{3}{4}$d. per "man" power. These meals cover the dietary needs of the given family except perhaps that vitamin C is low. It would be wise to add a bunch of watercress.

(*From a talk on February* 1)

Most of Reith's senior staff, from J. C. Stobart to Richard Lambert, saw cultural production as an arena of human activity independent of the logic of immediate affairs and attendant upon transcendental concerns. The BBC's attention to different mediums of art programming was predicated on the promise of aesthetic experience to illuminate and expand the mind without the laborious demands of traditional classroom education. Editorial reviews in the *Listener*, advertisements in the *Radio Times*, and proclamations on the Corporation's program policies in the *BBC Year Books* signaled trust in the power of art to constitute sensory and bodily experiences over and against contrived moral and pedagogical systems. Good taste—inculcated through tasteful programming that would familiarize audience with imaginative works—was endowed with the ability to generate a wider public appreciation for the here and now of life. Christopher Salmon's program proposals for the Talks department were based on the assumption that an expanded interest in "disinterested beauty" would inspire listeners to broaden their horizons.[20] Architect Halsey Ricardo spoke for Salmon when he told his audience, "Cultivate your powers of observation. Observation begets care—care begets insight into the conditions of production—and from thence follows judgment. Observation implies discrimination. ... Inspection is due the architect and craftsman who planned and erected the building" and who "will work ... for the work's sake."[21] A preparation for the radical aesthetic experience, understood as a dissociative experience that made one transcend normative appreciation (born of one's circumstance), was imagined to set the judgment of taste, long dormant in the British public, into play. Tasting (experiencing), recalling, imagining, reflecting, and finally judging (making meaning) were accepted as a form of knowledge that would support the intellect.[22]

III Preservation of England

The cover of the 27 February 1929 issue of the *Listener* featured a broadcast lecture by an architect, the retired arts and crafts practitioner Charles Robert Ashbee. This issue included a transcript of his appeal to the nation against the destruction of the English countryside, presented the Tuesday before. The broadcast was occasioned by a traveling exhibition titled the "Ugliness Exhibition," organized by the Council for the Preservation of Rural England. The brainchild of Clough Williams-Ellis, Patrick Geddes, and other prominent members of the Council, it was a collection of photographs and maps capturing the spoliation of the countryside by asphalt roads, petrol pumps, electricity poles, garbage, and inconsiderate picnickers. One of the last of the notable voices of the arts and crafts tradition, C. R. Ashbee had long romanticized localized, simpler, collective, guild-based life in the countryside that, to him, still glistened in the winding cobbled lanes of English medieval towns. His desire to continue to bask in this old-world charm in 1902 motivated Ashbee to move his guild, comprising some 150 men, women, and children, from London to the quaint town of Chipping Campden.[23] He had prepared the broadcast lecture in a picturesque house in Kent, covered with vines and roses and standing in a large garden surrounded by fields, where he had lived for a couple of years. Its grounds bordered Knole, the most spectacular of Tudor and Jacobean stately houses. For Ashbee, such houses were a perfect architectural expression of English spirit. He had brought to the microphone an enthusiasm for the large and deliciously rambling Victorian garden and a fascination with gardening that he had developed at his estate.[24] This new hobby reassured his long-standing trust in the power of rural pursuits to cure the aesthetic and social alienation of the newly franchised classes—their alienation caused, he suspected, by the terrible conditions of factory work, on the one hand, and life in industrial towns, on the other. He believed that gardening, swimming, cooking, home economics, carpentry, small lectures for and by friends, reviving dying crafts, local theater, and the rest, were the delights of human existence. They were essential to "the [full] life and duties of the citizen."[25]

Over the years, Ashbee had become uncertain of the wisdom of his Victorian elders who had fought the Tories tooth and nail to extend the right of self-determination beyond the aristocracy and landed gentry, to working-class men. In books and parliaments, at cricket matches and science meetings, at dinner and tea, the preceding generation of Liberals had argued that the extension of their cultured joys and privileges to the peasantry and factory workers would convert them from nuisances to patriotic citizens. The landless folk would then identify with the passions and furies of landed gentry, and take pride in the historic and natural riches of England.

Figure 3.4

Cover of a February 1929 *Listener* containing
C. R. Ashbee's broadcast review of an exhibition.
© Immediate Media Company London Limited.

Figure 3.5

Madresfield Court, a quintessential arts and crafts stately home; C. R. Ashbee designed its library. Courtesy: Michael Marrison.

Figure 3.6

A montage made out of images from the "Ugliness Exhibition," reviewed on air by C. R. Ashbee, *Listener*, February 1929. © Immediate Media Company London Limited.

Alas! To Ashbee, the "Ugliness Exhibition" indicated that the Victorian Liberals had been too hasty in spreading political rights. "The imposition of unsightly hoardings and petrol pumps, the curse of litter, the breaking up of historic estates, the sacrifice of fine old avenues of trees and so forth"[26] proved that Liberals had brought in a people without adequate preparation (culture and sensitivity) to bear the responsibilities that accompany freedom. "Democracy," noted the *Listener* editorial showcasing Ashbee's article, "has tended to spread the power to enjoy without providing a compensating restraint upon destructiveness."[27] In 1894, New Liberals had imposed death duties on inherited wealth in the form of great estates as a tax to pay for essential services for those who couldn't afford them. After the First World War, death duties had become one of the principal reasons for the breakup and neglect of large estates.[28] Where once there had been majestic roofs and soaring spires, manicured trees and pedicured grazing sheep, after death duties stood ruthless alterations and crumbling walls. Rising levies had so enfeebled estate owners' ability to maintain and control access to their property that they could neither shoo away picnic parties tearing up daffodils, nor keep their grounds in shape after trespassers carelessly left behind banana peels and dirty napkins.[29]

This unattractive picture turned a romantic socialist like Ashbee into a defender of private aristocratic property.[30] Having devoted himself to improving the quality of working-class life, though hobnobbing with the aristocracy at the same time,[31] in his retired life, Ashbee had become a critic of the redistributive radicalism of New Liberals. Although the legislation that imposed taxes on private property to pay for social services had been praised for its daring in the 1890s, Ashbee could no longer allow listeners to see it as a simple matter of equalizing the playing field between the rich and the poor. Its separation of private property

A Cottage by the Roadside — The Same Transformed

A Picturesque Tea-room

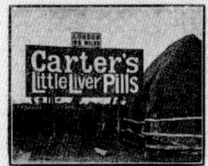

Roadside Advertisements

An 'Efficiency' Tea-room

Hoardings on the Iffley Road, Oxford (before removal)

A Railway Hoarding 'Landscape'

Bank-holiday Litter on Hampstead Heath
By courtesy L.G.O.C.

SCENES FROM THE 'UGLINESS' EXHIBITION

from public interest had proved to be shortsighted, as it had serviced neither the public nor the private property owner. Ashbee's New Way betrayed his divided loyalty to the poor and to the beauty of the countryside. And for the countryside, he felt that history had proved the aristocratic class to be the only reliable steward. As a result, he found himself declaring, "I am neither a Conservative, nor a Socialist, I am both":

> So I would do this: wherever there is a beautiful park or a historic house, and the owner, as he often does at present, is ready to give the public free run of either, I would go so far as to remit the estate duty. To so burden a public-spirited man that he has to sell the place up, thus often destroying the house and closing the park to the public, as is happening in many parts of England now, seems to me mere waste and folly.[32]

In this case, the public interest and private property, beauty and the taxation system were intimately entwined. Of the countryside, "or, as I prefer to say, England," he said:

> The great parks still left to us should be cherished for what they are—the remains of the old rights of chase, sacred to rich and poor alike. ...

> The beauty and history of England outside its landscape beauty is largely based on ancient methods of craftsmanship, on the way in which men made things with their hands, what men in English villages, or united in guilds in little towns up and down the country, fashioned for the joy of life, before the coming of machinery ... all the crafts that made for a self-dependent life. When we think of rural England we think of an England compact of such crafts, with the village church at its centre, the country-town near by, and the house of the squire, whose job was administration. There is no more squire now. The democracy has taken the job—the "R.D.C.," the "U.D.C.," the "statutory authority."[33]

Ashbee's England *was* the countryside. This England was not the discredited marker of accumulated wealth and power of landed gentry, as the constituency of the welfare state regarded it. It was the emblem of another England, an England of carefree and simpler times. There, masters and subjects were organically connected to one another in a Commonwealth of guilds and villages. There, between periods of sowing and reaping the crops, peasants became artisans. There, the population earned their living from farming (contact with land) and derived their happiness from making beautiful things with their hands. There, one was content to live for life's smallest pleasures, satisfied with fashioning inert natural matter into useful and meaningful stuff. There, arts and crafts, churches and homes, streets and fields, and parks and lakes knew nothing of the pomp and show of urban life in industrial cities. Mass production had trampled the rhythms of old life. Ashbee's England anticipated none of the shackles that would immobilize the imagination of the children of industrialization, none of the superfluousness of the new age. His England, surviving here and there, was a precious reminder of the lost liberty and pride of an organically evolved life amid land, gardening, and craft guilds. It saw everything from the romantic manor home to the much humbler cottage of the farmer-craftsman as united by the angel of beauty. It was the legacy of this England to which democracy must aspire and which it should preserve where it survived:

> I beg you, then, take a wider view. This is not a matter that affects merely our own firesides, or the street outside our house, our own particular party politics, or our business. It is an altogether greater matter. It touches us as Englishmen and at ever so many different points that seem at first to have no connection.[34]

Instead of assuaging the trauma of the mechanical organization of labor, blanket legislation had merely perpetuated it. The Labour government, which had inherited these laws from the New Liberals, had to show more foresight and discretion, he insisted. The private property owner should be encouraged to become a friend rather than foe of public interest. Laws should be the engine of order, harmony, and beauty, not divisive politics.

If the politicians did not have the foresight, then the task of recommending farsighted laws fell to the still-small voice of broadcasting insistent at the hearth. The first step in the process was to define etiquettes and a code of conduct for a world where the strangely discreet sounds of a box on the dresser had replaced the indiscreet sounds of rural church bells; where the land of law had replaced Ashbee's land of God.

The *Listener*'s editor, Richard Lambert, honored Ashbee as a visionary for the times. If in Ashbee's bygone world, it was the all-enveloping sound of church bells that anchored localism, imparted depth to the desire for rootedness, and offered the security of well-defined horizons, Lambert's protagonist Ashbee had to rekindle localism and nationalism via sounds that compressed all standing horizons and involved them in one another.[35]

The pages of the *Listener* portrayed the architect as the tough-minded hero-intellectual who realized

> broadcasting [as] the modern counterpart of the eighteenth century societies for the reformation of manners, which undertook to shame the public into decent behavior on … gross evils. These organizations acted upon the assumption that if one could awaken the educated and intelligent portion of society to the issues involved, they could influence or control the conduct of the rest.
>
> But the problem in our case is much greater, because it relates to questions of aesthetics and of manners, on which the right of private judgment usually goes unquestioned. … The truth is that in th[e] sphere of "public aesthetics" what is required is more standardization and less individualism. The "Ugliness" Exhibition is pointing the way to a new convention—to a new taboo, even. It should be forbidden, not by laws, but by the unseen pressure of opinion, to commit such offenses as the Exhibition pillories in the pictures shown elsewhere on these pages. … History reminds us that new conventions become established in stages. First the pioneers—such as the authors of the "Ugliness" Exhibition, the Council for the Preservation of Rural England and the National Trust—point the way; next the power of some mighty social instrument is used to publish and establish the new principle in the conscience of the nation. And last, the convention endures of itself without any pressure or advertisement, and habit makes the children that are to come forgetful even of the need, which originated it. The movement to save our countryside is still in the first of these stages; it must pass rapidly through the remainder if there is to be much countryside left to be saved for future generations.[36]

IV The Culture of Listening and the Debate on Flats versus Cottages

Every Thursday, after a long day of backbreaking work, Joe Brown left for home without lingering with other miners. (Joe is a composite character based on historical information on one segment of the audience that listened to architectural programs.) While his wife and daughter fixed dinner to the hum of a military band on the radio, he washed up, scrubbed the scum off his nails, and slipped out of his jumper into a white shirt, tie, and jacket. After dinner and tea, he skimmed through a BBC pamphlet, put on a hat and headed to the pub. Although going to the pub after dinner was his daily routine, on Thursdays he dressed up as if it were Sunday morning and he was off to church. For that day he was going to attend a weekly meeting to listen to a radio broadcast, made by the BBC with group listeners like him in mind. The radio set in the pub was nothing like his clunky homemade piece; it was a state-of-the-art transmitter with a crisp sound. The BBC engineering department had gifted it to the business in recognition of its generous hosting of the group. Not only that, they had also thrown in a free maintenance and replacement plan for the set. Their program developers had meticulously timed the evening series—every weekday in autumn, winter, and spring—to accommodate the weekday routine of working-class men.

It was the autumn of 1935. The group of twelve or fifteen of Joe's co-listeners settled down at a long table in one corner of the bar, just in time to listen to what promised to be a heated debate. Two opponents were discussing whether Britain should house its people in cities in modern flats with shared social facilities or in distinct, self-sufficient communities near towns, in arts and crafts cottages. G. M. Boumphrey, a prolific design columnist for the magazine *Spectator*, made a case for urban living in flats. He had written extensively on housing policies all around Europe and was greatly impressed by German and Czech company towns incorporating vertical housing. Sir Ernest Darwin Simon, a Liberal parliamentarian whose name was synonymous with Wythenshawe, the largest council housing garden city in Europe, located on the outskirts of Manchester, was making a case for suburban living in houses with private gardens.[37] The debate was presided over by the well-respected town planner, Professor Patrick Abercrombie. The founding editor of *Town Planning Review*, Abercrombie had earned public notice for schemes for the English towns and regions of Sheffield, Doncaster, Bristol, Bath, etc. A bitterly contentious issue, the question of flats

Figure 3.7
Locals in the Lion & Lamb, a pub in Hoxton, enjoying a broadcast. Courtesy: The English Heritage.

versus garden city had splintered British architects and planners into opposing ideological camps, with opposing views of communal life.

> **Simon:** The real value of the garden is … [in] its effect on family life. … The woman can do her housework, cooking, washing; the baby can be out in the garden perfectly safely, out in the open air, and she can be pottering in and out in between. … The husband while he is working in the garden can also be in and out—in touch with his wife. As one of them said: 'I can call out to my wife and ask where to plant the flowers. She can tell me what to do, and if I don't do it, she doesn't like the garden.' Mr. Boumphrey thinks that a garden two or three hundred yards away [from the kitchen] is equally good. Mr. Boumphrey's wife may perhaps be more tolerant than some of our wives.[38]

Simon had readily taken up the new medium. The fifty-six-year-old believed that the garden city offered the most decent housing solution for industrial workers. He had come to the microphone to prevail over what seemed to him a preposterous proposition by the forty-one-year-old Boumphrey, who felt that the English could learn something from the upstart architects and planners on the Continent. Simon capitalized on the existing prejudice of the English against flats. He portrayed their concrete and steel frames as menacing successors of the soulless tenements that his party had legislatively admonished since 1909. Like the monotonous streets of yesteryear, he maintained, flats crowded people together and severed what was already the working class's tentative relation to land and nature. Flats were still uneconomical to build with lifts; without them, women were mercilessly forced to take the stairs with children, prams, and groceries.[39]

Simon followed this damning indictment with a comforting proposition. He perfumed the air with dreams of cul-de-sacs, warm fireplaces, low-ceilinged parlors, cozy little pitched roofs, and picturesque bay windows. He lured Joe and his companions at the pub table into thinking that their spiritual and material growth could only be secured if the government took the responsibility of restoring the balanced life destroyed by a hundred years of private industrial activity. The government must give people the opportunity to revive their premodern habit of living in individual cottages surrounded by land and nature. Firmly anchored in earth and the vernacular building tradition, prettily surrounded by grass and trees, clearly separated from the street, nobly reticent—an

Figure 3.8

A winding street in Wythenshawe, Manchester, built in the 1920s, Ernest Simon's image of the better life available in council housing built for suburban living in the gardens. Against it, G. M. Boumphrey places the vertically stacked horizontal lines of flats in Kenner House, Manchester, built in the 1930s as a more prudent approach to housing. *Listener*, October 1935. © Immediate Media Company London Limited.

---

independent cottage, Simon argued, would reinforce their personal and communal growth. It would give them and their children the psychic and moral defense against the dehumanizing and impersonalizing forces of metropolitan life. Finally, listeners were given the impression that even if the cottages were subsidized by an external agency (in this case the state), their provision would reinforce workingmen's self-respect and capacity for initiative. Standing alone, the privacy of the cottages would encourage them to think for themselves, make them more family-oriented, and teach them to govern their own affairs.[40]

The group in the pub listened to Sir Ernest Simon while flipping through the accompanying pamphlet—a pocket-sized three-penny guide published thrice a year by the BBC publishing branch. The guides were sold at newsstands and available at polytechnics and public libraries in advance of each related series. Here, proud pictures of Wythenshawe accompanied related text and further bibliography. Joe and his co-listeners saw humbly sized double-story houses surrounded by flowerbeds, picket fences, and trees. On the next page, they were confronted by a picture of serenity—a wide curving street to one side of the houses, quietly punctuated by a beautiful leafy tree.

The picture painted by Simon did not convince Boumphrey. He did not see the single-family home as a vehicle for conserving the Englishman's humanity, nor did he believe that it would make the working class resistant to the alienation of the modern world. Boumphrey could not shake off the connection of

One of the wide roadways at Wythenshawe
By courtesy of the City Surveyor, Manchester

husband used to spend much of his time working in the garden. He feels lost without it. A boy of twelve likes carpentry. He cannot do it in a flat. The children have to be kept quieter than they ought to be and there are all sorts of other objections.

But there is one thing which is a major thing from the point of view of the ratepayer, and that is the cost of flats. A flat costs anything from £100 to £150 more than a cottage. A tremendous difference. It means at least three shillings extra on the rent. That is, if you have almost none of those numerous amenities —kindergartens, crèches and so on, which Mr. Boumphrey seemed to assume all flats automatically had. Last week I went over the latest block of flats to be finished in this country, in Manchester—the Smedley Lane flats. There was no crèche, no lift. There were not even window-boxes, because when they came to the cost they found they were too expensive. The Committee said: 'We cannot afford the extra cost of window boxes'. There was a communal laundry, and I asked a woman in the laundry what she did about the children while she was washing in that very beautiful laundry. She said: 'Well, I have three small children, and one girl of thirteen years. I could not bring them up here; there is nobody to look after them; so I keep my girl away from school to look after the other three children while I am washing here'. Had it been a cottage, she could have looked after them herself. The difference is three shillings a week without any of these amenities. If you had lifts, which are almost essential, the Housing Director in Manchester told me it would be half-a-crown extra on the rent. So there you are. Mr. Boumphrey, I think, admits lifts are necessary, but with them you would have to pay something like 6s. a week extra on the economic rents of these flats in the centre of Manchester, without reckoning for the cost of the ground, as against cottages in Wythenshawe—6s. a week, with no garden, not even a garden three hundred yards away in that case, and none of the advantages of family life in the cottage. I estimate that when you are building in the centre of a great town like London or Manchester, with heavy transport charges and high land values, you are forced to build flats, because people must be near their work. That is because we have these overgrown cities. Wythenshawe is a self-contained city, with a population of 100,000—twice the size of Gloucester. I hope Mr. Boumphrey will come and have a look at Wythenshawe, and tell us whether he thinks we are right in housing all these people in cottages with gardens right at their door.

BOUMPHREY: Sir Ernest Simon referred to Wythenshawe as a satellite town, but it seems to me if he had used the word stalactite town, it would have been nearer the mark, because Wythenshawe is not a satellite town at all. It is stuck on to the edge of Manchester—separated from Manchester merely by one of these green belts about a quarter of a mile wide, and the River Mersey. I should be all in favour of Wythenshawe if it were ten miles clear from Manchester, but all it has really done is to form a clot

Kennet House, Manchester—one of the latest blocks of flats
By courtesy of the City Surveyor, Manchester

against one side of Manchester. But, of course, we have both shirked the real issue of the development like that, and that is the question of land values in the towns. I know that, with the value of land in Manchester going up to the height it does, it would be almost impossible to build the sort of clearance I have in mind, but all that has to be done is to educate public opinion to the point where something will be done about these land values. I shall not go any deeper into that.

SIMON: Might I just reply to that point about the stalactite and clot—two very polite names which Mr. Boumphrey has bestowed on Wythenshawe? I don't know whether you are familiar with the parkways, which in fact we have borrowed from America. We have already planned, and already to some extent made, a broad road with parks on each side, on which cars can go through really beautiful surroundings, far more beautiful than the ordinary country road. You can motor or send your motor 'buses through fifty yards of park with trees on each side of the road into the country, and so far from putting the country further away, it affords actually more beautiful country to motor through when going into Cheshire than there was before Wythenshawe was built.

BOUMPHREY: But do you consider fifty yards of park really adequate? It doesn't seem to me that a fifty-yard belt of parkway can possibly be any recompense for the loss of the real open country.

As for gardens, I say by all means have them. I said that the weak point is that you cannot have them round your own door.

the freestanding house with English conservatism and its reactionary denial of contemporary challenges. He could not see any wisdom in forcing gardens and seclusion on people. Freestanding houses distanced work from home and destroyed the countryside. The cottage in the garden kept wives listening to their husbands and subjugated to the menial demands of housekeeping and childrearing. Far from making them independent-minded and critical of received opinion, it made them shortsighted and self-absorbed. Women's voting pattern showed that they consistently put their self- and family interests over the larger interests of the nation. Their aesthetic preferences stayed conventional; originality and novelty still bewildered them. For Boumphrey, a house in a garden—be it the grandest country estate, the old-fashioned middle-class cottage, or their most unassuming variety—was neither a nursery for healthy individuality nor a return to olden days of rural communal life. Instead, it was a factory manufacturing false consciousness.

Boumphrey wanted to pull the house out of the earth, literally. The higher the blocks of flats, he said, the more advantages they bore. They brought in air and light, provided combined services economically, and released much more ground for parkland.

> **Boumphrey:** For the working classes, flats can give the woman all sorts of luxuries she cannot hope for in a cottage … constant hot water at less than half the price, … [and a] properly equipped laundry and drying-room. A woman can leave her children in crèches and kindergartens, or turn them out into playgrounds where they will be looked after. All these things have been done with flats on the Continent: they are not just dreams.[41]

An impassioned supporter of Le Corbusier's proposal for the "Radiant City" and the International Congress of Modern Architecture's (CIAM) reflections on minimal housing, Boumphrey also disliked the garden city concept because of its threat to England's most precious resource: its countryside. "You don't solve the housing problem merely by building enough houses," he retorted, "if by doing it you lead to all sorts of trouble in other directions. The effect of … the three million houses we have built since 1919 … is obvious. The English landscape that many people, even foreigners, think the most beautiful thing in the world in its own way is being ruined."[42] Vertical living, as Boumphrey saw it, was also a planning strategy for the preservation of rural England. It killed two birds with one stone: it provided working classes the richer life they so rightly deserved, without the corollary destruction it had entailed until now. He choked with frustration. It was outrageous to portray flats as glorified slums and dehumanizing tenements without the charm of flowers and trees. For evidence, he said, "Look at page 29 and 30." Everyone flipped to the middle of the pamphlet. Here was an example of one of the latest blocks of flats in Manchester, built over the site of a shantytown. It showed two stacked walls of horizontal bands of white solids and dark shadows, separated by sunny bands of ground, footpaths, and freshly planted trees. Flowers blossomed in front of every entryway. On the next page, a sunny, wraparound balcony with deep shadows glistened with hope. Large glass doors connected the house to a breathtaking view of Oxford Street. Light Thonet furniture on the balcony gave the impression of comfort and openness. While listeners were looking at the pictures, he went on:

> Flats ... are not a means of crowding more people into a congested area. They are a means of releasing 80 to 85 per cent of that area for open space. By the proper use of flats we can have green towns, full of gardens, trees and parks, with roads wide enough to take even the far greater traffic of the future. We can do away with an immense amount of waste of time and money and unnecessary travelling. We can give the poorer classes a richer life, and the countryside can be saved for its proper purpose—agriculture. We can bring the real country back within reach of the town, and so let it fulfill its other purpose, as a place of recreation and a giver of mental peace—a peace that won't be found in the contemplation of any garden suburb.[43]

The difference in the two solutions put before Joe and other listeners should not distract us from noting that the housing critic and the MP had the same goal in housing and rehousing middle- and working-class tenants. Boumphrey, however, was adamant that the spiritual and economic potential of the ordinary man was best realized by living in flats. The program producers give the final word to Professor Abercrombie, who said:

> I have lived for twenty-five years, up to about a week ago, in a garden suburb—an old one, because the garden suburb is not a new invention. I have now moved into a London flat, and in twenty-five years from today I will tell you which I like the best. ... What I think we must all agree is that a great

advocating flats that don't exist, certainly not in this country. I am advocating cottages which do exist, and I am going to base my argument on the cottages at Wythenshawe. Wythenshawe is a so-called 'satellite garden town', built by Manchester

Balcony of a modern flat—Mount Royal, Oxford Street, London
By courtesy of 'The Architects' Journal' and Mr. Leonard Heywood, A.R.I.B.A.

just outside its own boundary. I must just try and tell you shortly what it is. Manchester has taken 5,000 acres, and has planned a satellite garden town that will have 25,000 houses, and will ultimately house a population of 100,000. It is what Mr. Boumphrey considers one of the large towns, to be planned by the best possible experience. Our chairman advised us on it in the early stages, and we planned it out with parkways, parks, open spaces, and with schools, so arranged that the children should not have to cross over the main roads as far as possible.

Now all the 100,000 people are going to live in cottages, unless Mr. Boumphrey can persuade the Manchester City Council that flats are preferable. Let us just consider first the question of land. According to Mr. Boumphrey, there is an enormous waste of good agricultural land. Most of these 5,000 acres ought to be growing wheat, or something of that sort. Now what do you think is happening there? The major part of the housing estates are, of course, gardens. The houses themselves occupy only about one-tenth of the area. The rest is occupied by gardens. The front gardens are almost always devoted to flowers. I remember the prize-winning garden in a competition at Wythenshawe last year. A man who had come out four years before from a slum, and had never had a spade in his hand, had produced a most beautiful garden—a blaze of colour—and it had made an immense difference to his life and his family's life. The back garden is generally devoted to vegetables, and the average value of the vegetables grown is about one shilling a week, which means fifty shillings a year. The vegetables grown in a housing estate, Sir Raymond Unwin pointed out, are worth a great deal more than the average product of the whole area, if it is a farm devoted to growing wheat and other things. So far as the produce is concerned, it is actually producing more vegetables (as well as producing flowers) than if it was entirely devoted to agriculture. That does not sound very much like wasted land. But the real value of the garden is not so much what it produces as its effect on family life. There is the garden right to your front door—right to your back door. The woman can do her housework, cooking, washing; the baby can be put out in the garden in the pram, children can be playing about in the garden perfectly safely, out in the open air, and she can be pottering in and out in between. Mr. Boumphrey did not admit it, but nobody can pretend that mothers, high up in flats, are not in constant fear of the danger of children falling downstairs. The husband while he is working in the garden can also be in and out—in touch with his wife. As one of them said: 'I can call out to my wife and ask where to plant the flowers. She can tell me what to do, and if I don't do it, she doesn't like the garden'. Mr. Boumphrey thinks that a garden two or three hundred yards away is equally good. Mr. Boumphrey's wife may perhaps be more tolerant than some of our wives.

This land devoted to gardens produces more actual food than agricultural land and it produces vitamins—I stand up for the vitamins, in spite of Mr. Boumphrey's mockery. It produces fresh vegetables for the children, which are extraordinarily good and extraordinarily important for them. It produces flowers in addition, which makes family life much happier and fuller. We have built two-and-a-half million houses with gardens of that sort since the War, but there are still millions of people who have not got them. So far from being wasted land, it seems that this land is by far and away the best used land in the whole country. The only pity is, there are still millions of people living in slums who cannot get such gardens. May I just give you one or two illustrations of that—how it works out with flats? Here is a woman with three children under school age,

The attraction of houses with their own gardens is shown at Wythenshawe
By courtesy of the City Surveyor, Manchester

living in a beautiful block of flats with a green grass courtyard—on the fourth floor. She is not very strong, she said; she cannot get them downstairs to play on the grass, because she is so far away; she cannot run up and down all the time. She says she sometimes wishes they could not see the grass, because it makes them want to get down to it. She had one sick child—very often ailing: whenever that child was ill—the very time when it was bad for the others to be indoors all the time—she was unable to let them go out at all.

I will give you just one more example. A family moved from Dagenham to Southwark, because they could not afford the fares. They said the children are not so well now. They used to be out of doors. The baby lived in the garden. Now he can only be put to sleep under the open window. The

Figure 3.9

Balcony of a modern flat in Mount Royal, Oxford Street, London (top left); cottages and gardens in Wythenshawe (bottom right); *Listener*, October 1935. © Immediate Media Company London Limited.

---

deal more study is required into this very urgent problem before we embark upon a gigantic policy of building flats or an equally gigantic policy of taking people out of the towns and putting them into the suburbs or into the satellites. That research we propose to do in the Housing Centre, and you will be interested to hear that in that work we shall have the help and guidance of Sir Ernest Simon and Mr. Boumphrey. Therefore we shall come to some satisfactory and solid conclusion.[44]

The town planner was agnostic. He did not see it as his place to steer public opinion in one direction or another. He saw his job as making sure his guests laid out their respective positions clearly, flushed out their intricacies, responded to criticism, and gave enough information to the listeners so they could make educated decisions and preferences about the options placed before them.

The flat-versus-cottage debate was clearly a matter of preference for towns or for suburbs, but it was also a burning political and policy issue. From 1935 to 1945, Britain was projected to raise two million new houses on top of the three million it had already built since the 1919 Addison Housing Act. While Tories, Liberals, and Labour had divergent ideologies on the provision of shelter, they all accepted state expenditure on better housing, which they deemed an expenditure on the prevention of crime, disease, immorality, laziness, and social instability. Better housing was also seen as a highway for the upward mobility of the working and middle classes.[45] Until 1935, the market had delivered a good part of the housing pie. But Tories and Labour, who then shared the rule, were compelled to pick up the tab for those of their constituents who fell below the radar of market initiatives.[46] The impact on taxes aside, the sheer immensity of the undertaking made housing strategies a quality of life issue not only for those to be housed in new developments, but also for those around them.

That Thursday's program punctuated a series called *Looking for the Town of Tomorrow*. It was part of the BBC wireless courses called broadcast syllabi, designed after the concept of weekly university lecture-seminars. Extended treatment of a single broadcast topic over six or twelve weeks was designed like a traditional course in continued education. The program was the proud work of the Department of Adult Education Broadcasts.[47] This subdepartment split the transmission year into terms, parallel to the academic calendar. It recruited the most reputable experts to acquaint the public with great literature, political concepts, economics, history, logic, ethics, and a basic understanding of science. Some of the transmissions focused on modern languages and the high arts, including sculpture, painting, architecture, drawing, and music. Still others encouraged hobbies like booklore, philately, woodcarving, carpentry, knitting, and weaving.[48]

The course *Looking for the Town of Tomorrow* had taken the shape of an oral travel narrative by G. M. Boumphrey, starting in September 1935. In the summer, the BBC had commissioned Boumphrey to fly to Europe. He visited five countries to research Continental experiments in standardized modules, industrial materials, aesthetic vocabulary, and planning strategies. Upon his return, he treated his listeners to vicarious trips to Germany, which had rejected its accomplishments in abstract modernism and International Style architecture in favor of a retrograde search for expressions of the homeland. Nazi Germany, the distressed broadcaster reported, had rejected the architecture that spoke of anonymous industrial origins for an architecture true to Aryan blood and soil. Boumphrey also walked Joe and his listening peers through the lavish flats with deep honeycomb balconies in a new street in Città degli Studi in Milan. Here were lessons the unwise Germans had forgotten but that a mature Britain must build on. Comparison of the industrial towns of Zlín in Czechoslovakia and Corby at home showed the results of diametrically opposed policies addressing the population explosion in the last few years: the first centrally planned, the second disjointedly developed. Boumphrey hailed Le Corbusier's proposal for a "Radiant City" on display in a Dutch gallery and dismissed the dark courtyard housing just built in Vienna. The previous three weeks, Joe and his friends had heard Boumphrey struggle to dispel public prejudice against flats. At stake were the form and shape of two million upcoming homes, their influence on the next generation, and their impact on the contours of the British landscape.

"Can Flats Solve the Housing Problem?" was a forty-minute-long unrehearsed debate, twice the length of usual shows. Perhaps the extra time was allowed because the producers had received too many complaints about the one-sidedness of Boumphrey's narrative; or perhaps, as demonstrated by the complaints, because it was a hot and topical subject that needed more time; or perhaps because they had at hand two passionate speakers who knew how to make great radio.

The program did not give Joe's listening group a measured quantity of subject matter. That was never the BBC's intention. It provided information its producers deemed necessary for their listeners' "expansion of mentality" and "enlargement of intelligence,"[49] so they could have a meaningful discussion on the virtues of cottages and flats and what they would, if given a chance, encourage their local councilors to push for.

At the end of the program, the listening group turned off the radio and opened up a moderated discussion. We know little about what they thought and discussed. What we do know is that their moderator was a local schoolteacher, trained by an advisory committee for the BBC's Department of Adult Education Broadcasts, who was on the BBC's payroll for this service. He was provided regular technical support and monitored by the advisory committee. Behind him sat two BBC field staff members who took notes on the quality of reception, the attention span of the audience, their preparation for the listening episode, their use of the pamphlets, the dress code at the meeting, and their points of interest, confusion, and debate.[50] With this, the BBC radio momentarily turned the informal meeting place of the pub into a formal debating society, both studied and recorded by BBC policy makers.

In 1938, the BBC divided the public into three broad groups: "intelligent and well-informed," "intelligent and not so well-informed," and the vast majority of "not-so-intelligent and mostly uninformed." These categories were descriptions of cultural rather than economic classes, and were created by the assistant director of Talks, Norman Luker, when he succeeded Christopher Salmon. Luker argued that wireless education could do little for the first group and was doing the most for the second group, but it was the third that ought to be its target.[51] The concept of group listening targeted this third segment of listeners.

Between 1927 and 1935, the BBC had been directly and indirectly running slightly fewer than three hundred such listening groups in all sorts of venues throughout Britain.⁵² It had first initiated this kind of listening-end management by drawing upon the impressive reserve of working men's organizations that had sprouted in the past forty years as part of social reform schemes.⁵³ These organizations had taken broadcasting into their preexisting classrooms for continued education. By 1935, the BBC had expanded the number of local partners: it coordinated with such associations of working-class men as the YMCA, activity clubs, village institutes, trade unions, adult schools, prisons, workhouses, and local businesses. Its main collaborator was the Workers Educational Association (WEA), the nation's leading institution of continuing adult education. Moreover, as early as 1928, 170 libraries were collaborating with the BBC. In addition to organizing and hosting listening groups, libraries advertised upcoming series via posters and postcards, carried pamphlets, and created supporting bibliographies for wireless classes. Most of their participants were working-class men. These three hundred or so BBC-initiated groups were multiplied by countless self-organized ones. The voluntary formal listening groups were offshoots of middle-class charities and ladies' clubs. They indicate the resonance of the BBC's approach to the cultural pedagogy in this class. Their members were not only listening together themselves, but took the radio set to hospitals, prisons, soup kitchens, women's associations, vocational centers, shops, and so on.⁵⁴

Early British radio was not just organizing adults around wireless listening; the BBC also established a department for children called School Broadcasts. This department accommodated its programs within the primary and grammar school curricula for children ages four to fourteen. Like the Department of Adult Education Broadcasts, it gave participating schools high-quality wireless sets, loudspeakers, equipment maintenance support, teacher training, and preparatory material. In 1928, the BBC was broadcasting to just a couple of London County Council schools on a trial basis. Starting with fifteen programs a week in 1928, by 1945 it was airing thirty to fifty-two shows a week. These included storytelling for five-year-olds, music lessons, and dramatized plays, debates, and talks for older kids, given by leading experts in the country. In 1927 the BBC was collaborating with 3,000 schools. At the outbreak of war in 1939, it had won the cooperation of the Board of Education and the figure had risen to 9,953 participating schools.⁵⁵ A little after World War II, 26,000 state schools, i.e., 75 percent of the total, were receiving daily School Broadcasts every afternoon. From 1929 onward, School Broadcasts worked with an auxiliary body called Central Council for Schools Broadcasting to assess and improve the effectiveness of their field activities. The council set up an extensive network of local committees extending, though unevenly, the length and breadth of the country. This network recruited teachers, lecturers, local education authorities, staff members of the Ministry of Education, parent associations, and numerous other groups invested in education reform.[56]

Three different formats of print publication circulated the wireless transmission of the spoken word. Programs were regularly recorded in the form of books and articles in the professional press. The books were published by the BBC and other presses, with other presses doing the bulk of the work. The *Listener* published abbreviated versions of talks one week after the broadcasts. Connected to the work in Adult Education and the Talks department, it was called a "hybrid between journalism and broadcasting."[57] Ninety percent of its content comprised translations of broadcasts, and ten percent were related articles and snippets that covered a wide variety of topics.[58] The *Listener*'s first editor, Richard Lambert, established a special section on visual arts, and periodically featured pieces like "Round the Exhibitions," book reviews, interviews, public art event news, and extracts from recent publications in the arts. The most peculiarly BBCesque of these publications, however, were the affordable, light pamphlets circulated to the members of listening groups, in advance of a particular broadcast series. Such a pamphlet was indispensable to broadcasts on visual arts.

The BBC's half-penny weekly *Radio Times* updated audiences about program schedules, while also publishing gossip columns on radio actors, singers, show hosts, newscasters, and other regular broadcasters. The weekly became the model of a whole horde of market-based magazines like *Radio Pictures*, *Radio City*, and *Wireless World*. In addition to pamphlets and books, the BBC's publication division produced supplementary material for school broadcasts: picture books for children and background notes for the teachers to help them integrate the programs with other reading material. They published three schedules or syllabi per year for Adult Education and illustrated its talks with eight or nine pamphlets per term on specific series, as well as providing posters for public libraries, leaflets, and colored postcards. Between autumn 1927 and summer 1928 alone, they circulated 261,000 study aids.[59]

Formal rituals of listening and its auxiliary practices left out most of the working- and lower-middle-class housewives and mothers. This demographic group was the most isolated from participation in civic and public life because

Figure 3.10

Pamphlet for School Broadcasts, 1933.
© Immediate Media Company London Limited.

---

of the obligations of domestic work. Domestic roles failed to generate the type of large organizations that brought men so continuously into public life, leaving many women out of the protocols of formal listening. Radio producers paid great attention to finding ways to bring public consciousness into the private domain, just as group listening was rendering private matters appropriate for discussion in public forums. For this, they generated an extensive body of literature and radio shows on the etiquettes of listening, including such advice as, "Make sure your set is working properly before you settle down to listen. Listen as carefully at home as you do in a theatre or concert hall. You cannot get the best out of a programme if your mind is wandering, or if you are playing bridge or reading. Give it your full attention."[60] Architects and architectural writers also contributed to this aspect of the BBC's efforts. The architect-historian John Summerson gave programs on the art of listening. "The worst thing which broadcasting has brought into modern life," he said, "is sheer indulgence in sound. … Listening is an art—the whole art of listening is to listen very little."[61] Early British radio producers desired the attention commanded by reading. In the years leading up to World War II, the British Broadcasting Corporation was an enormous reception-end organizer that created a unique culture of listening.

The London station also focused on the art of broadcasting. From the late 1920s to the mid-1930s, radio began to be talked of not only as a form of communication but also as a potential art form. Reith appointed Lance Sieveking to apply his knowledge of cinema and the theories of Vsevolod Pudovkin to radio production. Sieveking experimented with techniques of slow motion, close-up, dissolves, fades, mixes, and montage in the production of documentaries. Hilda Matheson brought her knowledge of language and the scholarship of Alan H. Gardiner to the production of Talks. She tried different transcription techniques to see if conversation could raise more healthy views on a subject than writing. In

An example of modern architecture praised by Sir Reginald Blomfield in a microphone discussion reproduced in this issue—the new Church of St. Esprit, in Paris (Architect, M. Paul Tournon)

By courtesy of 'L'Architecture'

Figure 3.11

The *Listener*, November 1934. © Immediate Media Company London Limited.

Figure 3.12

Pamphlet for School Broadcasts, 1936. © Immediate Media Company London Limited.

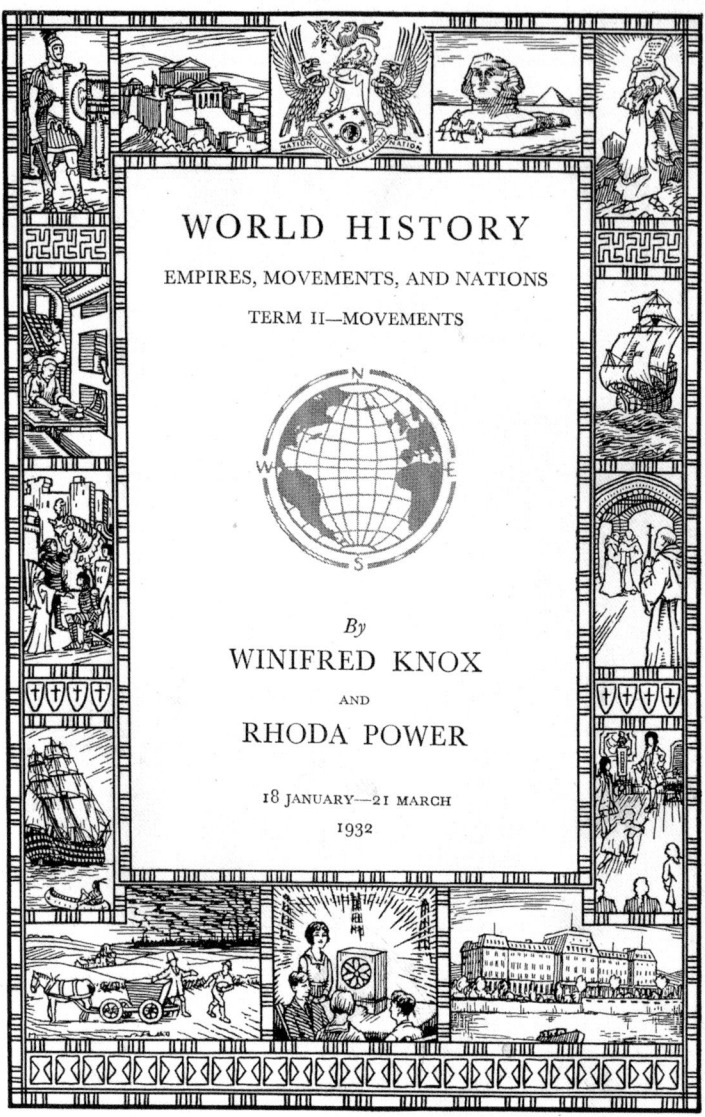

Price One Penny

Figure 3.13
Pamphlet for Adult Education, 1932.
© Immediate Media Company London Limited.

1930 the Talks department introduced "actuality" broadcasting: recording talks on location and combining sound effects to construct programs. Initial developments in the radio feature ranged from avant-garde techniques to plainspoken forms of social documentation and reportage. In 1936, the BBC commissioned art historian Herbert Read and musician Margaret Ludwig to translate Rudolf Arnheim's *Radio*, a book that provided techniques for creating different moods through sound and scene change in radio drama. Furnished with photographs of broadcasting studios in Savoy Hill and Broadcasting House, the translation demonstrated London's commitment to developing the art of broadcasting.

V Obstruction to Political Programming

Returning to our main topic, the BBC's body of architectural discourse was linked to John Reith's ambition to raise the standards of public discourse by providing balanced information in the form of news, political talks, location reporting, and the coverage of Parliament's proceedings. Responsible journalism could do much during this era when trade unions were pitting the interest of one industry against another, the urban poor were contesting the rights of rural poor, and the middle class, alarmed by the ever more assertive working class, found comfort in the bosom of conservatives. The aristocracy was scrambling to make up in financial power what it had lost in political power. In addition, the ballot results for most working- and some middle-class women substantiated liberals' worst fears that this segment of the electorate was going to be self-centered, bigoted, and prejudiced. It was precisely in anticipation of such tendencies that they had opposed women's suffrage. The picture was worsened when the latent conflict between the intellectuals' view of Labour as an assortment of high-minded and humanitarian lobbyists and the trade union vision of Labour as a party of working-class defense broke out into the open during the years of the second Labour government. The official agenda of the party for social and economic development now made no room for the high-minded impartiality of Charles Trevelyan, Stafford Cripps, and George Douglas Cole, who had switched parties. All in all, democracy had reduced the political arena to a battleground of the immediate and narrow interests of different classes and their subsets.[62] In *Broadcast over Britain*, Reith wrote that the BBC would provide

> direct information on a hundred subjects to innumerable people who thereby will be enabled not only to take more interest in events which formerly were outside their ken, but who will after a short time be in a position to make up their minds on many matters of vital moment, matters which formerly they had either to receive according to the dictated and partial versions and opinions of others, or to ignore altogether. A new and mighty weight of public opinion is being formed, and an intelligent concern on many subjects will be manifested in quarters now overlooked.[63]

Monopoly freed the Corporation from competition and the need to pander to sensational journalism. Right-to-license fees gave it financial freedom from advertisers and politicians.[64] But when Reith took charge of the BBC, he realized that he had little control over political journalism. News and opinion were dominated by the commercial and political affiliation of newspapers and politicians. As soon as the Post Office granted him the broadcasting license, the Newspaper Proprietors' Association and political parties joined forces against the BBC, convincing the Postmaster General to protect their market share against radio's technological superiority by limiting the scope of the Corporation news service. In *A Social History of British Broadcasting*, historians Paddy Scannell and David Cardiff describe the complicity of the Postmaster General and Parliament, which in 1927 enabled the press to maintain various degrees of restrictions on the BBC's right to the collection, editing, length, timing, and content of news.[65] The change of status from a company to a corporation did little for the BBC in this regard.

Due to these restrictions, the BBC was prohibited from making editorial comment on public policy and controversies. In addition to external constraints, though, the BBC also exercised self-restraint in matters sensitive for the government and politicians. In times of disagreement between the government and the unions, it followed the policy of supporting the representatives of the people over the people themselves. This demonstration of good and mature behavior earned them greater latitude from the government, and in 1928 Parliament lifted some of the bans.

Rushing to judgment, the News Section of the BBC misunderstood Parliament's latitude, seeing it as much-deserved recognition by the government: the Corporation had been accepted as a partner in communication with the electorate. But politicians and bureaucrats used broadcasting selectively. Clearly, in emergencies and the numerous moments of civil unrest in the early 1930s, the departmental bureaucracies and politicians preferred to channel news through radio because they favored a single source. At these times, it was difficult to separate the BBC's voice from that of the establishment. Yet the government or parties abdicated neither the control nor the stylization of information to the new disseminators of information. In normal situations, they still favored the press for the circulation of news. At these times, the BBC news bulletin became merely a notice board over which to announce all sorts of trivial communication; invitations to dinner events and social speeches were plentiful.

In their meticulous history of British broadcasting, Scannell and Cardiff reveal how limited the autonomy of the BBC was during the interwar period: "BBC's own efforts to open up the field of controversy on a broader basis were hampered by its commitment to consultation with the authorities, by complaints in the Commons and attacks in the national press, by outraged public opinion, by interference from government and—under the combined impact of all these pressures—by self-censorship, increasing caution and a retreat to safer ground."[66] Asa Briggs, the BBC's official historian, suggests that there was little improvement in the BBC's control over news management and political debate during the Second World War. Its six-member Board of Governors, appointed to protect the BBC from external interference, was shrunk to two members from 1939 to 1945, and subjugated to the Ministry of Information.[67]

Though political news was high up in the hierarchy of broadcast services, in these formative years the BBC was least effective in covering Parliament or the political parties. Retrospective assessments have been cognizant of this imbalance of power; Scannell and Cardiff note that the "BBC was the weakest of the players in the game," exposed to the strategic directives of the Post Office, press, and politicians on the one hand, and the cultural directives of the public on the other.[68] Though this was "a fact it had scarcely grasped by the mid-thirties," the Corporation enjoyed little more autonomy in this respect than when it had been a for-profit company.[69] The freedom of broadcasters was limited to the exploration of ways in which to incorporate the rules imposed upon them in news and the category of programming called talks.

VI The Necessity of Culture

In contrast to *political* transmissions, the Corporation enjoyed much greater power and control in defining the scope, form, and content of programming that loosely fell under the classification of cultural output. In 1926, an attorney for the BBC astutely anticipated that while "there might be control of the news," "a government was unlikely to bother with concerts, lectures, speeches or the weather."[70] Here the Corporation had the opposite problem. Most complaints were about misrepresentation or underrepresentation of the arts, rather than the right to represent.[71]

Daniel LeMahieu reminds us that broadcast culture bore the imprint of the "Victorian tradition of rational recreation":

> Reith viewed culture as a form of self-improvement, a means of personal and social discipline. "Enjoyment may be sought, not with a view to returning refreshed to the day's work but as a mere means of passing the time, and therefore of wasting it. ... On the other hand, it may be part of a systemic and sustained endeavor to re-create, to build up knowledge, experience and character." ... Reith placed culture within the context of moral character.[72]

The Reithian focus on moral character did not concern individuals alone, or some part or section of society; rather, it was essentially general.[73] The BBC's cultural programming sought to impose a cultural system that put the aesthetic and moral values of the educated classes above all others, within a political system where all citizens were equal before the law. Historian Ross McKibbin has argued that "Reith held so doggedly to the National Programme not because he wished to force an elitist culture upon the English, but because he wanted one audience to be aware of the tastes of another."[74] This was true only as long as it did not compromise Reith's commitment to "uplift." Part of his insistence on the National Programme was due to Reith's belief that "sedimentation of service and listeners would reflect tastes and interests as they were; 'national' programmes would develop tastes and interests dynamically. Broadcasting could enlarge horizons, both artistically and politically."[75] Reith's policies epitomize the humanist strategies to forestall the dangers and vulgarities of democracy.

The legitimate culture of his manifesto hinged on a specific conception of society that artfully welded the ideologies of meritocracy and natural talent. Society was no longer viewed as an extended procession, with the strongest pushing to the full limit of their powers, while the country to the rear was strewn with the dull-witted and thickheaded. Rather, society was a compact group, each member taken along and given every possible means to sharpen his or her ability to exercise private virtue and public morality. It had sufficient organization of schools, clubs, and associations to develop the natural talent of each member. The abilities and aptitude of its members were complementary to one another rather than identical. Each individual accepted the place given to her in society by her natural, God-given capacities, as just and useful to the collective advancement. Each performed his destined roles to the best of his abilities.

This society was managed and governed by its brightest and sharpest. The fruits of their expertise were absorbed from top to bottom, according to one's individual capacity. The BBC under the directorship of Reith was committed to the distribution of knowledge, not simply so that ignorant individuals would not burden society, but also for the survival of knowledge itself. For, in his view of society, it was not only the unexposed who were narrow-minded in their personal and public behavior, not only the imprudent who were overcome with distress and haste in their judgments, not only the simpletons who were prone to exploitation by the market and politicians. The concentration of knowledge not only allowed the complacent to shoot themselves in the foot but also the inquiring, and many of those whom it did not destroy it made redundant. Reith, and the young men and women he collected under his wing, recognized well that a concentration of knowledge not only destroyed the unquestioning, it manufactured them. It pushed the best brains in the country into ivory towers, and encouraged them to produce knowledge that was of use only to those with the cunning to convert it to their own profit and the manipulation of a defenseless public. Knowledge and society grew healthily only when they circulated in each other's veins.

The captains of this society, as the guest list of the BBC indicates, were professionals, writers, artists, journalists, and civil servants. From them, influence and morality would flow to the rest. Reform had to begin with individuals and private matters, because morality, it was believed, emanated from the private to the public. This formulation at once provided the BBC and its guests with a justification for their social roles and gave John Reith his entry and purpose. The simultaneous transmission of programs to the farthest corners of the country and the British Empire put radio at the service of the intellectual, politician, artist, economist, and journalist with public duty at heart to shape the polity in its image.

We must not understand the BBC's service to public discernment about the difference between culture and nonculture as merely a war of tastes between the cultural elite and the philistine classes. Ashbee, and after him the entire preservation movement to which the BBC opened its "back door," had become convinced that when the advance of democracy outpaced the progress of culture, democracy turned on culture and destroyed it. What it did not destroy, it maimed without remorse. This was the lesson the "Ugliness Exhibition" drove home. It motivated the writings of Strachey and Williams-Ellis, and concerned the competing opinions of Boumphrey and Simon. And it lay beneath the BBC's huge investment in programming about "good housekeeping." The "Ugliness Exhibition" sought to prove that when a populace unprepared for the responsibilities of freedom was given decision-making power, it displayed unrelenting intolerance for this invaluable mode of knowledge and being. It cared nothing for past and future, nothing for cultural continuity. Boumphrey was often heard complaining how the slightest mention in a local council committee room of the protection or production of beauty raised alarms. Advocates of beauty were chastised for aristocratism, conservatism, and antiprogressiveness. Not only that, with old patterns of patronage lost forever, a philistine democracy also stifled future artistic activity. A concerned Clough Williams-Ellis noted, "What is the use of artists doing beautiful things unless they have an appreciative audience behind them? Without that audience they would cease even to do them."[76]

Another architect, Halsey Ricardo, described the downward spiral of an uncultured society in the following words:

> To how many of my audience, in their walks or omnibus rides through our streets, does it occur to consider the general and particular effect of the buildings lining them? ... What sort of reply could you make to an inquiry as to what buildings caught your attention on the way from Oxford Circus to the Bank, and why? And yet this apathy, this shrinking of one's concern in citizenship, does matter very much. It leads to acquiescence in needless evil, to a kind of fatalism, to acceptance of things as they are, to false judgments and canons of taste.[77]

If the handful of examples given above indicates anything, it is that the stake in the reformation of manners and constitution of etiquettes in the age of their wireless dispersal was the monopoly over the cultural (informally codified) and political (legally determined) identity of Britain. The winner of the game took, to borrow an expression from Max Weber, the *monopoly* of the invention of "heritage"—worth requisition and spending public money—and of vigilant policing of the boundary between culture and its other. It involved dominion over the handling of individual and collective values, not to forget the hogging of institutional signs of cultural salvation. This was a project to teach men, women, and children respectability, a scheme for making known the spectrum of what a respectable people ought to value and reject, honor and ignore, love and fear. What was really at stake here was the very definition of modern England and Britain.

The construction of what Raymond Williams calls the "structure of feeling" of the wireless culture does not characterize only Ashbee or the other voices we have come across in the preceding pages.[78] We can interpret the entire fabric of public service broadcast, the collaboration and competition of the voices against each other, as an assertion of their monopoly over the handling of the cultural identity of Britain. It could clearly be seen as a collage of assertions of the relevance of artistic activity, both past and future, in a climate that seemed to have no place for it. It displayed liberal politics as they were at work through the uncharted medium of radio and showed how they were filtered through architectural discourse.

The definition of culture never fulfilled its political function so well as when it accommodated itself to democratic language. The English and England, the British and Britain, never fulfilled their social functions so well as when they gave the monuments of a splendid past to all as a public legacy. These values were never more compelling than when they fashioned the instruments of the sumptuous glorification of the great figures of bygone ages. They were indications of the magnificent possibilities that lay ahead for a nation that formally aspired to the rule of law. Wireless publication was an outwardly irreproachable means of justifying the monopoly of the cultured classes over values, identity, knowledge, manners, and taste without being inconsistent with the ideal of formal democracy. Did the BBC not justify its monopoly of the airwaves as a necessary evil for the eventual good of protecting public interest from commercial interest? This control would not be so strong if it did not aim at establishing, in the natural evolution of history, the sole right of the educated classes to appropriate culture to themselves symbolically, that is to say, in the only legitimate manner, in a society that pretends to yield to all, "democratically," the relics of an aristocratic past.

Shaping a public in the image of their own professed ideals through a cultural organ like radio was imperative for liberal intellectuals. Journalists, professionals, civil servants, artists, and aesthetes, whose ideals were unrepresented by the political parties, needed radio to do so. It was critical to their very existence. What else was going to distinguish and identify them, if not their definition of culture and progress? A world shaped by different ideals of equality, justice, and progress threatened to turn their civility, research, public duty, and sophistication of thought and style into parodies of a lost horizon. While "the elimination of the unfit" without social reform "is uncertain and capricious," Lyon Blease had cautioned, "[t]he deterioration of the fit is certain and remorseless."[79] These prewar words were more resonant after 1919 than they had been prior. They explain the sense of urgency and necessity that weighed upon the generation of Blease's children. The humanism of a liberal in the 1920s sprang from the same source as his or her fear. The sense of purpose was as driven by selflessness as it was by self-preservation. It was not just Boumphrey and Simon's flat-versus-cottage debate, Williams-Ellis and Strachey's myth of the accessibility of cultural artifacts, Ann Kindersley's instructions on the aestheticization of the home, and C. R. Ashbee's reclamation of the aristocratic and vernacular legacy of the English countryside as a public trust, through which the politics of a class that resisted a world divided into classes were at work. That these politics worked through the entire body of the BBC cultural output is beyond doubt.

The built environment endowed cultural topics with the political edge prohibited to the BBC. Many within the Corporation saw the BBC's agreement with the authorities to keep out direct political activism and controversy—mandated as much by law initially as by self-imposed discretion, and later by censorship—as a devil's pact. But when being forced into cultural instead of political programming took the form of architectural broadcasting, it turned out to be an angel's pact, for it not only consolidated a solid reputation for the Corporation, but it also gradually gathered all the liberties that its competitors at the national press had lobbied against and originally managed to deny it.

4 SPEAKING OF CONSERVATION: THE ORAL TRAVELOGUE AND BRITISH HISTORICAL IMAGINATION

I Oral Travel Guides

15 July 1936, 10:00 PM: Imagine the homemade sound box on the cabinet, delicately balanced to keep its batteries from leaking, as well as the stylish radio set with state-of-the-art speakers—bursting into song. The crash of the stock market was very good for the culture of listening. Radio became a source of consolation for 12 million license holders as well as uncounted homemade-set owners. The BBC took this development as an auspicious sign. It had become more daring in its presentation technique, though more timid in its content. This seemed to have been the trend for at least the past year or so. Storytelling—which loomed large in the atomized and monotonous world of agriculture and artisanship before print and industry—found a place for itself once again but now in an age of anxiety and distractions. Ideally, everyone on this warm Tuesday evening had settled, after dinner and cleanup, into their armchairs with a crossword puzzle or knitting project (or some similar civilizing hobby) when an announcer interrupted the music to announce the next program. A moment later, the familiar voice and electrifying presence of the forty-two-year-old G. M. Boumphrey filled the air. A mechanical tools inventor, children's storywriter,

furniture distributor, outdoor-sports enthusiast, design critic, advocate of flats (as featured in the last chapter), and impassioned preservationist, Boumphrey was giving a guided tour.[1] It was part of the ongoing series *Down River* on his recent adventures while canoeing through the picturesque terrain between Welshpool and Shrewsbury.[2] Next week, he was going to cover the notoriously monotonous stretch of river between Shrewsbury and Ironbridge. While *Down River* was an organized exploration of the countryside, it was at the same time a cautionary tale demonstrating the pitfalls of disorganized touring which, travel authors warned, produced "hazy confused impressions" of "topographical indigestion."[3] One example of "topographical indigestion" was described in part IV of the series:

> That third afternoon George and I began to have time to look about us a bit. We admired the superbly wooded hill behind Welshpool with Powis Castle on it and we saw with some pride that we were gradually working towards the end of Long Mountain on our right. Further ahead on that flank the Breidden Hill had come into view bearing an obelisk to the memory of Admiral Rodney in celebration of his victory over the French in 1781. As a matter of fact, Rodney himself had nothing to do with this part of the country. It has been cynically suggested that the pillar was put up by local squires as a thank-offering for the extraordinarily high price they had been able to get for their oak. The Admiral was a strong advocate of British oak for shipbuilding as against foreign stuff! Personally, I dislike the practice of building these impertinent landmarks on top of high and beautiful hills—and we saw quite enough of Rodney's Pillar for the next day or two to confirm our dislike. This hill and its sisters are beautiful with their thickly wooded slopes.[4]

Monday, 12 April 1937, 7:30 PM: A year later, travel programs were more frequent. That spring evening, the thirty-one-year-old John Betjeman treated both die-hard fans and casual listeners of the regional station "West of England" to a different kind of travelogue. As a minor poet, former assistant editor of the prestigious *Architectural Review* (1930–1935), author/editor of the *Shell Guides*, as well as an avid collector of architectural illustrations, Betjeman had a gift for invoking spaces and places. His narrative focused on towns in the West of England. There were reflections on England's best-kept tourist secret: Georgian

Figure 4.1

Ironbridge over the River Severn, Coalbrookdale, built 1781. Courtesy: Paul Clarke.

Figure 4.2

Tram lines in Bristol, 1932. Courtesy: "Collection of Nick Booker, original copyright holder unknown."

Bristol. In a reversal of tradition, his was a guide for the locals by a visitor. His *Town Tours* exhibited the pleasures elicited by a passerby and the pattern of change he noticed, invisible to the jaded local. Betjeman's project was to recondition the eye of the listener and make her the connoisseur (and critic) of given surroundings. This is his description of the first stop on a three-month-long town tour:

> Bikers, motorists, railway travelers see the villages they loved pulled down by local councils and built up by speculators; they see the familiar skyline strung with wires as though some dear old lady on her flight to heaven had left her knitting behind and it had stayed in mid-air. Tinned food, tinned brains, tinned souls—we are just beginning to look about us and see that "progress" is not to be measured in terms of scientific invention. We are beginning to see that people who lived a hundred years ago were perhaps wiser than we are today.[5]

A Thursday in May 1937, 8:30 PM: This evening, the regional channel of Manchester introduced a brand-new voice. It was the crisp, intelligent sound of John Summerson, a thirty-three-year-old architect turned architectural journalist and an aspiring historian. He zoomed in further than the previous tour givers and gave a vicarious tour of a conventional architectural monument, Newstead Abbey in Nottinghamshire, one of the great show houses of the country and one of the many stately houses he would describe to listeners in the next two months. The ancestral home of the revered and reviled romantic poet Lord Byron, it had been extensively renovated by subsequent owners in the nineteenth century and opened its gates to tourists from all over the world. After being

closed for a while, it was bought and donated to the Nottingham Corporation by the philanthropist Sir Julien Cahn in 1931. The show house, one of the ten most loved and famous Midlands houses, had recently been opened to the public by local authorities. Summerson visited it just the day before the broadcast in preparation for taking it to his listeners. In his narrative, the high and thick walls of the stately home divulged their secrets, offering up the mysteries and rumors surrounding the house to the probing eye of a systematic researcher:

> Byron lived here. But in telling you about the house this evening I am not going to put Byron too much in the foreground. I would rather you picture the house and its history as something with a much wider claim to your attention. The Byron episode will fit naturally into its place when we come to

Figure 4.3

Newstead Abbey, originally a twelfth-century monastery and later the seat of the Byron family. Courtesy: Kim Kiddle.

it. ... Originally an Augustinian priory, the Abbey is Henry the II's doing. He founded many monasteries to expiate his share in the murder of Thomas à Becket. ... Now let us look more closely at the house and try to picture it as Byron, the poet, knew it. ... But it is infinitely to the credit of pleasure-seekers, as well as to the tact and wisdom of Newstead's present guardians, that its character remains unspoiled. ... Whether we are drawn to Newstead by the beauty of its Gothic architecture or by its romantic and vivid associations with a great poet, we shall find it still lives up to its reputation as one of the strangest and most haunting of the great houses of Midlands.[6]

In twentieth-century Britain, no one did more to fix the nation's historical imagination in the built and landscape environment than Geoffrey Maxwell Boumphrey (1886–1960), Sir John Betjeman (1906–1984), and Sir John Summerson (1904–1992). Today, Betjeman, a poet laureate, is regarded as the most memorable poet of the century to be associated with the historic preservation movement in England. Summerson, in turn, is the most influential historian of British architecture.[7] The former was a founding member of the Victorian Society (founded 1958), the latter a founding member of the Georgian Group (1937); and both are remembered as architectural broadcasters. But in the 1930s and 1940s, it was Boumphrey who was heard most often on the radio. Responsible for an astonishing one-third of all the known BBC programs from 1927 to 1945, Boumphrey was far more active in weaving national identity with the history of architecture and landscape than is remembered today. Yet each of the three men updated the notion of heritage in different ways.

The principal aim of this chapter is to describe how each of these differently positioned architectural writers apprehended and represented built and topographical heritage. I look at what they included in it and what they left out. I ask how these guides represented social reality. How did they conceive the relation of the architectural community to the modern world and how did they interpret it to others? Boumphrey, Betjeman, and Summerson all supported the modern movement in the 1930s, praising its break from the tiresome imitation of the past. They admired its replacement of the rigid rules of Beaux-Arts composition with a functional approach, and they applauded its attention to contemporary problems. Yet when invited to broadcast, they settled on excursions into the rural past of Georgian towns and stately homes. Before 1945, broadcasters on the landscape and built environment used travelogues almost exclusively to represent historical physical environs in the countryside and small towns. The task at hand is to analyze how these champions of the modern movement understood and presented the value of rural and industrial Britain.

Travelogues were part of the BBC's burgeoning series produced for the outdoor months (April to October) annually. They were so popular that in the 1930s and 1940s they developed into a category of their own. While it is impossible to estimate the exact number of programs, we know that in the spring and summer of 1939 they were a daily occurrence during peak broadcasting times. The five regional stations allocated one day each week during this period to showcasing their localities. Scotland brought possible visitors to Dundee "up to date in their knowledge of the city: its history, industry, culture and amenity."[8] Wales invited the geologist W. F. Grimes to give tips on reading their caves in *How to Read the Welsh Countryside.*[9] The West of England station offered a tour of Falmouth and presented the "radio picture as it was in the olden days, and as it is today."[10] North Ireland displayed its special attractions. The Midlands tour took the format to a whole new level of exuberance. For example, one week its producers persuaded the Marquess of Northampton, the owner of the famous estate and stately home of Compton Wynyates, to allow local singers to present Elizabethan songs from this most Elizabethan of English mansions.[11] Another week they relayed Christopher Fry's pageant play *The Tower* for the travel slot. The play, acted out in front of the abbey in Tewkesbury festival, told the story of the construction, destruction, and ruthless reconstruction of the Norman abbey at Tewkesbury.[12] The Midlands station's "Ely Cathedral" pulled out all the stops. Part of *Sermons in Stone*, the forty-minute program was written and arranged by Robin Whitworth. Six presenters explained the impressive incidents down the ages as each approached and walked around the cathedral. An organ and a choir animated the story, from the cathedral's destruction in 1322 to current restoration. The program, recorded by the BBC Mobile Recording Unit, was the most expensive and laboriously rehearsed broadcast of the year.[13]

The BBC's travelogues drew aesthetes and intellectuals from all walks of life—professional travel journalists (S. P. B. Mais), civic-minded literary modernists (Geoffrey Grigson, Evelyn Waugh, E. M. Forster, and Rebecca West), and archaeologists (Bernard Ashmole and Stanley Casson). They showcased union-leaning clergymen, liberal-minded geologists, politicians, and lords and duchesses who were committed to the preservation of open land, coasts, commons, and riverbeds. The programs made historically valuable architecture a part of

Figure 4.4

Pamphlet, *Travel Talks*, 1937. © Immediate Media Company London Limited.

parliamentary debate. They introduced mixed preferences and taste for things past and present. Some contributors complained about tourists bathing in ponds or fouling places by relieving themselves in parks or discarding banana peels, and about dogs swimming in reservoirs; others were more restrained in their condemnation of public behavior. The message in all cases focused on the preservation of beauty and orderly exploration.

Our three broadcasters, Boumphrey, Betjeman, and Summerson, offered elaborate and competing disquisitions on architecture and topographical heritage. Their travelogues were, in effect, a type of backdoor activism for architectural preservation. They demonstrate that the British modernists, while not hostages to the past, were never able to shake off their Edwardian parents' and Victorian grandparents' reverence for the past. Not historicists, Boumphrey, Betjeman, and Summerson had a characteristically strong sense of history and historical continuity. As previous chapters indicate, they defended the modern movement as a reestablishment of the tradition of invention, lost either in the Renaissance or at the end of the gentlemanly Georgian era a hundred years ago. Their broadcasts support those theorists who insist that in interwar England the nexus of tradition and modernity—looking to the past and being up to date—and the preservation of history and progress in the future were not antagonistic endeavors. Against critical literature on "heritage," "Englishness," and conservation that view these ideas as oppositions, the broadcasts show that preservation of history and the modern movement's concern with the needs of the present and the future are of a piece. We will do well to remember that Geoffrey Boumphrey advocated the use of freestanding concrete-and-glass flats (introduced in the last chapter) not only because he was concerned with the aesthetic of light and simplicity and housing low-income populations in healthy environs. He was just as worried about asserting a distinct and visible boundary between country and city, as well as managing urban sprawl, for which he blamed the practices of garden city planning. High-density planning reduced urban sprawl and improved the preservation of countryside.[14] For this reason, the pioneer members of the MARS Group (1934), which broke with the norms of traditional practice in the name of duty to the future, were also the founding members of the conservationist Georgian Society (est. 1937). Amyas Connell's irreverence for Reginald Blomfield's revivalism and passion for the protection of the material examples of those revivals—preservation and development, history and modernity (mentioned in chapters 1 and 2)—went hand in hand. This generation's enthusiasm for what mostly amounted to an aristocratic property, be it parkland or built form, was tinged by a sense of public duty toward national heritage. It was precisely the same spirit that made the modern movement flavorful and the meaningless clichés of their elders distasteful to them. G. M. Boumphrey, John Betjeman, and John Summerson were three such modern critics, historians, and preservationists who looked backward in order to pave the way forward.

In the 1930s, preservation was a sticky and litigious issue. The first generation of radio broadcasters had inherited just as much political hostility toward preservation as their predecessors. Open-air leisure was both changing and growing in popularity. Between 1919 and 1939, urban excursions into the country accelerated as the ubiquity and reach of the motorcar opened new rural spaces for urbanite weekend trips. In 1939, the presence of two million cars virtually established a middle-class right of way on the road, while the popularity of bus trips facilitated working-class motor movement.[15] In 1930 came the formation of the Youth Hostels Association and the initial movement toward creation of the National Council of Ramblers' Federations, which became the Ramblers' Association (established in 1935). David Matless tells us that the vociferous geographer and preservationist Vaughan Cornish welcomed "a new development of great promise ... the formation of clubs and associations for touring the countryside under definite rules of conduct."[16] But this crowd was in no mood for definite rules. When preservationists told them to respect private property and refrain from trespassing, political tensions were heightened. And, indeed, the BBC received a swarm of angry and congratulatory letters alike on airing Cornish. When preservation bodies like the Commons and Open Spaces Society tried to dilute rights of access in the 1939 Access to Mountains Act, they were likewise met with tough opposition from the Ramblers' Association and accused of trying to slip in a clause that could make trespassing a criminal offense.[17] Preservationists were faced not by meek individuals seeking regulated education but by young communists who had a militant sense of their right to roam and who regarded right of access as a sacred issue of justice.

> I'm a rambler, I am a rambler from Manchester way
> I get all my pleasure the hard, moorland way
> I may be a wage slave on Monday
> But I am a free man on Sunday.[18]

It was onto this scene of popular consumption of the rural scenery that the interwar preservationists had to project their particular sense of modern nationalism and citizenship. Evan MacColl, the poet of the quatrain above, who believed in the public's right of way through commons and private estates, clearly drew upon the romantic socialism promoted by John Ruskin and William Morris. These nineteenth-century preservationists and their twentieth-century disciples in the arts and crafts movement gave MacColl a well-developed notion of the "people's heritage" that dissociated the English landscape and medieval towns from privilege and exclusion and forged them as the nation's past.[19] The arts and crafts intellectuals had convinced themselves that the aristocracy had been erased from the Old English countryside. They had believed that if they extended the benefits of scenic beauty from the few to the many, the people would learn to see the goodly heritage as their collective fortune and come to guard it. But the First World War distorted this dream. The interwar preservationists were isolated on the one side by a steadily trotting army of self-righteous and unaesthetic urbanites and suburbanites. On the other side they were crushed by the aggressive and shortsighted economic policies of Labour and Tories. In putting only a monetary value on every project, the Labour MPs regarded the spirit of preservation as antagonistic to the spirit of progress. The public also considered preservation and development irreconcilable. Boumphrey, Betjeman, and Summerson thus devised definitions of "heritage" that absorbed the materialist and populist critique of conservation.

These new preservationists inherited a movement that had undergone several revisions since its establishment in the 1860s. Its most important accomplishment was the founding of the National Trust for Places of Historic Interest or Natural Beauty at the turn of the century. The trust was a small coalition of aesthetes touched by a tincture of Morris's enthusiasm for medieval architecture and Ruskin's romanticism and belief in nature's civilizing and healthful effects on the laboring masses. Members were either socialists or Gladstone-variety radicals whose cultivation-oriented definition of progress and development had fallen out of favor with the new redistributive radicals who dominated the Liberal Party in the 1880s and 1890s. The Gladstonians argued for land, built fabric, and works of art—both in public and private possession—to be recognized as national "heritage" and preserved for the people. This required a different taxation system than the one proposed by New Liberals, which treated these items as national "wealth." New Liberals viewed the historic productions of artistic works and landscape as chattels that should be taxed to finance the navy, contain the grievances of occupying ratepayers, and pay for ambitious social reforms. They wanted property to be redistributed in ways that would contain the explicitly anti-landowner sentiment within the party without driving middle-class voters into the embrace of the Conservatives.[20] As discussed earlier, New Liberals placed the sale of historic art and architecture and the breakup of estates at the heart of popular governance and democratic finance. In consequence, the maintenance of inherited property became so costly that it hastened the momentum for preservation.

At variance with their party mates, Liberal landowners and activists who had voluntarily joined the trust to do good found themselves in bed with the trust's Tory members. Open to voluntary philanthropy, the Tories had joined the trust out of fear of confiscatory radicalism. The Liberals and socialists who cared for preservation periodically caught themselves on the wrong side of the bitter battle between aristocratic and popular rights, arguing for the maintenance of the old system of private ownership in the name of the people, and demanding tax concessions for the voluntary benevolence of public-spirited dukes and lords. Landlords who were to voluntarily share the joys of their possessions and stately homes with a ticket-paying public, they argued, could take on the role of duty-bound, enlightened custodians of public property.[21] C. R. Ashbee, introduced in chapter 3, was their classic remnant.

By the time wireless listening connected Britain, things had changed. The confrontation between the aristocracy and the people, which had animated British politics since 1880s, had subsided.[22] Land no longer bore the same political power. Thanks to successive series of franchise reforms, large landowners were now prepared to abandon the countryside for more lucrative forms of wealth and power. Many were feeling the pinch of rising expenses and inflexible incomes and were ruefully balancing their books. Weakened by a market economy, urbanization, agricultural depression, and heavy taxation, landowners found the staffing and maintenance of big country houses and estates to be a heavy economic burden. Old landed families were no longer willing to play the role of nurturers and furnishers of British landscape. Wrought by a different politics, they nevertheless shared the cultural indifference of radical Liberals; they viewed the countryside as private and disposable property to be converted into less binding assets. Land was still economically lucrative. Estates had been coming onto the market more rapidly since the Great Depression of the 1870s, but the flow increased during the First World War and rose to a flood in the postwar years.[23] Deals were being brokered all across Britain dividing large estates into lucratively sized properties. Other landowners negotiated leases with schools and hospitals. Between 1918 and 1921 alone, some six to eight million acres changed hands.[24] The *Estate Gazette* captured the changing scene with the headline "Revolution in Landowning."[25] The *Times* portrayed the buying and selling frenzy with the words "England is changing hands."[26] Small towns were going through no different a change. John Summerson lamented the effects: "Costly buildings rise every day from grotesque street plans and from boundary lines determined by the freaks and hazards of ownership over a period of centuries. At the same time, buildings which we have come to look upon as national possessions are being demolished for the mere speculative value of their sites."[27]

Landowners who could not or would not avail themselves of these escape routes began to entertain the propositions of old preservationists as lucrative options. By selling entry tickets to their homes and gardens, they could become cultural leaders and put their possessions to the good work of revamping their public image. The estate of Newstead Abbey, visited by John Summerson, was one of those homes open for exhibition and public recreation for a small fee. But to most landlords, the idea of becoming a custodian of a national trust was no longer a question of voluntary benevolence. Besides the indignity of succumbing to public pressure, they viewed this route as a mandatory order for turning private homes into public museums run by the government or a charity, and resented the idea. The whole thing smelled of nationalization, socialism, and exploitation—a path on which they believed Liberals and now Labour were determined to keep the country. They wanted no part of it. They instead tended to resist the Liberal argument about historical possessions altogether and were inclined to fall back on the Tory defense of private property.[28] As before the war, most "owners" after it "simply did not see cultural leadership as an obvious solution to their growing political and economic problems; it did not come naturally to the modern aristocrat, it seemed a waste of time and money or, worse, a dangerous concession to a rambling mob."[29]

The Conservative Prime Minister Stanley Baldwin is remembered for associating the country with the countryside: "England is the country and the country is England."[30] Yet he did not give preservation priority over the modernization of land. His ambitious electrification and massive road-building project of 1925–1926 brought the comforts of cities to the remotest villages and made them accessible to urban visitors. By this time, the Tories were seeking to shed their patrician image, and sacrificing the most privileged constituency (a small group) for that of the moderately privileged (larger). They raised death duties more unflinchingly than William Harcourt and gallantly left agriculture to the tender mercies of the free market.

The BBC's preservationists had witnessed the olde Isles of the prewar years give way to a New Britain of the interwar years. The Britain in which they were active was the conquered territory of an army of smallholding owners and mass tourists. Although the majority of the purchasers still consisted of sitting tenants, the symbolic ownership of the countryside had slipped into the hands of the urban middle class. Their victory came in the form of suburban estates, commuter trains, new roads, electrification, beach resorts, golf courses, and tennis courts—all indiscriminately placed. Speculative builders were all over the place. There were new inns, humble-sized cottages, road signs, billboards, and those unseemly petrol pumps.

As if the contest between middlebrow and highbrow cultural definitions was not enough, the interwar preservationists also had on their hands a new contender in hostility to its notion of heritage and progress: the Labour Treasury. Peter Mandler has noted that "the Treasury considered ancient monuments expenditures 'entirely a luxury,' and flatly refused 'to waste its resources on schemes which, however desirable from the aesthetic point of view, do not enrich the country or add to its commercial equipment.'"[31] In 1924, the Labour Party found its way into office on the basis of the critique that Liberals had not done enough for the welfare of the poor, that they had been too close to the rich and too restrained in compensating the common man for the unjust privileges the most powerful had enjoyed on the back of their constituency. Labour's goal was to convert the Liberal ladder to individual prosperity into a highway of class prosperity for the working classes, essentially measured by economic prosperity. Their confidence in material logic made the slightest mention of conservation sound like conservatism and brutally exposed the romanticism of socialist aesthetes. Labour and Tory political discourse separated the alleviation of poverty and the provision of "essential" welfare from the cultivation agenda (so sacred to Liberals). They portrayed the preservation of the countryside as irresponsible sentimentalism—an outmoded, even reactionary, fantasy of the old world despots.

As mentioned, this generation's case for preservation was not just attentive to the public opinion against it—it in part absorbed its logic, as seen in our three broadcasters. If there were any traces of aestheticism in Boumphrey, they were well submerged; his language gave little away. Betjeman shrouded his passion in a thick layer of humor and parody in order to be able to say what would not be taken seriously if said seriously. Summerson carefully regulated his romanticism with his autodidactic professionalism.[32] Their representations synthesized the old Gladstonian and New Liberal radicalism, in that they supplanted the antinomy between preservation, redistribution, and access. Unlike the Society for the Preservation of Ancient Buildings (SPAB), the three envisioned equipping the country—for the motorist, tourist, seasonal tenants, noise, speed, electricity, and picnicking—as preservation. They argued that the opening up of the natural and architectural treasures of the countryside, if well planned, could make development and preservation mutually beneficial. A full-minded scheme would rope in the frozen parts of the old countryside as tourist attractions and make them come alive. In this view, tourism was seen as an entirely positive phenomenon that would remedy its own ills. The steady stream of visitors, it was often pointed out, was dependent on the attractiveness of localities. With a little tempering and guidance in taste, the market would watch after beauty itself.

By 1930, preservationists like Noel Carrington saw preservation of the countryside as a crusade that could not be isolated from the beautification of the cities:

> The crusade [to preserve rural England] has enlisted many of the best minds of this country. It has secured legislation and is reinforcing legislation by making the public aware of the evil. Yet I think it true that the more active minds of the movement have come to the conclusion that mere preservation will achieve very little, if anything, of permanent value, as long as the

source of infection is left untouched. All these blights which descend on the countryside come from our cities, "those vast nurseries of industrial barbarians," as Mr. Williams-Ellis calls them, where generations have been left to grow in surroundings of squalor and ugliness.[33]

Most of Carrington's compatriots located the source of this crisis in the nineteenth-century towns, but he diagnosed the source of Englishmen's apathy to civilization in the decline of British Empire:

> If we have not quite the pride in our civilization that our fathers had, it is mostly because others are growing richer than us, and our "City" is growing dependant on Wall Street. That Stockholm is growing more beautiful or that Berlin more clean than London is a matter of indifference. We continue to accept our Sheffields and our Readings with a complacent shrug; we go further and create a Slough. All the world and his wife will be going to see the Exhibition of Italian art (if only because it is valued at fourteen millions Sterling), but how many will ask themselves how Piccadilly Circus compares with these lovely piazzas of Tuscany?[34]

If the preservationists, Carrington understood well, were to have any meaningful success, they must look not to the past but to the forces of revival in the future—not the Old England but a new England. His peers on the air appreciated modern technology and its powers. Though rather prematurely, Noel Carrington imagined a convergence of three political points of view:

> It is idle to think of England in terms of Georgian urbanity or of any other epoch we may fancy; life tomorrow, still today will be conditioned by the machine. Where the machine is frankly accepted, man has achieved a new and satisfying beauty. When it is accepted with shame and half-heartedly, it achieves the "Adam style," gas-fire or the imitation-half-timber villa on easy payment terms. The machine has also annihilated space (as we are reminded every day). The city has conquered the countryside. Accepting this as a fact to be faced, if not to be welcomed, we realize that our old conceptions of town and country are no longer valid. ... Our old conception of individual liberty—the liberty to abuse one's property as one likes—must almost certainly give way to acceptance of collective control inspired by civic pride.

> Capital and Labour are arriving at the same philosophy, the one calling it Rationalization and the other Nationalization.[35]

II Geoffrey Maxwell Boumphrey: Landscape as Event

A man of wide-ranging interests and immense missionary zeal, Geoffrey Maxwell Boumphrey would have passed through time without notice had radio in Britain not coincided with his talents and causes. The BBC first launched him on the national scene in 1931 in a broadcast called "The Modern Home." From then on he was a frequent presence in British households. In 1934 he aired a widely heard series on a walking expedition entitled *Along the Roman Roads*. Stretching from May to June, the series covered the famous stretches of Roman roads, Portway, Icknield Way, and Hadrian's Wall among them, as Boumphrey went in search of the physical remains of two-thousand-year-old paths that had first linked Wales, Scotland, and England into a trade and administrative network.[36] Hadrian's Wall and Avebury showed off the achievements of the Office of Works after an amending Act of 1931 and the Town and Country Planning Act of 1932: the ivy-laden remains and weed-covered surroundings of a four-thousand-year-old metropolis in Avebury had been cleaned up and made into an inviting tourist destination. The following year, the BBC flew Boumphrey to five countries in Europe where he visited modern towns and housing schemes including Tomáš Baťa's factory town in Zlín, Czechoslovakia. In the summer of 1936, he canoed through England with Geoffrey Humphrey, another writer on progressive housing. Together they produced eight episodes of *Down River*. Not to leave out the troubled Ireland, Boumphrey was contracted for the summer after to give a vicarious car tour through towns and country called "Ulster Holiday."

With the exception of *Looking for the Town of Tomorrow*, these travelogues offered glimpses of a pastoral country born out of the ideals of the most self-consciously progressive intellectuals in London. The programs put before listeners not the landscape disappearing from view but a modern one rising out of its ashes. Lying past the spoliation of suburbs, this landscape was dotted with inns, shops, and meals of boiled eggs for days on end. History had left its marks on it in the form of dark caves, strange stone "henges," crumbling castles, cottages with thatched roofs, iron bridges, and now row houses. It was populated with prospering farmers, struggling renters, and tenacious housewives. Its school girls were wiser than Boumphrey in navigating the rugged ground.[37] When clergymen and landed society surfaced in his travel account, they were a dishonorable lot who remorselessly burned down villages and destroyed towns to best each other in futile wars. The winds of time had delivered their spoils, the castles of blood and obelisks of greed, into the hands of sitting tenants, cobblers, and miners, all born and bred on the land. Here the conventional association between a history-conscious tourist and the nostalgia for the landed classes that had maintained the beauty of rural Britain came apart.

Boumphrey invoked churches and town halls, soaring Midlands spires and Worcester Cathedral not by their stylistic peculiarities but through sociopolitical anecdotes. He converted scenes and sights into historical accounts. His stories slowed down the passage of a twelfth-century abbey outside Sapperton and the leaning tower of Bridgnorth Castle into the mist. Framed by willows along banks, the scars of their glory and tumultuous past came to life in Boumphrey's descriptions:

> The river and a square church tower high on a hill ahead told us that we were not so far from Bridgnorth. There is a lot to be said for the taste of Charles I in preferring this town above any other place in his dominion. It returned the compliment by holding out stoutly for him against Parliamentarians, and paid the penalty by having its castle, dating from about 1100, mined and destroyed. Almost all that remains today is the tower, ruined and leaning at an angle which makes the more famous tower at Pisa seem almost vertical by comparison. Bridgnorth is unique in its situation for this country. The Upper Town is built all the way up and on top of a great cliff of red sandstone which rises precipitously almost 200 feet from the west bank of the river. Seen from below this is largely spoiled for me by that ugly tower of the church built by Telford, the great engineer—"in the Pagan manner" as my guide caustically puts it, or in other words incongruous Classic. If Telford had been content to build a church to do its job, no doubt he would have produced something as good-looking as his many beautiful bridges: his mistake was in thinking that a church must call for some mock-classic. A

Figure 4.5

Bridgnorth Castle's leaning tower, Shropshire, twelfth century. Courtesy: Shrewsbury Museums Service, photograph by P. Morris.

pity, because it has led people to think in spite of the evidence of his bridges, that an engineer cannot create beauty.[38]

Modernist as these assessments were, Boumphrey adopted no overt advisory posture toward his audience. Rather than taking a combative stance in his broadcasts on the contemporary production of flats and cottages, he employed a rather confident and exploratory tone to describe the wide-ranging landscape. The land he described was adventurous, participatory, and ready to reveal its riches and forgotten secrets to vigilant amateurs. It flourished over the ashes of an exclusive, fragmented, arrogant, and outmoded Britain. Stocking Green Close "shows the way in which history is being slowly pieced together," Boumphrey said in a show on "Hadrian's Wall."[39] He concluded:

> Let me end with the words of an eighteenth century antiquary written after he had made a tour of the [Hadrianic] Wall. "I hold myself obliged to preserve, as well as I can, the memory of such things as I saw; which, added to what future times will discover, will revive the Roman glory among us, and may serve to invite nobler minds to endeavor at that merit and public-spiritedness which shine through all their actions. This tribute at least we owe them, and they deserve it at our hands, to preserve their remains." We may not subscribe to every word of that; but surely the last sentence we can all agree with.[40]

This was Boumphrey's message all along: if the imperial nation was to revive its fading glory that had nourished public pride, it must preserve the memorials of that imperial time. But these concluding words of his popular series *Along the Roman Roads* were the only ones in the entire oeuvre of his travelogues in which he conspicuously, albeit cautiously, connected holiday travel to preservation and preservation to the preservationists' sense of public-spiritedness and citizenship. The rest of his broadcasts set an example of ways of seeing and being in the landscape, and described suitable manners for the appropriation of the countryside by new classes of visitors. Here was an exercise in crafting a new, conciliatory view of heritage.

These broadcasts constructed a countryside that brimmed over with optimism and now belonged to the entire nation and all classes. Week after week, year after year, region after region, Boumphrey's movement through the history and geography of Britain marked people's final triumph: "whole counties are spread at my feet."[41] Imbued with the moral language of fitness, honesty, and harmony, Boumphrey's broadcasts presented this material and picturesque landscape as the site where the popular consciousness of the British people was to be nationalized, the long forgotten recuperated, and the hitherto-private property made pertinent along new lines. The rivers and roads of this landscape became the arteries of national life; municipal museums surfaced as repositories of a collective consciousness; and the town and country of these broadcasts were now available for scientific planning and government management.[42] There, the past welcomed the present and the village hosted the city. On the Portway, he said, "the sites are nearly always beautiful, with immense views all round, and the solitude is impressive. One begins to feel very close to the past." Lincoln possessed "that feeling of unity that is one of the first things one looks for in a town. Its streets are full of lovely and sometimes quaint old houses." By evoking the countryside's open vistas and narrow paths, Boumphrey placed before his listeners a world available for the consumption and navigation of ever increasing numbers of tourists. Bursting with energy, it entertained motorists, bikers, railway passengers, amateur photographers, and archaeological detectives. It "was a place of recreation and a giver of mental peace—a peace that won't be found in the contemplation of any garden suburb."[43] Walks, cycling, camping, and map reading provided relief from the pressures of urban life.

This idealistic construction of rural Britain stood in sharp contrast with the equally idealistic countryside of the arts and crafts utopia. For all its romanticism, Boumphrey's vision rejected the previous generation's selective view of arts-and-craftsy village greens and manor houses at the heart of garden city planning. The past of Boumphrey's countryside was ruthlessly violent, full of betrayals and intrigues, and the predecessor of the current Great War:

> [T]he old town was for centuries the cock-pit of the Border Wars between Saxons and Britons, Normans and English and Welsh wars that only ended with the accession of a Welsh king, Henry VII, to the English throne. How much there is to be learned from these old struggles that might be applied to the state of Europe today! What is the result of it all—the raids and the burnings, the years of apprehension and poverty, of terror and anger and fierce revenge, the hundreds of thousands of wounded and tortured and

Figure 4.6
Badbury Rings, an Iron Age hill fort in east Dorset, dating from 800 BC. Courtesy: Committee of Aerial Photography, University of Cambridge. Photographed by Dr. J. K. St. Joseph.

> dead? A peaceful market town in a peaceful countryside that might have been there all the time! Are we never going to learn, I wonder?[44]

Elsewhere:

> I told George that he was sitting within a hundred yards or so of the place where King Alfred's generals brought the Danes to bay (they had landed from the Severn) and cut them to pieces, helped by the men of Powis. ... The whole of that countryside bears traces of a bloody history. ... If the story of all the entrenchments and ruined fortifications could be unraveled, it would make good reading.[45]

In Boumphrey's travelogues, one witnessed the return of the vitality that storytelling had had in oral societies. Dethroned by print as the primary mode of collective knowledge, storytelling came back victorious through the culture of wireless listening. Like the medieval storyteller, the modern broadcaster brought to listeners the lived and imagined experience of travels to different lands and various times.[46] He created a group sense among listeners, making a true audience of them. But wirelessly transmitted words created a community of immeasurable size whose members didn't share the physical proximity of earlier years. And unlike the transmission of memories and wisdom before, electronically diffused utterances betrayed the economy enforced on them by the fusion of orality and literacy.

These particular travelogues were alive to the protocols of verbal delivery. They recovered the "I" of the narrator, buried in textual travel guides, to good use. "I" stood in as the witness for the community of listeners whose bodily limits were exceeded by radio and required surrogates. No one understood the futility of talking in a passive voice on radio better than Boumphrey. He spoke of distinct events and gave exact descriptions that turned broadcast information into something more than a passing thought, and into abiding knowledge. "Rounding a bend suddenly" in one place provides a glimpse of "a couple of Brent geese—lovely great birds with their black heads and buff-coloured bodies."[47] Entire topographies were put forth as memorable sensory offerings. A short "climb" near the Welsh border reveals "as perfect a piece of pastoral England as one could want. On either side, stretches acres of flat fields golden with buttercups and studded with may-trees in full blossom."[48] "The tower of the cathedral and—yes, chimney against the sky—announces Worcester."[49]

Instead of the dull and long pedigrees, rent rolls, and abstract neutral lists at the heart of county guides, his outings relied on enthralling tales of human drama. Whereas the guides, printed since the end of the eighteenth century, depended on painstaking documentation, labels, and cross-references, oral travelogues turned not so much on accurate information as on infectiousness of emotion. If the former were enlivened by verifiable information—new data, charts, and precise diagrams—the latter were animated by Boumphrey's breath, warmth of voice, scripted excitement and trepidation, hesitance and confidence, and evident struggle for the right words.[50]

Boumphrey's prose did, however, possess an air of factuality. His descriptions were terse and colloquial. St. Mary Bourne was "a pleasant little village." The range of greens on Breidden hills was "marvelous, from the yellow bronze of the oaks, the grey-green of the willow, to the purer green of elm and ash and the deep blue-green of the maple."[51] The sight of flat walls and flat-roofed vernacular structures in an Ulster valley were cataloged amid the sounds of a surprised heron and a chattering blackbird, the taste of cheese from a nearby farm, the enthusiasm of kids waving from the banks of the Severn, and the smell of the wild flowers.[52] Boumphrey's travels turned the world into a picture of curiosities awaiting discovery:[53]

> Shrewsbury is not a town to be viewed by choice from its river. First of all comes a few houses, cheered by their gardens at this time of the year, then a succession of ugly industrial buildings of various kinds with hundreds of yards of drab streets and walls of bricks and stone. ... We endured a mile of this, ... and at last things began to improve: trees and land came into sight and, high on the south bank, the School. ... It is not much use trying to describe [the town] here, the narrow winding streets of black and white medieval houses, the castle and all the rest of it: they must be seen.[54]

Boumphrey the explorer followed the nature-loving ramblers who had been trickling into the countryside since the 1880s, abandoning himself to wherever the path took him. He placed before his listeners views that were entirely at the mercy of his mode of viewing. Sometimes the hopelessly coarse and harsh terrain made it impossible for him to look around, while at other times the smooth and flat surroundings freed him to enjoy the scenery. He rarely stopped to take stock of a bridge or tower:

> It was a superb day, bright sun and just enough clouds in the blue sky to give one a few minutes' shade every now and then. ... This part of Wales seems extraordinarily rich in prehistoric or barely historic remains. Almost every hill has its camp or castle lump. ... But the Severn in this part is not a river that gives its navigators much time to look about them. Another minor rapid bubbled into the view. ... I grounded on the shallows at the head, got out, paddled a few yards, got in again, shot down a small race, almost fouled a big turf of rushes, swept between two boulders with a narrow margin and got safely through. George picking his way delicately after me was horrified to see what he described as a large lobster looking at him threateningly from under a stone. I shouted to him to catch it; but it was too late—and so we missed a good crayfish for supper.[55]

Boumphrey's narratives adjusted the notion of heritage to suit the consumerist and inattentive society that was created in great part by the time- and space-altering technology of radio.[56] He fashioned the tourist as an amateur discoverer who complemented the expert, but he himself was not modeled after a scholar. His contributions were free from the pedantic detailing of the traveler who traveled solely for the sake of research.[57] In his travelogues, the scrutinizing gaze of antiquarian scholars gave way to the sketchy impressions of a hurried motorcar driver, an inexperienced canoeist, or a breathless hiker, equipped with little more than a camera, a guidebook, and curiosity. The creator of this heritage did not view things from a distance but was immersed in the setting, involved in it, with no privileged view from without. The portrayals in *Down River*, for example, were the impressions of an eye at the mercy of waters that were sometimes rough, at other times placid. It was an eye born of technological movement. Finally, broadcasts such as *Along the Roman Roads* bore a sense of place and time that was at once here and there, in our living rooms and on the scene. They at once perpetuated and freed listeners from the desire for a unified place, sequential time, and the experiencing, witnessing, sensing self.

III John Betjeman: Town as Scene

> Pines, rhododendrons, gorse, small oaks, tea places—a thirteenth century cottage fifty yards ahead—hoardings as frequently as trees, then fewer pines and small oaks, less gorse and less rhododendron, more hoardings and more tea places—enough tea brewed in a week to fill Poole Harbour: that is the impression I get when I motor to Bournemouth. Bournemouth begins almost where London ends. Down every main road the bungalows and villas spread. Ha! You think, here I am in the heart of the New Forest. ... But look through those oaks. Isn't that a modern sham-Tudor villa? Isn't that a retired civil servant mowing his lawn beneath yonder spreading oak? It is. The main roads to Bournemouth are houses most of the way.
>
> Now let's skip the Bournemouth suburbs and make straight for the sea-coast, for Bournemouth itself.[58]

John Betjeman offered impressions of a vacationer passing through small towns. From 1937 to the end of his life in 1984, he told stories that explored the synergy between poetry and radiophony. He spoke of town and country, discrete entities threatened by ribbon development growing like weeds between them. Rows of "houses that are no more Tudor than I am William Shakespeare" formed a cheerless, "rather grimy and unhappy" landscape that had "nothing worth looking at."[59] A new preservationist like Betjeman saw the vagueness of suburbia as both anti-city and anti-country. It was a rogue development that could only reap antisocial individualism and anticitizenship.

This was one of the subtexts of Betjeman's first appearance as a radio travel guide, on a 1937 show called *Town Tours* produced by J. C. Pennethorne Hughes. *Town Tours* included travelogues about "the most beautiful town" of Bristol, "the gentlemanly" "planned and composed" Exeter, and the "leafy" Bournemouth. These were accompanied by the "depressing" Swindon and "characterless" Plymouth. The first group composed a picture of an England that had held up its own in a changing landscape. There, the new happily assimilated to the old, as tasteful developers planned and constructed new buildings, while the second group was a victim of "speculators" who "thought of their money before other people's health and happiness."[60]

Figure 4.7

John Betjeman during the Second World War. Courtesy: simplymediarights.com.

The year after *Town Tours*, from mid-April to mid-May, Betjeman gave vicarious walks from his hotel room to a fictitious Seaview Holiday. In late August 1938, with a cheroot in his mouth and a map under his arm, he took listeners to an imaginary Ur-church of "Hagworthy St. Philip," explaining, "There isn't such a church nor such a place, but we'll invent one that stands for the typical English village church."[61] Betjeman's "Up to London" (1939), "Back to the Railway Carriage" (1940), and "Coming Home, or England Revisited" (1943) continued to be animated by the point of view of a curious visitor whose distancing nature turned the surroundings into scenery. Towns and villages became an assortment of visual surprises, phantasmagoria of stimuli, a theme park, and a bubbling museum. The charming artifacts of the crumbling past transported listeners into another time, denied to the jaded eye of the locals.

These travel broadcasts continued to thrive after 1945. The popularity of *Coast and Country* (1949–1951) kept the orator on air for nine consecutive seasons. By the time he broadcast *Buildings and Places* (1949) and *Landscapes with Houses* (1952), John Betjeman had become the official guide to both the real and the literary history of English counties and a historian of architecture and topography. Likewise, those who came to love England with Betjeman—its Victorian railway

Figure 4.8
Bedford Street, Plymouth, 1930. Courtesy: Richard and Gill Long.

stations, Georgian town halls, leafy suburbs, little shops, and local crafts—came to know and enjoy England as sightseers of the picturesque. At the heart of his tour guides was a campaign for the preservation not of the monumental churches and stately homes, but of the "rough stone walls popping here and there along a roadside"; "the silver featheriness of medieval stained glass" and the "woodwork [that] would remind ... our great-great-grandfather" of "the place he knew before he closed his eyes in the big box pew and slumbered away the parson's elevating sermon"; "the most beautiful" libraries and town halls of "local Renaissance architects"; the historic vernacular of towns and villages that was quietly giving way to modern vernacular "horrors" "dropped ... for all the world like huge slices of cake on the tops of hills by some mad celestial picnic party."[62]

Betjeman's descriptions cut through two divisions. They ignored, first, the conventional hierarchy between architecture and building and, second, that between building and built fabric—in both cases, in favor of the latter. "The idea of this talk and of the subsequent ones I hope to give on West Country towns," he clarified in his first soundings on Bristol, "is to help you to look about you when you are in a town." The obvious historic monuments of a place did not need to be noted: "What do need noticing, are the squares and streets," the "unpretentiousness" of the everyday environs. The verbal image of Bristol was brought into play not as a gem but as a necklace elegantly composed of stones almost unknown to anyone outside the city—the recently preserved "cleaned up and painted" parish church; "that amazingly delicate suspension bridge" to Clifton; the panoramic view of the city revealing a "forest of towers, spires and the masts of vessels" when seen from the hills; "the exquisitely proportioned tower of St. Paul's church rising tier on tier, tower on tower, out of all that stateliness"; "Doric cemetery gates"; and "Dr Pymotre's Gothic house." Betjeman's amusement park

Figure 4.9
The rural vernacular captured in John Betjeman's article "The Passing of the Village," *Architectural Review*, September 1932. Courtesy: *Architectural Review*.

was not the spectacular, dazzling city but decisively more subdued, intimate, feminine, and personable.[63]

It was this undervalued and threatened vernacular that "isn't a museum of showpieces, but a living thing, still in use," lying in the interstices of the handful of "inert monuments," that gave the town its flavor and pride. The codes of the distant, aestheticizing eye that Boumphrey had denied himself allowed Betjeman to dissociate this memorial to the subtle tastes of gentlemanly Britain from its particular class and hold it as a disinterested standard of taste for the British of all creeds and classes. The tourist's eye—inquisitive, restless, and probing, all at once—allowed him to treat the midscale historic vernacular as the inheritance proper of mass culture.

Betjeman argued that it was the village and town "churches of England [that] are the story of England. They alone remain islands of calm in the seething roar of what we now call civilization. They are not backwater," he insisted, "but strongholds. ... A church isn't just an old building which interests pedantic brass rubbers, but a living building with history written all over it and history that, with very little practice, becomes easy and fascinating reading."[64] Betjeman's infamous flirtations with religion and the Church of England aside, for him the value of a church lay in its contribution to the scenery of English towns. Likewise, the railway station, the seaside resorts, the cinema hall, the pub, and the bookshop were important in his oeuvre not in their sociological function but in how they provided purely scenic pleasure. It was to the institutionalization of this new "sign economy"—a touristic collection of signs by which cultural heritage was established—that Betjeman dedicated his oral travelogues.

This touristic glance was nothing but modern. The authentic experience, paramount for Betjeman, is a major goal of twentieth-century tourism.[65] His

Photograph by F. R. Yerbury.
A village built in a GREENSAND district. Whitchurch, Bucks.

Photograph by B. C. Clayton.
A village built in a CHALK district. Haughley, Suffolk.

Photograph by Dolby Bros.
A village built in an OOLITE district. Ufford, Northants.

outings had none of the ideology of the elite amateur's Grand Tour and cultural self-certification. There was no antiquarian gaze that spent all its energy tiresomely documenting a single "Romanesque tympanum," or an art historian's ordering eye that was only interested in a locality for "a particular phase of baroque," or an architect's selectiveness that went straight "for le Corbusier."[66] In their place he instituted a deliberate seeking out of the visceral experience of the entire town, transcending a tedious routine. His outings stirred the romantic hope of historic continuity and the fiction of unity, little different than Boumphrey's. But while Boumphrey insisted on the present and the "contemporary" landscape, Betjeman took the listener to another time—a past world with an authenticity that was missing, sick, or dead in the present moment. And yet he illustrated how the relics of the past were intimately intertwined with the here and now.

If Boumphrey the engineer championed matter-of-fact language, Betjeman the poet summoned unrestrained sentimentality. Whereas Boumphrey's prose exuded a sense of realism, seriousness, and masculine exteriority, Betjeman's appraisals revealed a tender, subtle, internal affection for places. Haunted churches and abandoned railways were infused with life through literary association. But his descriptions did not aim for nostalgia; they exhibited a craving not for the age of unwavering faith but for the free play of sensory joy. Every twist and turn of phrase, every indentation and variation of pitch, and each telling silence were geared to elicit an emotional response. The experience of desire, pleasure, horror, anger, disgust, and sorrow was an end in itself.[67]

Language—not just the choice of words but the very medium itself—was integral to this ambition. Witty puns magically relieved these middle-class symbols of inequality and exclusivity of their historical burden and made them available for poetic affection and a display of sentimentality. In Betjeman's travelogues was heard the full force of metaphor and suggestion. It was this transformative power of words that made him the darling of England and the image of patriotism.[68] While his connoisseur's enthusiasm was unfashionable in disciplinary circles and shunted by his more somber-minded friends into the archives of nineteenth-century romanticism, Betjeman purposefully cultivated it to encourage popular excursions into the past over those of the experts. "Antiquarians," he complained, had "made architecture incredibly boring. They have turned what should have been part of the enjoyment of England's beauty into a wretched wrangle over medieval dates."⁶⁹ In a broadcast entitled "Seaview," he urged listeners:

> Do you like to lean over the edge of a dinghy on a calm day and see at the bottom of the green water the remains of walls on what was once dry land? Do you want to get away from the noise of cars and things, like me talking to you now, and telephones and aeroplanes and the other inestimable advantages of our civilization?
>
> If so, go to the Scilly Isles. There aren't many of them that are inhabited so you can't go to all, even if you can afford it. But they are all they're cracked up to be. There are haunted uninhabited islands with ruins of houses on them. There's St Mary's (the biggest island) with Hugh Town, the little capital, a place with hardly one ugly building in it … St Agnes, which is like an unspoiled Cornwall; Annet, where you crush birds eggs with every step you take on the spongy thrift …⁷⁰

Recent scholarship has characterized John Betjeman's writing and broadcasting as richer in charm than in historical information, and rather amateurish in its treatment of buildings. Much has been made of the fact that this great promoter of historical imagery of buildings was wanting in architectural and art historical knowledge.⁷¹ What they neglect to state is that Betjeman's anti-intellectualism was entirely principled. His life's mission, of which the oral travelogues were a principal component, was to free architecture from the emotionally neutral observation of scholarly reading rooms, to wrest it from the "secret language of experts," and situate it squarely within the realm of hearty emotion and the vibrant appreciation of a noncontextualizing and nonhistoricizing viewer. His speech was devoted to assimilating vernacular architectural tradition into the tradition of books illustrated "for drawing room consumption" as opposed to those "written for the study or the library." "The chief job of criticism," he would later ruminate, "is to communicate enthusiasm rather than to find fault."⁷² He never aspired to give historical information for its own sake, but rather included it to convey a literary feeling for the material residue of history. Historical knowledge and sentimentality had the same purpose in these programs: to bridge the gap between the literary eye (envisioning) and bodily experience (seeing), to illuminate vision, and to revive "the tradition of polite pleasure that all men and women of taste drew from looking at buildings before 1914."[73]

His BBC series *Town Tours* and the programs "Back to the Railway Carriage" and "Some Comments in Wartime" all belonged more intimately to the hearer than to a viewer. Words constructed anonymous buildings and squares. They overcame the opacity of materiality and corporeality, and selectively presented the English tradition to the eye. On Betjeman's lips, words did not transgress from the norms of vision, but fulfilled them.

What till then had been the practice of an elite Grand Tourist, with his wireless travelogues, became a dominant aspect of the middle-class tourist experience. "The tourist gaze," John Urry notes, "is directed to features of landscape and townscape that separate them off from ordinary experience. … Places are chosen … because there is anticipation … of intense pleasures." Such anticipation, Urry goes on, "is constructed and sustained through a variety of non-tourist practices [that] construct and reinforce [the] gaze."[74] For Betjeman, this "non-tourist practice" was constituted by historical knowledge. The purpose of history, for him, was to establish historic sites as places for the recovery of enjoyment and pleasure—those most primal and moderate of human faculties. Tourism, as Miles David Samson tells us, "can be observed as liminal behavior, in that it is [a] temporally constrained, socially tolerated period of wish fulfillment. It involves the search for something new."[75] These qualities of tourism were not lost on Betjeman, who saw mass architectural tourism as a modern instrument of breaking with everyday life and bringing joy, a final frontier of the resistance of humanness against the onslaught of "tinned food, tinned brains, tinned souls."[76] When history exceeded this purpose, he insisted, it became laborious, pedantic, and redundant.

Railway and the car, catalysts in the spoliation of town and country, were praised in Betjeman's travelogues for their role in reconditioning the public eye. In "Back to the Railway Carriage," he told listeners that the railway carved "out a landscape of its own": "Railways were built to look from and to look at. They still provide those pleasures for the eye."[77] They offer an "unfamiliar view of a place one knows well from the road." They magically turn the lackluster into radiant, the dull into rich, and the dead into live. "Trains were made for meditation," Betjeman commented.[78] Railways provided riders with relief from the mounting bleakness that was swallowing English towns and cities in the name of technological progress.

The same was true for the chief culprit of what Betjeman called "petrol-clouded civilization"—the motorcar.[79] These oral guides were an extension of his *Shell Guides*, guidebooks commissioned by the British and Dutch company Shell Petroleum to encourage the use of motorcars. There, Betjeman sang the praises of the automobile's contribution to the touristic gaze. The *Shell Guides* were written with the hope that motor travel would bring an equally nuanced and sensitive exploration of the less trodden Britain. To consult a *Shell Guide* as a map for a trip, Timothy Mowl tells us, "was to become an informed convert to architecture and an aficionado of the environment."[80] A "petrol-clouded civilization," Mowl claims, made "dim counties like Berkshire, Derby and Durham seem as exotic, as characterful, and as crammed with potential discoveries as the conventional holiday lands of Cornwall, Devon and Dorset."[81] Modern technology was worth using because it turned our everyday world into a touristic scene.

The greatest challenge to Betjeman's quest for the preservation of the human, the visceral, the experiential, the emotive, the bodily, and the poetic came from nothing less than his medium of dissemination itself. For radio is first and foremost a method of transmission; and transmission, which is movement, involves separation. Its transportation of audition overcomes not just distance but the natural limitations placed on hearing by the body. Thus, what radio overcomes is the body itself. Not only that; radio also involves the atrophy of experience and the disintegration of place as understood by the humanist tradition. Nevertheless, Betjeman's quest belongs more properly to the psychodynamic of radio than to that of print, for radio returns to his speech and sounded words the temporality and evanescence that they lose in writing. In addition to giving his words the character of action rather than of thought, radio also endows them with the quality of an event rather than assimilating them to print on a piece of paper. The technological diffusion of the organic rhythms of his voice overcame the distance between Betjeman the narrator and the listeners at home, placing his voice before them as if they were in the company of an intimate friend. Betjeman's transmissions signify better than anything the uncertainty that lies at the heart of the culture of wireless listening.

Figure 4.10

Thomas Tresham, Triangular Lodge at Rushton Hall, Northamptonshire, 1593–1597. Courtesy: Kelvin Barber.

IV John Summerson: Stately Heritage as Library

The last time I saw it was on a still Thursday evening late in the year. Long shadows stretched across the walls, exaggerating the grotesque intricacies of the detail. The air was full of nightmare brilliance of Autumn decay and it struck me that the lodge itself was the sort of thing you might very well come across in a nightmare. It is loaded with ornaments, yet there are no real windows, only three sides, so the corners are sharp and menacing. At the top is a cluster of nine tiny gables—three on each side—with a great chimney disguised as a pinnacle rising from the midst of them.

What is the meaning of it all?[82]

In the middle of the three-month-long, purposefully indulgent *Town Tours* by John Betjeman, the BBC introduced yet another voice that took on the triad of architectural heritage, tourism, and preservation. This was the aspiring architectural historian John Summerson. Like Boumphrey's and Betjeman's broadcasts, his was a highly personal, eyewitness survey that liberally used the license of picturesque language to capture the quality of architecture. But unlike Boumphrey, who did not discriminate between what came his way, and Betjeman, who was primarily concerned with the neglected and overlooked, Summerson, the only architect in the group, offered architecture-centric tours. He focused on the canonic, spectacular architectural sites. If Boumphrey and Betjeman inhabited architectural history as amateur critics, Summerson inhabited the radio travelogues as a professional architectural historian in the making. His descriptions scrutinized architecture and pinpointed its springs.

The excerpt above described Summerson's visit to the estate of Rushton Hall in Northamptonshire. Aired on the evening of 23 June 1937, it related his impressions of the famous Triangular Lodge on its grounds, designed and built by Sir Thomas Tresham, a prominent sixteenth-century trader and devout Roman Catholic. "I chose Rushton," Summerson clarified at the top of the program, "because of the special alliance of architecture with history there. It is one of those houses which calls up vividly a particular age and particular people."[83] The Triangular Lodge demonstrated that buildings explained, and were explained by, the social and economic relations in society. It was a reminder of the antagonistic relationship between the Roman Catholics and Queen Elizabeth in the late sixteenth century, for Tresham had conceived the lodge while imprisoned for fifteen years for refusing to convert to Protestantism.[84] It was built, probably as a place of prayer, between 1593 and 1597 after he was freed. Summerson explained its grotesque imagery and its obsession with the number three—three sides, three floors, trefoil windows, and three triangular gables on each side—as recalling the Holy Trinity. He touched upon the history of the main house laid in 1438, its expansions, neglect, rehabilitations, and preservation by subsequent owners and lodgers.

The place had been embellished with anecdotes; poets had written poems on it, novelists had set plots for books there, and so on. Rushton Hall emerged as much as an embodiment of historical events as a product of ongoing writing and rewriting. The broadcast concluded: "It is still the figure of Sir Thomas Tresham which emerges most clearly from the past of Rushton Hall. His anxiety to record in solid stone the symbolism of his faith and his own passionate belief in it has had its reward—to anybody who has been to and penetrated the thickets which hide the Triangular Lodge, to anybody who has been to the forlorn but beautiful ruin of the New Building at Lyveden, Thomas Tresham is a very real and admirable person."[85] The material survival of the building extended an otherwise transitory moment and life into the future beyond their natural course; the stones immortalized the man.

Historiographers know Summerson for his masterful combinations of formal reading with sociological and cultural analysis. He has taught us how to read the history of a people through the study of plans, sections, and construction drawings. But his broadcasts did something else. They exhibited no desire to walk the audience through buildings, and they made little attempt to describe the visual properties of structures. Instead, they subjugated formal descriptions to stories. Space was animated by the events it hosted, both now and before. Summerson's analysis did not aim for a sound and comprehensive thesis but for humor and intelligence, warmth and force. His narratives took advantage of what spoken words did best—create compelling atmospheres. These travelogues developed media-appropriate narratives. They freed architectural history from subservience to design practice and asserted it as an accessible scholarly endeavor.

Listeners heard about his anticipation of a trip, arrival at a site, and his frustrations. Summerson spoke of difficulties in finding an entrance, of getting caught in the rain, and of shortness of breath while cutting through a property. Each week chapels and libraries appeared out of nowhere. Indirect connections pervaded the accounts; for example, Summerson started out: "Instead of telling you at once about the building, I am going to ask [you] to picture in your minds a painting which I saw there the other day."[86] Impressions of the haunted Ashby castle, the quiet and dignified Cottonian library, or the charming Wren churches were the norm:

> Last week I went to Blenheim again to refresh my memory for this talk. The first thing that struck me was this—that in laying out the grounds with those interminable avenues, Vanbrugh might almost have been looking forward to an age when people would be able to see Blenheim from the air. It is only from the air that you can see the house, the gardens and park as a pattern—and a very splendid and majestic pattern they make. On foot, although you miss the symmetry, the scene is of course, more picturesque—more inviting. You see parts of the Palace emerging from the trees—steep, pinnacled towers with something military about them—not fortress-like, but with the pomp and discipline of a full dress parade. Even as you come to the entrance and pass through into the court, you don't get a full idea of the building's extent. But this court opens into another and here you really are at the center of things. On your right is the park with a mile-long avenue vanishing to a memorial column across the bridge. On your left a broad flight of steps leads up to the portico.[87]

Summerson employed deceptively simple prose and an open-ended style. He drew upon his training in architectural journalism and learned much from the best of amateur architectural authors like H. S. Goodhart-Rendel (the RIBA's president whose complaint about speech was discussed in chapter 1) and Robert Byron (a travel writer). He relished posing questions and happily leaving them unanswered. Acts of visiting and looking, on his lips, became not so much reading as conversation with the past.[88] History, both written and built, no longer sounded like an ossified relic to be worshipped, imitated, or bulldozed. It was an active event to be engaged knowledgably, creatively, and intuitively.

The result was gripping shows that held the attention and suspense of exhausted listeners at 9:45 PM every Wednesday. They were respectable by academic standards and attractive by broadcast standards. Thrilled, the Regional Director at Birmingham announced that he had found a gem! "Not a word edited … a new star is born,"[89] he wrote proudly to his superiors in London. He recommended his find for future use. For the BBC broadcast management, minus a glitch or two, the series *Famous Midland Houses* had hit the perfect note. Summerson had tried to solicit work with the BBC since 1931. The resourceful Sir Reginald Blomfield had put in a strong word for him, but nothing came of it.[90] But from the start of this series, and especially with the outbreak of the war, he would become a regular presence in the studios and wrote frequently for the *Listener*.

"Rushton Hall" was fourth of the ten famous Midlands houses Summerson was commissioned to visit for the regional station of Midlands. Other notable houses in the series included Compton Wynyates, Newstead Abbey, Kentchurch Court, Holme Lacy, Haughton Hall, Condover Hall, Castle Ashby, and Blenheim Palace. All of them were private homes whose owners, either of necessity or commercial prowess, had opened them to public viewing. But they were still at an early stage in their history of commercialization, not yet fully assimilated into the consumption patterns of mass tourism that flourished after 1945.

In 1930s Britain, a scientific study of past structures was predominantly a matter of measurement and visual and empirical documentation. It was dominated by the demands of pattern books that provided historicist practitioners with tracings and details to be manipulated. But broadcasts about buildings cut loose from the insularity of traditional research. Free of any visual component, they turned the face of architectural history away from the drafting board and toward pressing cultural debates. With this came a change in the fortunes of architectural historians, who till then were the most obscure of all cultural producers.[91]

Summerson's travelogues were an exercise in a "new architectural history." This history brought together the accessibility of English amateur architectural

Figure 4.11
John Vanbrugh, Blenheim Palace, Oxfordshire, 1705–1724. Courtesy: Kathy Pearmain

journalism with the concerns of German art history—which had landed in London at the Warburg Institute around 1933—and a light, humanistic Marxism blowing through the English avant-garde of the 1930s. Summerson took iconic buildings that in British disciplinary circles were discussed mainly for their importance in the history of styles and artistic pedigree and reframed them as determinations of power relations and artistic talent, describing them as the material residue of the friction between the nobility and the rising merchant class, the shifts in the system of patronage, and the state of architectural production—as well as the artist's will and control over its scale and proportions, and the skill of the artisans in detailing and finishes. Summerson animated these static images as case studies in human behavior. Their analysis, he demonstrated, must draw on both anthropology and aesthetics. As Caroline van Eck notes, for him the task of an architectural historian was the revelation of "what is in effect an extra dimension of history—the history of form."[92] Week after week, Summerson dug out of the National Archives family documents and the diaries of owners, builders, and proprietors.

The "splendid" Blenheim, "the symbol of its age," offered a tale of the precarious relationship between the queen (the provider of state funds for the palace) and the duchess of Marlborough (the recipient of these funds), the conflicting choice of architects and the tastes of the duke and the duchess, and the animosity between the duchess and the architect, John Vanbrugh. Competing worldviews and the battle of wills were set in place. But all this was shot through with a history of the featured houses' architecture, which Summerson constructed as a history of genius and mediocrity. He crowned John Vanbrugh as "the only Englishman who ever raised architecture to something near the Shakespearian plane," yet also reminded listeners that Blenheim was often ridiculed "for its size and heaviness."[93] Kentchurch Court showed "merciless reconstruction; but after all you couldn't expect the eighteenth-century Scudamores to live in a medieval museum."[94] Summerson seized on the stately Midlands homes as products of contemplation and chance, success and failure. Houses and gardens were ledgers of the history of ideas, changing conceptions of architecture and the tastes to express it: "The great home of Castle Ashby recalls in its fabric and furnishing, every phase of this ancient dynasty. ... Tudors, Stuarts, Georgians, Victorians; each has contributed something to the shape of the Castle Ashby."[95] Condover Hall, the grand sixteenth-century manor house in Shropshire, exemplified how "the Elizabethans loved symmetry—the more elaborate and precise the better. It was part of their discovery that house-building was not only useful and necessary but rather amusing as well." The destinies of these houses were ever changing: "Today [Condover Hall] is a hospital for ladies suffering from nervous breakdowns—its quietness and dignity made it well-fit for such a purpose."[96] Newstead Abbey, which "still lives up to its reputation as one of the strangest and most haunting of the great houses of Midlands," was originally a monastery founded, along with many other monasteries, by Henry II "to expiate his share in the murder of Thomas à Becket."[97] Summerson principally constructed an impression of buildings via parables, legends, and myths. "There is a very strange story," started his introduction to the show on Condover Hall, "of how Mr. Thomas Owen came to possess Condover. It has been handed down through generations of Shropshire folk and if we are to credit them with more imagination, perhaps, than historical accuracy, it doesn't make the story much less worth telling." At play here was romantic materialism; Summerson's program on "Compton Wynyates" captured the mark of history left on its red walls and in the hollow places where medieval Englishmen had planted their vineyards. But Summerson read impressions left in the house by England's past in a typically antimaterialist and English aestheticist manner.[98] With this, he conveyed at once a very acute sense of how buildings were a product of men's fates, actions, and talents and how they shaped men's fates and actions. This approach made him a forerunner of the British Marxist historians, such as R. E. Warner, Alick West, and Ralph Fox, all of whom reconciled materialist and idealist historiographic traditions.

After the bombing of London during the Second World War, Summerson gave tours of the "Ruins and the Future" (1941). "Ruins are disturbing things, they make you think. They [arouse]—your anger, certainly—but your critical faculty as well."[99] "Bombed Architecture in the West" (1942) was a survey of lost and saved buildings in "great western cities whose appearance has been horribly altered by the raiders." It included obituaries of conspicuous but also inconspicuous buildings in Plymouth. "Plymouth Rebuilding Plan" (1944) and "Nash's Terraces in Regent's Park" (1945) took listeners on trips to the past to evaluate future developments. Of the latter, Summerson said, "I walked through the area this morning. The great terraces, in spite of their battered state, are still glorious in the Autumn sunshine. The streets and squares behind, for all their dismal shabbiness, still remind one that Nash's ... plan ... by the standards of its own day was a good plan."[100] Against it, Summerson evaluated the new planning scheme produced by St. Pancras' Labour Council to rehabilitate the ter-

Figure 4.12

Compton Wynyates, Warwickshire, dating from at least 1204 AD. Photographer unknown.

races: "The new plan is also a good plan by the standards of our own day. ... It offers to exchange good planning of the past for good planning of the present."[101] The series *Western Men* introduced "John Wood: Architect and Planner of Bath" (1945) in the same manner as a walking tour through Bath. After the war, Summerson's *On the Map* (1946) surveyed twenty-four British towns as a family album of architecture, followed by the broadcast "Getting the Most out of Looking at a Town" (1946). By "St. Stephen, Walbrook: A Revaluation, I—History of the Church" (1947) and "Historic Houses of England" (1947), this was the standard approach of Summerson's Home Service broadcasts.

Summerson was a good friend of John Betjeman. The two shared the goal of bringing architectural heritage out of the musty old books into the new world of popular consumption. However, for Summerson, the problem was not the overintellectualization that Betjeman saw, but a lack thereof; he believed architectural historians and antiquarians had not treated their subject intellectually enough to make it pertinent to anyone other than themselves. Whereas Betjeman demanded an abandoning of oneself to imagination and feelings in front of a building, Summerson took as his task the furnishing of what Carlo Olmo calls "patient ... interpretations that deliberately set out to be educative." The intellectual process had to be evident and pertinent to a "consumerist and inattentive society."[102]

Summerson imagined a probing, more cerebral pleasure which "combine[d] amusement with instruction." Looking ought to become "a sporting event—something between a walking marathon and a cross-word puzzle,"[103] he argued. Pleasure in one's surroundings was not an act of resistance to the mechanical age but a way in which different classes of the nation could identify with one another. Looking about oneself, one would discover that the buildings of "older towns ... make a glorious family album of architecture."[104]

Yet the three competing visions of the architectural heritage shared faith in the redemptive qualities of modern tourism. For each, tourism provided the fresh eye that would help the public realize that buildings were both political products and the trappings of life. "Looking at the past of the town gives you some confidence in judging what is appropriate for the present,"[105] Summerson said, and observing the past was also vital because "man can form no picture of the future except by reference to the past."[106] Later, postwar reconstruction would give the wirelessly educated audience an occasion to decide how buildings

Figure 4.13

Moundfield Road, Stamford Hill, showing the destruction of the English built landscape during the war. Courtesy: Duncan.

governed their lives. Looking about themselves transformed passive spectators into active citizens.

Boumphrey the adventurer, Betjeman the poet, and Summerson the historian were also on the same page in their affirmation that "there is more to looking at a town than just looking at the ancient monuments which are given in guide books."[107] Summerson echoed the other two: "older buildings make better exemplifying architecture as living art than contemporary ragbag." But his interest in preservation was motivated by an architecture-centered desire to save only the best examples of originality and man's ingenuity.[108] The three broadcasters agreed that there was "a good deal of pleasure to be got from looking at towns, looking at them with understanding eyes, seeing them as a record of the race to which we belong."[109] Again to borrow the words of Carlo Olmo, their broadcasts had the quality of "moral action,"[110] for they made the built environment the site of the intersection of national past, present, and future; the debate over national identity; the disputes over history and modernity; and the emergent ideals of citizenship.

5 THE BOX ON THE DRESSER: THE SACRALIZATION OF CONTEMPORARY EVERYDAY SPACES

I The Street in the Age of Its Radiophonic Diffusion

One warm evening in June 1933, everyone who was tuned into the National Programme in London was privy to a tug of war over the character of the street. A recurring topic on air, that evening it was an argument between Frank Pick, the fifty-five-year-old chief executive of London Transport, and his interviewer John Gloag.

> **Pick:** All sorts of things are dumped into the street without order and without planning by a whole lot of public utility undertakings or departments of local authorities, until the street becomes thoroughly untidy, as you say. Let our listeners go out and use their eyes on the main street outside their homes, and just list the clutter of stuff for themselves. Every street should be deliberately planned from the start, with all its equipment properly located and coordinated, for all these things may be wanted.
>
> **Gloag:** But so far you have only mentioned the comparatively minor details, which contribute to the street's untidiness. I'm still thinking of the sides of the street.

Figure 5.1

Frank Pick on the cover of *Architectural Review*, August 1942. Courtesy: *Architectural Review*.

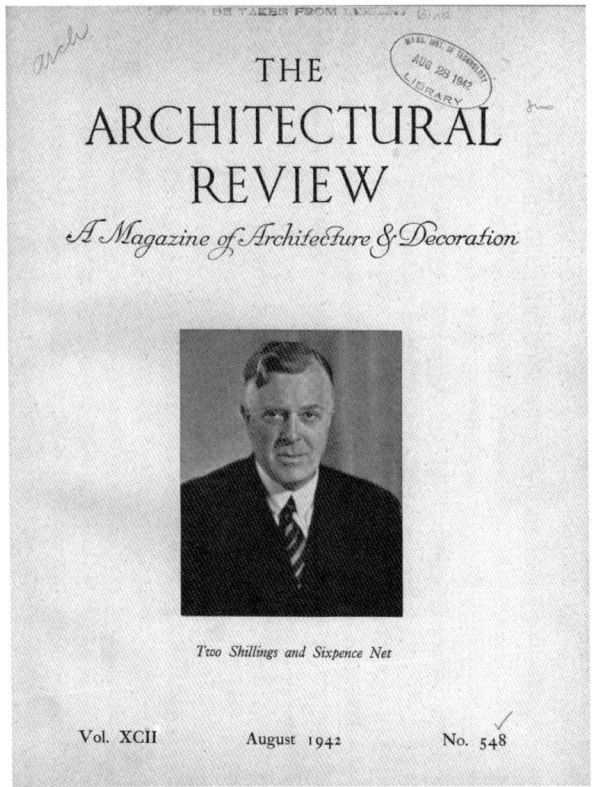

Pick: Before we think of the sides of the street we should finish off the things which complicate its surface. Now one of the worst bothers with streets is the frequency with which islands are placed in them. Islands take up so much of the space of the street, destroying its capacity.[1]

The thirty-seven-year-old Gloag, who had taken to broadcasting like a fish to water, was an architect turned advertising agent. He wanted his guest to explain the character of the street in terms of the surrounding facades. He pushed his interlocutor to talk about the static view of the street, that is, the architecture that constituted its walls. But Pick was unwavering. He was adamant that a street was first and foremost an affair of traffic and movement. He kept on pointing to the hierarchy of road widths, the use of cul-de-sacs, the way pedestrian and vehicular circulation were divided, and how street signs, lighting, benches, fire hydrants, and parks responded to the need for passage through the city. Gloag finally conceded that his guest had really come to get this point across.

Gloag: It seems that all the time I have been picking your brains on the subject, one dominating thing emerges, that traffic is controlling the whole plan and character of the modern city ...

Pick: All is traffic, even if it is not on wheels.[2]

This twenty-minute interview was broadcast during peak listening hours. The Adult Education department had created it as part of its well-publicized series *Design in Modern Life*, a collection of interviews covering an assortment of opinions about the notion of art in contemporary life. Week after week, architects—including Robert Atkinson, Wells Coates, and Maxwell Fry—and housing specialists, such as Elizabeth Denby, explained their particular medium of artistic expression in the age of industrial production. Some stressed the endurance of cultural production in the face of challenges posed by the mass market; others were emboldened by broadcasting's ability to transport their ideas into homes previously inaccessible to them. Most celebrated the possibility, for the first time since the Middle Ages, of fusing art and life, and expressed their dreams of creating a community intersubjectively connected by taste, manners, and knowledge. The public art of a community formed by industrial production, broadcasting, and popular democracy, they insisted, would not be the expression of the mighty alone, but of leaders and followers alike. It would bear the stamp of its consumers as much as that of its producers. The most civic-minded among them insisted on an art open to everyone.

After his interview, Pick came back for the concluding segment of the series. The most dynamic and visible public administrator of the period, he was given the last word on the larger topic of design. He finished the eleven-part series for producer Charles Siepmann with musings on the "Meaning and Purpose of Design." Pick, whom Winston Churchill called the "brick layer,"[3] came to the microphone not as a corporate leader but as a founder of the Design and Industries Association (DIA).[4] Arguably one of DIA's most powerful members, he was educated, as were many in the group, in the ideals of the romantic corporatism of the greatest of Victorian artists and socialists—John Ruskin and William Morris. These men had attacked industrial capitalism because its division of labor detached thought and personality from products. Ruskin instead promoted a community organically bound by faith, land, and joy in self-realizing work. Morris's arts and crafts movement emerged from these ideals. Like Morris, Pick was an impassioned spokesman of purposeful design. Through his patronage of art he tried to reconcile romantic corporatism with corporate business interests.[5] The first had been the basis of his education, while the second constituted his immediate circumstances. Yet unlike Ruskin and Morris, but like many of their interwar followers and liberal intellectuals, he accepted industrial capitalism, believing that it could be a means to higher ends if one only had the will to infuse mass-produced commodities with artistic spirit.

Pick regarded his work as an executive of the Underground Group, run as a commercial enterprise, and the government-run London Transport as a divine calling. He reshaped the transportation system and the city of London into an integrated work of art, fashioning London's transportation as the nervous system of the city. The system developed a unified design—from the ticket layout to underground platforms—that gave the sprawling city a visually coherent entity. Pick's ambition was to make art a part of everyone's daily experience. It is to Pick that we owe the famous logo of London Transport and the stylization of the London Underground map. By commissioning collaborative work, he turned painters into designers of bus upholstery and posters, and he told architects to consider nothing too insignificant a formal challenge.

Pick's two contributions to *Design in Modern Life*—the conversation with Gloag and the closing lecture—gave a full airing to his beliefs.[6] Pick was a shrewd publicist—in fact, he had first made his reputation as the publicity officer responsible for marketing the underground. He handled radio as a platform to impose his definition of the architect and architecture, using it as a tool for regulating the relationship between design arts and the public. Pick adeptly broadened the definition of design work from making monuments to creating the ubiquitous everyday environment.

The small segment of the audience that was actually embroiled in disciplinary battles over approaches to town planning would have instantly discerned that by taking circulation as the generative principle of urban design, Pick was drawing a line in the sand between his own concept of the city and academic conceptions. Pick saw the city as a single organic entity kept alive by a strong circulation system, rather than as an aggregation of separate mechanical parts. The spatial organization of his city was determined by function rather than by the rules of symmetry, balance, and proportions that were emphasized in the classical tradition. The anonymity of the street, at least in theory, provided a more equitable and yet readable organizing principle than Beaux-Arts traditional hierarchies based on discrete focal points. Finally—and what Gloag didn't appreciate—emphasis on movement and traffic as opposed to street facades gave Pick a crucial strategic advantage. It allowed him to define design and its place in modern life without getting tangled up in the historicist debate on styles.

In the interview on 6 June 1933, Pick called for the street to be designed according to the type of movements he meant to encourage:

> The shopping streets ... should be streets in which it is possible to loiter and gossip, to look at the shop windows without being jostled. Wide foot walks are wanted. There is no reason why a shopping street should not have a promenade up the middle like the Unter den Linden in Berlin. ... Where a shopping street is a wide street with through traffic, it is almost impossible to pass from side to side so as to look at the shops in comfort, and without risk. No one wants to risk his life to look at the latest confection over the road. ... There seems to be no reason why illuminated signs should be restricted in such streets. All that is necessary is that the buildings should be designed to carry them properly.[7]

Here design emerged as the elegant coordination of practical challenges, not a quest after ideal forms. It was the incorporation of the mundane into the work

Figure 5.2

An early London Underground map, commissioned by Frank Pick and designed by Harry Beck in 1933. Courtesy: Tricia Wang.

Figure 5.3

Posters commissioned by Frank Pick, Dover Street Underground station, 1930s. Courtesy: London Transport Museum.

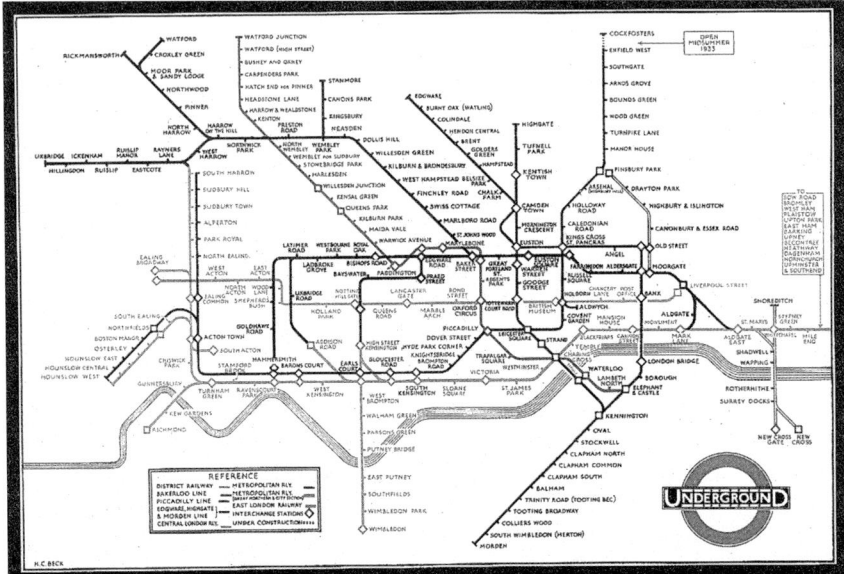

of art—the shop and street signs, garbage bins, telephone booths, water and vegetation, manholes, and fire hydrants that had been dumped willy-nilly onto the street in recent years. In "Design in the Street," Pick was critical of the purely literary or academic point of view of the vast majority of the profession. Most architects were trained to judge a work by the facility of its creator with archaeological knowledge, above all. They could not conceptualize these lowly features—or their promise to give the urban fabric a preliterate vitality—because this vitality didn't fit within the framework of their literate and abstracted aesthetic preoccupations. While the revivalists saw the street as a composition of individual aesthetic spectacles for judicious contemplation, Pick insisted on its total experience. Urban space, to him, was no longer a panorama for the distancing act of inspection. It was an all-encompassing environment, negotiated from within by automatic reflexes. His description acted upon the mind and spirit of his listeners by emphasizing the city street's clarity of purpose, elimination of redundancy, improvement of mobility, purification of air, and introduction of light. Gone was the halted, awestruck spectatorship of the intellectual idealists bestowing dignity on works. It was now through preliterate involvement, through use and active apprehension that art was realized. The broadcast privileged the vast majority of distracted and unlearned listeners over the culturally educated. It made engrossment the matrix from which all attitudes toward works of art were to be issued in the future.[8]

For Frank Pick, the Edwardian child of Victorian liberals, the unsightliness of the English town and countryside and the accompanying moral morass were not only the fault of the academic conception of design. He also blamed market-based developments, which had been subjected to very little oversight by both Liberal and Conservative governments. In his interview with Gloag and elsewhere, he nodded to the recently issued Town and Country Planning Act of 1932, which expanded the power of local councils to plan public space more comprehensively than ever before.[9] It rendered the open spaces between buildings—the interstices of the urban form—as socially neutral breathing spaces rather than social arenas. This was an ongoing process, initiated by the Public Health Act of 1875, and justified on the grounds of advancing moral improvement and relieving congestion.[10] But now it was also seen as mitigating daily hassles and improving the efficient flow of goods, services, and bodies. Efficiency became a crucial element in the enjoyment of towns. A work of art was now judged not by what Walter Benjamin called its "cult-value" but by its entertainment value.[11]

Figure 5.4

Street signs pictured in Frank Pick's article "Design in the Street," in John Gloag, ed., *Design in Modern Life*, 1934. Courtesy: Taylor & Francis Books (UK).

Pick's closing broadcast, "The Meaning and Purpose of Design" on 27 June 1933, directly advanced the definition of design he had suggested in "Design in the Street" three weeks earlier. The concept was explained in terms of "efficiency and balance," which were open to a variety of visual interpretations, instead of the study of historic style. Pick's examples emphasized the ordinary over the exceptional, the ubiquitous over the unique, and the everyday over monumental spaces. It was lost on no one that this move made abstract concepts accessible and made design as relevant to those who never thought of it as it was to those who took pains with it. Design now did not rely on sudden encounter to mesmerize and didn't need to shock people to awaken their senses. Instead, it aimed for regular and continuous contact. In the modern world, connected wirelessly, the usual mode of mastering cultural information would occur not through deciphering its hidden codes but by overcoming the distance necessary for such reading. Design would be absorbed through habit.

"Design is nothing abstruse at all," Pick said. Its source was no longer the undisciplined and unverifiable impulse of a pencil stroke: "Design is applied science. It is only a matter of using our brains, of bringing thought to bear upon the making and fashioning of things for everyday use." As Pick was at pains to point out, the word "design"—which started being widely used in England in the eighteenth century—was a replacement of that much-maligned word "art," which was redolent of old-world cultivation. "The illustrations I have chosen," he emphasized, "have been from homely and familiar things that have nothing to do with art or aesthetics, or beauty in itself."[12] One of his DIA compatriots, Anthony Bertram, would second him on this issue a few years later: "Design is integral to life. ... It is not like literature or music or painting which you need not have at all if you don't want to. ... [In the case of design] if you don't get it good you will get it bad."[13] Pick presented design as a way to reconnect artistic expression to life as it was unfolding at the moment. Design was art, updated to be industrial and commercial. As such, design posed new problems to an artist: it touched everyone; it spiritualized the everyday; it gave artists an ability to turn radio listeners into consumers of their products. As a result, design, on air, became tantamount to large-scale manufacturing.

Listeners were given the impression that the achievements of a wireless university were no longer to be measured by a handful of masterpieces but by mass-produced consumer goods. On radio, "design" suggested affordable art, with shop windows as the museums of the twentieth century and mass consumers

Figure 5.5

Thinking through consumer goods to explore what the public wants, in Anthony Bertram, *Design in Everyday Things*, 1937. © Immediate Media Company London Limited.

elevated to the status of patrons.[14] The marketplace placed cultural products, artistic experiments, and revolutionary talent within the reach of more people. As Anthony Bertram said, the word signaled the artistic community's acknowledgment of "the importance of giving beautiful, dignified and efficient homes to all our people."[15] This is certainly not the reality of modern architecture, but it was definitely the ideal that popularized it and made its principles applicable to everything from the largest to the smallest scale of things in modern life. Pick highlighted the role of shoppers in reforming the arts:

> You must first startle your shop-keeper by asking questions, in the fashion of the dialogues you have heard Tuesday after Tuesday for the last 10 weeks, and then he will startle the manufacturer by passing them on, and the manufacturer will be compelled to look about for designers skilled and competent to embody the answers which you want in things themselves. The movement starts with you, the consumer or user.[16]

This was to be a grassroots reform: consumers educated by the BBC would rejuvenate the shape and shade of the land.

Other voices also supported these ideas. Holbrook Jackson, just as great a Morrisian enthusiast, joined the chorus, elaborating on what the marketplace could do for the reform of arts: "It is not altogether a misfortune that the aesthetically deficient should be relieved of the responsibility of choice. It should be clear," he continued, "that although a shop is a mechanism for the distribution of merchandise, it can in proper hands and with a little imagination, approximate, if not to a work of art, at least to a gallery of the Arts and Crafts."[17]

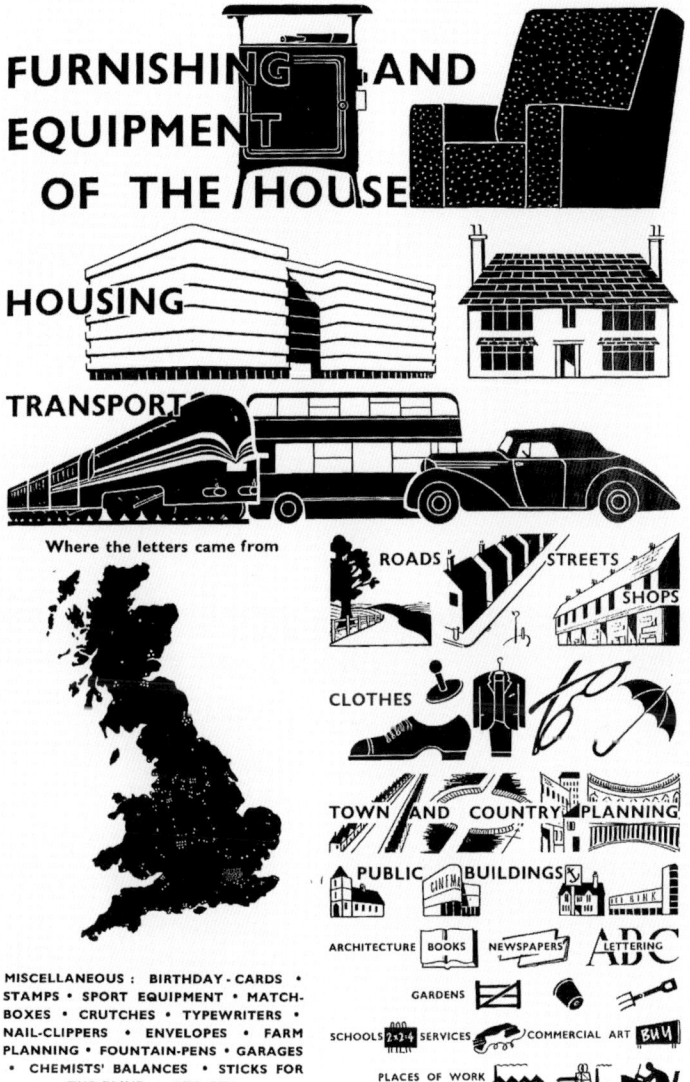

Figure 5.6

Unit furniture, illustrated in Anthony Bertram, *Design in Everyday Things*, 1937. © Immediate Media Company London Limited.

VI. Unit furniture in oak with walnut base designed by Bowman's Ltd., and here arranged for a bachelor's one-room flat. Unit furniture is a modern development in flexible design for an unsettled age.

Most of the broadcasters invited to speak on modern art and design gave elaborate discourses on standardization. Here, of course, they veered far from the fundamentals of Ruskin and Morris, arguing that taste was not personal and that form followed rigorous rules. Standardized design was discussed as a way out of the problem of capricious consumption. Jackson hoped that standardized goods would improve "popular appreciation, or, at least, acceptance of form (I mean the shape of things) as distinct from ornament; also, a quickening of the colour sense." Industrial art had created "a new sense of design, comfort and convenience." It broke down class divisions, which Morris and Co. had failed to do. Jackson even ventured: "It is not, perhaps, extravagant to hope that [with industrial design] the British Commonwealth may one day become a Commonwealth of Taste."[18] Once mass production set the standards and the market helped them get widely absorbed, individuals could once again exercise freedom intuitively—the freedom that the industrial revolution had granted them rather prematurely. Standardization of goods, likeminded broadcasters estimated, was going to "replace the good old traditions as well as the bad old habits." Jackson and Pick thus made the discourse on symbolic form identical with the discourse on modern taste.

Radiophonic works cleared the ground for a theory of art and architecture that found the locus of creativity in the demands of the present rather than the mimesis of tradition. A radiophonically educated consumer culture would convert art from the private testimonial of an artist to the corporate logo of a people. It would transform art from an exclusive club to a bottom-up, participatory enterprise. Art would step out of musty institutions and sit in the agora, submitting itself to the judgment of all those educated in the wireless university.

Radiophonic work—that is, a concept of work born of the logic of the broadcast word—assigned the power of meaning to everything. On radio the accent on the word "design" concerned itself not with individual taste but with a public aesthetic. Speakers from Pick to Gloag to Bertram and Barton concluded that all the variety in individual taste must spring from baseline "standards of beauty." With a standard, they would be able to reel in the capriciousness of English buyers that had been pumped by the rogue individualism nurtured by the nineteenth century.

It never crossed these men's minds that radio's promise for steering culture could also standardize minds. How could the use of a nonvisual medium for the reformation of the visual world carry that danger? After all, it was the medium par excellence of imagination. A broadcast therefore must be open to a variety of formal interpretations. And hence, with all seriousness, Frank Pick publicly embarked upon his romantic conceptualization of a wirelessly connected Britain as a group portrait of integrated inhabitants. Who would have thought that the rise of mass listening and mass shopping would rekindle the Victorian dream of modeling the nation after thirteenth-century rural England?

II The Town in the Age of Its Wireless Dispersion

Pick's ideas were representative of a radiophonic discourse on contemporary production. More than 80 percent of all invitations to broadcast on current problems in practice focused on the principles of good design. Surely the topic was borrowed from contemporary architectural debates already going on in print. What was particular to radio was the singularity of emphasis. Other contributions to the topic by the Adult Education department included *Art and Industry* (1932) and *Design in Everyday Things* (1937). The first was a group of weekly lectures by four different speakers that was broadcast on the occasion of the publication of the Gorell Report for the Board of Trade on how applied arts could make competitive British products for the international market. *Art and Industry* considered the lack of correspondence between industrial manufacturers and the artistic community. This, speakers found, was not a matter of superficial difficulties or a lack of good will, but the result of a deep-seated distinction between what constituted fine arts and applied art. The renowned art critic Roger Fry regretted that manufacturers were suspicious of art, regarding it as a strange, incomprehensible factor and its creators as peculiar and unaccountable. The series pointed to what the collaboration between designers and industrial manufacturers could do for social reconstruction and the expansion of the share of British goods in the world market.

The second series, *Design in Everyday Things*, was a combination of lectures and interviews that gave voice to the authorities most directly responsible for the appearance of the built environment. A three-month-long course, its topics covered different building typologies (domestic, work, recreation) and scales of design challenges (urban, architectural, industrial products). Speakers enumerated the virtues of advance planning. "Your Home and Mine" took the topic to schoolchildren, and "Good Housekeeping" presented it to women. The news periodically reviewed exhibitions of working-class furnishings and interior design, architectural drawings at the Royal Institute of Art, an exhibition of "Ideal Homes," and the RIBA's annual displays, announcements of awards, and notices of centennials of famous architects, from the same perspective. The series came up in the discussions of the activities of the Modern Architecture Research Group (MARS Group) and its planning proposals for Bethnal Green.[19] Finally, it also took the form of sound bites between longer programs, such as discussions on books by Nikolaus Pevsner and Herbert Read on art, industry, and the poor standards of English taste.

> If a woman, living in the centre of Belfast, bemoans the fact that though she lives in the greenest island in the world her days are spent among bricks and stones; if she longs sometimes to sit in a garden rather than stand at her open street door; if she worries about her children who so soon run off into the noisy and dangerous streets, she is simply saying in her own words that town life as we know it in our large industrial cities is unbalanced and barbarous. And it is only another way of saying the same thing for a Cabinet Minister to deplore the way the beauties of the Antrim coast have been spoilt by the indiscriminate erection of bungalows, caravans, and huts.[20]

These were the opening words of the opening broadcast of a series called *Town Planning in Ireland* by another confidant of Frank Pick—Maxwell Fry, the architect-planner and member of the DIA, speaking three years after Pick. A man of affairs, groomed for the petty politics of art and industry by none other than Pick, Fry spent his days in the corridors of the foreign office, the military headquarters, and the Board of Industries and Commerce, and his evenings in the hippest art circles in Chelsea.[21] He was the slickest architect whom the director of the regional station of Northern Ireland (there were five such regional stations at the time) could fly in from London. Fry was to give a series of six talks on town planning as the grand finale series of the winter of 1936. The Minister for Home Affairs for Northern Ireland, Sir Richard Dawson Bates, introduced the ensemble. The regional station had flown Fry all over the island in order to broadcast specific proposals for different types of settlements in Northern

Figure 5.7

G. M. Boumphrey, *Your Home and Mine*, BBC pamphlet, 1937. © Immediate Media Company London Limited.

Ireland (large cities, small towns, villages, commons open land). The BBC headquarters in London, in a gesture of recognition, arranged for the *Listener* to print the series in full. An introductory editorial made sure that listeners who had neglected to tune in to the Northern Ireland frequency in the past few weeks had an opportunity to see it in text. Fry also furnished Richard Lambert, the *Listener*'s editor, with explanatory photographs and a bibliography. As with all series, its primary audience comprised the formally organized listening groups, but it certainly wanted to have a more far-reaching effect. Among other things, *Town Planning in Ireland* was a testament to the growing intimacy and trust between the DIA and the BBC.

The BBC had given Maxwell Fry a medium of mass communication whose total "field" character tended to eliminate the fragmented specialties of town and country and emphasized their continuities. Radio made it easier for him to stress the connection between architecture and planning, and to remind his urban and rural listeners of the interconnectedness of the changes in their respective environs. The key to both architecture and planning, for example, "lies in the relationship that each part seeks with another and all parts with the whole, the harmony to which Corbusier never tired of referring."[22] The compression of space and distance by the railway, motorcar, and radio transmission, Fry asserted, had made it impossible to consider the town as a self-contained environ. Surely one should get rid of ribbon development and establish the city as a discrete entity situated firmly and distinctly in the countryside, but only to establish and clarify the dialogue between them. Town planners had to acknowledge that modern technology had interwoven the destinies of town and country; the barbarous streets of Belfast and the spoiled coast of Antrim were linked with one another. Both were integral components of the body of the nation. Fry's

Town Planning in Northern Ireland

Can Belfast Be Reshaped?

By E. MAXWELL FRY

BELFAST. One of the great cities of the world; sixth port in the United Kingdom. I recall with great affection how I first saw you from that curve in the Crumlin Road, lying grey and inert under your pall of workmen's houses. Tramcars clanged, crowds thronged the too narrow pavements, mean shops one after another strung out unendingly. The hills seemed far away, and the Lough Water forgotten. I was in an industrial town.

The heart of Belfast where 'roads cease to straggle and fall into a geometric pattern of straight wide thoroughfares . . . of which Donegall Square is the head!'

For a long time I walked the streets where most Belfast people live. The houses in them were not much different from their counterpart in St. Helens or Leeds. A very narrow front, just wide enough to take a window, a door and sufficient brickwork to hold the house together: a room in front—half a room behind, a dark well of a yard behind that again, and a narrow passage. Then the same thing was repeated backwards, and so you had one block of dwellings. A narrow street with narrow pavements completed the picture.

In these houses that form the greater part of Belfast, the means of decent living are almost entirely lacking, and I thought to myself both from a sociological and technical point of view, that they were rather a poor sort of thing to have been turned out by the same people who have built great ships of which they are so proud. The ships sail away, but the houses remain.

smoke that mingled with the September mist. Everything before me was grey . . . everything but the faint glint of Lough Water, and the soft green of the hills sloping down into the grey city. I thought, as I looked down, that it was a mighty work that had been done by those two centuries of busy men. What force and what power it was that brought the city together out of nothing, filled it with life, and sent its works and men to every corner of the earth. Who am I—who are *we*, that can hope to reshape the vastness of this solid creation, at this eleventh hour?

And then I followed the Crumlin Road down the hillside and into the city, and as I went down the green gave way to grey, the pall of smoke closed over me, and soon there was nothing to be seen but the hard walls of factories and the factory-made streets of

'Nobody planned the living town'

Photos: Aerofilms

Figure 5.8
Page from Maxwell Fry's article "Can Belfast Be Reshaped?," *Listener*, November 1936.
© Immediate Media Company London Limited.

quest was to ensure that his listeners understood that planning concerned separate but interconnected entities with separate but interconnected roles; and these interconnections made sense only within the larger context of regional and national planning. A modern town ought to be understood as part of an all-inclusive, ongoing process. Like a sculpture, it was a work of art. But unlike a sculpture that evolved in the artist's mind and studio, a town was not a free-floating signifier; it was realized as part of a national landscape. A "town" in Fry's sense was at once dialogical, discrete, and a fragment of a larger entity.

Fry's lectures for *Town Planning in Ireland* never mentioned the relationship between edifice and void, routes and pivot focal points, that so bedeviled men like Sir Reginald Blomfield, Edwin Lutyens, and H. S. Goodhart-Rendel. Such aesthetic considerations now had to be justified by scientific research into the topography, economic conditions and industry, land values and demographics, and the need for agricultural land around the city. Planning was now, first and foremost, studied thought that wrestled with aesthetic and extra-aesthetic requirements. Only thence was a contemporary work of art produced.

The *Listener* editorial on the series highlighted that Fry's broadcasts did not concern fictive dreams of "visualiz[ing] an ideal town in which all the buildings are charming, the parks well placed, the means of communication perfectly adjusted." Instead, Fry dealt with the humbler but more challenging task of "improving the external amenities of daily life." While the previous generation had seen the art of town building as an exercise on a white sheet of paper to which the site and context were accommodated, a modern planner's "calling [was] grounded," as all art should be, "in a struggle to approach the certainties, the verities, that give life its meaning."[23] On the urban fabric, it was actions of policy that must speak. This new emphasis of planning turned individuals into a group

Figure 5.9

Scenic setting of Portrush, Northern Ireland, representing town and country as discrete entities. Courtesy: National Library of Ireland.

that retained all their individuality, not by symbolic statements of style but by the operative mechanism of organization.

When *Town Planning in Northern Ireland* told listeners about the width and lay of the street, the location and scale of open space, the situation of town hall and railway stations, it broke with the idea of visually composing a city. The series did not consider the city as spreading outward from its visible and dominating monuments (established practice since medieval times) or from a network of squares and imposing vistas (as in classical towns). All recommendations for town planning were now prompted by the separation of traffic and the principal functions of the city so as to create distinct zones of work, housing, and recreation. Based on a pure abstraction of human life in cities, modern town planning was conceived as the art of building a machine. As Fry put it:

> The heart of this machine is in the people ... the ... element, which binds the whole together, gives it life and movement, and defines its form: the element of communication. Work, Shelter, Relation and Communication—there you have the complete town. If one part is lacking or falls into decay the rest must suffer; and upon the quality of each ... depends the health and vigour, the intelligence and happiness of the people.[24]

Those who tuned into the Northern Ireland frequency were told that they should remember that towns were artificial growths. They involved complex organization. They imposed rules. They curtailed individual freedom. But they didn't repress the most natural desires and instincts of inhabitants: "As our towns have grown in size ... the organization upon which [the town] now depends is extremely complicated." But "in spite of this complexity, we still keep, as human beings, many of our natural or animal desires, and suffer intensely if these remain unsatisfied."[25] All town planners necessarily designed machines. But Fry specified that good town planners never lost sight of the fact that they designed machines that provided for primal human instincts:

> It has been the gravest mistake of the nineteenth-century industrialism to imagine that the artificial town can be carried to any lengths. It can't. There is a point where people begin to lose all contact with nature, and at that point nature revolts and people suffer. ... Not only in Belfast but in many a smaller town in Ulster, people are so crowded together that they have too

little pure air to breathe, and not enough light. As a result, they are poor in body and mind, easy victims to disease, and poor citizens into the bargain. And so … when we build up our complicated cities and towns … our organization must be balanced between the artificial creation of a social machine and the satisfaction of human nature.[26]

Fry made the best of the reach of the radio as a talking machine and its ability to mime the biological aspect of communication repressed by the printed word. He exploited the voice and the auditory and mimetic worlds to his advantage. He had come to convince the Irish that they should no longer let a town grow by the logic of industry. Towns shouldn't be allowed to expand as an agglomeration of factories, a repetitive and impersonal rhythm of rows upon rows of company or council housing:

> Now if work is the chief reason for there being a town at all, the next thing we come to is housing, by which I mean dwellings of every possible kind. This element is the largest in point of mere size, and we can imagine a town built up of these two elements—work and housing alone. It would consist of a factory and its housing nearby. There are indeed such places to be found in the industrial north of England: wicked and squalid remains of a brutal past.[27]

What should be done instead? A city, in Fry's estimate, was clearly made out of the inert and mechanical services, hygiene, running water, and safe streets. But a city worth living in was one that blew life into these mechanical parts, gave poetry to its "wires" and "pipes" and treated them in ways that gave character and intimacy to a neighborhood. Fry's mechanically transmitted voice assured its listeners that a modern planner must "design" this machine so that it could become a living organism: "It will help you to realize what town planning is, if you will think of a town as a machine—not a mechanical machine, but a machine like the human body, delicate, complex, organic and constantly being renewed."[28]

Only a self-sustaining, organic machine, the talking machine said, could repair the social web of kinship. Only a machine harmoniously aligned to its intended destiny, the electronically delivered voice assured, could repair the fragmentation and rogue individualism instituted by industrialization. The message

Figure 5.10

Ribbon development as an inadequate response to the congestion of cities, causing the destruction of the countryside. Courtesy: Länsmuseet Gävleborg.

of the breath severed from the body was the remarkable proximity of the mechanical and the organic to one another.

The association of the quality of the space with the quality of citizens squarely placed Maxwell E. Fry within the tradition of British liberalism. He had come to see the city as an organism, by his own admission, through the teachings of the multitalented Scottish scholar and town planner Patrick Geddes. The founding director of the German Bauhaus, Walter Gropius (who escaped Germany in 1933 and joined Fry as a design partner from 1933 to 1936), taught Fry that designers and planners were involved not in the business of building spaces but in the creation of society. From the plan for the Ville Radieuse by Le Corbusier (Fry's future collaborator for the planning of Chandigarh), he learned the balance between collective and personal needs. The art of town planning was to find a happy equilibrium between administrative order and family life.[29] Fry brought ten years of experience in a planning office to the series of *Town Planning* talks. Having started in the neo-Georgian tradition, he found that his ideas quickly became at odds with those of other practitioners at work. Not only that, he was also disillusioned with the idea of garden cities.[30] His three-year partnership with Walter Gropius was thus a meeting of the minds. Two years before, Fry had coordinated the first MARS Group exhibition. Instead of focusing on satellite towns, the exhibition, an offshoot of the International Congress of Modern Architects (CIAM), brought the ambitions of garden city planning to the problems of inner cities and urban slums. He presided over a group whose replanning of the tough working-class neighborhood of Bethnal Green in East London was animated by the desire to bring the invisible hand of free competition under the guiding hand of experts. He reassured the modern architects of their moral authority and their belief that only experts should govern society's productive capacities and provide for its needs.[31] Using enormous charts and demographic surveys to explain design decisions, he and his peers showed that planning had become the provenance of a diagnostician-artist.[32]

In the second half of the nineteenth century, the investment in urban settlements had led to an all-around improvement in the living conditions of the urban working classes.[33] But early twentieth-century planners and policy makers became even more concerned with living conditions because of the connection they saw between such conditions and instilling family values in the working classes. This burning issue was part of the period's obsession with national efficiency and the maintenance of an imperial race. Before World War I, the delivery of housing was informed by the antiurbanism of garden cities. Whatever their theory, in practice garden cities moved housing away from the workplace. Prewar planners hedged their bets, anticipating that the government would take action to get factories to move near housing, and in this way they would return the industrial towns to village communes. Homely hobbies like gardening, reading, and so on, planners calculated, would create a socially adjusted and content electorate. Unfortunately, the bet came to nothing but soulless suburbanization. After the war, planners returned their attention to cities, proposing to excise the "plague spots" and bring open air, greenery, small town flavor, and contact with land to the city. Fry argued that the imperial race had to be put on the path of individual development and collective purification in a setting that did not fragment life into different compartments but where men and women would be involved in diverse activities simultaneously.[34]

Whereas the generation of Sir Raymond Unwin, the first planner of garden cities, had envisioned reform in the self-sufficient capsules of satellite towns, the next generation imagined a utopian society in which the nuclear family was incubated in judiciously spaced urban flats.[35] These would have collective amenities, social rooms, and public nurseries. In an interview he gave John Gloag two years earlier for *Design in Modern Life*, the same series that had showcased Frank Pick, Fry had broadcast his contempt for Unwin and garden cities: "The early reformers," instead "of doing anything effective at the centre ... turned their eyes away towards the outskirts, and using a romantic notion of architecture then prevalent, worked out the system of garden city suburb development upon which the movement has now been based."[36] He blamed satellite towns for failing to remain satellite towns. They quickly became menacing suburbs, extending the city oppressively. Unwin and Barry Parker had envisioned a model of town planning that, in Fry's opinion, ruined cities and destroyed society. They scattered men over the land, fanning the flames of lawless self-indulgence, chaos, and social unrest.

Contrary to what the propagandists for garden cities said, Fry was adamant that towns did not necessarily produce dullness and inefficiency. The slovenly and debauched men and women seen about the town were a historical creation. In the eighteenth century, when cities were small, they had harmonious social relations, with man and his surroundings reinforcing each other. Civility was the order of the day, Fry claimed:

In [eighteenth-century] society everyone knew their place. The rich and landed aristocracy took the social and cultural lead as by natural right. This society, when it built or designed nearly any mortal thing, had a fine sense of order, which owed its direction and its force to classic or Roman culture. The distinguishing trait of classic culture is breadth, repose, symmetry, a sense of scale—that is to say, the easy fitting of one part to another—and a fine reticence of expression. ... Then into the midst of this well-ordered though top heavy society ... there was an explosion which wrecked the balanced society of the past and in its place grew up a teeming population of factory and mineworkers, an eruption of industrial towns. Lancashire, the Black Country, the North East Coast, South Wales[,] all those dirty crowded places, which are today the seats of unemployment, and the subject-matter of slum clearance, were at that time the happy hunting grounds for a new type of individualism that knew no laws and had no taste.[37]

The garden city movement, in Fry's estimate, could not be called a planning movement because it evaded the problems of planning created by industrial towns. The more complicated conditions of twentieth-century society, the continuity between city and society and of the different elements within a city, required the ordering and far-seeing eye of an expert planner. The modern art of town building resided in reconstructing the twentieth-century town in the image of the eighteenth-century town. The modern town, he held, was not a socialist sea of undifferentiated parts; it was modeled on the human body, in which every part was unique, irreplaceable, and interdependent. "Planning" brought together the different elements in a city to "give rise to a new set of relationships" that were "the product of new attitudes to light and air, to changing social habits, to freedom of movement hitherto channeled by social conventions."[38] Fry did not recognize the relationship between the functional city's division of daily functions into different spaces and the industrial mindset that broke every action into distinct components. He instead focused on the interdependence of these components. Functional separation confirmed that each individual had a role in the larger whole, and endowed daily strife with a sense of greater purpose and common good. The purpose of planning was to improve the conditions of life, remove the most crippling burdens of poverty, enable individuals to take charge of their lives, and strengthen their capacity to compete for self-interest in the fierce environment of the free market. A modern city was an enabling city.

It did not control but guided citizens on how to fully realize their natural talents and destinies. This mechanical artifact restored the natural order of things. It served the unaddressed needs of progress rather than convention. It fused hierarchy and mutuality, the spatial and social, the mechanical and organic into a well-coordinated entity. Could the mechanical in Fry's mechanically transmitted voice reach any greater heights?

III The English House in the Age of Its Wireless Dispersion

On Tuesday evenings in a certain year, a serene, almost still voice emanating from the sound box on the table interrupted everyone's routine. With no care for occasion or one's station in life, it spoke to all indiscriminately, yet it possessed the rehearsed intimacy of face-to-face conversation. Self-assured in its command, like Sunday morning church bells, it asked every household from England to Ireland, whether comfortable or struggling, to leave aside the back-breaking and enslaving cyclicality of domestic labor for the next twenty minutes. "Turn off the lights, gaze into the fire and enjoy the mood that is presented to you," it said. The controllers of broadcasting were not unmindful. They realized that the more they pulled the listener out of herself and her immediate circumstances, and the more they made her self-forgetful, the more deeply what she heard would be impressed upon her memory. The room was then filled with fantasies and dreams of the house of the future, built with new economical materials and unfettering building technology. The house of the future took shape as the locus of planned comfort, studied ease, feather-light eloquence, and careful self-display. There was no more wasted effort, rotten food, and clutter. A new age of machines that made prefitted furniture, mechanical appliances, and larger windows had been ushered in. Rather than dragging wardrobes from rental to rental and living amid thoughtless acquisitions or the burdens of antiques, homemakers decorated their houses and flats with thoughtfully picked bargains.

The purpose of design in the living room, the listeners were told, was the production of space, while the goal of kitchen planning ought to be the management of time. The same technology that had put a small wireless set within reach of listeners' pockets was also placing bigger commodities like these houses within their grasp.

One Tuesday evening in March 1933, listeners heard a conversation between two likeminded thinkers, the engineer-turned-design-critic G. M. Boumphrey and Canadian engineer-turned-architect Wells Coates, who was working on the interior design of the BBC's Broadcasting House as he spoke into one of its microphones.

> **Boumphrey:** What do you consider are the challenges in the conditions of life today, which call for a change in the design of dwelling?
>
> **Coates:** In the first place ... we don't possess our homes in the old, permanent, settled sense. ... We get rid of our belongings, if we can, and make for a new, an exciting kind of freedom. ... We want to make flexible arrangements about our homes. ... We don't want to feel tied down. ... I think it will be useful if we agree to keep to the one word dwelling—a good Anglo-Saxon word which originally means a place where one lingers or tarries—to include all types of dwelling-units: houses, flats, tenements.[39]

Boumphrey had brought the thirty-eight-year-old Coates on air to tactfully present a delicate issue. He had to convince an across-class, home-centered people[40] to celebrate the circumstances that unbeknown to them had changed the function of the house in their lives. Coates unleashed the full range of his persuasive powers; today, he argued, "time and space are being measured in a new way," as both physical and psychological mobility had accelerated. Now "we move from place to place, to find work, or to find new surroundings." Cinemas, shopping arcades, and accessible sea shores had robbed the home of its entertainment function; public transportation, improved schools, and distant workplaces, in turn, had done away with the home's centrality in work and education. Servants had disappeared. Children were moving out sooner than before. No one wanted to live in an extended family arrangement. Together these changes had given the world a newfound freedom, delivering people from the demands of the house of old. Coates told Boumphrey, "Our freedom as workers—and still more as holiday-makers and week-enders—very greatly alters our attitude to our dwellings."[41] Boumphrey wanted to make sure the most wary and skeptical among their audience understood the depth of Coates's observation. "The pace

Figure 5.11

Home listening, circa 1935–1940. Courtesy: Bryan Costin.

Types of simple electric-light fittings by Troughton & Young, Ltd. New designs for a new source of light.

XII.

Below, left to right. A simple lamp standard in wood; a very cheap table lamp in chromiumed steel; a gas-fitting which avoids the old unsightliness.

Figure 5.12

Modern domestic equipment as great bargains available in the market, illustrated in Anthony Bertram, *Design in Everyday Things*, 1937. © Immediate Media Company London Limited.

at which life is lived today," he underlined, "makes it essential for us to spend as little time as possible on the routine of existence—washing, dressing, writing letters, and so forth."[42] Designers of domestic space should no longer concern themselves with their mastery of Vitruvian proportions or the expression of eternal truths. Now, the contingent needs of anonymous and temporary occupants were to be the matrix from which all solutions to the problem of modern living were to be given.

The purpose of a modern dwelling place, the interviewer and interviewee insisted, was to emancipate humanity from its burdens; irrespective of class, everyone should be able to outsource cooking, cleaning, groceries, laundry, and child rearing to someone outside the home, clearing it for relaxation and self-display. The talent of a designer was displayed by his ability to tastefully minimalize the house and "make the real comfort, quiet, and convenience required in our dwellings during the short periods we spend in them, an essential purpose in our design."[43] A good example could be found in a recently completed housing complex in Liverpool. To Boumphrey and Coates, the traditional notion of the house gave way to that of a hotel—a minimal occupancy space, taken up momentarily. For these two CIAM faithfuls, enthused by the audaciousness of CIAM ideas about minimal dwelling, a house was no longer where one lived but where one merely stayed. It was now in this impersonal "nowhere" that our passions, our character, our uniqueness, and our preferences were to be expressed. It was ridiculous, Coates said satirically, to drag a heavy "Jacobean dining-room set, mass-produced like hundreds of thousands of others," into these momentary rest areas. The only way we can make this space our own is with the light touch of "our good manners; our taste in clothes; our crockery, glassware and other small objects of personal choice or vanity."[44]

This interview was part of an impressive body of programming on the transformation of the concept, function, and shape of the oldest building typology of the house at the moment when electronic mass diffusion had entered into it. The radio had entered the home after its noteworthy duty for the military during the First World War. As the apparatus of the wireless set took its place in the home as a conventional piece of furniture or a box on the dresser, it became the auditory center of the wireless community. It took over the hearth as the psychological core of the home. If the hearth had enhanced a family's sense of distinctiveness, made it appear nuclear to itself and others, the radio set magically transported the family to the expanded public sphere of a boundless auditorium. It did so without drawing family members out of the domestic shell into the sociality of coffee shops or the decorum of salons. Nor did it commit them to the withdrawn and inward activity of reading. Radio rekindled localism among what Coates astutely identified as a nomadic people. Modernity has put us in perpetual circulation. It has ruptured distinctions that were critical to shaping identity before the invention of electronic media by involving the intimate and foreign, inside and outside, individual and typical in one another's constitution in ways unknown to print culture.

A mere three decades before the scripted conversation between Boumphrey and Coates resonated in millions of British living rooms and bedrooms, a German architect, Hermann Muthesius, had eulogized a handful of quaint-looking country houses built in the arts and crafts tradition. He regarded the tailor-made cottages and stately homes by Norman Shaw, Phillip Webb, M. H. Baillie Scott, William Lethaby, and Charles Voysey as refuges from the alienating forces of the modern metropolis. In these homes, inhabitants comfortably concluded the day's work uninterrupted from without, settled among family, with a book by an oil lamp: "Here, in the heart of his family, self-sufficient and feeling no great urge for sociability, pursuing his own interests in virtual isolation, he finds his happiness and his spiritual comfort."[45]

By the time Coates and Boumphrey came along, the mass medium of electronic diffusion had disrupted this blissful and coherent picture of the English house. That radio consolidated and expressed mass culture forced the definition of culture to be channeled not through iconic works but through the entire built fabric. Suddenly, domesticity did not seem to have cultivated a collectively

Figure 5.13

Example of type dwelling: Gerrard Gardens, tenement housing, Liverpool. Courtesy: Twentieth Century Images.

beneficial self-interest. On the contrary, it had harbored an antisocial individualism. J. E. Barton, the art educator and polemicist mentioned earlier, used the microphone to condemn the institution of the home for "sentiment stirring."[46] John Gloag portrayed it as "ancestor worship."[47] Anthony Bertram dismissed its contemporary iteration as a "fancy dress show." The parade of little Tudoresques along the bypass road represented, in his view, nothing but fear of living in the present moment and dreams of escape: "People in the past did not imitate what had gone before. Why did the tradition stop then? Why, at the end of [the eighteenth] century, did people begin to build imitation Gothic, imitation castles, and why did they get worse until we have the by-pass villa style of today?" He grumbled, "I believe that if everybody really knew what a house was and insisted on getting it, we should not have to put up with all the bad imitations that most of us occupy." In addition, he argued, it is "a very extravagant way of building and all that extra money is being spent to escape from our own age; I believe we shall never really get an honest and efficient and beautiful modern style until we have thoroughly got rid of this unhealthy craving for the past."[48] Wells Coates made fun of the Englishman's fantasies about possessing large, unwieldy, cumbersome homes—"or at the least what they call in the advertisements a 'baronial hall'—to give him a feeling of stability, security and individuality. It is amazing how many discomforts he will put up with to secure this."[49] Whereas in Muthesius's partial view, the freestanding English house conserved the inhabitant's true being and selfhood in the face of anonymous work and an alienating city, it had now become the symbol of English conservatism and reactionary denial of modernity. Individuality without a larger sense of collective responsibility had become the English nightmare. From the grandest country estates to the quaint-looking middle-class cottages mushrooming around the nation to the humblest tenements, an English house was no nursery for budding individuality; instead, it was a factory for the manufacture of false consciousness and the primary target of reform.

Unlike the structure of thinking informed by the book or the professional press, the platform structured by radio was intolerant of the ideal of the house as a tailor-fit suit. A custom-made design was an exclusive paradigm, bound to personal taste, and a particular point of view. It resisted generalization. The wireless auditorium, instead, favored the law of averages. Accordingly, in broadcasts the ideal of the house became one of loose fit. "A really satisfactory house and its furniture must be made," said Bertram, "like a suit round a body." However, "the average man must be contented with a ready-made type-dwelling."[50] A "type-dwelling" had a modest scale, broad appeal, and the potential of a greater ripple effect. A discourse on it was like news and weather; it theoretically involved everyone in the audience. It was better endowed with the power to get everyone deeply involved in cultural production and with the illusion of good taste burgeoning from below as opposed to an enterprise imposed from above. Most importantly, unlike the discussion on public spaces, streets, and the town, a discourse on the house magically turned passive receivers of information into active practitioners of taste.

The transmission of the type dwelling surrendered the private "client" in favor of the anonymous "user." In broadcast discourse on form, the intricacy of patterned wallpaper was abandoned in favor of the beauty and abstraction of white walls. The imperfections of handicrafts gave way to a preference for the precision of machine-made items. The cult of things was replaced by the cult of space, collectibles replaced by disposables. Applied ornament was chastised against the innate richness of natural and synthetic materials. Furniture and furnishings were now typically referred to as "equipment." In discussions of plans, impersonal arrangements were favored over a personal touch. The renowned critic Herbert Read distinguished the standardized dwelling from a country house by virtue of the former's "complete suppression of all individuality. Such houses [were] built, not by the foot, but by the mile." Furthermore, Read remarked, "In the first case, we must remember that the constructional unit is the town," not the house.[51] According to Bertram, type dwellings were "designed not for a particular family but for a social group."[52] "I should say," seconded Coates, "that one of the first demands, since we don't live in one place all our lives, is to get rid of some of the many personal effects we carry about from one place to another."[53] Read insisted that monotony was avoided by recessing these urban building blocks among trees, gardens, and playing fields. "Their long straight lines" became the antidote to "many acres of chaotic villadom," for type dwellings "harmonize[d] well with the towering business blocks in the distance." The application of modern technology created not a bland, characterless house but a "natural plan achieved with efficiency and with fervor."[54]

The broadcasters painstakingly screened, edited, and censored by Reith's staff favored high-rise dwelling. Geoffrey Boumphrey and Maxwell Fry spoke enthusiastically about the vertical apartment living proposed by Le Corbusier and Walter Gropius. As mentioned in chapter 3, Boumphrey pointed out the

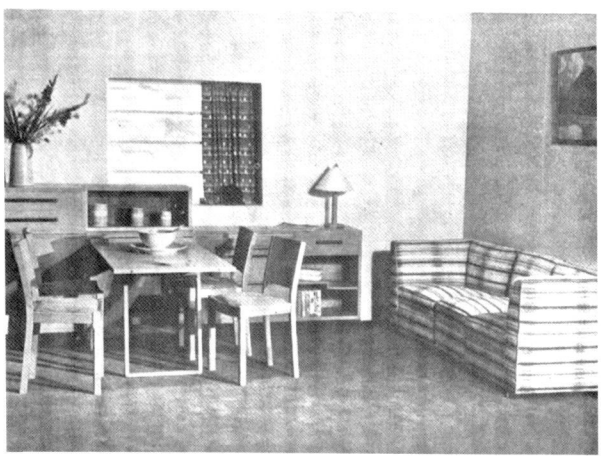

11. The cluttered drawing-room of the past, and (*below*) a modern living-room, with dining-table that folds away. Our restless age calls for restfulness in the home. Victorian leisure and domestic staffs could cope with Victorian acquisitiveness and display. We cannot: and we travel lighter.

Figure 5.14

A comparison of the cluttered Victorian home to the spacious type dwelling, illustrated in Anthony Bertram, *Design in Everyday Things*, 1937. © Immediate Media Company London Limited.

---

many advantages of living in blocks of flats, which allowed for the economical provision of services. Unlike the garden city developments that sucked up land from farmers, apartment buildings "release[d] much more ground."[55] It was as if man's freedom from English conventionality and taste was at stake in the choice between flats and cottages dispersed in gardens. There were many who were critical of the apartment blocks. "All that I have ever heard reduces to the same complaint; it is just like a box!" said Read in defending the type house of Le Corbusier. "But, as Mr. Bernard Shaw once said, what is wrong with a box. If the proportions are right, such a box on a hillside will look as well as a yacht at sea. It is only necessary to get rid of our prejudices."[56]

Reviewing an exhibition of the prairie-style houses of Frank Lloyd Wright, Maxwell Fry found that he had no use for Wright's earth-hugging planes or (morally) grounding fireplaces. He preferred innovations in flats that severed that relation and wove architecture out of "the complete economics of industrialized life." He accused the sensuality of the Robie House and the romanticism of Fallingwater of weighing down man. Their rather expensive example could not lead the generation of architects who wanted to resolve the riddle of mass living, for such architects, he contended, had to put the challenges of the real over and above the ideal. The freedom of Wright's spatial and structural innovations from "the vigorous attendant economics of the inevitably organic modern industrial system" made these houses "rather vegetable than organic"![57] An organic approach did not privilege the individual, Fry argued: "In the state of the world today ... the individual is less important than the whole." It was financial necessity that converted people from a mechanical aggregate of distinct parts into a Darwinian whole, a coordinated and healthy body. It was only architecture that grew out of financial logic that had "nearly universal validity."[58]

Others insisted that a house should be a throw-away commodity, with a given expiration date and shelf life, rather than an inheritance to be cherished and passed on to posterity.

> **John [Gloag]**: When an architect designs a house, he should approach it in the feeling that he is doing something that is going to be permanent. ... Let it at least be a thing that people can take pride in—that I can take pride in ...
>
> **Sinclair [Wood]**: This is, you know, one point I don't understand. Even if it is necessary for posterity to see one's architecture—and I don't accept that—but even if it is necessary ... why leave up a kind of museum, and make people go on living in a museum, just so that posterity may know how you designed buildings and how you built them?[59]

"Permanence in Building" was a dramatization of a three-sided debate between a man who revered the traditional concept of art (Gloag), an uncompromising utilitarian (Wood), and a man who wanted to free art from traditional limitations so it could serve new obligations (Whittaker). It was written by John Gloag (the interviewer of Frank Pick) and produced by the Department of Broadcast Talks in 1937. The three discussants argued over permanence and transience in human abode. "John," modeled after the honorable and uncompromising Sir Reginald Blomfield (played by Gloag himself), insisted that any house worth its salt should possess heritage value that would appeal to posterity. It must embody timeless truths and undying values that steered clear of the accidents of history. The other two men, irreverent and seemingly cavalier, took the opposite position. They insisted that a house "ought to come down within periods of, say, ten years or something like that."[60] The purpose of a house was not to mummify life but to sustain it, make it comfortable and pleasurable. A house was good only as long as it fulfilled the needs of the moment and fashioned the lifestyles of the time. The moment it lagged behind developments in building technologies, stopped influencing cultural opinions, and could not address the latest currents in social relations, it became obsolete. Sinclair argued: "I don't think that a building should be allowed to remain up for all time, because that must make it inefficient. I mean, to translate this into simple terms—if you put

Figure 5.15

Frank Lloyd Wright, Robie House, Chicago, 1909. Courtesy: Library of Congress Prints and Photographs Division, Washington, D.C.

up a house for people to live in." John snarled: "Well, of course, that really is the barrack ideal, isn't it." In fact, "you have got what I call the 'motor-car [or obsolescence] complex' about that."[61] Gloag gave the last word to James, who wanted to relieve the idea of the house from the architectural complex: "I think when you talk about permanence in building, it must be sort of divided into groups."[62]

Compelled by the argument, John finally conceded, "Yes, of course. Actually the question of permanence should not affect the domestic side so much." A dwelling should be like a car, traded in and turned into scrap once it exhausted its usefulness. In a wirelessly connected world, the canonical criterion by which a house was judged was not going to be what Walter Benjamin calls "cult value" but its "contemporariness-value."

Emotional indulgence was reserved only for discourse on historical houses. Among the radiophonic discussants of contemporary and future housing, one heard no one longing for the typically English picture of crackling and blazing Dickensian fires with the cat on the mat and chestnuts to roast. As Bertram said in "What Is a House?":

> [The] Hearth … was where the head of the family laid down the law. Now, of course … it is only ghosts that occupy the hearth. … [T]oday … the open fire should be regarded, not as a source of heat but as a decoration, with immense psychological value, when you do happen to be in for a "long uninterrupted evening." … But of course they are not always that uninterrupted nowadays. When we come back from the cinema we rather prefer a switch to a heap of dead ashes.[63]

Nostalgia and "irrelevant sentimentality" were accused of being unsound living tradition.

Herbert Read suggested that the house of tomorrow ought to be conceived in the spirit of a cabin in an ocean liner, with the city block thought of as the liner. The sanction for these parallels had come from the master merchant of dreams of the future, Le Corbusier, who had seen the great passenger ship as a model for the modern house and city block when he traveled from France to the distant shores of South America in 1929. A well-designed cabin made a few cubic feet of space into an ideal machine to live in. There is "not a movement in man's daily life," Read noted in his "Weekly Notes on Art," "that has not been considered in the disposition of the cabin's furniture. He was looked after by an excellent steward, and in the ship's restaurant he could find a variety of food and drink such as no private house could offer. ... For exercise there were the long, clean decks, a gymnasium, and a swimming-bath."[64] "The House of To-morrow" was going to be as spatially stringent as a cabin. Yet it had to account not just for the regularities of daily routines but also for its contingencies, its surprises and accidents.

Radio listeners routinely heard qualities of the car attributed to the house. "Why should it be a merit in a house to be old or imitation old, and not in a car?," Bertram asked.[65] Why was a car expected to change its appearance every so often, while the tamest nuance in the design of a house was met with utter disapproval? The changes in the car design, in this line of argument, did not take place to create an insatiable appetite for the latest fashion, or fill the pockets of manufacturers; it was a frank expression of progress in technology. House design must have the same pragmatic shrewdness and economy as the design of a car. Like a Rolls Royce, its appearance must appeal to both museum-goers and those who never go to museums. At the same time, while it won this universal appeal, it must constantly and regularly change to come out with new and improved models. It must show the forward march of rationality. Both the house and the car ought to be fiats of industry, developments in materials, engineering, and structures, not archaeology or vernacular knowledge. "The perfect house, simply works like a Rolls Royce," Bertam concluded.[66] Building a mantelpiece for a movable electric heater was as absurd as "fitting shafts and a nosebag to a car."[67] The comparison of dwelling space with the cabin, car, and ocean liner was telling. A work must possess transience, movement, and lightness. Remember Frank Pick's words, "All is traffic, even if it is not on wheels." Distance would hold no problem for the radiophonic dwelling. Like an ocean liner cabin, it would draw its identity not from a locality but from its ability to transcend locality and site. As a result, the definition of context changed from locality to site. The house would be (un)local and generic. It would be unrooted and uprooting, both physically and conceptually. It was the nonspecificity and absence of relation to locality that would give the place an identity. Bertram asked,

> "What sort of building for what sort of humans?" It seems simple enough—twentieth-century building and twentieth century humans—but it is generally forgotten. Perhaps that is why Le Corbusier invented his phrase about a machine for living in. This is a machine age: he wants to bring the idea of

a house into line with it. He wants a house in its way to be as efficient and comfortable as a car, and, like a car, to look what it is and not be tricked out in the costume belonging to a dead way of life and a dead technique.[68]

Also gone were all notions of the house as wearing a decorous mask. Voices lamented the missteps taken by both the English picturesque practices and their opponent, neoclassical architecture. Both treated the facade as a two-dimensional affair. The picturesque movement had turned the face of the house into a charming painting; neoclassical architecture, into a generalizable mask to be worn in public to protect privacy. Both hid the life they enclosed. With a charming grimace, someone on air retorted, these masks suggested what might have happened to the buildings, but actually did not. The exterior, broadcast voices insisted, was a three-dimensional affair that should not hide but announce. It should use a logically deduced vocabulary, and display the values and needs of the lives that lay within. Its shape was to be generated from internal planning. It must grow from the inside out. It had to represent its occupants; otherwise it was only a pantomime. A residential facade was no longer meant to guard privacy but now should exhibit it, wearing the inside out.

The broadcast discourse on contemporary design transformed the ideal of a work of art from a unique, stand-alone monument to an everyday, mass-produced and anonymous environ. The consistent profanation of the concept of the house, the city, and the street was no radical act of sacrilege. The increasingly mundane nature of the criteria of good design was not an avant-garde maneuver; it was nothing like Marcel Duchamp's exhibition of a urinal that lay bare the devices of the edifice of fine art. Nor did it forecast the next generation's valorization of popular consumption, technological communication, and mobility to undermine the hierarchy between high and low cultural production, as Archigram's pamphlets would do in the 1960s. It was a ritual act that, far from dropping art as one worldly thing among others, provided its belief with a new basis. It was the recalibration of the institution of art so that its operative hierarchies could continue to function in a world transformed by radiophony. For Pick,

> Design is something more than just using material aright, or showing skill in its use to bring out its beauty. It is something more than serving a purpose. It is something more than ensuring tidiness and order. It is also expression. It is the designer saying something for himself. The further we get

away from use, the more we seek expression. Fitness for purpose must transcend the merely practical and serve a moral and spiritual order as well.[69]

For Bertram,

> All design is everybody's business. I would almost go so far as to say that design in its widest scope really means civilization. If everyone had their house in order, I believe we should soon have the world's house in order. … It is well to remember, now and then, that behind all this business of taps and teapots and where to put electric light, there lies a very big idea—the idea of man planning and making civilized life.[70]

The discourse on the house capitalized on the British people's legendary love affair with homes. As the whole nation woke up and slept to fantasies of a glorious present and a future of good living, John Reith calculated, this discourse would sponsor an intersubjective understanding in a political community currently plagued by juvenile class conflict.

In "The Curves of the Needle" (1928) the influential German music critic and cultural theorist Theodor Adorno approved of the "positive tendency of consolidated technology to present objects themselves in as unadorned [realist] a fashion as possible." But this recommendation came with a warning, for this predisposition of technology was nevertheless "traversed by the ideological need of the ruling society, which demands a subjective reconciliation with these objects" via none other than the "reproduced voice": "The ambiguity of the results of forward-moving technology—which does not tolerate any restraint—confirms the ambiguity of the process of forward moving rationality as such."[71]

Reith fully grasped that the burgeoning culture of listening was changing the experience of learning quite independently of the home and school. This strengthened his resolve to replace the familial small talk at the fireplace with the radio's purposeful conversations and music:

> It is glorious to blaze a trail through virgin forests, overcoming the obstacles of Nature, combating disease, avoiding the dangers of marsh and flood, procuring food as may be possible, opening up and developing for commercial purposes that which was barren and desolate before. But it is more wonderful still when the opposition comes, not from the blind forces

Evolution of the house, from the fortified Norman castle to the twentieth-century le Corbusier villa

to make it look as if it were built differently from how it is. The house, of course, really does not look in the least like a timber-frame house. But supposing, as in the more expensive type of bogus Tudor, it really is a timber-frame construction and the beams really are supporting the house, so that it is an honest construction, does that make it an honest house? I doubt it. Because the interior is not planned as a Tudor house, nor is it occupied by Tudor people. Besides, it is a very extravagant way of building and all that extra money is being spent to escape from our own age. I believe we shall never really get an honest and efficient and beautiful modern style until we have thoroughly got rid of this unhealthy craving for the past.

But what methods of construction, broadly, have we today? I would say four that are at all common: all brick, or all concrete, and a steel or concrete frame (rather like the old timber frame) with brick filling. Steel frame is not practicable for the ordinary small house and we need not consider it here. Now each of the three methods left has a different character. To take one example, in an all-brick house the walls have to carry their own weight and support the upper floors and the roof, so it is obvious that there are strict limits to the amount of opening you can have for doors and windows ('voids' is the architectural term), but in a concrete-frame house the walls need only be screens to keep the elements out. They can hang from the ceiling if you like. They can be all glass if you like. The house can be supported on posts at certain points only. You can do almost anything about the proportion of void to solid. For instance, le Corbusier designed a house which is entirely supported on

Figure 5.16
Anthony Bertram, illustration showing the evolution of the house starting with the fortified Norman castle and culminating in Le Corbusier's Villa Stein, in "What Is a House?," *Listener*, October 1937. © Immediate Media Company London Limited.

of Nature, but from the indifference or ignorance or hostility of man; when the roads to be laid are not merely passages of transport wagons or railways, but for influences and developments which shall be permanent and good and widespread, in the sphere of the things to remain.[72]

Public discussions listened to at home would remove the British public's myopic outlook born of limited exposure to art and culture and prepare everyone across classes for decorous participation in political and cultural life.[73] Implicit in Reith's language is the belief that this participation and opening up of the mind must be a colonizing endeavor. To keep democracy from becoming a mob rule, to make it a civilizing and enlightening force, the forces of virtue must colonize public decision making and everyday life.

This was a distasteful idea for Reith's Victorian forebears. If not in practice, they at least in theory had regarded the domestic realm as off-limits to public law and interference. But this twentieth-century son of theirs had found a magic box that had the power to touch the most intimate chords lying dormant in one's heart, surreptitiously and without arousing suspicion. The public faculty of audition, on his watch, was not going to preserve but would conquer and colonize the home's bookish isolation, if only to structure privacy afresh amid a crowd.

CONCLUSION:
NOTES ON METHOD AND
OTHER THINGS

Broadcast buildings are pure simulacra. They drift through the nonspace of wireless transmission and give architecture a taste for flight. They relieve the object from its relationship to a unique place and a specific function and usher it into the system of free-floating signs. Architecture is freed from the conventional idea of site and gravity, and enabled to take on new roles and forge relations with mass consumption. Readings, scripted conversations, and Betjeman's poems dismiss the lowly controls of working drawings and study models. It is not wind and sun movement but the movement of voice that creates pictures. Telling silences and catchy anecdotes adjust the listener's eye to the vicarious images dancing in front of her.

Radiophonic constructions make the distinction between the referent and the reference meaningless. They embolden orators to make impossible architectural propositions, imagine audacious possibilities for the city, and evoke untested scientific reasoning. Satire, suspense, and commentary throw caution to the wind and flirt with the boundary between wish and fact. Children's stories give fantastic descriptions of buildings. Fictional travelogues make brilliant aesthetic assertions. Mock debates make excellent propositions. These historic and futuristic statements can also be enjoyed as teenage romance and science fiction for their fusion of the wishful, the imaginary, and the plausible. Listening to

G. M. Boumphrey, John Betjeman, and John Summerson is like listening to dramatists, poets, and storytellers who twist and turn ideas in thrilling sequence. They deliberately and effectively blur the line between the real and the made-up: tangents multiply, anecdotes accumulate, and by the end all threads come together to reinforce a single fiction.

Yet their ideas are not presented as word play but delivered as common sense. The BBC's reputation for objectivity and public service veils the independence of the reference from the referent and encourages the narrators to see themselves not as fiction writers but as social scientists and public experts. Orators earnestly believe that their positions are born of scientific and historic facts rather than the demands and politics of broadcasting. Radio's confluence of rationalism and organism, mechanization and psychology, magic and science, mystery and clarity ensures that narrator and narration are judged on the terms proposed by orators.

It is little surprise that their stories are awash with manifestos, cautionary tales, and wisdom from near and afar. Some of them weave fictions about happy futures, others about health and comfort, and still others about the sack of architectural motifs left to us by history. Yet the goal of all the stories ultimately remains to answer the same questions: What should architecture be? How can we distinguish architects from nonarchitects and culture from nonculture? What ought to be the criteria for judging works? The parable is the same—what must architects do and not do?

These simulations are not a marginal form of architectural construction. They yielded enormous influence on the material production of new towns, twentieth-century picturesque planning, postwar preservation, and welfare housing. The radiophonic call for architecture as a mass-produced, mass-consumed, all-encompassing, everyday, and authorless commodity was a precursor of the experimental efforts of English architects of the cold war era. The aestheticization of politics by Hitler and politicization of aesthetics by Stalin and Mussolini discredited concepts of ideal beauty and truth. In their place, characteristics like ephemerality, flight, and inherent obsolescence stepped in. Those who grew up during evacuations and woke up daily to news of anticolonial movements and the crown's brutality also woke up to the exploitative role of architecture, not only in totalitarian regimes, but also in liberal democracies and colonies. The political and economic experiments of the first half of the twentieth century emphasized the vulnerability of culture to other forms of power. If British artists and intellectuals between 1927 and 1945 had called upon art to spiritualize mass commodities, the cold war generation of the Independent Group and later that of Cedric Price and Archigram reached out to disposable commodities to relieve architecture from its material and artistic burden. Hardbound collectible treatises gave way to the ephemerality of pamphlets. Total design submitted to throwaway equipment. The stillness of monuments relented to movable planes and dynamic force fields, and the misplaced pomposity of old values was replaced with a knowing hedonism.

In 1936, the renowned perceptual psychologist Rudolf Arnheim described radio as a magical medium that would endow radio's simulations with redemptive force. Radio, Arnheim gathered, would emancipate humanity from the tyranny of vision and mimetic thought, and return our primordial instincts to us. With "the new aural education by wireless," we would not only "get a feeling for the musical in natural sounds" but also "feel ourselves back in that primeval age where the word was still sound, the sound still void."[1] This cheerful assessment of modern technology was translated from German into English by Margaret Ludwig and the art critic Herbert Read, a weekly columnist for the *Listener*. The BBC, motivated by the same optimism, sponsored the book.

Historians of signs, who have inherited the Holocaust and other catastrophes as legacies of electronically connected humanity, cannot be as celebratory. Those of us schooled by the master thinker Jean Baudrillard would say that Arnheim would not have been so sanguine had he considered the relationship of radiophonic signs to reality as an unfolding of the history of capitalist consumption. Grasping society merely from the outside as an already configured spectacle where human beings just slip into roles with preestablished destinies, they would see the oral travelogues and advice on good design by Frank Pick, John Gloag, G. M. Boumphrey, and John Summerson, among others, only as a mechanical working out of the independent logic of virtual products, quite apart from the constraints of architecture's materiality. Wireless sites would simply indicate the independence of architectural thought and material objects, relieving them of the duty of representing the constraints of materiality, social position, local knowledge, and organic needs. As pure simulacra, scholars would pronounce, they are dead signs—arbitrary, meaningless, and interchangeable. Baudrillard arrives at the opposite conclusion to Arnheim; far from injecting reason into politics and culture, electronic media has foreclosed the very possibility of culture and politics. Baudrillard writes,

"The medium is the message" signifies not only the end of the message, but also the end of the medium. There are no longer media in the literal sense of the term (I am talking above all about the electronic mass media)—that is to say, a power mediating between one reality and another, between one state of the real and another—neither in content nor in form. ... This critical—but original—situation ... is the only one we are left with. It is useless to dream of a revolution through content or through form, since the medium and the real are now in a single nebulous state whose truth is undecipherable.[2]

Despite all the overlaps between my study of wireless sites and Baudrillard's theory of simulacra, I do not follow his conclusion. My book shows that radiophonic constructions improved the authority of a marginal intervention into culture like architecture, especially in comparison to other mediums of cultural production (art, music, philosophy). This was something that architecture's physical existence and the "reality" of architectural practice at the moment did not possess. But to conclude that we have reached the end of meaning and the end of human intervention leads us to a kind of nihilism all too familiar in the "radical chic" schools of architecture today while leaving intact the power of electronically diffused signs.

Simulacra are not just imposed upon us by an omnipresent and invasive media with a power of its own; they are socially and historically bound inventions. They both shape and are shaped by the habitus of participants and the competition over definitions—in this case, over the definition of the architect and architecture, over the definition of the profession of broadcast journalism, and so on. Their fate is bound to what listeners make of them and how they use them (I, for example, use them differently than a couple listening to Elizabeth Denby for ideas to redo their kitchen). And finally, they are at the mercy of the tools with which the person listening to them decodes what is being said.

Media historians and theorists cannot make the Baudrillardian assumption that cultures of scarcity restricted signs and symbols to an idyllic state of symbolic exchange or the faithful recording of an inalienable reality. For this idea is as hopelessly romantic as the belief that signs and symbols in precapitalist societies stood for a pregiven organic identity of people and mirrored their preexisting social place after the fact. Whether capitalist or agrarian, representation has never been separable from what people regard as reality. Not only are the two intimately bound up with one another, but actually, reality is nothing but a representation.

What that representation may be has been challenged by people throughout history. Reality varies with the viewpoint from which socially and historically situated agents make meaning of the world. It is ironic that this point is exposed nowhere as vividly as in a contested cultural terrain like architecture, whose objects are unrecognizable without the institutional authority to affirm the singularity of its artistic condition.

It is also naïve and erroneous to think that objects in a culture of abundance relinquish symbolic exchange to the abstraction of economic and sign exchange. My analysis of architecture's involvement with radio insists that cultural activity not only perseveres in the age of its mass reproduction but has also flourished in its incredible ability to mutate with new circumstances. Far from leaving us with images devoid of symbolic properties, radio did not merely represent architects as artists and buildings as works but contributed to their objective existence as such.

Radio broadcasts turned new classes of people into consumers of culture and heightened the power of architects and critics to translate external determinations into conformity with their own social practices. We find a correlation between radio's contribution to the development of the art market and the power of architects and critics to affirm the irreducibility of the work of art to the status of a simple article of merchandise. It is not insignificant that the omnipresence of mass media coincides with the professionalization of architectural production and the emergence of a new class of architects and critics: professionals who are less inclined to recognize rules other than the specifically intellectual or artistic traditions handed down by their predecessors that serve as a point of departure or rupture. And it is precisely this that constitutes an objectively autonomous field of cultural production!

This "blossoming" of architectural enterprise over the course of the twentieth century has found expression in calls for critical practice and illuminating theory. It has also created a fatalistic and paralyzing criticality on the one hand and a cynical indulgence on the other. However, none of these developments have prevented architecture from playing a key role in yielding symbolic violence and perpetuating relations of domination, nor have they made it resilient to the reifying effects of modern and postmodern media. No mode of design activity—withdrawn or engaged, critical or receptive—has been immune to cooption. Architecture, by the very nature of its object and the location of its practitioners in the hierarchy of power dynamics, will remain an eminently political activity and arena of political thought. It will never fulfill the dream of those who strive for neutral, detached, apolitical objects. It will never reach, as Gaston Bachelard saw well, the "uncontroversial" status of the natural sciences. Yet architecture is still capable of becoming a shield against the forms of mystification and symbolic domination perpetuated by those who sat in front of the BBC microphone.

Needless to say, this optimistic claim runs counter not just to Baudrillard but also to the Marxist principle that dismisses culture as superstructure, ideology, and false consciousness. My approach to media studies takes culture as an active ingredient in social relations of production, equal to social factors such as wealth and profession. I also depart from those media historians who place the burden of receptivity squarely on media instead of on media's dialectical relationship with the "interests" and "competence" that different segments of the population bring to media and their products, which are necessary for their inescapable influence.

We can prevent the business of architecture from becoming either an instrument of consumption that naturalizes class distinctions or an accomplice to tourist distractions prone to obfuscate the recognition of our complicity in the repressive mechanisms of the culture industry. But we cannot do this by privileging this or that critical strategy for design, for at least two reasons. The first reason is that this solution puts undue faith in the will of the all-knowing hero-architect to overcome the structural adversity of submitting his works to the overarching logic of mass consumption. It revives all the myths of the architect as a unique individual standing outside of history, pushing it forward into an ever-refined state of consciousness. Second, the efficacy of a work of art does not lie in the work itself but in the microcosm within which architects, critics, and historians struggle, in the name of truth and in the progressive institutionalization of works' discourse. It is this truism that makes us keep one eye on cultural institutions and one on their products.

We must work concretely to secure and safeguard the social and institutional conditions under which the moral agency of critical work is possible and can take effect. This requires the deconstruction of the mechanisms and representations by which architecture has now become an instrument of the privileged and the powerful so as to be able, within limits, to transform its allegiances by transforming its representation. Disciplinary reflexivity, it cannot be stressed enough, is not a matter of the will of the artist or critic. Its origins do not lie in human "faculty" or nature. Nor is it the product of photography, television, or the Internet. If we shed these "naturalist" or "mediatic" assumptions, we will see that such reflexivity is a social invention, inseparable from the autonomization of architecture. If we accept disciplinary autonomy, not merely as an illusion or farce but as a social and historical invention that is vital for critical activity, we must be prepared to recognize that this puts us in the company of the disciplinary activists studied in this book. We would take this step without compelling our moral agency to be as bound to our cultural, educational, or economic class as it was in the case of our predecessors—not because we are superior human beings, but because we exist in a state of the discipline that benefits from a number of mechanisms for reflexivity that our disciplinary grandparents did not have. "Freedom," Löic Wacquant reminds us, "is not a given but a conquest, and a collective one."[3]

NOTES

Introduction

1. K. Michael Hays, *Architecture's Desire: Reading the Late Avant-Garde* (Cambridge, Mass.: MIT Press, 2010), 7.

2. Victor Hugo, "This Will Kill That," in *The Hunchback of Notre Dame* (Philadelphia: Carey, Lea and Blanchard, 1834); also see Neil Levine, "The Book and the Building: Hugo's Theory of Architecture and Labrouste's Bibliothèque Ste-Geneviève," in Robin Middleton, ed., *The Beaux Arts and Nineteenth-Century French Architecture* (Cambridge, Mass.: MIT Press, 1982).

3. We don't know the exact number of these programs, as they are archived under different categories. The figure of six hundred comes from pulling together information from transcripts, *Radio Times*, the *Listener*, BBC books and pamphlets, and written correspondence between BBC executives and broadcasters.

4. The wartime debates on urbanism and reconstruction were as commonly played out in the BBC's weekly *Listener* as in the *Architectural Review*. See, for example, Jeremy Melvin, "Publishing Architecture in the 1930s: The Architectural Press and the Modern House," in *F. R. S. Yorke and the Evolution of English Modernism* (Chichester: Wiley-Academy, 2003), 31; Jules Lubbock, *The Tyranny of Taste* (New Haven: Yale University Press, 1995); Alan Powers, "Search for a New Reality," *Twentieth Century Society* (1984): 18–39; James M. Richards, "Radio Station: A New Building Typology," *Architectural Review* (March 1931).

5. The best-known of these texts include Herbert Read, *The Meaning of Art* (London: Faber & Faber, 1931) and John Summerson, *The Classical Language of Architecture* (Cambridge, Mass.: MIT Press, 1963). Both were commissioned by the BBC. Stephen Games, *Pevsner on Art and Architecture: The Radio Talks* (London: Methuen, 2002), reminds us that many of Pevsner's canonical texts, like *The Englishness of English Art* (London: Architectural Press, 1956), began as lectures on radio. While these texts are more widely known, specialists on Britain have long known about the collaboration between architects and the BBC. There are a number of obituaries of architects and critics written by the BBC personnel and vice versa.

6. On the role of modern media in the history of architecture, see seminal works including Hélène Lipstadt, "The Building and the Book in César Daly's *Revue Générale de l'Architecture*," in Beatriz Colomina and Joan Ockman, eds., *Architectureproduction* (New York: Princeton Architectural Press, 1988); the Princeton Ph.D. architectural students' traveling exhibition, "The Radical Architecture of Little Magazines: Periodicals as Sites of Innovation" (2007–2009), http://soa.princeton.edu/content/clipstampfold-radical-architecture-little-magazines-196x-197x (accessed 24 June 2013); and Tim Benton, "Dreams of Machines: Futurism and l'Esprit Nouveau," *Journal of Design History* 3 (1990): 19–34.

7. Raymond Williams, *Culture and Society* (Harmondsworth: Pelican, 1963), 325, 329.

8. John Reith, *Broadcast over Britain* (London: Hodder & Stoughton, 1924), 173–177.

9. Reith, quoted in Paddy Scannell and David Cardiff, *A Social History of British Broadcasting: Serving the Nation 1922–1939* (Oxford: Blackwell, 1991), 7.

10. Susan Pedersen and Peter Mandler, introduction to Pedersen and Mandler, eds., *After the Victorians: Private Conscience and Public Duty in Modern Britain* (London: Routledge, 1994).

11. Reith, *Broadcast over Britain*, 16.

12. See Stefan Collini, *Public Moralists: Political Thought and Intellectual Life in Britain, 1850–1930* (New York: Oxford University Press, 1991), 121–169.

13. Peter Stansky, *Gladstone: A Progress in Politics* (Boston: Little, Brown, 1979), 3–26.

14. John Stuart Mill, *Considerations on Representative Government* (London: Parker, Son, and Bourn, 1861), 115–164.

15. John Stuart Mill, "Inaugural Address Delivered to the University of St. Andrews" (1867), quoted in Collini, *Public Moralists*, 71.

16. Norman Luker, departmental memorandum on Talks Standards addressed to Sir Richard Maconachie, 25 November 1938, BBC Written Archives Centre, Caversham Park, Reading (subsequently cited as WAC), R51/397. He described these groups as Groups A, B, and C, respectively.

17. From 1929 to 1940, the weekly program output on National Service, transmitted from London, grew from 89.5 hours to an average of 121.33 hours. This figure does not include the production of several new regional services and the Forces Service established between 1927 and 1945. In 1927, the Corporation was launched with 773 people. By the end of World War II, it employed nearly 10,000 people. There were 2,178,259 wireless license holders on the eve of its establishment. By 1

September 1939, these had increased to 9,082,666. For a bird's-eye view of the speed of the BBC's growth, see Asa Briggs, *The BBC: The First Fifty Years* (Oxford: Oxford University Press, 1985); Briggs, *Governing the BBC* (London: British Broadcasting Corporation, 1979); Briggs, *The History of Broadcasting in the United Kingdom* (London: Oxford University Press, 1961–1995), vols. 1 and 2; and Jennifer Doctor, *The BBC and Ultra-Modern Music, 1922–1936: Shaping a Nation's Tastes* (Cambridge: Cambridge University Press, 1999), 13–21. For a revealing picture of the impact of the Corporation's monopoly on freelance broadcasting societies and the geography of distribution of the reception service in Britain, see Mark Pegg, *Broadcasting and Society, 1918–1939* (London: Croom Helm, 1983).

18. The BBC's pedagogic ambitions were unchallenged in the domestic market, but they were given a good run for their money by the continental stations of Radio Luxembourg and Radio Normandy. These channels influenced the presentation and content of the BBC's educational programming, as chronicled by Daniel LeMahieu, *A Culture for Democracy* (Oxford: Oxford University Press, 1988).

19. Richard Stanton Lambert, *Ariel and All His Quality: An Impression of the BBC from Within* (London: V. Gollancz, 1940), 25.

20. Fred Hunter, "Matheson, Hilda (1888–1940): Intelligence Officer and Director of Radio Talks," *Oxford Dictionary of National Biography Online*, http://www.oxforddnb.com/view/article/49198 (accessed 20 August 2009); also see Fred Hunter, "Hilda Matheson and the BBC, 1926–40," in Sybil Oldfield, ed., *This Working-day World: Women's Lives and Culture(s) in Britain, 1914–1945* (London: Taylor & Francis, 1994), 169–174.

21. Richard J. Meyer, "Charles A. Siepmann and Educational Broadcasting," *Educational Technology Research and Development* 12:4 (Winter 1964): 413.

22. Allan Jones, "Mary Adams and the Producer's Role in Early BBC Science Broadcasts," *Public Understanding of Science* 21:8 (November 2012).

23. Lambert, *Ariel and All His Quality*, 9–41.

24. For short professional profiles of the BBC's most powerful staff members who shaped its program policy, see the rich index in Doctor, *The BBC and Ultra-Modern Music*. Though Doctor is most interested in the figures influencing music policy, she covers most of the towering figures in the pioneering generation of the Corporation.

25. On Reith's desire to distinguish the BBC from existing models of broadcasting in the United States and Europe, see Briggs, *The BBC: The First Fifty Years*, and John Reith, *The Reith Diaries* (London: Collins, 1975).

26. On the corporation's financial arrangements and Board of Governors, see Briggs, *Governing the BBC*.

27. Hilda Matheson, *Broadcasting* (London: Thornton Butterworth, 1933), 206.

28. J. C. Stobart to Reith, memorandum entitled "Wireless University," 8 October 1926, p. 2, Education—Adult Education, Papers and Reports 1924–1934, R14/145/1, File 1a, BBC WAC.

29. Ibid.

30. For contemporary views on the relationship between art and competing models of governance in the interwar years, see J. M. Keynes (Introduction), N. Milyutin (Russia), G. Duthuit (France), R. Hinkel (Germany), L. Mumford (America), F. T. Marinetti (Italy), and Clive Bell (Conclusion), "Art and the State," *Listener* 7:398–406 (1936).

31. Letter from Mr. Gill to H. S. Goodhart-Rendel, 15 October 1938, Goodhart-Rendel Papers, General Correspondence British Broadcasting Corporation, Various Departments, Letters of Congratulation 1937–56 (2), G-ReH/15/2, Royal Institute of British Architects (RIBA) Collections, London.

32. Stobart to Reith, "Wireless University."

33. For the zealous ideals of BBC personnel and associates on the use of broadcasting to create a cultured and enlightened polity, see D. G. Bridson, *Prospero and Ariel: The Rise and Fall of Radio* (London: Gollancz, 1972); Matheson, *Broadcasting*; Roger Huxley Eckersley, *B.B.C. and All That: Autobiographical Reminiscences* (London: Sampson Low, Marston, 1946); Hilda Jennings and Winifred Gill, *Broadcasting in Everyday Life* (London: BBC, 1939); Lambert, *Ariel and All His Quality*; and Reith, *Broadcast over Britain* and *Into the Wind* (London: Hodder & Stoughton, 1949). Charles A. Siepmann wrote several articles on this topic, as well: "Wireless and Adult Education in Great Britain," *Journal of the American Association of University Women* 22 (January 1929): 57–60; "The Mechanization of Education," *Spectator* 147 (28 November 1931): 728–729; "Can Radio Educate?," *Education by Radio* 11 (First Quarter 1941): 25–26; and "Can Radio Educate?," *Journal of Educational Sociology* 14 (February 1941): 346–357. These records show the BBC's attempts to make public education, the market economy, and the ideal of a good society all mutually supportive.

34. Martin J. Daunton, "Housing," in F. M. L. Thompson, ed., *The Cambridge Social History of Britain, 1750–1950* (Cambridge: Cambridge University Press, 1990), 204.

35. Madge Dresser, "Housing Policy in Bristol, 1919–30," in Martin J. Daunton, ed., *Councillors and Tenants: Local Authority Housing in English Cities, 1919–1939* (Leicester: Leicester University Press, 1984); Andrzej Olechnowicz, *Working-Class Housing in England between the Wars: The Becontree Estate* (New York: Oxford University Press, 1997); David Matless, *Landscape and Englishness* (London: Reaktion Books, 1998).

36. Pedersen and Mandler, *After the Victorians*.

37. Lambert writes: "From that time onwards, a steadily growing wave of attacks upon the BBC for the 'redness' or the 'pinkness' of broadcast talks rose up in the Press, and extended to Parliament. ... Again and again the most trivial errors were magnified into examples of 'left-wing bias'" (*Ariel and All His Quality*, 76). Also see Reith, *Broadcast over Britain*, on complaints (littered throughout the book) of bias in cultural programming.

38. See Ross McKibbin, "Why Was There No Marxism in Great Britain?," *English Historical Review* 99 (1984): 297–331. In this most influential essay, McKibbin argues that even the Labour Party was not a socialist party.

39. On the attitude of liberal intellectuals toward working-class culture, see Peter Stansky, *On or about December 1910: Early Bloomsbury and Its Intimate World* (Cambridge, Mass.: Harvard University Press, 1996).

40. Scannell and Cardiff, *A Social History of British Broadcasting*, 3–22.

41. Ibid., 290–291.

42. "The Ullswater Report," quoted in Lord Simon of Wythenshawe, *The BBC from Within* (London: Victor Gollancz, 1953), 30–31.

43. According to Scannell and Cardiff, "The Talks Department was always more at home with public figures and men of letters. It was less successful than other departments in bringing the ordinary men and women to the microphone, though not for want of trying" (*A Social History of British Broadcasting*, 171). Also see Ross McKibbin, *Classes and Cultures: England 1918–1951* (Oxford: Oxford University Press, 1998), 460.

44. Walter J. Ong, *Orality and Literacy: The Technologizing of the Word* (London: Routledge, 1982). Ong's theories are now thirty years old but still far from outdated.

45. G. K. Chesterton, "Review of Architectural Books," 9 January 1933 (BBC recording reference: 194); Sir Giles Gilbert Scott, "Speech at the Banquet of the Royal Institute of British Architects," 22 November 1934 (BBC recording reference: 35); Sir Reginald Blomfield and Amyas Connell, "New Homes for Old" (BBC recording reference: 35); John Gloag, Sinclair Wood, and James Whittaker, "Permanence in Building," in *Men Talking*, no. 5 in series, 4 February 1937 (BBC recording reference: 14212); Rt. Hon Herbert Morrison, "A Green Belt round London" in *Topical Talk*, 22 January 1935 (BBC recording reference: 60).

46. Allen S. Weiss, "Radio Icons, Short Circuits, Deep Schisms," in Weiss, ed., *Experimental Sound and Radio* (Cambridge, Mass.: MIT Press, 2001), 3.

47. Samuel Weber, "On Television," in Weber, *Mass Mediauras: Form, Technics, Media*, ed. Alan Cholodenko (Stanford: Stanford University Press, 1996), 115.

48. Ibid., 117.

49. Allen S. Weiss, *Phantasmic Radio* (Durham: Duke University Press, 1995), 7.

50. Its floor plans and facade treatment were the work of the architect, painter, and sculptor Col. George Val Myer. Myer had received the commission on the strength of his current multistory office projects in London. When the facility opened in 1932, it was widely acclaimed as a fiat of functionalism. Robert Byron saw the building's aesthetic modernity as the result of a conflict between moribund traditionalism and inventive modernism that was won by the latter. Robert Byron, "Broadcasting House," *Architectural Review* (August 1932): 47.

51. Most of the offices, studios, meeting rooms, and circulation and waiting areas were detailed and furnished by a group of younger architects under the supervision of the Austrian architect Raymond McGrath. McGrath was an active member of the Cambridge-based intellectuals and artists called the Twentieth Century Group. He brought to the commission two of its other members, the Canadian Wells Coates and Russian Serge Chermayeff. They were three of the most vocal modernists based in Britain, experienced in industrial production, radio set design, knowledge of the latest materials, expressive use of color and pattern, and efficient planning. Edward Maufe and Dorothy Trotter, who brought yet other design ideas to the interior, accompanied them. The *Architectural Review* issue published in August 1932 provides us with the most detailed documentation of Broadcasting House when it was first built.

52. Howard Robertson, "In and Out of Broadcasting House—II. The Structure of the Building," *Listener* 8:184 (20 July 1932): 86.

53. Ibid.

54. Wells Coates, "The Studio Interiors," *Architectural Review* (August 1932): 60.

55. For more information on Coates's approach to modern architecture, see Sherban Cantacuzino, *Wells Coates: A Monograph* (London: G. Fraser, 1978); and Laura Cohn, *The Door to a Secret Room: A Portrait of Wells Coates* (Brookfield: Ashgate, 1999).

56. "The enlightenment which the BBC employs in its programmes, it has also employed in its buildings." "The New Tower of London," *Architectural Review* (August 1932): 43.

57. This area had been laid out and developed by John Nash for the Prince Regent in the nineteenth century.

58. For the best discussion of the "phantasmagoric" attributes of the medium, see Weiss, *Phantasmic Radio*, and his chapters in *Experimental Sound and Radio*.

59. Charles Reilly, "In and Out of Broadcasting House—I. The Architecture of the Building," *Listener* 8:183 (13 July 1932): 54. To another observer it looked like a "naval aircraft carrier": "The new building parts the road like a battleship floating towards the observer" ("The New Tower of London," 46).

60. The exterior announced its function through the academically sanctioned device of reliefs and sculptures. The south side swept in a bold curve like an overblown corner that was heavily modeled with a coat of arms. Val Myer carved the balcony frieze with static stone reliefs, while Eric Gill punctuated the entrance on the south with a sturdy primitivist bronze group. Gill's other sculpture, in the niche above the entrance door, portrayed Ariel hearing celestial music. It was accompanied by a nearby freestanding sculpture of Ariel and Prospero.

61. Val Myer subordinated the structural grid to the jigsaw-puzzle organization of the program and the imposed regularity of the outer surface. As a contemporary observer put it, Broadcasting House stood as "a rival and a more prepossessing monster to Langham Hotel." But it was a conciliatory rival. Its window type, for example, preferred affinity with the Langham and other surrounding buildings, to fidelity to structural logic. Also see Robert Byron, "Broadcasting House," *Architectural Review* (August 1932): 47.

62. During a visit to New York City, the architect had been much impressed by the variety in its skyscrapers. However, unlike their verticality, his eight-story massing had a decidedly horizontal thrust.

63. Marshall McLuhan, "Radio: The Tribal Drum," in *Understanding Media: The Extensions of Man* (1964; repr., Cambridge, Mass.: MIT Press, 1991), 297–307.

64. For a good discussion of how these institutions proliferated after the enabling legislation of the mid-nineteenth century and turned into training grounds for the development of imagination, feeling, and a fixed moral order, see Kate Hill, *Culture and Class in English Public Museums, 1850–1914* (Aldershot, England; Burlington, Vt.: Ashgate, 2005); Mark Swenarton, *Artisans and Architects: The Ruskinian Tradition in Architectural Thought* (New York: St. Martin's Press, 1988).

1 Figure of Speech: The Place of Radio in the Space of Architecture

1. H. S. Goodhart-Rendel, "Architecture in a Changing World," *Listener* 20:509 (13 October 1938): 759–760, broadcast lecture, 4 October 1938, transcript BBC WAC, and H. S. Goodhart-Rendel Papers, Lectures on Art and Architecture to Various Societies 1906–1959, G-ReH/33/2/17, RIBA Collections, London.

2. For the history of architects concerned about the role of language in architecture, see Adrian Forty, *Words and Buildings: A Vocabulary of Modern Architecture* (New York: Thames & Hudson, 2000), 10–117.

3. Sir Edwin Landseer Lutyens, quoted in Andrew Saint, *The Image of the Architect* (New Haven: Yale University Press, 1983), 107–108.

4. The invitation to the representative of RIBA architects to speak to the nation on the occasion of the Registration Bill was one of the most visible marks of the improving position of the profession.

5. See Samuel Weber, "Mass Mediauras; or Art, Aura and Media in the Work of Walter Benjamin," in Weber, *Mass Mediauras: Form, Technics, Media*, ed. Alan Cholodenko (Stanford: Stanford University Press, 1996), 76–107.

6. John Evelyn, introduction to *A Parallel of the Ancient Architecture with the Modern ... To Which Is Added an Account of Architects and Architecture by John Evelyn Esq.*, by Freart de Chambray R., trans. J. Evelyn (London, 1664), in Forty, *Words and Buildings*, 11.

7. Ibid.

8. John Lanshaw Austin, *How to Do Things with Words* (Cambridge, Mass.: Harvard University Press, 1962). The book is the posthumous collection of Austin's lectures given at Oxford University in 1946.

9. Roger Hinks, "Can Art Be Subversive?," *Listener* 17:424 (24 February 1937): 339.

10. Paddy Scannell and David Cardiff, *A Social History of British Broadcasting: Serving the Nation 1922–1939* (Oxford: Blackwell, 1991), 151.

11. Maxwell Fry, correspondence with Assistant Director of the Talks Department in 1932, Maxwell Fry, Personal File 1931–1940, P.E.1, BBC WAC.

12. Letter from H. S. Goodhart-Rendel to Captain R. Parker, 17 October 1938, Goodhart-Rendel Papers, General Correspondence British Broadcasting Corporation, Various Departments, Letters of Congratulation 1937–56 (2), G-ReH/15/2, RIBA Collections, London.

13. Letter from Mr. Gill to H. S. Goodhart-Rendel, 15 October 1938, Goodhart-Rendel Papers, General Correspondence British Broadcasting Corporation, Various Departments, Letters of Congratulation 1937–56 (2), G-ReH/15/2, RIBA Collections, London.

14. The most detailed account of this debate can be found spread through the years in *RIBA Journal*. Norman Shaw, ed., *Architecture: A Profession or an Art; Thirteen Short Essays on the Qualifications and Training of Architects* (London: J. Murray, 1892), presents the position of architects at the turn of

the century who saw architecture as an art. Barrington Kaye, *The Development of the Architectural Profession in Britain: A Sociological Study* (London: George Allen & Unwin, 1960), does a good job of organizing the RIBA archive on this issue and supplementing it with the legislative and key demands. Mark Crinson and Jules Lubbock, *Architecture—Art or Profession? Three Hundred Years of Architectural Education in Britain* (Manchester: Manchester University Press, 1994), 38–114, describes the form the debate took from 1834 to 1938. They sketch the competing conceptions of architectural education, especially those held by the arts and crafts architects, who, loyal to the guild structure, insisted on pupilage and neoclassicists at the RIBA. Impressed by the French Beaux-Arts academic model, the RIBA sought to institute a more public and closely regulated system.

15. Kaye, *The Development of the Architectural Profession in Britain*, does a good job of organizing the RIBA archive on this issue and supplementing it with legislative and other key demands.

16. Goodhart-Rendel to Captain R. Parker, 17 October 1938.

17. H. S. Goodhart-Rendell in a letter to Mrs. Smith of Talks Department, 28 October 1939, General Correspondence, British Broadcasting Corporation, Various Departments, Letters of Congratulation 1937–56 (1) G-ReH/15/1, RIBA Collections.

18. By 1945 the GPO had issued 10.8 million radio licenses.

19. One can find maps of the geographical distribution of signal transmission polls and radio sets across United Kingdom in Mark Pegg, *Broadcasting and Society, 1918–1939* (London: Croom Helm, 1983). By 1935 the disparity of licenses across England, Wales, and Scotland had also been reduced.

20. Scannell and Cardiff, *A Social History of British Broadcasting*, 356–357.

21. For transmission hours and content, also see *Program Indexes* (London: British Broadcasting Corporation, 1927–1945). These increased from 40 hours to 121 hours a week in the 1930s.

22. Asa Briggs, *The Golden Age of Wireless* (London: Oxford University Press, 1965), vol. 2 of his *The History of Broadcasting in the United Kingdom*; and Jennifer Doctor, *The BBC and Ultra-Modern Music, 1922–1936: Shaping a Nation's Tastes* (Cambridge: Cambridge University Press, 1999), 13–21.

23. Asa Briggs, *The BBC: The First Fifty Years* (Oxford: Oxford University Press, 1985), and Briggs, *The Golden Age of Wireless*, offer rich information on the beginnings of broadcast television in the 1930s.

24. Ross McKibbin, "Listening In," in *Classes and Cultures: England 1918–1951* (Oxford: Oxford University Press, 1998), 457.

25. Edmund and Ruth Frow, "The Spark of Independent Working-Class Education: Lancashire, 1909–1930," in Brian Simon, ed., *The Search for Enlightenment: The Working Class and Adult Education in the Twentieth Century* (London: Lawrence & Wishhart, 1990), traces the introduction of visual aids and lantern slides by professors from elite universities in WEA classes.

26. A question in a *Listener* editorial hints at the reason for this overlap: "Who it may be asked is to do the training? Those who have specialized in the subject and those who have made it their profession." Editorial, "The Shape of Things to Use," *Listener* 18:452 (8 September 1937): 490.

27. *Artists at Work* was a set of interviews of contemporary artists conducted by the renowned archaeologist and specialist on Greek and modern sculpture, Stanley Casson. As he wrote in the introduction to the book, Casson felt that broadcasting could solve a glaring deficiency in the scholarship on art. He wrote, "Of all the literature on art that contributed by artists is by far the smallest. For an artist seldom has either the time or inclination to write." As a result, "many artists have been 'written up' by admiring jackals. ... Their authentic views are obscured by the professional edition of their admirers." A radio interview, in the economy of a conversation, could elicit and record the "authentic views" of artists and correct the understanding of the problems in art as practitioners saw them. Stanley Casson, *Artists at Work: Based on a Series of Broadcast Dialogues between the Editor and Frank Dobson, Henry Rushbury, Albert Rutherston and Edward Halliday* (London: G. G. Harrap, 1933).

28. Daniel LeMahieu, *A Culture for Democracy* (Oxford: Oxford University Press, 1988), describes the BBC's rivalry with the more entertainment-oriented stations of Radio Luxembourg and Radio Normandie. These are the only exceptions to the rule.

29. Kate Whitehead, *The Third Programme: A Literary History* (Oxford: Clarendon Press 1989); Doctor, *The BBC and Ultra-Modern Music*; Jules Lubbock, *The Tyranny of Taste: The Politics of Architecture and Design in Britain, 1550–1960* (New Haven: Yale University Press, 1995), chapter 3 and 4.

30. Arts Council of Great Britain, *The Public and the Arts* (London: Arts Council of Great Britain, 1953), quoted in the editorial "Patronage and the Arts," *Listener* 50:1286 (22 October 1953): 674. The Arts Council newsletter noted, "As a diffuser of the arts the BBC is already an exemplary patron." For the BBC's commentary on the Arts Council's acknowledgment of the uniqueness of its patronage, see the *Listener's* editorial.

31. Lord Reith's long relationship with the RIBA and architecture is mentioned by Reith's biographers Peter Clarke and Ian McIntyre. Shortly after Churchill forced him to resign from the BBC in 1938, Reith was appointed the chair of the town planning commission, where he collected the brightest brains in the profession during and after the war. Peter Clarke, *Hope and Glory: Britain 1900–1990* (London: Penguin Press, 1996); Ian McIntyre, *The Expense of Glory: A Life of John Reith* (London: HarperCollins, 1993). The RIBA officially recognized his patronage by offering him an honorary membership in the institute in 1940.

32. "Appreciation of the Physical Environment" (London: CEAPE, 1942), Education: General: Council for Education in Appreciation of Physical Environment, 1942–1945, Rib/61, BBC WAC

33. "Patronage and the Arts," 674.

34. The particular grievances of the profession and their sense of frustration can be found most concretely in the minutes of professional meetings printed in the *RIBA Journal* for the years concerned.

35. John W. Simpson, "The Unification and Registration of the Architectural Profession," *Journal of the Royal Institute of British Architects* 28 (30 July 1921); Frank Jenkins, *Architect and Patron: A Survey of Professional Relations and Practice in England from the Sixteenth Century to the Present Day* (London: Oxford University Press, 1961), 228–246; Kaye, *The Development of the Architectural Profession in Britain*.

36. Goodhart-Rendel, "Architecture in a Changing World," 760.

37. Francis Skinner, memorandum for discussion at an ATO meeting on 11 February 1935 at Conway Hall, BAL Archive, Sir Ove Arup Papers, ArO/2/14/1, cited in Allan, *Berthold Lubetkin*, 324.

38. Edward Carter, "Politics and Architecture," a retrospective issue on the 1930s, *Architectural Review* (November 1979): 324.

39. John Summerson, quoted by John Gloag, "The Architect and the Future Public," *Journal of the Royal Institute of British Architects* 55 (September 1948): 509.

40. Despite fears, the electronic production of music did not close the music halls, but boosted their attendance. See claims in John Reith, *Broadcast over Britain* (London: Hodder & Stoughton, 1924), 101–107.

41. Briggs, *The Golden Age of Wireless*, 200–226.

42. Ibid.

43. Hinks, "Can Art Be Subversive?," 339. Also see the fray between Geoffrey Grigson and Stanley Casson, "Points from Letters: Oxford Architecture," *Listener* 16:401 (16 September 1936), *Listener* 16:403 (30 September 1936), and *Listener* 16:405 (14 October 1936); as well as the heated debate between John Summerson and Reginald Blomfield, "Points from Letter: British Architecture at the Royal Academy," *Listener* 17:420 (27 January 1937) and *Listener* 17:421 (3 February 1937). Richard Stanton Lambert, *Ariel and All His Quality: An Impression of the BBC from Within* (London: V. Gollancz, 1940), lays out the complaints of the Royal Academy and others against the BBC's modernist bias.

44. John Summerson, "Extracts from Sir John Summerson Royal Gold Medal Address," *Journal of the Royal Institute of British Architects* 83 (December 1976): 495.

45. Charles Reilly, "Propaganda and Publicity," *Journal of the Royal Institute of British Architects* (27 August 1921): 547.

46. Pierre Bourdieu, in Pierre Bourdieu and Loïc J. D. Wacquant, *An Invitation to Reflexive Sociology* (Chicago: University of Chicago, 1992), 148.

47. See Frank Salmon, ed., *Summerson and Hitchcock: Centenary Essays on Architectural Historiography* (New Haven: Yale University Press, 2006).

48. Francis Skinner, memorandum, cited in Allan, *Berthold Lubetkin*, 324.

49. J. E. Barton, *Purpose and Admiration: A Lay Study of the Visual Arts* (London: Christophers, 1932), 21–22.

50. Hélène Lipstadt, "The Experimental Tradition," in Lipstadt and Barry Bergdoll, eds., *The Experimental Tradition: Essays on Competitions in Architecture* (New York: Princeton Architectural Press, 1989), 16.

51. J. E. Barton, "Will the New City Make New Men?," *Listener* 7:167 (23 March 1932): 412–414; broadcast lecture, part VI of *Modern Art*, 22 March 1932.

52. John Summerson, "Creative Housing," *Listener* 18:447 (4 August 1937): 223.

53. In "Creative Housing," Summerson complained,

> The Minister of Health is, no doubt, justified in pointing with pride (as he constantly does) to the sum total of over three million dwellings which represents the nation's housing achievement in the post-War period. As an economic achievement it is certainly pretty formidable. It reflects a high level of prosperity. ... But once you look at this achievement as a concrete affair of structures and lay-outs the inglorious truth emerges that it has been possible to construct three million tolerably substantial dwellings and yet create absolutely nothing. Our towns remain much what they were, the only change being that their girth has bulged, or straggled into the country, as one estate after another has become ripe for profit-making. (Ibid.)

54. Robert Atkinson, "Design in Public Buildings," *Listener* 9:231 (14 June 1933): 928; broadcast lecture, part IX of *Design in Modern Life*, 13 June 1933, transcript BBC WAC; also published in John Gloag, ed., *Design in Modern Life* (London: G. Allen & Unwin, 1934), 83.

55. Clough Williams-Ellis, "Putting Architecture in Its Place," *Listener* 10:235 (12 July 1933): 71.

56. Frederic Towndrow, "The Revolution in Architecture," *Listener* 1:8 (6 March 1929): 281; broadcast talk, part II of *Adventures in Architecture*, 3 March 1929.

57. John Dower, "Architecture and Aerodromes," *Listener* 4:85 (27 August 1930): 322; and Sydney N. Bushell, "The Maidless House," *Listener* 2:36 (18 September 1929): 390.

58. Webb J. Laing and E. Thole, "The House that Jack Built," broadcast lecture, 27 April 1936, transcript BBC WAC.

59. Doreen Joad, "Garden Design," *Listener* 1:11 (27 March 1929): 403; broadcast lecture, 27 March 1929.

60. Geoffrey M. Boumphrey, "Damp in the House," part IV of *A Man about the House*, broadcast talk, 29 October 1932, transcript BBC WAC.

61. Anthony Bertram, from the series *Design in Everyday Things*, 1937, transcript BBC WAC; and Ivor Thomas, "Housing the Working Classes," *Listener* 15:370 (12 February 1936): 308, part III of *The Public Social Services*.

62. John Summerson, "An Archive for Architecture," broadcast talk, 25 September 1944, transcript BBC WAC; and John Summerson, "Reconstruction: Plymouth Rebuilding Plans," broadcast talk, 4 May 1944.

63. John Summerson, "An Archive for Architecture," broadcast talk, 25 September 1944, transcript BBC WAC.

64. Herbert Read, "How Shall We Rebuild?," *Listener* 24:615 (24 October 1940): 587.

65. David Matless, "Ordering the Land: The 'Preservation' of the English Countryside, 1918–1939" (Ph.D. diss., University of Nottingham, 1990), 25–61.

66. The phrase "form follows function" was first introduced by the American architect Louis Sullivan. In Britain it first joined the arts and crafts concept of purposeful design and then the modernist principles of unadorned, mass reproducible design.

67. Clough Williams-Ellis and Amabel Strachey, "Pleasures in Architecture," broadcast conversation, 6 January 1927, transcript BBC WAC, based on Clough Williams-Ellis and Amabel Strachey, *Pleasures of Architecture* (London: J. Cape, 1924).

68. Towndrow, "The Revolution in Architecture," 281.

69. Hon. Humphrey Pakington, "Tradition and Experiment," *Listener* 3:68 (30 April 1930): 768–769; broadcast talk, part I of *To-day and To-morrow in Architecture*, 29 April 1930, transcript BBC WAC.

70. Howard Robertson, "Structure and Material," *Listener* 3:69 (7 May 1930): 803–804; broadcast talk, part II of *To-day and To-morrow in Architecture*, 6 May 1930, transcript BBC WAC.

71. Maurice Webb, "The Future of the Skyscraper," *Listener* 3:71 (21 May 1930): 881; broadcast talk, part IV of *To-day and To-morrow in Architecture*, 20 May 1930, transcript BBC WAC.

72. Harold Tomlinson, "The New Spirit in Design," *Listener* 3:70 (14 May 1930): 840; broadcast talk, part III of *To-day and To-morrow in Architecture*, 13 May 1930, transcript BBC WAC.

73. Alan Powers, *Serge Chermayeff: Designer, Architect, Teacher* (London: RIBA Publications, 2001), 32.

74. R. A. Duncan, "The Architecture of the Future," *Listener* 3:73 (4 June 1930): 973; broadcast talk, part VI of *To-day and To-morrow in Architecture*, 3 June 1930, transcript BBC WAC.

75. Sir Reginald Blomfield and A. D. Connell, "For and Against Modern Architecture," *Listener* 12:307 (28 November 1934): 885.

76. A. E. Richardson, in Reginald Blomfield et al., "Is Modern Architecture on the Right Track?—A Symposium," *Listener* 10:237 (26 July 1933): 126.

77. M. H. Baillie Scott, in Blomfield et al., "Is Modern Architecture on the Right Track?," 127.

78. Maxwell Fry, in Blomfield et al., "Is Modern Architecture on the Right Track?," 129.

79. Wells Coates, in Blomfield et al., "Is Modern Architecture on the Right Track?," 132.

80. Fry, in Blomfield et al., "Is Modern Architecture on the Right Track?," 129.

81. Coates, in Blomfield et al., "Is Modern Architecture on the Right Track?," 132.

82. Sir Raymond Unwin, "Architecture Symposium—A Summing-Up," *Listener* 10:239 (9 August 1933): 213.

83. Sir James Maude Richards, "Architectural Criticism in the Nineteen-Thirties," in John Summerson, ed., *Concerning Architecture: Essays on Architectural Writers and Writing Presented to Nikolaus Pevsner* (London: Allen Lane, 1968), 252–257.

84. In 1944, when the BBC had begun to move from the collectivist vision of Reith to a more individualistic broadcasting approach, Sir Giles Gilbert Scott's presentation on his design for the Liverpool Cathedral was the only exception to this practice. Sir Giles Gilbert Scott, "Liverpool Cathedral," broadcast lecture, 16 July 1944, transcript, Scott Family Papers, ScGG/230/1, RIBA Collections, London.

85. Reilly, "Propaganda and Publicity," 547.

86. Ibid.

87. See the observations of Leonardo da Vinci on the preservative and ephemeral aspects of sight and sound respectively when he compares painting and music: "Painting is superior to music, it does not have to die as soon as it is born. ... Music which is consumed in the very act of its birth is inferior to painting which the use of varnish has rendered eternal." Leonardo da Vinci (*Trattato* I, 29), quoted in Walter Benjamin, "Art in the Age of Mechanical Reproduction," in Benjamin, *Illuminations*, ed. Hannah Arendt, trans. Harry Zohn (New York: Schocken Books, 1968), 249, n. 15.

88. See Roger Chartier, *The Order of Books: Readers, Authors and Libraries in Europe between the Fourteenth and Eighteenth Centuries* (Stanford: Stanford University Press, 1994), on the culture of reading among French peasants.

89. Walter J. Ong, introduction to his *Orality and Literacy: The Technologizing of the Word* (London: Routledge, 1982.

90. Elizabeth Eisenstein, *The Printing Press as an Agent of Change: Communications and Cultural Transformations in Early Modern Europe* (Cambridge: Cambridge University Press, 1979); Hadley Cantril and Gordon W. Allport, "The Mental Setting of Radio," in *Psychology of Radio* (New York: Harper & Brothers, 1935).

91. Ibid.

92. Ibid.

93. Howard Robertson, "Modern Architecture in Europe," *Listener* 3:72 (28 May 1930): 930; broadcast talk, part V of *Architecture To-day and Tomorrow*, 27 May 1930, transcript BBC WAC.

94. John Gloag, "Design in Everyday Life," broadcast talk, part V of *Art for Everyone*, 1944, transcript BBC WAC; based on Gloag's book *The House We Ought to Live In* (London: Duckworth, 1923).

95. Maxwell Fry and John Gloag, "The Design of Dwellings," broadcast interview, part IV of *Design in Modern Life*, 9 May 1933, transcript BBC WAC; also published in Gloag, *Design in Modern Life*, 35.

96. Elizabeth Denby and Geoffrey Boumphrey, "The Kitchen," *Listener* 9:227 (17 May 1933): 782; broadcast interview, part V of *Design in Modern Life*, 16 May 1933, transcript BBC WAC; also published as "Design in the Kitchen" in Gloag, *Design in Modern Life*, 97–108.

97. G. M. Boumphrey, "Your Dwelling House: How a House Is Built," in *The House—Inside and Out*, second impression (London: George Allen & Unwin, 1936), 49; broadcast interview of Maxwell Fry by Boumphrey, "An Architect's Advice on a House," part I of *Inside and Out*, 11 February 1935, transcript BBC WAC.

98. Ibid.

99. Geoffrey M. Boumphrey, "The Look of a House" in *The House—Inside and Out*, 22–23; broadcast conversation between G. M. Boumphrey and Maxwell Fry, "The Look of a House," part II of *Inside and Out*, 18 February 1935, transcript BBC WAC.

100. Robert Furneaux Jordan, "Building in Timber," *Listener* 16:395 (5 August 1936): 267–269; broadcast lecture, part II of *Design in Wood*. Jordan was the author of a well-known history of architecture following the model established by Banister Fletcher.

101. F. R. Yerbury, "Experiments in Housing: Some Suggestions from Sweden," *Listener* 32:817 (7 September 1944): 263; broadcast talk, "Housing and Social Conditions in Sweden," 22 August 1944, transcript BBC WAC, 2–3.

102. Ibid.

103. John Summerson, "Bombed Architecture in the West," broadcast talk, 6 April 1942, transcript BBC WAC.

104. H. S. Goodhart-Rendel, "Build or Restore," broadcast lecture, 26 January 1941, transcript BBC WAC, 4–5.

105. Ibid.

106. John Summerson, "John Wood, Architect and Planner of Bath," broadcast talk, part III of *Western Men*, 7 September 1945, transcript BBC WAC.

107. See Clough Williams-Ellis's book review of Fredric Towndrow, *Architecture in the Balance* (London: Chatto & Windus, 1933), in Williams-Ellis, "Putting Architecture in Its Place," 71.

108. E. H. Gombrich, "Art and Propaganda," *Listener* 22:569 (7 December 1939): 1118.

109. Ong, *Orality and Literacy*, 136.

110. Ibid.

2 The Order of Things: The Place of Architecture in the Space of Radio

1. Richard Lambert, "Are Talks Too Highbrow?," editorial, *Listener* 3:67 (23 April 1930): 116.

2. Arno Schirokauer, "Art and Politics in Radio," in Anton Kaes, Martin Jay, and Edward Dimendberg, eds., *The Weimar Republic Sourcebook* (Berkeley: University of California Press, 1994), 609.

3. Kurt Tucholsy, "Radio Censorship," in Kaes, Jay, and Dimendberg, *The Weimar Republic Sourcebook*, 603.

4. For Eric Gill's disapproval of the BBC's cultural and political ambitions, see the correspondence between Charles Siepmann and Stanley Casson, Stanley Casson, Personal File 1931–1940, P.E.1, BBC WAC.

5. Walter Benjamin, "Reflections of Radio," in *Walter Benjamin: Selected Writings*, vol. 2, ed. Michael Jennings and Marcus Bullock (Cambridge, Mass.: Harvard University Press, 1996), 543–544.

6. Frank Warschauer, "The Future of Opera on the Radio," in Kaes, Jay, and Dimendberg, *The Weimar Republic Sourcebook*, 607. In the same compilation, Bertolt Brecht, in "The Radio as an Apparatus of Communication," 597–599, perceived an automatic synergy between instruction via radio and the efforts of modern artists to give art an instructive character. Arno Schirokauer, in "Art and Politics in Radio," 609–610, anticipated that the public nature of radio art would necessarily assume a different character from the one art possessed when it was a predominantly private enterprise. In "The Writer Speaks and Sings on Gramophone Records," W. E. Williams anticipated that radio and gramophone would enrich sensory perception. Rudolf Arnheim, *Radio*, trans. Margaret Ludwig and Herbert Read (London: Faber and Faber, 1936), hoped that the mode of expression demanded by the microphone would personalize political expression and political debate. See also Bertolt Brecht, *Brecht on Film and Radio*, ed. and trans. Marc Silberman (London: Metheun, 2000).

7. Warschauer, "The Future of Opera on the Radio," 607.

8. The correspondence between the BBC staff and speakers reveal these to be the primary concerns of the staff. Charles Siepmann to Stanley Casson in 1931, Stanley Casson, Personal File 1931–1940, P.E.1, BBC WAC.

9. Doreen Joad, "Garden Design," *Listener* 1:11 (27 March 1929): 403; broadcast lecture, 27 March 1929.

10. Geoffrey Boumphrey, Edward Halliday, and John Gloag, "What's Wrong with Design Today?," *Listener* 9:223 (19 April 1933): 610; broadcast the week of 19 April 1933, transcript BBC WAC.

11. Herbert Read, "An Enquiry into Public Taste," *Listener* 18:443 (7 July 1937): 31; Sir Charles Holmes, "'Why the English Have No Taste,'" *Listener* 14:346 (28 August 1935): 352. Holmes's views were confirmed by Margaret H. Bulley, "A Test in Taste," *Listener* 10:259 (27 December 1933): 1001.

12. Herbert Read, "Methods in Art Criticism," *Listener* 3:59 (26 February 1930): 371.

13. Cyril Burt, "Psychology of Art," *Listener* 9:211 (25 January 1933): 138; broadcast talk, 24 January 1933.

14. Roger Fry, "The Meaning of Pictures," *Listener* 2:39 (9 October 1929): 467; broadcast talk, part III of *The Meaning of Pictures*, 2 October 1929.

15. J. E. Barton, "Do We Use Our Eyes?," *Listener* 7:164 (2 March 1932): 312; broadcast lecture, part III of *Modern Art*, 1 March 1932.

16. Robert Lyon, "An Experiment in Art Appreciation," *Listener* 13:333 (29 May 1935): 909.

17. Fry, "The Meaning of Pictures," 467.

18. J. E. Barton, "What Is Taste?," *Listener* 7:165 (9 March 1932): 346; broadcast lecture, part IV of *Modern Art*, 8 March 1932.

19. Eric Newton and R. H. Wilenski, "The Modern Critic Explains His Creed," *Listener* 13:322 (13 March 1935): 452; broadcast interview, part IV of *The Artist and His Public*, 12 March 1935.

20. G. M. Boumphrey and Maxwell Fry, "The Look of a House," broadcast interview, part II of *Inside and Out*, 18 February 1935; published in Boumphrey, *The House—Inside and Out* (London: George Allen & Unwin, 1936), 30–31.

21. Frederick Etchells, "Architecture and the Average Man," *Listener* 10:242 (30 August 1933): 316.

22. John Reith, "What Is Our Policy?," *Radio Times* 2 (14 March 1924): 442; quoted in Jennifer Doctor, *The BBC and Ultra-Modern Music, 1922–1936: Shaping a Nation's Tastes* (Cambridge: Cambridge University Press, 1999), 26.

23. John C. W. Reith, *Broadcast over Britain* (London: Hodder and Stoughton, 1924), 130.

24. "The policy of the Company being to bring the best of everything into the greatest number of homes, it follows that if this policy be carried out, that many educative influences must have been stirred." Reith, *Broadcast over Britain,* 147.

The first recorded connection between Reith's policies and the Arnoldian ideal of intermixing culture with service was made in the Annan Report (*Report of the Committee on the Future of Broadcasting* [London: HMSO, 1977], 14, 80). Paddy Scannell and David Cardiff, *A Social History of British Broadcasting: Serving the Nation 1922–1939* (Oxford: Blackwell, 1991), 9–10, also acknowledges this connection. They consider how Arnold's radical position, namely, that the state should use its authority to act as the guardian of culture in the national interest, resurfaced in the programming practices at the BBC. For more on the continuities between the nineteenth-century cultural theorist and the first twentieth-century electronic mass media, see Timothy Burns, *BBC: Public Institution, Private World* (London: Macmillan, 1977).

25. J. Dover Wilson, introduction to Mathew Arnold, *Culture and Anarchy* (Cambridge: Cambridge University Press, 1960), xi. Reith uses precisely the same words in *Broadcast over Britain*, 147–154, when he entitles one of the chapters "The Best of Everything" to articulate his position.

26. Christopher Salmon, Memorandums to Director of Talks (1927–1931), BAC: Talks Policy, File 1, BBC WAC; Hilda Matheson, *Broadcasting* (London: Thornton Butterworth, 1933).

27. Unit One was a short-lived consortium of a handful of modern artists, sculptors, and architects in the early 1930s; and Modern Architectural Research Group was the English chapter of Congrès Internationaux d'Architecture Moderne (CIAM), founded in 1933.

28. Asa Briggs, *The Golden Age of Wireless*, vol. 2 of *The History of Broadcasting in the United Kingdom* (London: Oxford University Press, 1965); and Doctor, *The BBC and Ultra-Modern Music*.

29. This scene is a source-based simulated ethnographic construction inspired by Pierre Bourdieu's emphasis on the "weight of the world narrative." See Pierre Bourdieu, *The Weight of the World: Social Suffering in Contemporary Society* (Cambridge: Polity, 1999).

30. Charles Siepmann to Stanley Casson in 1931, Stanley Casson, Personal File 1931–1940, P.E.1, BBC WAC.

31. Casson to Siepmann, 6 May 1931, Stanley Casson, Personal File 1931–1940, P.E.1, BBC WAC.

32. Stanley Casson and C. Cox, "Why Bother about Art?," *Listener* 7:170 (13 April 1932): 533; broadcast dialogue, part I of *Artists at Work*, 12 April 1932.

33. Ibid.

34. Read, "An Enquiry into Public Taste," 31.

35. Eric Newton, "The Artist and His Public," *Listener* 13:313 (9 January 1935): 63; broadcast lecture, part I of *The Artist and His Public*, 7 January 1935.

36. Anthony Blunt, "How I Look at Modern Painting," *Listener* 20:496 (14 July 1938): 74; broadcast talk, week of 14 July 1938.

37. Casson's advice came in response to a question—"How are we to tell whether a work is sincere or not?"—in "A Discussion between Stanley Casson and a Philistine." The role of the skeptical philistine in the conversation was played by a friend of Casson. Casson and Cox, "Why Bother about Art?," 533.

38. Newton, "The Artist and His Public," 63.

39. Margaret H. Bulley, "A Test in Taste," *Listener* 10:259 (27 December 1933): 1001.

40. Herbert Read, "On Looking at a Picture," *Listener* 5:108 (4 February 1931): 193–194.

41. Anthony Bertram, "Design Everywhere," broadcast lecture, part VIII of *Design in Everyday Things*, 20 December 1937, transcript BBC WAC; also published in Anthony Bertram, *Design* (Harmondsworth: Penguin, 1938), 99.

42. Frank Pick, "The Meaning and Purpose of Design," *Listener* 9:233 (28 June 1933): 1016; broadcast lecture, part XI of *Design in Modern Life*, 27 June 1933. Also published in John Gloag, ed., *Design in Modern Life* (London: George Allen & Unwin, 1934), 134.

43. Hon. Humphrey Pakington, "Tradition and Experiment," *Listener* 3:68 (30 April 1930): 769; broadcast talk, part I of *To-day and To-morrow in Architecture*, 29 April 1930, transcript BBC WAC.

44. Ibid., 768.

45. Etchells, "Architecture and the Average Man," 316.

46. John Summerson, "An Archive for Architecture," broadcast talk, 25 September 1944, transcript BBC WAC.

47. A. E. Richardson, "The Railway Station of Tomorrow," *Listener* 15:377 (1 April 1936): 619.

48. *BBC Yearbook* (London: British Broadcasting Corporation, 1926).

49. Ibid.

50. For every nine programs on architecture-related topics, there were two programs on art and sculpture.

51. John Summerson, "Creative Housing," *Listener* 18:447 (4 August 1937): 223.

52. Hilda Matheson, BBC memo, 1929, John Gloag, Personal File 1928–1932, BBC WAC.

53. J. E. Barton, *Purpose and Admiration: A Lay Study of the Visual Arts* (London: Christophers, 1932), 37.

54. Eric Newton and H. S. Goodhart-Rendel, "Artist and Architect," *Listener* 23:578 (8 February 1940): 263; broadcast discussion, part III of *The Artist in the Witness Box*, 6 February 1940.

55. Pakington, "Tradition and Experiment," 768.

56. Maxwell E. Fry, "Frank Lloyd Wright," *Listener* 21:540 (18 May 1939): 1050.

57. John Gloag, "Ancestor Worship in Design," *Listener* 8:192 (14 September 1932): 364; broadcast lecture, part I of *Design in Industry*, broadcast 7 September 1932.

58. Sir Reginald Blomfield in Blomfield et al., "Is Modern Architecture on the Right Track?—A Symposium," *Listener* 10:237 (26 July 1933): 123.

59. H. S. Goodhart-Rendel, quoted by M. H. Baillie Scott in Blomfield et al., "Is Modern Architecture on the Right Track?," 129.

60. Charles Holden in Blomfield et al., "Is Modern Architecture on the Right Track?," 125.

61. John Summerson, "Model Villages," broadcast talk, 10 April 1942, transcript BBC WAC.

62. Herbert Read, "The International Style," *Listener* 13:332 (22 May 1935): 866.

63. Geoffrey M. Boumphrey, "Leaders and Followers," in *Your Home and Mine*, broadcast lectures, between 24 September 1935 and 10 December 1935; published in Geoffrey M. Boumphrey, *Your House and Mine* (London: George Allen & Unwin, 1938). Also see Casson and Cox, "Why Bother about Art?," 533.

64. Boumphrey, "Leaders and Followers."

65. Maxwell Fry in Blomfield et al., "Is Modern Architecture on the Right Track?," 127.

66. Geoffrey M. Boumphrey, "Your Home and Mine," broadcast lecture, between 24 September 1935 and 10 December 1935; published in Boumphrey, *Your House and Mine*, 201.

67. P. Morton Shand, "The Changing Bridge—I," *Listener* 18:456 (6 October 1937): 723; broadcast talk, 4 October 1937.

68. Maxwell Fry, "Modern Town Planning," *Listener* 19:246 (13 January 1939): 661; broadcast talk, 11 January 1939.

69. Reginald Blomfield in Blomfield et al., "Is Modern Architecture on the Right Track?," 124. An elaboration of his position here can be found in Reginald Blomfield, *Modernismus* (London: Macmillan, 1934).

70. Amyas Connell in Sir Reginald Blomfield and Amyas D. Connell, "For and Against Modern Architecture," *Listener* 12:307 (28 November 1934): 886. Broadcast as "Discussion: New Homes for Old," 24 November 1934, transcript BBC WAC.

71. F. R. S. Yorke, quoted in David Dean, *Architecture of the 1930s: Recalling the English Scene* (New York: Rizzoli, 1983), 38. Also see 37–42, where Dean places Yorke's inversion of the relationship between modern and traditional approaches to architecture in a larger context of similar attempts. For findings of other historians on the issue, see Hélène Lipstadt, "Polemic and Parody in the Battle for British Modernism," *AA Files*, no. 3 (January 1983): 68–76; Alan Powers, "John Betjeman and Modern Architecture," in *First and Last Loves: John Betjeman and Architecture* (London: Soane Gallery, 2006), 31–40; John Summerson, "Extracts from Sir John Summerson Royal Gold Medal Address," *Journal of the Royal Institute of British Architects* 83 (December 1976): 494; Michael T. Saler, *The Avant-Garde in Interwar England: Medieval Modernism and the London Underground* (New York: Oxford University Press, 1999).

72. Anthony Bertram, "What Is a House?," *Listener* 18:457 (13 October 1937): 780–782; broadcast talk, "The House," Part II of *Design in Everyday Things*, 11 October 1937, transcript BBC WAC; also published in Bertram, *Design*, 61.

73. Boumphrey, *Your House and Mine*, 209.

74. Frederic Towndrow, "The Revolution in Architecture," *Listener* 1:8 (6 March 1929): 281; broadcast talk, 3 March 1929.

75. Hon. Humphrey Pakington, "Tradition and Experiment," *Listener* 3:68 (30 April 1930): 768–769; broadcast talk, part I of *To-day and To-morrow in Architecture*, 29 April 1930, transcript BBC WAC.

76. Maxwell E. Fry and John Gloag, "The Need for Planning Town and Countryside," *Listener* 9:232 (21 June 1933): 971; broadcast interview, part X of *Design in Modern Life*, 20 June 1933, transcript BBC WAC; also published in Gloag, *Design in Modern Life*, 111–124.

77. Richard Lambert, "Are We Becoming Vulgar?," editorial, *Listener* 3:53 (15 January 1930): 100.

78. J. E. Barton, "Will the New City Make New Men?," *Listener* 7:167 (23 March 1932): 412; broadcast lecture, part VI of *Modern Art*, 22 March 1932.

79. Reith, *Broadcast over Britain*, 28.

80. Samuel Weber, *Mass Mediauras: Form, Technics, Media*, ed. Alan Cholodenko (Stanford: Stanford University Press, 1996), 66.

3   The Politics of Broadcasting and the Broadcasting of Politics

1. See Ross McKibbin, "Listening In," in McKibbin, *Classes and Cultures: England 1918–1951* (Oxford: Oxford University Press, 1998), 457–458.

2. Clough Williams-Ellis, *Architect Errant* (London: Constable, 1971), 72.

3. Clough Williams-Ellis and Amabel Strachey, "Pleasures of Architecture," broadcast conversation, 6 January 1927, transcript BBC WAC; based on Clough Williams-Ellis and Amabel Strachey, *Pleasures of Architecture* (London: J. Cape, 1924), 155–156.

4. Williams-Ellis and Strachey, *Pleasures of Architecture*, 156–157.

5. Ibid.

6. Ibid., 72, 80–81.

7. Ibid., 70.

8. Ibid., 164.

9. Geoffrey M. Boumphrey, "Your Home and Mine," broadcast lecture, between 24 September 1935 and 10 December 1935, published in Geoffrey M. Boumphrey, *Your House and Mine* (London: George Allen & Unwin, 1938), 209.

10. Sir William Rothenstein, "Entry into Art," *Listener* 14:353 (16 October 1935): 650; broadcast lecture, week of 16 October 1935.

11. Sir Charles Holmes, "'Why the English Have No Taste,'" *Listener* 14:346 (28 August 1935): 352.

12. George Furlong, "Is Modern Art Unintelligible?," *Listener* 20:503 (1 September 1938): 450.

13. Sir Michael Sadler, "Conclusion and Comment," *Listener* 22:559 (28 September 1939): 616; broadcast lecture, part XII of *Art in Education*, week of 28 September 1939.

14. Ibid., 615.

15. Williams-Ellis and Strachey, *Pleasures of Architecture*, 164.

16. Halsey Ricardo, "The Value of Public Opinion," broadcast of a public lecture delivered at the RIBA, 18 May 1922, *Journal of the Royal Institute of British Architects* 29 (June 1922): 502.

17. Herbert Read, "Art in Education," *Listener* 22:551 (3 August 1939): 215.

18. For continuities between nineteenth-century Victorian and twentieth-century modern liberalism, see Stefan Collini, *Public Moralists: Political Thought and Intellectual Life in Britain, 1850–1930* (New York: Oxford University Press, 1991). W. Lyon Blease, *A Short History of English Liberalism* (New York: Putnam, 1913), remarked upon a similar persistence of ideas across generations in British politics and state policies. For a contesting view, see George Dangerfield, *The Strange Death of Liberal England* (New York: Capricorn Books, 1935).

19. Ann Kindersley, "Handicrafts in Colour," *Listener* 1:7 (27 February 1929): 255; broadcast lecture, part II of *About the Household*, 23 February 1929.

20. Christopher Salmon, memorandums to Director of Talks (1927–1931), BAC: Talks Policy, File 1, BBC WAC.

21. Ricardo, "The Value of Public Opinion," 502.

22. Salmon, memorandums to Director of Talks (1927–1931).

23. Fiona MacCarthy, *The Simple Life: C. R. Ashbee in the Cotswolds* (Berkeley: University of California Press, 1981).

24. Alan Crawford, *C. R. Ashbee: Architect, Designer and Romantic Socialist* (New Haven: Yale University Press, 2005), 195–206.

25. C. R. Ashbee, quoted in Peter Stansky, *William Morris, C. R. Ashbee and the Arts and Crafts* (London: Nine Elms Press, 1984).

26. Richard Lambert, "The Ugliness Exhibition," editorial, *Listener* 1:7 (27 February 1929): 240.

27. Ibid.

28. Gordon E. Mingay, *A Social History of the English Countryside* (London: Routledge, 1990), 205.

29. Peter Mandler, *The Rise and Fall of the Stately Home* (New Haven: Yale University Press, 1997), 109–152; Martin Daunton, "The Political Economy of Death Duties: Harcourt's Budget of 1894," in Negley Harte and Roland Quinault, eds., *Land and Society in Britain, 1700–1914* (Manchester: Manchester University Press, 1996), 137–171.

30. Crawford, *C. R. Ashbee*, 16.

31. Stefan Muthesius, "Review: *C. R. Ashbee: Architect, Designer and Romantic Socialist* by Alan Crawford," *Oxford Art Journal* 9:2 (1986): 82–84.

32. C. R. Ashbee, quoted in ibid.

33. C. R. Ashbee, "Ugliness Exhibition," *Listener* 1:7 (27 February 1929): 234; broadcast, 23 February 1929.

34. Ibid.

35. For the role of bells in local identity in the nineteenth century, see Alain Corbin, "The Auditory Markers of the Village," in Corbin, *Village Bells: Sound and Meaning in the Nineteenth Century French Countryside*, trans. Martin Thom (New York: Columbia University Press, 1998), 95–101.

36. Lambert, "The Ugliness Exhibition," 240.

37. See Ernest Darwin Simon, *The Rebuilding of Manchester* (London: Longmans, Green, 1935).

38. Ernest Darwin Simon in G. M. Boumphrey, E. D. Simon, and P. Abercrombie, "Can Flats Solve the Housing Problem?," *Listener* 14:355 (30 October 1935): 741–744; unrehearsed debate between Geoffrey M. Boumphrey and Simon, moderated by Patrick Abercrombie, postscript of *Looking for the Town of Tomorrow*, 19 October 1935, transcript BBC WAC.

39. Ibid.

40. Ibid.

41. Geoffrey M. Boumphrey in Boumphrey et al., "Can Flats Solve the Housing Problem?," 741.

42. Ibid.

43. Ibid., 743.

44. Patrick Abercrombie in Boumphrey et al., "Can Flats Solve the Housing Problem?," 744.

45. Andrzej Olechnowicz, *Working-Class Housing in England between the Wars: The Becontree Estate* (New York: Oxford University Press, 1997).

46. Martin J. Daunton, "Housing," in F. M. L. Thompson, ed., *The Cambridge Social History of Britain, 1750–1950* (Cambridge: Cambridge University Press, 1990).

47. This section was originally developed as an organ of the elaborate and ever-growing department of Broadcast Education, but three years earlier, in 1932, it had been absorbed by the creative and ambitious Hilda Matheson into her department of Talks and News.

48. "Broadcast Adult Education, Early Stages," 13 May 1940, 6–7, Education—Adult Education, Papers and Reports 1935–1940, BAC R14/145/2, File 1b, BBC WAC.

49. J. C. Stobart, R14/145/2, File 1b, BBC WAC.

50. "Broadcast Adult Education, Early Stages."

51. Norman Luker, report to Sir Richard Maconachie (director of Talks since 1935), 25 November 1938, BAC R51/397, BBC WAC. The report proposed ideas for inspiring programming.

52. Asa Briggs, *The Golden Age of Wireless*, vol. 2 of his *The History of Broadcasting in the United Kingdom* (London: Oxford University Press, 1965), 219–221.

53. Blease, *A Short History of English Liberalism*, 1–42.

54. Ibid.

55. Briggs, *The Golden Age of Wireless*, 189.

56. John Scupham, "School Broadcasting in Great Britain," broadcast, 13 and 14 April 1951, Education—Educational Broadcasting—Articles and Speeches—1933–54, BAC R16/121, BBC WAC. Scupham, who was the head of School Broadcasting in 1951, was reporting on the history of School Broadcasting from 1924 to 1951.

57. Richard Stanton Lambert, *Ariel and All His Quality: An Impression of the BBC from Within* (London: V. Gollancz, 1940), 126.

58. The *Listener* was a nonprofit enterprise that was run at a loss throughout the 1930s. It had a small readership, topping at 50,670 in 1934; BAC R43/67, BBC WAC.

59. "British Broadcasting Corporation: Summary of Adult Education Work," June 1928, Education—Adult Education, Papers and Reports 1924–1934, BAC R14/145/1 File 1a, BBC WAC.

60. *BBC Year Book* (London: British Broadcasting Corporation, 1930), 60.

61. John Summerson, "The Critics: Radio," Sir John Summerson Papers, Broadcast Talks SuJ/10/17, broadcast undated, transcript V&A and RIBA Collections, Victoria and Albert Museum, London (further referenced as RIBA Collections).

62. Susan Pedersen and Peter Mandler, introduction to Pedersen and Mandler, eds., *After the Victorians: Private Conscience and Public Duty in Modern Britain* (London: Routledge, 1994), 9, 10.

63. John C. W. Reith, *Broadcast over Britain* (London: Hodder and Stoughton, 1924), 18–19.

64. The BBC's pedagogic approach to broadcasting was challenged by Radio Luxemburg and Normandy. Daniel LeMahieu, *A Culture for Democracy* (Oxford: Oxford University Press, 1988), discusses the influence of these radio stations on the BBC's presentation and content organization.

65. Paddy Scannell and David Cardiff, *A Social History of British Broadcasting: Serving the Nation 1922–1939* (Oxford: Blackwell, 1991), 8.

66. Ibid., 56.

67. Asa Briggs, *The War of Words* (London: Oxford University Press, 1970), and Briggs, *Governing the BBC* (London: BBC, 1979).

68. Scannell and Cardiff, *A Social History of British Broadcasting*, 50.

69. Ibid. The first three chapters of the book provide a rich account of the BBC's struggle for independence from the newspaper lobby, the Post Master General, and other government offices.

70. James Curran and Jean Seaton, *Power without Responsibility: The Press and Broadcasting in Great Britain* (London: Routledge, 1988).

71. The only notable exceptions to this rule were the music organizations. An account of their worries about and resentment toward radio, especially the formation of the BBC orchestra, can be found in Reith, *Broadcast over Britain,* chapter 1–3. Briggs, *The Golden Age of Wireless*, 185–226, shows that their resistance was short lived and preemptive in nature. For the most comprehensive account of the BBC's relationship to the music industry, see Jennifer Doctor, *The BBC and Ultra-Modern Music, 1922–1936: Shaping a Nation's Tastes* (Cambridge: Cambridge University Press, 1999), 3–21.

72. Reith, *Broadcast over Britain*, 18; quoted in D. L. LeMahieu, "John Reith," in Pedersen and Mandler, *After the Victorians*, 195.

73. On the generality of culture in the history of ideas of Matthew Arnold and other liberal British cultural theorists of the nineteenth century and the first half of the twentieth, see Raymond Williams, *Culture and Society: 1780–1950* (New York: Columbia University Press, 1958), 115.

74. McKibbin, *Classes and Cultures*, 273.

75. John Reith, quoted in Kate Whitehead, *The Third Programme: A Literary History* (Oxford: Clarendon, 1989), 7.

76. Clough Williams-Ellis, "Architectural Appreciation," *Journal of the Royal Institute of British Architects* 51 (February 1944): 81.

77. Ricardo, "The Value of Public Opinion," 504.

78. Raymond Williams, *The Long Revolution* (New York: Columbia University Press, 1961), 64–65.

79. Blease, *A Short History of English Liberalism*, 340.

4 Speaking of Conservation: The Oral Travelogue and British Historical Imagination

1. Geoffrey Maxwell Boumphrey holds patents for a number of agricultural tools registered in the United Kingdom and Canada.

2. Geoffrey M. Boumphrey, *Down River*, *Listener* 16:391 (8 July 1936) to 16:398 (26 August 1936), broadcast from 29 May to 17 July 1936, transcript BBC WAC.

3. Tom Stevenson, ed., *The Countryside Companion* (London: Odham's Press, 1939), 18.

4. Geoffrey M. Boumphrey, "From Ironbridge to Worcester," *Listener* 16:394 (29 July 1936): 219; broadcast travelogue, part IV of *Down River*, 19 June 1936, transcript BBC WAC.

5. John Betjeman, "Bristol," broadcast travel guide, part I of *Town Tours*, 12 April 1937, transcript BBC WAC; published in Betjeman, *Trains and Buttered Toast: Selected Radio Talks*, compiled by Stephen Games (London: John Murray, 2006), 55. Subsequent references are to the published version.

6. John Summerson, "Newstead Abbey," broadcast travelogue, part II of *Famous Midland Houses*, Sir John Summerson Papers, SuJ/10/1, broadcast undated, transcript RIBA Collections.

7. John Summerson was celebrated as CBE in 1952, knighted in 1958, and awarded the RIBA Silver and Gold Medals in 1937 and 1971, respectively, for his service to architecture. John Betjeman was also CBE, knighted in 1969, and created Poet Laureate in 1976.

8. R. L. Mackie, "Dundee," broadcast from Scotland, 15 August 1939, 7:50 PM; see *Program Index* (London: British Broadcasting Corporation, 1939).

9. W. F. Grimes, "The Gope Cape," broadcast from Wales, 21 July 1939, 7:30 PM; see *Program Index*.

10. Bernard Fishwick and Pat Beech, "Falmouth," broadcast from West, 9 August 1939, 8:15 PM; see *Program Index*.

11. John Summerson, "Compton Wynyates," broadcast travelogue, part I of *Famous Midland Houses*, Sir John Summerson Papers, SuJ/10/1, broadcast May 1937, transcript RIBA Collections.

12. "The Tower," produced by E. Martin Brown, broadcast from Midlands, 20 July 1939, 8:25 PM; see *Program Index*.

13. Robin Whitworth, "Ely Cathedral: Sermons in Stone," broadcast from Midlands, 27 August 1939, 9:05 PM; see *Program Index*.

14. Geoffrey Boumphrey in Boumphrey, E. D. Simon, and P. Abercrombie, "Can Flats Solve the Housing Problem?," *Listener* 14:355 (30 October 1935): 741–744; unrehearsed debate between Geoffrey M. Boumphrey and Ernest Darwin Simon, moderated by Patrick Abercrombie, postscript of *Looking for the Town of Tomorrow*, broadcast on 19 October 1935, transcript BBC WAC.

15. David Matless, *Landscape and Englishness* (London: Reaktion Books, 1998), 63–67.

16. Ibid., 75; also see Vaughan Cornish, *National Parks, and the Heritage of Scenery* (London: Sifton, Praed & Co., 1930).

17. Matless, *Landscape and Englishness*, 72.

18. From "Manchester Rambler," by Evan MacColl, cited in Matless, *Landscape and Englishness*, 72.

19. For the opposition between aristocratic and people's heritage in the 1930s, see Peter Mandler, *The Rise and Fall of the Stately Home* (New Haven: Yale University Press, 1997); Martin Daunton, *Trusting Leviathan: The Politics of Taxation in Britain, 1799–1914* (Cambridge: Cambridge University Press, 2007); Gordon E. Mingay, *A Social History of the English Countryside* (London: Routledge, 1990); and Matless, *Landscape and Englishness*.

20. Daunton, *Trusting Leviathan*, 242.

21. Mandler, *The Rise and Fall of the Stately Home*, 171–172.

22. Ibid., 225–263.

23. Mingay, *A Social History of the English Countryside*, 205.

24. Ibid.

25. Cited in ibid., 208.

26. *Times* (London), May 1919, quoted in ibid., 207.

27. John Summerson, "Premises Coming Down," *Listener* 17:425 (3 March 1937): 393.

28. Mandler, *The Rise and Fall of the Stately Home*, 109–152.

29. Ibid., 217.

30. Stanley Baldwin, "Speech on England" (May 1924), in *On England, and Other Addresses* (Harmondsworth: Penguin, 1938), 6–7.

31. Mandler, *The Rise and Fall of the Stately Home*, 240.

32. John Summerson, "The Romantic Element in Architecture," *Architectural Design and Construction* 2 (March 1932): 228. See also Alan Powers, "John Summerson and Modernism," in Louise Campbell, ed., *Twentieth Century Architecture and Its Histories* (Utley: Society of Architectural Historians of Great Britain, 2000), 153–172.

33. Noel Carrington, "Need Our Cities Be Ugly?," *Listener* 3:54 (22 January 1930): 149.

34. Ibid.

35. Ibid.

36. Geoffrey M. Boumphrey, "Along the Roman Roads," *Listener* 11:280 (23 May 1934) to 12:286 (4 July 1934); broadcast from 23 May to 4 July 1934; published as Geoffrey M. Boumphrey, *Along the Roman Roads* (London: George Allen & Unwin, 1935).

37. Geoffrey M. Boumphrey, "Ulster Holiday," *Listener* 18:449 (18 August 1937): 330; broadcast travel guide, part II of *Out of Doors*, undated.

38. Boumphrey, "From Ironbridge to Worcester," 220.

39. Geoffrey M. Boumphrey, "Hadrian's Wall," *Listener* 12:286 (4 July 1934): 12; broadcast travel guide, part VII of *Along the Roman Roads*, week of 4 July 1934.

40. Ibid., 16.

41. Geoffrey M. Boumphrey, "On the Portway," *Listener* 11:280 (23 May 1934): 857; broadcast travel guide, part I of *Along the Roman Roads*, week of 23 May 1934.

42. Geoffrey M. Boumphrey, "Down Ermine Street," *Listener* 11:283 (13 June 1934): 993; broadcast travel guide, part IV of *Along the Roman Roads*, week of 13 June 1934.

43. Geoffrey M. Boumphrey, "On the Portway," *Listener* 11:280 (23 May 1934): 857; broadcast travel guide, part I of *Along the Roman Roads*, week of 23 May 1934.

44. Geoffrey M. Boumphrey, "From Welshpool to Shrewsbury," *Listener* 16:392 (15 July 1936): 123; broadcast travel guide, part II of *Down River*, 5 June 1936, transcript BBC WAC.

45. Ibid.

46. Ruth Crosby, "Oral Delivery in the Middle Ages," *Speculum* 11 (1936): 88–110.

47. Boumphrey, "From Welshpool to Shrewsbury," 124.

48. Ibid.

49. Boumphrey, "From Ironbridge to Worcester," 221.

50. Elizabeth L. Eisenstein, *The Printing Press as an Agent of Change: Communications and Cultural Transformations in Early Modern Europe* (Cambridge: Cambridge University Press, 1979), 225–272.

51. Boumphrey, "From Welshpool to Shrewsbury," 124.

52. Geoffrey M. Boumphrey, "Ulster Holiday," *Listener* 18:448 (11 August 1937): 275; broadcast travel guide, part I of *Out of Doors*, undated.

53. Wolfgang Schivelbusch has identified the development of the conception and perception of the world as if it were a picture rather than concrete places as a result of railway travel. Wolfgang Schivelbusch, *The Railway Journey: The Industrialization of Time and Space in the Nineteenth Century* (Berkeley: University of California Press, 1986).

54. Geoffrey M. Boumphrey, "From Shrewsbury to Ironbridge," *Listener* 16:393 (22 July 1936): 173; broadcast travel guide, part III of *Down River*, 12 June 1936, transcript BBC WAC.

55. Geoffrey M. Boumphrey, "The Start at Newtown," *Listener* 16:391 (8 July 1936): 54; broadcast travel guide, part I of *Down River*, 29 May 1936, transcript BBC WAC.

56. As an example, Boumphrey commented that Potters Hill showed how much could be learned about England's past "due to one man keeping his eyes open. The process would be speeded up if more people visited museums occasionally and learned the sort of things to look out for." Ibid.

57. Malcolm Andrews, *The Search for the Picturesque: Landscape Aesthetics and Tourism in Britain, 1760–1800* (Stanford: Stanford University Press, 1989), 24–38.

58. John Betjeman, "Bournemouth," broadcast travel guide, part IV of *Town Tours*, 28 May 1937, transcript BBC WAC; published in Betjeman, *Trains and Buttered Toast*, 72.

59. John Betjeman, "Swindon," broadcast travel guide, part III of *Town Tours*, 8 May 1937, transcript BBC WAC; published in Betjeman, *Trains and Buttered Toast*, 69–70.

60. Ibid.

61. John Betjeman, "How to Look at a Church," *Listener* 20:504 (8 September 1938): 484–486; broadcast 31 August 1938, transcript BBC WAC; later published in Betjeman, *Trains and Buttered Toast*, 231.

62. John Betjeman, "Conclusion," broadcast, Part VI of *Town Tours*, 24 June 1937, transcript BBC WAC; published in Betjeman, *Trains and Buttered Toast*, 82.

63. Betjeman, "Bristol," 60.

64. Betjeman, "How to Look at a Church," in Betjeman, *Trains and Buttered Toast*, 234.

65. Dean MacCannell, *The Tourist: A New Theory of the Leisure Class* (New York: Schocken, 1976), 6; John Urry, *The Tourist Gaze*, 2nd ed. (London: Sage Publications, 2002), 2, 9.

66. John Betjeman, *The English Town in the Last Hundred Years: The Rede Lecture* (Cambridge: Cambridge University Press, 1956), 4–5.

67. It seemed to be Betjeman's facility with language in invoking architecture that carried him through his broadcasting career, for years later his producers would still complain about his speech delivery. Stephen Games, in his introduction to Betjeman, *Trains and Buttered Toast*, 6, reports that "David Winter, the last producer to work with him in the mid-1970s, commented that 'his voice was technically unexciting, lacking in dynamic range and trapped in a camp Oxbridge accent.' Winter continued, however, that Betjeman had 'a completely distinctive broadcasting style' and that his voice 'was undeniably arresting to the ear. The listener was invited to share his boyish enthusiasms and fascinations. And there was, of course, that quite wicked sense of humor, made all the more mischievous by the artless way in which the barbs were delivered.'"

68. Betjeman would write in 1972, "The camera can lie almost as much as the perspective draughtsman. So what are we left with but words? And when it comes to words describing architecture,

adjectives become disproportionately important." John Betjeman, "On Writing about Architecture," *Architect* (March 1972): 24.

69. Betjeman, *The English Town in the Last Hundred Years*.

70. John Betjeman, "Seaview," broadcast, Part IV of *Beside the Seaside*, 11 May 1937, transcript BBC WAC; published in Betjeman, *Trains and Buttered Toast*, 106–107.

71. See Timothy Mowl's comparison of Betjeman to Nikolaus Pevsner in Timothy Mowl, *Stylistic Cold Wars: Betjeman versus Pevsner* (London: John Murray, 2000); and Mark Girouard, introduction to *First and Last Loves: John Betjeman and Architecture* (London: Soane Gallery, 2006), 7–10.

72. Betjeman, "On Writing about Architecture," 24.

73. Ibid., 25.

74. Urry, *The Tourist Gaze*, 3.

75. Miles David Samson, "Philip Johnson and the Museum of Modern Art's 'Grand Tour' Modernism," paper presented at the annual conference of the Society of Architectural Historians, Pasadena, 2–5 April 2009.

76. Betjeman, "Bristol," 55.

77. John Betjeman, "Back to the Railway Carriage," broadcast travelogue, 10 March 1940, transcript BBC WAC; published in Betjeman, *Trains and Buttered Toast*, 125.

78. Ibid.

79. Betjeman, "Bristol" 55.

80. Mowl, *Stylistic Cold Wars*, 58.

81. Ibid.

82. John Summerson, "Rushton Hall," broadcast travelogue, part IV of *Famous Midland Houses*, Sir John Summerson Papers, SuJ/10/1, broadcast 23 June 1937, transcript RIBA Collections.

83. Ibid.

84. "Sir Thomas Tresham," National Trust website http://www.nationaltrust.org.uk/main/w-vh/w-visits/w-findaplace/w-lyvedennewbield/w-lyvedennewbield-history/w-lyvedennewbield-history-thomas_tresham.htm, accessed 4 April 2009.

85. Summerson, "Rushton Hall."

86. John Summerson, "Kentchurch Court and Holme Lacy," broadcast travelogue, part III of *Famous Midland Houses*, Sir John Summerson Papers, SuJ/10/1, 6 June 1937, transcript RIBA Collections.

87. John Summerson, "Blenheim Palace," broadcast travelogue, part VII of *Famous Midland Houses*, Sir John Summerson Papers, SuJ/10/1, 4 August 1937, transcript RIBA Collections.

88. This observation was first made by Christy Anderson as an attribute pervading all of Summerson's future scholarship as well. Christy Anderson, "A Very Personal Renaissance," in Frank Salmon, ed., *Summerson and Hitchcock: Centenary Essays on Architectural Historiography* (New Haven: Yale University Press, 2006), 82.

89. BBC memo, 1935, John Summerson, Personal File 1937–1944, 24 May 1937, BBC WAC.

90. Reginald Blomfield, 1934 letter to the BBC Talks Assistant Director, John Summerson, Personal File 1937–1944, 24 May 1937, BBC WAC.

91. Peter Mandler, "John Summerson," in Susan Pedersen and Peter Mandler, eds., *After the Victorians: Private Conscience and Public Duty in Modern Britain* (London: Routledge, 1994), 233.

92. Caroline van Eck, "Artisan Mannerism: Seventeenth-Century Rhetorical Alternatives to Sir John Summerson's Formalist Approach," in Salmon, *Summerson and Hitchcock*, 87–88.

93. Summerson, "Blenheim Palace."

94. Summerson, "Kentchurch Court and Holme Lacy."

95. John Summerson, "Castle Ashby," broadcast travelogue, part VI of *Famous Midland Houses*, Sir John Summerson Papers, SuJ/10/1, 18 July 1937, transcript RIBA Collections.

96. John Summerson, "Condover Hall," broadcast travelogue, part V of *Famous Midland Houses*, Sir John Summerson Papers, SuJ/10/1, 6 July 1937, transcript RIBA Collections.

97. Summerson, "Newstead Abbey."

98. Raymond Williams has argued that the Marxist interpretation of culture that became widely effective in England from the 1930s onward viewed the arts as "dependant upon social change." But Marxists who were characteristically English could not agree about the passivity of this dependence. Raymond Williams, *Culture and Society: 1780–1950* (New York: Colombia University Press, 1958), 265–284.

99. John Summerson, "Ruins and the Future," broadcast travelogue, Sir John Summerson Papers, SuJ/10/1, 30 March 1941, transcript RIBA Collections.

100. John Summerson, "Nash's Terraces in Regent's Park," broadcast travelogue, Sir John Summerson Papers, SuJ/10/1, 6 October 1942, transcript RIBA Collections.

101. Ibid.

102. Carlo Olmo argues that while Summerson "accepted" his task as the writing of "culture for mass market society" and, as we know, succeeded in reaching wide audiences through radio, television, and journalism, he still conceived of his work as an "intellectual process." Carlo Olmo, "International Architecture, Historical Research and Working Critique," *Zodiac*, no. 18 (September 1997–February 1998): 89; cited in Hélène Lipstadt, "Celebrating the Centenaries of Summerson and Hitchcock: Finding a Historiography for the Architect-Historian," in Salmon, *Summerson and Hitchcock*, 347.

103. John Summerson, "How to Look at a Town," broadcast travelogue, Sir John Summerson Papers, SuJ/10/1, 10 February 1945, transcript RIBA Collections.

104. Ibid.

105. Ibid.

106. John Summerson, "An Archive for Architecture," broadcast, Sir John Summerson Papers, SuJ/10/1, 25 September 1944, transcript RIBA Collections.

107. Summerson, "How to Look at a Town."

108. Ibid.

109. Ibid.

110. Olmo, "International Architecture, Historical Research and Working Critique," 89.

5 The Box on the Dresser: The Sacralization of Contemporary Everyday Spaces

1. Frank Pick and John Gloag, "Design in the Street," *Listener* 9:230 (7 June 1933): 988; broadcast interview, part VIII of *Design in Modern Life*, 6 June 1933, transcript BBC WAC; also published in John Gloag, ed., *Design in Modern Life* (London: George Allen & Unwin, 1934), 97–108.

2. Ibid.

3. Quoted in Maxwell E. Fry, *Autobiographical Sketches* (London: Elek, 1975), 137.

4. The DIA, modeled after the Deutscher Werkbund, was established in London in 1915. Its purpose was to improve standards of design in the manufacturing industry and everyday life. The association sought to promote better understanding between manufacturers, designers, and retailers and to foster "a more intelligent understanding amongst the public for what is best and soundest in design." Pick served as its president in 1928. http://designmuseum.org/design/frank-pick (last accessed 4 July 2013).

5. Michael T. Saler, *The Avant-Garde in Interwar England* (New York: Oxford University Press, 1999), 95, notes that Pick saw the essence of art in its conception rather than its manual creation, and felt that it did not matter if the execution of design was carried out by hand or machine.

6. See Nikolaus Pevsner on Pick, quoted in Jane Fraser and Liz Paul, "The Living Tradition: Modernism and the Decorative Arts," *Twentieth Century Society* 20 (1984): 52.

7. Pick, in Pick and Gloag, "Design in the Street," in Gloag, *Design in Modern Life*, 97–108.

8. A year earlier, in 1932, J. E. Barton, a prolific critic, had told his radio audience something consistent with these ideas: "I hope to show, by illustrations from our own age, that this genuine creative spirit of today is … not an affair of galleries or museums, but part and parcel of all the life that is surrounding you. It is appearing in your streets, shops, factories, hotels, cinemas, and homes." Like Pick, Barton's definition of design overcame the social distance that gave the compositional formu-

lae of neoclassical architects their authority. J. E. Barton, "Purpose Made Visible," *Listener* 7:162 (17 February 1932): 224–226; broadcast lecture, part I of *Modern Art*, 16 February 1932, transcript BBC WAC.

9. For a summary on the ambitious scope of planning schemes extended by the 1932 Act, see Samuel Hill, "Town and Country Planning Act, 1932," *Journal of the Royal Society for the Promotion of Health* 54:2 (1933): 100–116.

10. Martin J. Daunton, "Housing," in F. M. L. Thompson, ed., *The Cambridge Social History of Britain, 1750–1950* (Cambridge: Cambridge University Press, 1990), 204. Daunton provides a valuable description of the changing experience of public and private space from the late nineteenth century to the end of World War II with the expansion of state intervention, the housing market, and the development of a property-owning democracy.

11. Walter Benjamin, "The Work of Art in the Age of Mechanical Reproduction," in Benjamin, *Illuminations: Essays and Reflections*, ed. Hannah Arendt (New York: Schocken Books, 1968), 239–240.

12. Frank Pick, "The Meaning and Purpose of Design," *Listener* 9:233 (28 June 1933): 1016; broadcast lecture, part XI of *Design in Modern Life*, 27 June 1933; also published in Gloag, *Design in Modern Life*, 133. Subsequent references will be to the essay's publication in Gloag's book.

13. Anthony Bertram, "What Does the Public Want?," *Listener* 18:456 (6 October 1937): 709; broadcast conversation between Anthony Bertram and F. C. Hooper, part I of *Design in Everyday Things*, 4 October 1937, transcript BBC WAC.

14. Geoffrey Boumphrey, "Your Home and Mine: Leaders and Followers," broadcast 24 September 1935 to 10 December 1935, published in Boumphrey, *Your House and Mine* (London: George Allen & Unwin, 1938), 175–178. John Gloag, "Who Knows What the Public Wants?," in Gloag, *Design in Modern Life*, 17–28, broadcast talk by Gloag, "Ancestor Worship," part I of *Design in Industry*, 7 September 1932; also published as Gloag, "Ancestor Worship in Design," *Listener* 8:192 (14 September 1932): 364.

15. Anthony Bertram, "Housing the Workers," *Listener* 18:461 (10 November 1937): 1007; broadcast lecture, Part III of *Design in Everyday Things*, 7 November 1937, transcript BBC WAC; also published as "Working Class Housing," in Bertram, *Design* (Harmondsworth: Penguin, 1938), 33.

16. Pick, "The Meaning and Purpose of Design," 133.

17. Halbrook Jackson, "Shopping and Taste," *Listener* 17:427 (17 March 1937): 487.

18. Ibid.

19. Modern Architectural Research Group (MARS Group) was the English chapter of Congrès Internationaux d'Architecture Moderne (CIAM) founded in 1933.

20. Maxwell E. Fry, "What Planning Means," *Listener* 16:409 (11 November 1936): 886; broadcast talk, part II of *Town Planning in Northern Ireland*, 11 November 1936.

21. Fry, *Autobiographical Sketches*.

22. Maxwell E. Fry and John Gloag, "The Need for Planning Town and Countryside," *Listener* 9:232 (21 June 1933): 971; broadcast interview, part X of *Design in Modern Life*, 20 June 1933, transcript BBC WAC; also published in Gloag, *Design in Modern Life*, 111–124.

23. "Week by Week," editorial, *Listener* 16:409 (11 November 1936): 890–891.

24. Fry, "What Planning Means," 886–887.

25. Ibid., 886.

26. Ibid., 887.

27. Ibid.

28. Ibid.

29. Fry, *Autobiographical Sketches*.

30. Ibid.

31. The best description of Fry's role in CIAM is found in John Allan, *Berthold Lubetkin: Architecture and the Tradition of Progress* (London: RIBA, 1992).

32. Ibid.

33. Daunton, "Housing," 208. For improvement in nineteenth-century housing conditions, see A. Errazurez, "Some Types of Housing in Liverpool, 1785–1890," *Town Planning Review* 19 (1943): 68; and Sir Robert Giffen, *The Progress of the Working Classes in the Last Half Century* (London: G. Bell and Sons, 1884), 13.

34. Fry and Gloag, "The Need for Planning Town and Countryside," in Gloag, *Design in Modern Life*, 111–124.

35. Valentine Williams and Sir Raymond Unwin, "The Future of Housing," *Listener* 20:499 (4 August 1938): 240; broadcast interview, 2 August 1938.

36. Fry and Gloag, "The Need for Planning Town and Countryside," in Gloag, *Design in Modern Life*, 111–124.

37. Ibid.

38. Ibid.

39. Geoffrey Boumphrey and Wells Coates, "Modern Dwellings for Modern Needs," *Listener* 9:219 (24 March 1933): 819; broadcast interview, part VI of *Design in Modern Life*, 23 March 1933.

40. See Peter Clarke, "Bricks and Mortar," in Clarke, *Hope and Glory: Britain, 1900–1990* (London: Penguin, 1996); and Daunton, "Housing."

41. Wells Coates in Boumphrey and Coates, "Modern Dwellings for Modern Needs," 819.

42. Geoffrey Boumphrey in ibid., 820.

43. Coates in ibid.

44. Ibid.

45. Hermann Muthesius, *The English House* (New York: Rizzoli, 1987), 7.

46. J. E. Barton, "What Is Taste?," *Listener* 7:165 (9 March 1932): 346; broadcast lecture, part IV of *Modern Art*, 8 March 1932.

47. Gloag, "Who Knows What the Public Wants?," in Gloag, *Design in Modern Life*, 17–28.

48. Anthony Bertram, "What Is a House?," *Listener* 18:457 (13 October 1937): 780–782; broadcast talk, "The House," Part II of *Design in Everyday Things*, 11 October 1937, transcript BBC WAC; also published as "In the House," in Bertram, *Design*, 67–97.

49. Coates in "Modern Dwellings for Modern Needs," 819.

50. Bertram, "In the House," 67.

51. Herbert Read, "The House of To-morrow," *Listener* 5:111 (25 February 1931): 324.

52. Bertram, "In the House," 67.

53. Coates in "Modern Dwellings for Modern Needs," 819.

54. Read, "The House of To-morrow," 324.

55. Geoffrey M. Boumphrey, "Flats or Garden-Cities?," *Listener* 14:351 (2 October 1935): 556; broadcast travelogue, part II of *Looking at the Town of Tomorrow*, 2 October 1935, transcript BBC WAC.

56. Read, "The House of To-morrow," 324.

57. Maxwell E. Fry, "Frank Lloyd Wright," *Listener* 21:540 (18 May 1939): 1050.

58. Ibid.

59. John Gloag, Sinclair Wood, and James Whittaker, "Permanence in Building: Should Houses Be Built to Last," part V of *Men Talking*, 4 February 1937, at 2:51 PM, British Library Sound Archives, London, transcript BBC WAC.

60. Ibid.

61. Ibid.

62. Ibid.

63. Bertram, "In the House," 82–83.

64. Read, "The House of To-morrow," 324.

65. Bertram, "What Is a House?," 780.

66. Ibid.

67. Anthony Bertram, "Heat, Light and Sound in the Home," *Listener* 18:460 (3 November 1937): 971–972; broadcast talk, "The House," Part V of *Design in Everyday Things*, 1 November 1937, transcript BBC WAC; also published in Bertram, "In the House," 84.

68. Bertram, "Architecture: The House?," 61–62.

69. Pick, "The Meaning and Purpose of Design," 127; and broadcast interview between John Gloag and Frank Pick, "The Meaning and Purpose of Design," part XI of *Design in Modern Life*, 8 November 1937, transcript BBC WAC.

70. Bertram, "Housing the Workers," 1005.

71. Theodor W. Adorno, "The Curves of the Needle," in Anton Kaes, Martin Jay, and Edward Dimendberg, eds., *The Weimar Republic Sourcebook* (Berkeley: University of California Press, 1994), 606. First published as "Nadelkurven," *Musikblätter des Anbruch* 10 (February 1928): 47–50.

72. John C. W. Reith, *Broadcast over Britain* (London: Hodder and Stoughton, 1924), 28.

73. For the earliest proclamations of the BBC on its commitment to becoming an engine for supplanting the hearth (a key element in the architectural theory of Gottfried Semper and the houses of Frank Lloyd Wright) and making the radiophonic hearth the engine for engendering a democratic culture, see the manifesto of its first director general (DG), John Reith, before he took on that role, in Reith, *Broadcast over Britain*, 15–19.

Conclusion: Notes on Method and Other Things

1. Rudolf Arnheim, *Radio*, trans. Margaret Ludwig and Herbert Read (London: Faber and Faber, 1936), 35.

2. Jean Baudrillard, *In the Shadow of the Silent Majorities; or, The End of the Social, and Other Essays*, ed. Paul Foss and John Johnston, trans. Paul Patton (New York: Semiotext(e), 1983), 102–103.

3. Pierre Bourdieu and Löic Wacquant, *An Invitation to Reflexive Sociology* (Chicago: University of Chicago Press; Cambridge: Polity Press, 1992), 58.

BIBLIOGRAPHY

Adorno, Theodor W. *Aesthetic Theory*. Minneapolis: University of Minnesota Press, 1997.
Allan, John. *Berthold Lubetkin: Architecture and the Tradition of Progress*. London: RIBA Publications, 1992.
Anderson, Christy. "A Very Personal Renaissance." In Frank Salmon, ed., *Summerson and Hitchcock: Centenary Essays on Architectural Historiography*, 69–84. New Haven: Yale University Press, 2006.
Andrews, Malcolm. *The Search for the Picturesque: Landscape Aesthetics and Tourism in Britain, 1760–1800*. Stanford: Stanford University Press, 1989.
Annan, Noel Gilroy. *Report of the Committee of Inquiry on the Future of Broadcasting*. London: HMSO, 1977.
Annan, Noel Gilroy. *Our Age: English Intellectuals between the World Wars—A Group Portrait*. New York: Random House, 1990.
Arnheim, Rudolf. *Radio*. Trans. Margaret Ludwig and Herbert Read. London: Faber and Faber, 1936.
Arnold, Matthew. *Culture and Anarchy*. Cambridge: Cambridge University Press, 1960.
"The Artist in the Witness Box." Editorial. *Listener* 22 (567) (23 November 1939): 1004.
Ashbee, C. R. "Ugliness Exhibition." *Listener* 1 (7) (February 27, 1929): 233–235.
Atkinson, Robert. "Design in Public Buildings." *Listener* 9 (231) (14 June 1933): 928–931.
Austin, John Lanshaw. *How to Do Things with Words*. Cambridge, Mass.: Harvard University Press, 1962.

Baldwin, Stanley. "Speech on England." In *On England, and Other Addresses*. Harmondsworth: Penguin Books, 1938.
Barton, J. E. "Art Begins at Home." *Listener* 7 (163) (24 February 1932): 278–280.
Barton, J. E. "Do We Use Our Eyes?" *Listener* 7 (164) (2 March 1932): 312–314.
Barton, J. E. *Purpose and Admiration: A Lay Study of the Visual Arts*. London: Christophers, 1932.

Barton, J. E. "Purpose Made Visible." *Listener* 7 (162) (February 17, 1932): 224–226.
Barton, J. E. "What Is Taste?" *Listener* 7 (165) (9 March 1932): 346–348.
Barton, J. E. "When Shall We Be Civilized?" *Listener* 7 (166) (16 March 1932): 378–380.
Barton, J. E. "Will the New City Make New Men?" *Listener* 7 (167) (23 March 1932): 412–414.
Baudrillard, Jean. *In the Shadow of the Silent Majorities; or, The End of the Social, and Other Essays*. Ed. Paul Foss and John Johnston. Trans. Paul Patton. New York: Semiotext(e), 1983.
Baudrillard, Jean. *Simulations*. New York: Semiotext(e), 1983.
BBC Year Book. London: British Broadcasting Corporation, 1930.
Becherer, Richard. "Past Remembering: Robert Mallet-Stevens's Architecture of Duration." *Assemblage* 31 (December 1996): 17–41.
Bell, Clive. "The Failure of State Art." *Listener* 16 (406) (21 October 1936): 745–748.
Benjamin, Walter. *Illuminations*. Ed. and intro. Hannah Arendt. Trans. Harry Zohn. New York: Schocken Books, 1968.
Benjamin, Walter. *Selected Writings*. Vol. 2. Ed. Michael Jennings and Marcus Bullock. Cambridge, Mass.: Harvard University Press, 1996.
Benton, Tim. "Dreams of Machines: Futurism and l'Esprit Nouveau." *Journal of Design History* 3 (1990): 19–34.
Bertram, Anthony. "The Art of Paul Nash." *Listener* 8 (200) (9 November 1932): 662.
Bertram, Anthony. "Bedrooms and Bathrooms." *Listener* 18 (459) (27 October 1937): 910–911.
Bertram, Anthony. *Design*. Harmondsworth: Penguin, 1938.
Bertram, Anthony. *Design in Everyday Things*. London: British Broadcasting Corporation, 1937.
Bertram, Anthony. "From Aeroplanes to Nutcrackers." *Listener* 18 (467) (22 December 1937): 1385.
Bertram, Anthony. "Heat, Light and Sound in the Home." *Listener* 18 (460) (3 November 1937): 971–972.
Bertram, Anthony. *The House: A Machine for Living in; A Summary of the Art and Science of Homemaking Considered Functionally*. London: A. & C. Black, 1935.
Bertram, Anthony. "Housing the Workers." *Listener* 18 (461) (10 November 1937): 1005–1007.
Bertram, Anthony. "Living-Rooms and Kitchens." *Listener* 18 (458) (20 October 1937): 840–841.
Bertram, Anthony. "Our Streets." *Listener* 18 (463) (24 November 1937): 1125.
Bertram, Anthony. "Places of Pleasure." *Listener* 18 (466) (15 December 1937): 1324.
Bertram, Anthony. "Places of Work." *Listener* 18 (465) (8 December 1937): 1261–1263.
Bertram, Anthony. "Public Buildings." *Listener* 18 (464) (1 December 1937): 1188–1190.
Bertram, Anthony. "What Does the Public Want?" *Listener* 18 (456) (6 October 1937): 709–711.
Bertram, Anthony. "What Is a House?" *Listener* 18 (457) (13 October 1937): 780–782.
Betjeman, John. "Back to the Railway Carriage." *Listener* 23 (585) (28 March 1940): 621.
Betjeman, John. "The Death of Modernism." *Architectural Review* 70 (December 1931): 161.
Betjeman, John. "An English Heritage." *Listener* 4 (93) (22 October 1930): 662.
Betjeman, John. *The English Town in the Last Hundred Years: The Rede Lecture*. Cambridge: Cambridge University Press, 1956.
Betjeman, John. *Ghastly Good Taste; or, A Depressing Story of the Rise and Fall of English Architecture*. London: Chapman & Hall, 1933.
Betjeman, John. "How to Look at a Church." *Listener* 20 (504) (8 September 1938): 484–486.
Betjeman, John. "On Writing about Architecture." *Architect* 2 (3) (March 1972): 24–25.
Betjeman, John. "The Passing of the Village." *Architectural Review* 72 (1932): 89–93.
Betjeman, John. *Selected Poems*. Ed. Alan Powers. London: Folio Society, 2004.

Betjeman, John. *Trains and Buttered Toast: Selected Radio Talks*. Comp. Stephen Games. London: John Murray, 2006.
Betjeman, John. "The Truth about Waterloo Bridge." *Architectural Review* 71 (April 1932): 125–127.
Betjeman, John. "Waterloo Bridge Is Falling Down." *Listener* 7 (163) (24 February 1932): 260.
Blease, W. Lyon. *A Short History of English Liberalism*. New York: Putnam, 1913.
Blomfield, Reginald. *Modernismus*. London: Macmillan, 1934.
Blomfield, Reginald, and Amyas Connell. "For and Against Modern Architecture." *Listener* 12 (307) (28 November 1934): 885–888.
Blomfield, Reginald, Charles Holden, Wells Coates, Maxwell E. Fry, Joseph Emberton, A. E. Richardson, and M. H. Baillie Scott. "Is Modern Architecture on the Right Track?—A Symposium." *Listener* 10 (237) (26 July 1933): 123–132.
Blunt, Anthony. "The Art of Diego Rivera." *Listener* 13 (327) (17 April 1935): 652–653.
Blunt, Anthony. "Cross-Section of Art in England Today." *Listener* 19 (492) (16 June 1938): 1280–1281.
Blunt, Anthony. "How I Look at Modern Painting." *Listener* 20 (496) (14 July 1938): 74–75.
Boumphrey, Geoffrey M. *Along the Roman Roads*. London: George Allen & Unwin, 1935.
Boumphrey, Geoffrey. *British Roads*. London: T. Nelson and Sons, 1939.
Boumphrey, Geoffrey. "Commonsense in City Housing." *Listener* 12 (301) (17 October 1934): 660.
Boumphrey, Geoffrey. "Does Town Life Mean Race Deterioration?" *Listener* 14 (362) (18 December 1935): 1111.
Boumphrey, Geoffrey M. "Down River." *Listener* 16 (391) (8 July 1936): 53–56.
Boumphrey, Geoffrey M. "Flats or Garden-Cities?" *Listener* 14 (351) (2 October 1935): 555–558.
Boumphrey, Geoffrey M. "From Ironbridge to Worcester." *Listener* 16 (394) (July 29, 1936): 219–222.
Boumphrey, Geoffrey M. "From Shrewsbury to Ironbridge." *Listener* 16 (393) (22 July 1936): 173–176.
Boumphrey, Geoffrey M. "From Welshpool to Shrewsbury." *Listener* 16 (392) (July 15, 1936): 123–126.
Boumphrey, Geoffrey. "Furnishing Workers' Homes." *Listener* 17 (439) (9 June 1937): 1126.
Boumphrey, Geoffrey M. *The House—Inside and Out*. London: George Allen & Unwin, 1936.
Boumphrey, Geoffrey. "Industry Comes to Corby." *Listener* 13 (322) (13 March 1935): 430–434.
Boumphrey, Geoffrey. "Inside London's New University." *Listener* 17 (422) (10 February 1937): 247.
Boumphrey, Geoffrey M. "The Last Stage to Goring Gop." *Listener* 16 (398) (August 26, 1936): 393–396.
Boumphrey, Geoffrey. "Post-War Housing in Germany." *Listener* 14 (350) (25 September 1935): 510.
Boumphrey, Geoffrey. "Revolution in the Home: New Order of Simplicity and Common Sense." *Listener* 6 (132) (22 July 1931): 144–145.
Boumphrey, Geoffrey M. "Round about Oxford." *Listener* 16 (397) (August 19, 1936): 356–358.
Boumphrey, Geoffrey M. "The Start of the Thames." *Listener* 16 (396) (August 12, 1936): 308–311.
Boumphrey, Geoffrey. "Thought for Tomorrow." *Listener* 13 (329) (1 May 1935): 735–737.
Boumphrey, Geoffrey. *Town and Country Tomorrow*. London: T. Nelson and Sons, 1940.
Boumphrey, Geoffrey M. "Ulster Holiday." *Listener* 18 (449) (18 August 1937): 330.
Boumphrey, Geoffrey M. *Your House and Mine*. London: George Allen & Unwin, 1938.
Boumphrey, G. M., and John Cadbury. "Suburbs or Satellites?" *Listener* 13 (320) (27 February 1935): 347–349.
Boumphrey, G. M., and Wells Coates. "Modern Dwellings for Modern Needs." *Listener* 9 (219) (24 March 1933): 819–822.
Boumphrey, Geoffrey M., and Elizabeth Denby. "The Kitchen." *Listener* 9 (227) (17 May 1933): 782–784.

Boumphrey, G. M., E. Halliday, and J. Gloag. "What's Wrong with Design Today?" *Listener* 9 (223) (19 April 1933): 607–610.
Boumphrey, Geoffrey, and A. B. Read. "Commonsense in Lighting." *Listener* 9 (229) (31 May 1933): 847–850.
Boumphrey, G. M., E. D. Simon, and P. Abercrombie. "Can Flats Solve the Housing Problem?" *Listener* 14 (55) (30 October 1935): 741–744.
Bourdieu, Pierre. *Distinction: A Social Critique of the Judgment of Taste*. Cambridge, Mass.: Harvard University Press, 1984.
Bourdieu, Pierre. *The Field of Cultural Production: Essays on Art and Literature*. New York: Columbia University Press, 1993.
Bourdieu, Pierre. *In Other Words: Essays Towards a Reflexive Sociology*. Stanford: Stanford University Press, 1990.
Bourdieu, Pierre. *The Logic of Practice*. Stanford: Stanford University Press, 1990.
Bourdieu, Pierre. *On Television*. New York: New Press, 1998.
Bourdieu, Pierre. *Outline of a Theory of Practice*. Cambridge: Cambridge University Press, 1977.
Bourdieu, Pierre. *The Rules of Art: Genesis and Structure of the Literary Field*. Stanford: Stanford University Press, 1996.
Bourdieu, Pierre. *Sociology in Question*. London: Sage, 1993.
Bourdieu, Pierre. *The Weight of the World: Social Suffering in Contemporary Society*. Cambridge: Polity, 1999.
Bourdieu, Pierre, and Jean-Claude Passeron. *Reproduction in Education, Society and Culture*. London: Sage Publications, 1977.
Bourdieu, Pierre, and John B. Thompson. *Language and Symbolic Power*. Cambridge, Mass.: Harvard University Press, 1991.
Bourdieu, Pierre, and Loïc J. D. Wacquant. *An Invitation to Reflexive Sociology*. Chicago: University of Chicago, 1992.
Boyer, M. Christine. *The City of Collective Memory: Its Historical Imagery and Architectural Entertainments*. Cambridge, Mass.: MIT Press, 1994.
Brecht, Berthold. *Brecht on Film and Radio*. Ed. and trans. Marc Silberman. London: Methuen, 2000.
Bridson, D. G. *Prospero and Ariel: The Rise and Fall of Radio*. London: Gollancz, 1972.
Briggs, Asa. *The BBC: The First Fifty Years*. Oxford: Oxford University Press, 1985.
Briggs, Asa. *The Birth of Broadcasting*. Vol. 1 of *The History of Broadcasting in the United Kingdom*. London: Oxford University Press, 1961.
Briggs, Asa. *The Golden Age of Wireless*. Vol. 2 of *The History of Broadcasting in the United Kingdom*. London: Oxford University Press, 1965.
Briggs, Asa. *Governing the BBC*. London: British Broadcasting Corporation, 1979.
Briggs, Asa. *The War of Words*. London: Oxford University Press, 1970.
Bull, Michael, and Les Back. *The Auditory Culture Reader*. Oxford: Berg, 2003.
Bulley, Margaret H. "A Test in Taste." *Listener* 10 (259) (27 December 1933): 1001.
Burke, Edmund. *A Philosophical Enquiry into the Origin of Our Ideas of the Sublime and Beautiful*. New York: Columbia University Press, 1958.
Burns, Timothy. *BBC: Public Institution, Private World*. London: Macmillan, 1977.
Burt, Cyril. "Psychology of Art." *Listener* 9 (211) (25 January 1933): 138–140.
Bushell, Sydney N. "Choosing a Home." *Listener* 2 (35) (11 September 1929): 350.

Bushell, Sydney N. "The Maidless House." *Listener* 2 (36) (18 September 1929): 390.
Byron, Robert. "Broadcasting House." *Architectural Review* 72 (August 1932): 47–52.

Cairns, Julia. "Colour in the Home." *Listener* 1 (11) (27 March 1929): 404.
Calhoun, Craig, Edward LiPuma, and Moishe Postone, eds. *Pierre Bourdieu: Critical Perspectives*. Chicago: University of Chicago Press, 1993.
Cantacuzino, Sherban. *Wells Coates: A Monograph*. London: G. Fraser, 1978.
Cantril, Hadley, and Gordon W. Allport. *Psychology of Radio*. New York: Harper & Brothers, 1935.
Carrington, Noel. "History through Architecture." *Listener* 7 (159) (27 January 1932): 136–137.
Carrington, Noel. "Need Our Cities Be Ugly?" *Listener* 3 (54) (22 January 1930): 149.
Carter, Edward. "Politics and Architecture." *Architectural Review* 166 (November 1979): 324.
Casson, Stanley. *Artists at Work: Based on a Series of Broadcast Dialogues between the Editor and Frank Dobson, Henry Rushbury, Albert Rutherston and Edward Halliday*. London: G. G. Harrap, 1933.
Casson, Stanley. "On Using Our Eyes." *Listener* 6 (146) (28 October 1931): 720–722.
Casson, Stanley, and C. Cox. "Why Bother about Art?" *Listener* 7 (170) (13 April 1932): 531–533.
Castle, Graham, and G. M. Boumphrey. "Village Life Today." *Listener* 13:323 (20 March 1935): 493.
Chartier, Roger. *The Order of Books: Readers, Authors and Libraries in Europe between the Fourteenth and Eighteenth Centuries*. Stanford: Stanford University Press, 1994.
Chermayeff, Serge. "Away with Snobbery, Sentiment and Stupidity." *Listener* 7 (193) (21 September 1932): 393–395.
Chesterton, G. K. "Architecture in Search of a Style." *Listener* 9 (210) (18 January 1933): 109.
Chesterton, G. K. "Review of Architectural Books." Broadcast, 9 January 1933. Sound Archives, London.
Chesterton, G. K. "Books and Authors: Architecture in Search of a Style." *Listener* 9 (210) (18 January 1933): 109.
"Civic Centres Exhibition." Editorial. *Listener* 16 (409) (11 November 1936): 889.
Clarke, Peter. *Hope and Glory: Britain 1900–1990*. London: Penguin Press, 1996.
Coates, Wells. "The Dramatic Control Room No. 1." *Architectural Review* 72 (August 1932): 60.
Cohn, Laura. *The Door to a Secret Room: A Portrait of Wells Coates*. Brookfield: Ashgate, 1999.
Collini, Stefan. *Public Moralists: Political Thought and Intellectual Life in Britain, 1850–1930*. New York: Oxford University Press, 1991.
Colomina, Beatriz. *Privacy and Publicity: Modern Architecture as Mass Media*. Cambridge, Mass.: MIT Press, 1994.
Colomina, Beatriz, and Jennifer Bloomer, eds. *Sexuality and Space*. New York: Princeton Architectural Press, 1992.
Colomina, Beatriz, and Joan Ockman, eds. *Architectureproduction*. New York: Princeton Architectural Press, 1988.
Cook, Chris. *A Short History of the Liberal Party, 1900–2001*. New York: Palgrave, 2002.
Corbin, Alain. *Village Bells: Sound and Meaning in the Nineteenth-Century French Countryside*. Trans. Martin Thom. New York: Columbia University Press, 1998.
Cornish, Vaughan. *National Parks, and the Heritage of Scenery*. London: Sifton, Praed, 1930.
Crawford, Alan. *C. R. Ashbee: Architect, Designer and Romantic Socialist*. New Haven: Yale University Press, 2005.
Crinson, Mark, and Jules Lubbock. *Architecture—Art or Profession? Three Hundred Years of Architectural Education in Britain*. Manchester: Manchester University Press, 1994.
Crosby, Ruth. "Oral Delivery in the Middle Ages." *Speculum* 11 (1936): 88–110.

Curran, James, and Jean Seaton. *Power without Responsibility: The Press and Broadcasting in Great Britain*. London: Routledge, 1988.
Curtis, William J. R. *Modern Architecture since 1900*. London: Phaidon, 1996.

Dangerfield, George. *The Strange Death of Liberal England*. New York: Capricorn Books, 1935.
Daunton, Martin J. "Housing." In F. M. L. Thompson, ed., *The Cambridge Social History of Britain, 1750–1950*, 195–250. Cambridge: Cambridge University Press, 1990.
Daunton, Martin. "The Political Economy of Death Duties: Harcourt's Budget of 1894." In Negley Harte and Roland Quinault, eds., *Land and Society in Britain, 1700–1914*. Manchester: Manchester University Press, 1996.
Daunton, Martin. *Trusting Leviathan: The Politics of Taxation in Britain, 1799–1914*. Cambridge: Cambridge University Press, 2007.
Davies, Kevin. "Finmar and the Furniture of the Future: The Sale of Alvar Aalto's Plywood Furniture in the UK, 1934–1939." *Journal of Design History* 2 (11) (1998): 145–156.
Davies, Peter. "In Defence of Not-So-Modern Houses." *Listener* 18 (464) (1 December 1937): 1187–1188.
Dean, David. *Architecture of the 1930s: Recalling the English Scene*. New York: Rizzoli, 1983.
Dellheim, Charles. *The Face of the Past: The Preservation of the Medieval Inheritance in Victorian England*. Cambridge: Cambridge University Press, 1982.
Doctor, Jennifer. *The BBC and Ultra-Modern Music, 1922–1936: Shaping a Nation's Tastes*. Cambridge: Cambridge University Press, 1999.
Dower, John. "Architecture and Aerodromes." *Listener* 4 (85) (27 August 1930): 322.
Dresser, Madge. "Housing Policy in Bristol, 1919–30. In Martin J. Daunton, ed., *Councillors and Tenants: Local Authority Housing in English Cities, 1919–1939*. Leicester: Leicester University Press, 1984.
Duncan, R. A. "The Architecture of the Future." *Listener* 3 (73) (4 June 1930): 973.
Duthuit, G. "Art and the State—III. France." *Listener* 16 (400) (9 September 1936): 474–476.
Dutton, David. *A History of the Liberal Party in the Twentieth Century*. New York: Palgrave Macmillan, 2004.

Eckersley, Roger Huxley. *B.B.C. and All That: Autobiographical Reminiscences*. London: Sampson Low, Marston, 1946.
Edwards, Norman. "The Problem of the Talks." *Listener* 3 (67) (23 April 1930): 717.
Eeles, F. C. "What to Look for in Churches." *Listener* 18 (446) (28 August 1937): 197–199.
Eisenman, Peter. "The End of the Classical: The End of the Beginning, the End of the End." *Perspecta* 21 (1984): 155–173.
Eisenstein, Elizabeth. *The Printing Press as an Agent of Change: Communications and Cultural Transformations in Early Modern Europe*. Cambridge: Cambridge University Press, 1979.
Errazurez, A. "Some Types of Housing in Liverpool, 1785–1890." *Town Planning Review* 19 (1943): 57–68.
Etchells, Frederick. "Architecture and the Average Man." *Listener* 10 (242) (30 August 1933): 316.

Forty, Adrian. *Words and Buildings: A Vocabulary of Modern Architecture*. New York: Thames & Hudson, 2000.
Foucault, Michel. *Discipline and Punish: The Birth of the Prison*. New York: Pantheon Books, 1977.
Fowler, Bridget. *Reading Bourdieu on Society and Culture*. Oxford: Blackwell Publishers/Sociological Review, 2000.

Fraser, Jane, and Liz Paul. "The Living Tradition: Modernism and the Decorative Arts." *Twentieth Century Society* 20 (1984): 52–67.
Freeden, Michael. *Liberalism Divided: A Study in British Political Thought, 1914–1939*. Oxford: Oxford University Press, 1986.
Frow, Edmund, and Ruth Frow. "The Spark of Independent Working-Class Education: Lancashire, 1909–1930." In Brian Simon, ed., *The Search for Enlightenment: The Working Class and Adult Education in the Twentieth Century*. London: Lawrence & Wishhart, 1990.
Fry, Maxwell. *Autobiographical Sketches*. London: Elek, 1975.
Fry, Maxwell E. "Can Belfast Be Reshaped?" *Listener* 16 (410) (18 November 1936): 961–963.
Fry, Maxwell E. "English Town Hall Architecture." *Listener* 11 (275) (18 April 1934): 649–651.
Fry, Maxwell E. "Frank Lloyd Wright." *Listener* 21 (540) (18 May 1939): 1050–1052.
Fry, Maxwell E. "Modern Town Planning." *Listener* 19 (246) (13 January 1939): 661.
Fry, Maxwell E. "A Plan of Action for Ulster." *Listener* 16 (415) (23 December 1936): 1199–1200.
Fry, Maxwell E. "Saving the Coastline's Beauty." *Listener* 16 (412) (2 December 1936): 1040.
Fry, Maxwell E. "Town Planning in Northern Ireland: What Planning Means." *Listener* 16 (406) (18 November 1936): 886–887.
Fry, Maxwell E. "What Planning Can Do for Small Towns." *Listener* 16 (414) (16 December 1936): 1147–1148.
Fry, Maxwell E. "What Planning Means." *Listener* 16 (409) (11 November 1936): 886.
Fry, Maxwell E., and John Gloag. "The Need for Planning Town and Countryside." *Listener* 9 (232) (21 June 1933): 970–973.
Fry, Roger. "The Meaning of Pictures." *Listener* 2 (39) (9 October 1929): 467–469.
Furlong, George. "Is Modern Art Unintelligible?" *Listener* 20 (503) (1 September 1938): 450.

Games, Stephen. *Pevsner on Art and Architecture: The Radio Talks*. London: Methuen, 2002.
Gandelsonas, Mario. "Linguistics in Architecture." *Casabella* 374 (February 1973): 17–31.
Gaze, John. *Figures in a Landscape: A History of the National Trust*. London: Barrie & Jenkins in association with the National Trust, 1988.
Giffen, Robert. *The Progress of the Working Classes in the Last Half Century*. London: George Bell and Sons, 1884.
Girouard, Mark. Introduction. In Tim Knox, ed., *First and Last Loves: John Betjeman and Architecture*. London: Soane Gallery, 2006.
Gloag, John. "Advertising in the 3D." *Architectural Review* 72 (November 1933): 79–82.
Gloag, John. "Ancestor Worship in Design." *Listener* 8 (192) (14 September 1932): 364–366.
Gloag, John. "The Architect and the Future Public." *Journal of the Royal Institute of British Architects* 55 (September 1948): 509–511.
Gloag, John. "A Broadcast Commentary." *Listener* 13 (313) (9 January 1935): 52.
Gloag, John, ed. *Design in Modern Life*. London: George Allen & Unwin, 1934.
Gloag, John. "Design in Wood." *Listener* 16 (394) (29 July 1936): 194.
Gloag, John. "Geoffrey M. Boumphrey, 1894–1969." *Architectural Review* 147 (February 1970): 162, 164.
Gloag, John. *The House We Ought to Live In*. London: Duckworth, 1923.
Gloag, John. "The Machine Age Gone Gay." *Listener* 21 (542) (1 June 1939): 1139.
Gloag, John, Sinclair Wood, and James Whittaker. "Permanence in Building." Part V of *Men Talking*, BBC series, 4 February 1937. British Library Sound Archives, London; transcript BBC WAC.

Gloag, John, and G. G. Wornum. "New Building for a New Age." *Listener* 25 (641) (24 April 1941): 583.

Gombrich, E. H. "Art and Propaganda." *Listener* 22 (569) (7 December 1939): 1118.

Goodhart-Rendel, H. S. "Architecture in a Changing World." *Listener* 20 (509) (13 October 1938): 755–760.

Goodhart-Rendel, H. S. "Build or Restore." Broadcast lecture, 26 January 1941. Transcript BBC WAC.

Grigson, Geoffrey, and Casson, Stanley. "Points from Letters: Oxford Architecture." *Listener* 16 (401) (16 September 1936): 539, 16 (402) (23 September 1936): 590, and 16 (403) (30 September 1936): 639.

Gropius, Walter. "Rehousing in Big Cities—Outwards or Upwards?" *Listener* 11 (279) (16 May 1934): 814.

Habermas, Jürgen. *The Theory of Communicative Action*. Boston: Beacon Press, 1984.

Halliday, Edward, and Gordon Russell. "The Living-Room and Furniture." *Listener* 9 (225) (May 3, 1933): 695–698.

Hays, K. Michael. *Architecture's Desire: Reading the Late Avant-Garde*. Cambridge, Mass.: MIT Press, 2010.

Hill, Kate. *Culture and Class in English Public Museums, 1850–1914*. Aldershot, England; Burlington, Vt.: Ashgate, 2005.

Hill, Samuel. "Town and Country Planning Act, 1932." *Journal of the Royal Society for the Promotion of Health* 54(2) (1933): 100–116.

Hinkel, R. H. "Art and the State—IV. Germany." *Listener* 16 (401) (16 September 1936): 514–517.

Hinks, Roger. "Can Art Be Subversive?" *Listener* 17 (424) (24 February 1937): 339–341.

Hinks, Roger. "Text and Image." *Listener* 22 (556) (7 September 1939): 484.

Holmes, Charles. "Can Taste Be Taught?" *Listener* 9 (210) (18 January 1933): 76.

Holmes, Charles. "An Experiment in Artistic Taste." *Listener* 9 (210) (18 January 1933): 76.

Holmes, Charles. "Which Do You Prefer?" *Listener* 9 (210) (January 18, 1933): 77–82.

Holmes, Charles. "'Why the English Have No Taste.'" *Listener* 14 (346) (28 August 1935): 352–354.

Houfe, Simon, John Wilton-Ely, and Alan Powers. *Sir Albert Richardson 1880–1964*. London: Heinz Gallery, 1999.

Howe, Irving. *Modern Literary Criticism: An Anthology*. Boston: Beacon Press, 1958.

"How the Public Responds to Broadcasting." Editorial. *Listener* 14 (351) (2 October 1935): 559.

Hunter, Fred. "Hilda Matheson and the BBC, 1926–40." In Sybil Oldfield, ed., *This Working-Day World: Women's Lives and Culture(s) in Britain, 1914–1945*. London: Taylor & Francis, 1994.

Hunter, Fred. "Matheson, Hilda (1888–1940): Intelligence Officer and Director of Radio Talks." In *Oxford Dictionary of National Biography Online*. http://www.oxforddnb.com/view/article/49198 (accessed 20 August 2009).

Jackson, Holbrook. "Shopping and Taste." *Listener* 17 (427) (17 March 1937): 487.

Jarzombek, Mark. *The Psychologizing of Modernity: Art, Architecture, and History*. Cambridge: Cambridge University Press, 2000.

Jenkins, Frank. *Architect and Patron: A Survey of Professional Relations and Practice in England from the Sixteenth Century to the Present Day*. London: Oxford University Press, 1961.

Jennings, Hilda, and Winifred Gill. *Broadcasting in Everyday Life*. London: British Broadcasting Corporation, 1939.

Joad, Doreen. "Garden Design." *Listener* 1 (11) (27 March 1929): 403.
Jones, Allan. "Mary Adams and the Producer's Role in Early BBC Science Broadcasts." *Public Understanding of Science* 21:8 (November 2012).
Jordan, Robert Furneaux. "Building in Timber." *Listener* 16 (395) (5 August 1936): 267–269.

Kaes, Anton, Martin Jay, and Edward Dimendberg, eds. *The Weimar Republic Sourcebook*. Berkeley: University of California Press, 1994.
Kaye, Barrington. *The Development of the Architectural Profession in Britain: A Sociological Study*. London: George Allen & Unwin, 1960.
Keynes, J. M. "Art and the State—I." *Listener* 16 (398) (26 August 1936): 371–374.
Kindersley, Ann. "Handicrafts in Colour." *Listener* 1 (7) (27 February 1929): 255.
Knox, Tim, ed. *First and Last Loves: John Betjeman and Architecture*. London: Soane Gallery, 2006.

Laing, Webb J., and E. Thole. "The House that Jack Built." Broadcast lecture, 27 April 1936. Transcript BBC WAC.
Lamb, W. "Art in Industry at the Royal Academy." *Listener* 13 (313) (9 January 1935): 47–51.
Lambert, Richard. "Are Talks Too Highbrow?" Editorial. *Listener* 3 (67) (23 April 1930): 116.
Lambert, Richard. "Are We Becoming Vulgar?" Editorial. *Listener* 3 (53) (15 January 1930): 100.
Lambert, Richard Stanton. *Ariel and All His Quality: An Impression of the BBC from Within*. London: V. Gollancz, 1940.
Lambert, Richard. "The Ugliness Exhibition." Editorial. *Listener* 1 (7) (27 February 1929): 240.
Lancaster, Osbert. "The Changing Spirit of Architecture." *Listener* 30 (760) (8 May 1943): 160.
Lange, Alexandra. "This Year's Model Representing Modernism to the Postwar American Corporation." *Journal of Design History* 19 (3) (Autumn 2006): 233–248.
LeMahieu, Daniel. *A Culture for Democracy: Mass Communication and the Cultivated Mind in Britain between the Wars*. Oxford: Oxford University Press, 1988.
LeMahieu, Daniel. "John Reith." In Susan Pedersen and Peter Mandler, eds., *After the Victorians: Private Conscience and Public Duty in Modern Britain*. London: Routledge, 1994.
Levine, Neil. "The Book and the Building: Hugo's Theory of Architecture and Labrouste's Bibliothèque Ste-Geneviève." In Robin Middleton, ed., *The Beaux Arts and Nineteenth-Century French Architecture*. Cambridge, Mass.: MIT Press, 1982.
Levita, Cecil. "Housing and Civic Responsibility." Part V of *Other People's Houses. Listener* 9 (214) (February 15, 1933): 233–235.
Lewis, Leslie. "Furnishing in Sunshine." *Listener* 2 (27) (17 August 1929): 101.
Lipstadt, Hélène. "The Building and the Book in César Daly's *Revue Générale de l'Architecture*." In Beatriz Colomina and Joan Ockman, eds., *Architectureproduction*. New York: Princeton Architectural Press, 1988.
Lipstadt, Hélène. "Celebrating the Centenaries of Summerson and Hitchcock: Finding a Historiography for the Architect-Historian." In Frank Salmon, ed., *Summerson and Hitchcock: Centenary Essays on Architectural Historiography*, 331–350. New Haven: Yale University Press, 2006.
Lipstadt, Hélène. "Polemic and Parody in the Battle for British Modernism." *AA Files*, no. 3 (January 1983): 68–76.
Lipstadt, Hélène, and Barry Bergdoll. *The Experimental Tradition: Essays on Competitions in Architecture*. New York: Princeton Architectural Press, 1989.

Lubbock, Jules. *The Tyranny of Taste: The Politics of Architecture and Design in Britain, 1550–1960*. New Haven: Yale University Press, 1995.
Lubetkin, Berthold. "Lubetkin's Letter to Wells Coates." *Architectural Review* 330 (November 1979): x.
Lyon, Robert. "An Experiment in Art Appreciation." *Listener* 13 (333) (29 May 1935): 909–911.

MacCannell, Dean. *The Tourist: A New Theory of the Leisure Class*. New York: Schocken, 1976.
MacCarthy, Fiona. *The Simple Life: C. R. Ashbee in the Cotswolds*. Berkeley: University of California Press, 1981.
Maclagan, Eric. "Church Building through the Centuries." *Listener* 18 (464) (1 December 1937): 1200.
Mainds, Allan D. "Charles Rennie Mackintosh." *Listener* 10 (236) (19 August 1933): 98.
Mandler, Peter. *Aristocratic Government in the Age of Reform: Whigs and Liberals, 1830–1852*. Oxford: Clarendon Press, 1990.
Mandler, Peter. *The English National Character: The History of an Idea from Edmund Burke to Tony Blair*. New Haven: Yale University Press, 2006.
Mandler, Peter. *History and National Life*. London: Profile Books, 2002.
Mandler, Peter. *Liberty and Authority in Victorian Britain*. New York: Oxford University Press, 2006.
Mandler, Peter. *The Rise and Fall of the Stately Home*. New Haven: Yale University Press, 1997.
Marinetti, F. T. "Art and the State—VI. Italy." *Listener* 16 (405) (14 October 1936): 730–732.
Matheson, Hilda. *Broadcasting*. London: Thornton Butterworth, 1933.
Matless, David. *Landscape and Englishness*. London: Reaktion Books, 1998.
Matless, David. "Ordering the Land: The 'Preservation' of the English Countryside, 1918–1939." Ph.D. diss., University of Nottingham, 1990.
McIntyre, Ian. *The Expense of Glory: A Life of John Reith*. London: HarperCollins, 1993.
McKenzie, D. F. *Bibliography and the Sociology of Texts*. Cambridge: Cambridge University Press, 1999.
McKibbin, Ross. *Classes and Cultures: England 1918–1951*. Oxford: Oxford University Press, 1998.
McKibbin, Ross. "Why Was There No Marxism in Great Britain?" *English Historical Review* 99 (1984): 297–331.
McLuhan, Marshall. *Understanding Media: The Extensions of Man*. 1964. Cambridge, Mass.: MIT Press, 1991.
Melvin, Jeremy. *F. R. S. Yorke and the Evolution of English Modernism*. Chichester: Wiley-Academy, 2003.
Mendelsohn, Erich. "In Defense of the New Architecture." *Listener* 4 (84) (20 August 1930): 278.
Menzies, Leslie. "The Fireplace in Summer." *Listener* 1 (23) (19 June 1929): 874.
Menzies, Leslie. "Painted Furniture." *Listener* 1 (4) (6 February 1929): 150.
Menzies, Leslie. "Repairing Furniture." *Listener* 1 (12) (3 April 1929): 440.
Meyer, Richard J. "Charles A. Siepmann and Educational Broadcasting." *Educational Technology Research and Development* 12 (4) (December 1964): 413.
Mill, John Stuart. *Considerations on Representative Government*. London: Parker, Son, and Bourn, 1861.
Milyutin, N. "Art and the State—II. Russia." *Listener* 16 (399) (2 September 1936): 423–426.
Mingay, Gordon E. *A Social History of the English Countryside*. London: Routledge, 1990.
Morrison, Herbert. "A Green Belt round London." *Topical Talk*, 22 January 1935. Sound Archives, London.
Morrison, Herbert. "Planning London." *Listener* 13 (335) (12 June 1935): 987.
Mowl, Timothy. *Stylistic Cold Wars: Betjeman versus Pevsner*. London: John Murray, 2000.
Mumford, L. "Art and the State—V. America." *Listener* 16 (404) (7 October 1936): 549–552.

Muthesius, Hermann. *The English House*. New York: Rizzoli, 1987.
Muthesius, Stefan. "Review: C. R. *Ashbee: Architect, Designer and Romantic Socialist* by Alan Crawford." *Oxford Art Journal* 9 (2) (1986): 82–84.
Myer, G. V. "Modern Architecture and Tradition." *Listener* 8 (185) (27 July 1932): 324–326.

Neumann, Dietrich, and Donald Albrecht. *Film Architecture: Set Designs from* Metropolis *to* Blade Runner. New York: Prestel, 1999.
"New Architecture in London, The." Editorial. *Listener* 7 (165) (9 March 1932): 335.
Newton, Eric. "The Artist and His Public." *Listener* 13 (313) (9 January 1935): 63–64.
Newton, Eric. "Artist in the Witness Box." *Listener* 23 (582) (7 March 1940): 480.
Newton, Eric. "Centre Party vs. Left Wing." *Listener* 23 (576) (25 January 1940): 163–165.
Newton, Eric. "Medium and Craftsmanship." *Listener* 13 (317) (6 February 1935): 241–243.
Newton, Eric, and J. L. Beddington. "Art and Propaganda." *Listener* 23 (579) (15 February 1940): 304–306.
Newton, Eric, and Reginald Blomfield. "This Modernismus." *Listener* 13 (320) (27 February 1935): 371–373.
Newton, Eric, and H. S. Goodhart-Rendel. "Artist and Architect." *Listener* 23 (578) (8 February 1940): 263–265.
Newton, Eric, and R. H. Wilenski. "The Modern Critic Explains His Creed." *Listener* 13 (322) (13 March 1935): 452–454.
"New Tower of London, The." *Architectural Review* 72 (August 1932): 43.

O'Donovan, Donal. *God's Architect: A Life of Raymond McGrath*. Wicklow: Kilbride Books, 1995.
Olechnowicz, Andrzej. *Working-Class Housing in England between the Wars: The Becontree Estate*. New York: Oxford University Press, 1997.
Olmo, Carlo. "International Architecture, Historical Research and Working Critique." *Zodiac*, no. 18 (September 1997–February 1998): 89.
Ong, Walter J. *Orality and Literacy: The Technologizing of the Word*. London: Routledge, 1982.
Orwell, George. "The Frontiers of Art and Propaganda." *Listener* 25 (646) (29 May 1941): 768.

Pakington, Humphrey. "Tradition and Experiment." *Listener* 3 (68) (30 April 1930): 768–769.
Panofsky, Erwin. *Gothic Architecture and Scholasticism*. New York: Meridian Books, 1957.
"Patronage and the Arts." *Listener* 50 (1286) (22 October 1953): 674.
Pedersen, Susan, and Peter Mandler, eds. *After the Victorians: Private Conscience and Public Duty in Modern Britain*. London: Routledge, 1994.
Pegg, Mark. *Broadcasting and Society, 1918–1939*. London: Croom Helm, 1983.
Petrie, Maria. "Architecture and Everyman." *Listener* 6 (135) (12 August 1931): 263.
Pevsner, Nikolaus. *The Englishness of English Art*. London: Architectural Press, 1956.
Pevsner, Nikolaus. *Pevsner on Art and Architecture: The Radio Talks*. Ed. Stephen Games. London: Methuen, 2002.
Pevsner, Nikolaus. *Pioneers of the Modern Movement from William Morris to Walter Gropius*. London: Faber & Faber, 1936.
Pevsner, Nikolaus. *Worcestershire*. Harmondsworth: Penguin, 1968.
Pick, Frank. "At the Paris Exhibition." *Listener* 17 (436) (19 May 1937): 971–973.
Pick, Frank. "The Meaning and Purpose of Design." *Listener* 9 (233) (28 June 1933): 1016–1018.

Pick, Frank, and John Gloag. "Design in the Street." *Listener* 9 (230) (7 June 1933): 895–898.
Piper, John. "The English and Their Architecture." *Listener* 31 (804) (8 June 1944): 640–642.
Powers, Alan. *Eric Ravilious: Imagined Realities*. London: Philip Wilson, 2004.
Powers, Alan. *H. S. Goodhart-Rendel: 1887–1959*. London: Architectural Association, 1987.
Powers, Alan. *In the Line of Development: FRS Yorke, E Rosenberg and CS Mardell to YRM, 1930–1992*. London: RIBA Heinz Gallery, 1992.
Powers, Alan. "John Betjeman and Modern Architecture." In Tim Knox, ed., *First and Last Loves: John Betjeman and Architecture*, 31–40. London: Soane Gallery, 2006.
Powers, Alan. "John Summerson and Modernism." In Louise Campbell, ed., *Twentieth Century Architecture and Its Histories*, 153–172. Utley: Society of Architectural Historians of Great Britain, 2000.
Powers, Alan. *Oliver Hill, Architect and Lover of Life: 1887–1968*. London: Mouton Publications, 1989.
Powers, Alan. "Search for a New Reality." *Twentieth Century Society* 20 (1984): 18–39.
Powers, Alan. *Serge Chermayeff: Designer, Architect, Teacher*. London: RIBA Publications, 2001.
Powers, Alan. *Twentieth Century Houses: From the Archives of Country Life*. London: Aurum, 2004.
Powers, Alan, and Morley Von Sternberg. *Modern: The Modern Movement in Britain*. London: Merrell, 2005.
"Preservation of Rural England: Draft of New Council Prepared." [London] *Times* 8 (November 1926): 11.
Program Indexes. London: British Broadcasting Corporation, 1927–1945.

"Radical Architecture of Little Magazines, The: Periodicals as Sites of Innovation." Princeton Ph.D. architectural students' traveling exhibition. (2007–2009).
Raphael, W. S. "The Art of Easing Housework." *Listener* 2 (39) (9 October 1929): 485.
Ratner, Harry. *Language and Thinking*. New York: Insight Media, 1992.
Read, Herbert. *Anarchy and Order: Essays in Politics*. Boston: Beacon Press, 1971.
Read, Herbert. "Architecture and Sculpture." *Listener* 4 (81) (30 July 1930): 169.
Read, Herbert. *Art and Society*. New York: Schocken Books, 1966.
Read, Herbert. "Art in Education." *Listener* 22 (551) (3 August 1939): 215.
Read, Herbert. *Child Art: The Beginnings of Self-Affirmation*. Berkeley, Calif: Diablo Press, 1973.
Read, Herbert. "The City of To-morrow." *Listener* 5 (110) (18 February 1931): 272–273.
Read, Herbert. "The House of To-morrow." *Listener* 5 (111) (25 February 1931): 324.
Read, Herbert. *Education through Art*. New York: Pantheon Books, 1958.
Read, Herbert. "An Enquiry into Public Taste." *Listener* 18 (443) (7 July 1937): 31.
Read, Herbert. *The Green Child*. New York: New Directions, 1948.
Read, Herbert. "How Shall We Rebuild?" *Listener* 24 (615) (24 October 1940): 586–587.
Read, Herbert. *Icon and Idea: The Function of Art in the Development of Human Consciousness*. Cambridge, Mass.: Harvard University Press, 1955.
Read, Herbert. *The Innocent Eye*. New York: H. Holt, 1947.
Read, Herbert. "The International Style." *Listener* 13 (332) (22 May 1935): 866–868.
Read, Herbert. *Meaning of Art*. London: Faber & Faber, 1931.
Read, Herbert. "Methods in Art Criticism." Listener 3 (59) (26 February 1930): 371.
Read, Herbert. "On Looking at a Picture." *Listener* 5 (108) (4 February 1931): 193–194.
Read, Herbert. *To Hell with Culture, and Other Essays on Art and Society*. New York: Schocken Books, 1963.
Reiach, Alan. "The Buildings We Live With." *Listener* 26 (657) (14 August 1941): 234.
Reilly, Charles. *Architecture as a Communal Art*. London: B. T. Batsford, 1944.

Reilly, Charles. *Charles Reilly and the Liverpool School of Architecture, 1904–1933.* Liverpool: Liverpool University Press; National Museums & Galleries on Merseyside, 1997.

Reilly, Charles. "In and Out of Broadcasting House—I. The Architecture of the Building." *Listener* 8 (183) (13 July 1932): 52–55.

Reilly, Charles. "Modern Movements in Architecture." *Listener* 25 (636) (20 March 1941): 399.

Reilly, Charles. "Propaganda and Publicity." *Journal of the Royal Institute of British Architects* 29 (August 27, 1921): 547.

Reith, John C. W. *Broadcast over Britain.* London: Hodder and Stoughton, 1924.

Reith, John C. W. *Into the Wind.* London: Hodder & Stoughton, 1949.

Reith, John. *The Reith Diaries.* London: Collins, 1975.

Reith, John C. W. "What Is Our Policy?" *Radio Times* 2 (14 March 1924): 442.

Ricardo, Halsey. "The Value of Public Opinion." *Journal of the Royal Institute of British Architects* 29 (June 1922): 502–507.

Richards, James M. "Architectural Criticism in the Nineteen-Thirties." In John Summerson, ed., *Concerning Architecture: Essays on Architectural Writers and Writing Presented to Nikolaus Pevsner*, 252–257. London: Allen Lane, 1968.

Richards, James M. "Radio Station: A New Building Typology." *Architectural Review* 69 (March 1931).

Richardson, A. E. "The British Railway Station." *Listener* 15 (375) (18 March 1936): 519–522.

Richardson, A. E. "The Charm of Old London." *Listener* 19 (476) (23 February 1938): 405.

Richardson, A. E. "The Railway Station of Tomorrow." *Listener* 15 (377) (1 April 1936): 618–620.

Richardson, A. E. "Railway Stations Abroad." *Listener* 15 (376) (25 March 1936): 574–576.

Richmond, Zoe. "A Small Space and a Small Purse." *Listener* 1 (5) (13 February 1929): 187.

Robertson, Howard. "In and Out of Broadcasting House—II. The Structure of the Building." *Listener* 8 (184) (20 July 1932): 86–89.

Robertson, Howard. "Modern Architecture in Europe." *Listener* 3 (72) (28 May 1930): 930.

Robertson, Howard. "Structure and Material." *Listener* 3 (69) (7 May 1930): 803–804.

Rothenstein, William. "Entry into Art." *Listener* 14 (353) (16 October 1935): 650–651.

Rothenstein, W., W. Lewis, G. Grigson, A. K. Lawrence, and R. Blomfield. "Traditional versus Modern Art." *Listener* 21 (543) (8 June 1939): 1191.

Sadler, Michael. "Conclusion and Comment." *Listener* 22 (559) (28 September 1939): 616.

Saint, Andrew. *The Image of the Architect.* New Haven: Yale University Press, 1983.

Saler, Michael T. *The Avant-Garde in Interwar England: Medieval Modernism and the London Underground.* New York: Oxford University Press, 1999.

Salmon, Frank, ed. *Summerson and Hitchcock: Centenary Essays on Architectural Historiography.* New Haven: Yale University Press, 2006.

Samson, Miles David. "Philip Johnson and the Museum of Modern Art's 'Grand Tour' Modernism." Paper presented at the annual conference of the Society of Architectural Historians, Pasadena, California, 2–5 April 2009.

Scannell, Paddy, and David Cardiff. *A Social History of British Broadcasting: Serving the Nation 1922–1939.* Oxford: Blackwell, 1991.

Schirokauer, Arno. "Art and Politics in Radio." In Anton Kaes, Martin Jay, and Edward Dimendberg, eds., *The Weimar Republic Sourcebook*, 609–610. Berkeley: University of California Press, 1994.

Schivelbusch, Wolfgang. *The Railway Journey: The Industrialization of Time and Space in the Nineteenth Century.* Berkeley: University of California Press, 1986.

Scott, Giles Gilbert. "Liverpool Cathedral." Transcript, Scott Family Papers, ScGG/230/1, RIBA Collections, London.

Scott, Giles Gilbert. "Speech at the Banquet of the Royal Institute of British Architects," 22 November 1934. Sound Archives, London.
Shand, P. Morton. "The Changing Bridge—I." *Listener* 18 (456) (6 October 1937): 722–724.
Shand, P. Morton. "The Changing Bridge—II." *Listener* 18 (457) (13 October 1937): 796–798.
Shand, P. Morton. "Whither Church Architecture? I." *Listener* 10 (259) (27 December 1933): 972.
Shand, P. Morton. "Whither Church Architecture? II." *Listener* 11 (260) (3 January 1934): 18.
"The Shape of Things to Use, The." Editorial. *Listener* 18:452 (8 September 1937): 490–491.
Shaw, Norman, ed. *Architecture: A Profession or an Art; Thirteen Short Essays on the Qualifications and Training of Architects*. London: J. Murray, 1892.
Siepmann, Charles. 1941. *"Can Radio Educate?" Education by Radio 11*., 25–26. First Quarter.
Siepmann, Charles. "Can Radio Educate?" *Journal of Educational Sociology* 14 (February 1941): 346–357.
Siepmann, Charles. "The Mechanization of Education." *Spectator* (London) 147 (28 November 1931): 728–729.
Siepmann, Charles. "Wireless and Adult Education in Great Britain." *Journal of the American Association of University Women* 22 (January 1929): 57–60.
Simon, Brian. *The Search for Enlightenment: The Working Class and Adult Education in the Twentieth Century*. London: Lawrence & Wishart, 1990.
Simon, Ernest Darwin. *The Rebuilding of Manchester*. London: Longmans, Green, 1935.
Simon, Melanie. "Ranges of Light and Time: What Can Alan Ward's Photography Teach Landscape Architects?" *Landscape Architecture* 19:3 (2000): 122–123.
Simon of Wythenshawe, Lord (Ernest Darwin Simon). *The BBC from Within*. London: Victor Gollancz, 1953.
Simpson, John W. "The Unification and Registration of the Architectural Profession." *Journal of the Royal Institute of British Architects* 28 (July 30, 1921): 497–500.
Skeaping, John. "The Relation of Sculpture and Architecture." *Listener* 11 (270) (14 March 1934): 456.
Smith, Janet Adam. "Experiment in Art Appreciation." *Listener* 19 (480) (23 March 1938): 625.
Stansky, Peter. *Gladstone: A Progress in Politics*. Boston: Little, Brown, 1979.
Stansky, Peter. *On or About December 1910: Early Bloomsbury and Its Intimate World*. Cambridge, Mass.: Harvard University Press, 1996.
Stansky, Peter. *William Morris, C. R. Ashbee and the Arts and Crafts*. London: Nine Elms Press, 1984.
Stevenson, Tom, ed. *The Countryside Companion*. London: Odham's Press, 1939.
Stoller, Ezra. "Photography and the Language of Architecture." *Perspecta* 8 (1963): 43–44.
Street, A. G., et al. "Good Manners in the Countryside." *Listener* 12 (292) (15 August 1934): 264.
Summerson, John. "Abstract Painters." *Listener* 21 (531) (16 March 1939): 574.
Summerson, John. "Architecture: A Changing Profession." *Listener* 21 (536) (20 April 1939): 830–832.
Summerson, John. "Architecture at the Empire Exhibition." *Listener* 19 (488) (18 May 1938): 1064–1066.
Summerson, John. *Architecture in Britain, 1530 to 1830*. London: Penguin Books, 1953.
Summerson, John. "An Archive for Architecture." Broadcast talk, 25 September 1944. Transcript BBC WAC.
Summerson, John. "Bombed Architecture in the West." Broadcast talk, 6 April 1942. Transcript BBC WAC.
Summerson, John. "Building Boom—I." *Listener* 18 (468) (29 December 1937): 1418–1420.
Summerson, John. "Building Boom—II." *Listener* 19 (469) (5 January 1938): 20–22.
Summerson, John. *The Classical Language of Architecture*. Cambridge, Mass.: MIT Press, 1963.

Summerson, John, ed. *Concerning Architecture: Essays on Architectural Writers and Writing Presented to Nikolaus Pevsner*. London: Allen Lane, 1968.

Summerson, John. "Creative Housing." *Listener* 18 (447) (4 August 1937): 223–225.

Summerson, John. "The Critics: Radio." Undated broadcast. Sir John Summerson Papers, Broadcast Talks SuJ/10/17. Transcript V&A and RIBA Collections, Victoria and Albert Museum, London.

Summerson, John. "Extracts from Sir John Summerson Royal Gold Medal Address." *Journal of the Royal Institute of British Architects* 83 (December 1976): 495.

Summerson, John. "Famous Midland Houses." Broadcast May 1937. Sir John Summerson Papers, SuJ/10/1. Transcript RIBA Collections.

Summerson, John. "The Fate of Modern Architecture." *Listener* 23 (593) (23 May 1940): 1002–1003.

Summerson, John. "Forty Years of British Architecture." *Listener* 17 (418) (13 January 1937): 60–62.

Summerson, John. *Georgian London*. New York: C. Scribner's Sons, 1946.

Summerson, John. *Heavenly Mansions, and Other Essays on Architecture*. New York: W. W. Norton, 1963.

Summerson, John. "How to Look at a Town." Broadcast travelogue, 10 February 1945. Sir John Summerson Papers, SuJ/10/1. Transcript RIBA Collections.

Summerson, John. "John Wood, Architect and Planner of Bath." Broadcast talk, 7 September 1945. Transcript BBC WAC.

Summerson, John. *The Life and Work of John Nash, Architect*. Cambridge, Mass.: MIT Press, 1980.

Summerson, John. "London Hereafter." *Listener* 28 (719) (22 October 1942): 532.

Summerson, John. "London Regrouped." *Listener* 30 (755) (1 July 1943): 16.

Summerson, John. "Model Villages." Broadcast talk, 10 April 1942. Transcript BBC WAC.

Summerson, John. "Mr. Voysey—Gold Medallist." *Listener* 23 (582) (7 March 1940): 479–480.

Summerson, John. "Nash's Terraces in Regent's Park." Broadcast travelogue, 6 October 1942. Sir John Summerson Papers, SuJ/10/1. Transcript RIBA Collections.

Summerson, John. "Norman Shaw: Master of Design." *Listener* 25 (638) (3 April 1941): 493.

Summerson, John. "Norwich City Hall." *Listener* 20 (512) (3 November 1938): 934–935.

Summerson, John. "Paper Architecture." *Listener* 25 (630) (6 February 1941): 189.

Summerson, John. "Reconstruction: Plymouth Rebuilding Plans." *Listener* 31 (799) (4 May 1944): 491.

Summerson, John. "Premises Coming Down." *Listener* 17 (425) (3 March 1937): 390–393.

Summerson, John. "Rebuilding the City." *Listener* 32 (815) (24 August 1944): 216.

Summerson, John. "The Romantic Element in Architecture." *Architectural Design and Construction* 2 (March 1932): 228

Summerson, John. "Royal Gold Medal Award: Sir John Summerson's Tribute to Nikolaus Pevsner." *Architect's Journal* 145:26 (28 June 1967): 1523–1524.

Summerson, John. "Ruins and the Future." Broadcast travelogue, 30 March 1941. Sir John Summerson Papers, SuJ/10/1. Transcript RIBA Collections.

Summerson, John. "Sir Edwin Lutyens: 1869–1944." *Listener* 31 (783) (13 January 1944): 46.

Summerson, John. *The Unromantic Castle and Other Essays*. New York: Thames and Hudson, 1990.

Summerson, John. "The Villa Vernacular." *Listener* 22 (550) (27 July 1939): 188–190.

Summerson, John, and Reginald Blomfield. "Points from Letter: British Architecture at the Royal Academy." *Listener* 17 (420) (27 January 1937):178, 17 (422) (10 February 1937): 278, and 17 (424) (24 February 1937): 374.

Swenarton, Mark. *Artisans and Architects: The Ruskinian Tradition in Architectural Thought*. New York: St. Martin's Press, 1988.

Thomas, Ivor. "Housing the Working Classes." *Listener* 15 (370) (12 February 1936): 307–309.

Thompson, F. M. L. *Land and Society in Britain, 1700–1914*. Manchester: Manchester University Press, 1996.

Tomlinson, Harold. "The New Spirit in Design." *Listener* 3 (70) (14 May 1930): 839–840.
Towndrow, Frederic. "The Revolution in Architecture." *Listener* 1 (8) (6 March 1929): 281–282.

Unwin, Raymond. "Architecture Symposium—A Summing-Up." *Listener* 10 (239) (9 August 1933): 213.
Unwin, Raymond. "Property and Prosperity." *Listener* 11 (280) (23 May 1934): 853.
Unwin, Raymond. "The Proposed National Housing Board." *Listener* 9:220 (29 March 1933): 473–475.
Unwin, Raymond, and Thomas Adams. "What London Might Be." *Listener* 6 (133), Supplement 15 (29 July 1931): i–xii.
Unwin, Raymond, and R. A. Livett. "Towards a Healthy Social Life." *Listener* 18 (462) (17 November 1937): 1069.
Urry, John. *The Tourist Gaze*. 2nd ed. London: Sage Publications, 2002.

van Eck, Caroline. "Artisan Mannerism: Seventeenth-Century Rhetorical Alternatives to Sir John Summerson's Formalist Approach." In Frank Salmon, ed., *Summerson and Hitchcock: Centenary Essays on Architectural Historiography*, 85–104. New Haven: Yale University Press, 2006.

Warschauer, Frank. "The Future of Opera on the Radio." In Anton Kaes, Martin Jay, and Edward Dimendberg, eds., *The Weimar Republic Sourcebook*, 607–609. Berkeley: University of California Press, 1994.
Watkin, David. *The Rise of Architectural History*. London: Architectural Press, 1980.
Webb, Maurice. "The Future of the Skyscraper." *Listener* 3 (71) (21 May 1930): 881.
Weber, Samuel. *Mass Mediauras: Form, Technics, Media*. Ed. Alan Cholodenko. Stanford: Stanford University Press, 1996.
"Week by Week." Editorial. *Listener* 16 (409) (11 November 1936): 890–891.
Weiss, Allen S., ed. *Experimental Sound and Radio*. Cambridge, Mass.: MIT Press, 2001.
Weiss, Allen S. *Phantasmic Radio*. Durham: Duke University Press, 1995.
Whitehead, Kate. *The Third Programme: A Literary History*. Oxford: Clarendon Press, 1989.
Williams, Raymond. *Culture and Society: 1780–1950*. New York: Colombia University Press, 1958.
Williams, Raymond. *The Long Revolution*. New York: Columbia University Press, 1961.
Williams, Valentine, and Sir Raymond Unwin. "The Future of Housing." *Listener* 20 (499) (4 August 1938): 240–242.
Williams-Ellis, Amabel. "Say It in Pictures." *Listener* 8 (202) (23 November 1932): 756.
Williams-Ellis, Clough. *Architect Errant*. London: Constable, 1971.
Williams-Ellis, Clough. "Architectural Appreciation." *Journal of the Royal Institute of British Architects* 51 (February 1944): 79–83.
Williams-Ellis, Clough. "Art for the People." *Listener* 17 (436) (19 May 1937): 974–976.
Williams-Ellis, Clough. "Fitness for Purpose." *Listener* 7 (164) (2 March 1932): 315.
Williams-Ellis, Clough. "Imaginary Interview with Sir Christopher Wren." *Listener* 29 (731) (14 January 1943): 43.
Williams-Ellis, Clough. "London Scenes: Hyde Park." *Listener* 15 (383) (13 March 1936): 906.
Williams-Ellis, Clough. "Putting Architecture in Its Place." *Listener* 10 (235) (12 July 1933): 71.
Williams-Ellis, Clough. "The Riddle of Charing Cross Bridge." *Listener* 2 (49) (18 December 1929): 813.
Williams-Ellis, Clough. "Vigour and Invention." *Listener* 8 (190) (31 August 1932): 315.
Williams-Ellis, Clough, and Amabel Strachey. *Pleasures of Architecture*. London: J. Cape, 1924.

Yates, Lucy. "Bright Ideas for Dull Houses." *Listener* 2 (25) (3 July 1929): 29.
Yerbury, F. R. "The Architecture of the Future." *Listener* 3 (53) (15 January 1930): 95–97.
Yerbury, F. R. S. "Experiments in Housing: Some Suggestions from Sweden." *Listener* 32 (817) (7 September 1944): 263.

INDEX

Aalto, Alvar, 47, 105
Abercrombie, Patrick, 4, 139, 145
Adams, Mary, 12
Addison Housing Act, 147
Adorno, Theodor W., 259
Adult Education broadcasts, 4, 12, 92, 100, 148–151, 219, 230. *See also* education: adult
Adventures in Architecture, 61, 101
advertising, 11, 70, 71, 219
advice literature, 34
aesthetic experience, 130
aesthetic production, 116
aesthetics, 89, 90, 95, 115–116, 121, 126, 131, 138, 210, 225, 264
Allport, Gordon W., 72
All Souls Church, London, 25, 27
Alma-Tadema, Lawrence, 111
Along the Roman Roads, 185, 188, 193
applied art, 31, 91–92, 95, 100, 115–116, 124, 230
appreciation, aesthetic, 51, 86, 89, 95, 109, 115, 116, 119, 125

appreciation, architectural, 50, 59, 61, 62, 103, 116, 119, 121, 124, 125, 126
appreciation, ordinary, 89, 130, 201, 229
Archigram, 258, 265
architect, 25, 35–39, 47, 51, 59, 62, 70, 72, 75, 90, 92, 100–105, 111, 119–121, 126, 130, 158, 163, 170, 204, 210, 213, 219, 231, 244, 248, 254, 268. *See also* journalism, architectural
  definition of, 8, 53, 66, 77, 105, 116, 221, 266, 268
  role of, 4, 53–55, 59, 68, 138
Architects and Technicians Organization, 113
Architectural Association, 92, 105
architectural history, 1, 58, 65, 77, 80, 105, 111, 125, 174, 204, 207, 208
Architectural Review, 25, 47, 111, 113, 121, 168
Architecture Club, 121
"Architecture in a Changing World," 38, 42
"Archive for Architecture, An," 58
Ariel and Prospero, 27
aristocracy. *See* social class
Arnold, Matthew, 91

art deco, 27
Art in a Changing World, 103
Art in Education, 126
"Artist and His Public, The," 94
Artist in the Witness Box, 87
Artists at Work, 47
art market, 38, 80, 267
arts and crafts movement, 76, 105, 115, 130–131, 137, 139, 179, 189, 220, 226, 248
Arts Council, 50
Ashbee, Charles Robert, 59, 130–138, 162–164, 180
Ashmole, Bernard, 105, 175
Ashmolean Museum, 11, 92
Atkinson, Robert, 53, 219
Auden, W. H., 47
autonomy, disciplinary, 39, 265, 269
autonomy, of art, 94, 105, 115–116, 130
autonomy, of BBC, 17, 159–160

Bachelard, Gaston, 268
"Back to the Railway Carriage," 195, 202
Baillie Scott, M. H., 4, 67, 248
Baldwin, Stanley, 182
Barton, J. E., 52–53, 89, 103, 116–117, 229, 250
Baťa, Tomáš, 185
Bates, Sir Richard Dawson, 231
Bath, 77, 139, 213
Baudrillard, Jean, 265–266, 268
BBC Written Archives, Caversham Park, 18
Beaux-Arts, 121, 174, 221
Belfast, 231, 233, 237
Benjamin, Walter, 29, 86, 223, 256
Bertram, Anthony, 34, 55, 105, 111, 225–226, 229, 250, 251, 256–257, 259
Bethnal Green, 231, 240
Betjeman, John
  broadcasts, 4, 8, 33, 75, 204, 263–264
  career as critic and broadcaster, 77, 101, 168, 170, 174, 194–196, 215
  on preservation, 75, 174, 177–179, 183, 194–204, 213
  publications and broadcasts, 7, 47, 203, 213
  as tourist, 198–200, 202

Beveridge, Sir William, 47
Blease, Lyon, 164
Blenheim Palace, 207–210
Blomfield, Reginald, 4, 66–67, 105, 111, 113, 178, 208, 235, 254
Bloomsbury, 91
Blunt, Anthony, 94
Board of Education, 11
board of governors, BBC, 14, 159
"Bombed Architecture in the West," 211
Boult, Sir Adrian, 91
Boumphrey, Geoffrey Maxwell
  biography, 167–168
  broadcasting as civic service, 73, 162
  as design critic, 7, 33, 47, 55, 59, 75, 174, 183, 185
  on flats and modern dwelling, 139–149, 164, 177, 244–248, 251
  as modernist, 90, 109, 111, 125, 174, 178
  travel guides and national heritage, 148, 168, 177, 179, 185–193, 198, 200, 204, 264–265
Bourdieu, Pierre, 8
Bournemouth, 194
Breidden hills, 168, 192
Breuer, Marcel, 77
Bridgnorth Castle, 186
Bristol, 89, 103, 139, 170, 194, 196
Broadcasting House, 19–29, 47, 100, 157, 244
Buckingham Palace, 100
Builder, 121
built environment, 2, 4, 7–8, 18, 29, 33, 41, 43–44, 66, 95, 100, 116, 128, 165, 174, 215, 230
Bulley, Margaret H., 95
Burt, Cyril, 42, 87
Bushell, Sydney N., 55
Byron, George Gordon, Lord, 170–174
Byron, Robert, 208

Cahn, Sir Julien, 172
"Can Flats Solve the Housing Problem?," 149
Cantril, Hadley, 71–72
Cardiff, David, 41, 158–160
Carrington, Noel, 101, 183–184

Casson, Stanley, 47, 61, 91–94, 175
Castle Ashby, 207–210
"Castles of Scotland," 101
censorship, 17, 41, 159, 165, 251
Central Council for Schools Broadcasting, 150
Chermayeff, Serge, 34, 101, 105
Children's Hour, 101
Chipping Campden, 131
"Christian Tradition in Architecture," 101
Churchill, Winston, 42, 220
CIAM (Congrès internationaux d'architecture modern, International Congress of Modern Architecture), 4, 144, 240, 247
citizenship, 9, 14, 16, 66, 84, 126–127, 131, 161, 163, 179, 188, 194, 215, 238, 240, 243
city, 1, 25, 58, 67, 77, 100, 107, 139, 141, 144, 148, 151, 175, 178, 184, 189, 194, 196, 198, 219–223, 233–242, 250, 253, 256, 258, 263
Clark, Edward, 12
Coates, Wells, 4, 22, 25, 67–68, 72, 77, 106, 219, 244–251
cold war, 264–265
"Coming Home, or England Revisited," 195
commodification, 33–34, 38
communism, 2, 9, 12, 17, 179, 264
Compton Wynyates, 175, 208, 211
Condover Hall, 208, 210–211
Connell, Amyas, 4, 34, 66, 101, 111, 178
conservatism, 136, 157
  Conservative Party, 16–17, 121, 180, 182, 223
consumerism, 12
consumers, 34, 44, 73, 80, 92, 113, 220, 225–226, 229, 267
Cornish, Vaughan, 178
corn subsidies, 75
Cornwall, 201, 203
cottage, 137, 142–144, 147, 164, 194
Cottonian library, 207
Council for Adult Education, 103
Council for Education in Appreciation of Physical Environment, 50

Council for the Preservation of Rural England, 50, 121, 131, 138
country house, 121, 170, 181, 204–215, 248, 251
countryside, 42, 130, 131, 136, 138, 144–145, 164, 168, 175, 189–191
  country estates, 4, 121, 144, 181, 204–215, 250–251
  modernization of, 59, 178–179, 180–184, 188, 192, 202, 242
  preservation of, 136, 138, 144–145, 177–178, 183
  radiophonic construction of, 101, 185–189, 194–196, 223
county guides, 192
cultural legitimacy, 89
cultural production, 70, 79–80, 116, 130, 219, 251, 258, 266–267
culture of listening, 2, 40, 44, 94, 126, 139, 153, 167, 230, 259

Da Ponte, Lorenzo, 84
death duties, 75, 134, 182
debates, on architecture and arts, 8, 31, 33, 66, 79, 96, 139, 147, 149, 164, 208, 215, 221, 230, 254, 263
dehumanization, 142, 145
democracy, 2, 10, 11, 14, 16, 76–77, 115–116, 125, 127, 134, 136–137, 158, 161–162, 164, 219, 216
democratic culture, 14, 116
Denby, Elizabeth, 73, 219, 266
design, 4, 25, 34, 38, 40, 46–47, 49, 51, 55, 58–62, 65, 68–70, 73, 76, 79, 87, 101, 109, 115, 124–125, 128, 139, 168, 220–231, 238, 240, 243–247, 250–251, 257–259, 267, 268
  of Broadcasting House, 20, 22, 25
  contemporary, 16, 33, 66, 105, 121, 229, 258
  good design, 7, 52, 53, 87, 230, 258, 265
  industrial design, 31, 105, 115, 229
  practice, 40, 42–43, 66, 207
  urban design, 221
Design and Industries Association (DIA), 34, 220, 225, 231, 233

designers, 4, 20, 22, 44, 47, 50–51, 53, 62, 66, 70, 72, 79, 94, 105, 107, 113, 220, 226, 230, 240, 247, 258
Design in Modern Life, 58, 219–220, 241
Dobson, Frank, 92
do-it-yourself, 16
domesticity, 9–10, 16, 49, 84, 96, 117, 153, 230, 243, 247–248, 256, 261
Donald, Dorothy, 93
Dower, J., 55
Down River, 168, 185, 193
Duchamp, Marcel, 258
Duncan, R. A., 66
dwelling, 68, 244, 247, 251, 256–257
  minimal, 247

economy, 4, 16, 47, 75, 111, 126, 181, 191, 198, 257
educated classes. *See* social class
education
  adult, 4, 11–12, 70, 92, 100, 103, 148–151, 219, 230
  architectural, 50–51, 66, 103, 113
  children's, 4
  cultural, 7, 12, 70, 86, 96, 179, 269
  home as site of, 244–261
  public, 11, 52, 115, 161–162, 208, 261, 264
  radio as instrument of, 10–16, 46, 148–151, 265
  reform, 151
  schools, 93, 96, 119, 125–126, 127, 130, 220, 230
  wireless classroom, 46, 59
  wireless university, 14, 225, 229
Edwardian era, 17, 37, 62, 106, 115, 177, 223
eighteenth century, 76, 101, 138, 188, 192, 210, 225, 241–242, 250
Eisenstein, Elizabeth, 71
electronic communication, 2, 11, 18–19, 22, 46, 191, 238, 248, 265–266
Eliot, T. S., 47
Emberton, Joseph, 67
Etchells, Frederick, 90, 96
event, 2, 9, 52, 84, 151, 185, 203, 208, 213

everyday life, 4, 8, 14, 16, 34, 46, 66, 86, 91, 105, 106, 125, 196, 202–203, 225, 230, 261, 264
everyday space, 217, 221, 225, 258
Exeter, 194
exhibitions, 4, 43–46, 66, 70, 83, 94, 101, 105, 131, 181, 231, 240, 253, 258

Fallingwater, 253
Famous Midlands Houses, 172, 208
fascism, 2, 9, 12, 14, 18, 148, 240, 264
fine arts, 31, 91, 100, 105, 230
"fitness for purpose," 107, 259
flats, 55, 139–149, 168, 177, 181, 241, 243–244, 253
Fleet Street, 11, 58
Fletcher, Sir Banister, 61, 101
Forster, Edward Morgan, 175
Fourth Reform Act of 1918, 127
Fry, Maxwell, 4, 42, 59, 67, 73, 100, 106, 109, 219, 230–241, 251, 253
Fry, Roger, 89, 230
functionalism, 67–68, 76, 94–95, 107–109
Furlong, George, 126

garden cities, 139–141, 144, 178, 189, 240–242, 253
gardening, 16, 41, 131, 137, 241
Geddes, Patrick, 131, 240
Georgian era, 20, 168, 177, 210
Georgian Group, 174, 178
Georgian towns, 174, 184, 196
Gielgud, Val, 12
Gill, Eric, 47, 51, 84, 92
Gladstone, William Ewart, 9–10, 14, 180
glass painting, 128
Gloag, John, 7, 34, 47, 53, 58, 72, 77, 87, 100, 105, 217–221, 223, 229, 241, 250, 254, 256, 265
Goodhart-Rendel, Harry Stuart, 16, 37–39, 42–43, 50, 76–77, 80, 101, 103, 105, 207, 235
Grand Tour, 200, 202
Great Depression, 44, 50, 53, 181
Green, W. Curtis, 67

Grigson, Geoffrey, 91, 175
Gropius, Walter, 47, 105, 240, 251
Guardian, Manchester, 46, 90, 94

Hadrian's Wall, 185, 188
Halliday, Edward, 87, 92
Harcourt, Sir William Vernon, 182
Hastings, Hubert de Cronin, 49
Haughton Hall, 208
Hays, K. Michael, 1
Health Ministry, 100
hearing (listening), 18–19, 31, 34, 71–72, 81, 84, 86, 94, 121, 149, 153, 203
hearth, 2, 9, 14, 17, 137, 248, 256
heritage, national, 2, 16, 18, 33, 58, 76, 80, 163, 174, 177–180, 182, 188, 193, 198, 204, 213, 254
Hinks, Roger, 40
Holden, Charles, 67, 107
Holme Lacy, 208
Holmes, Sir Charles, 87, 126
house
    architect- or developer-built, 35, 38, 53, 61, 66, 68, 72–76, 109–113
    functional or aesthetic problems, 55, 58, 100–101, 211
    function of, 244
    with gardens, 139, 142–150, 192, 194–195, 210
    mass-produced, 73–76, 101, 243–244
    meaning of, 125, 211
    modern, 243, 247–259
    old, 189, 192, 196, 201, 210–211
    row houses, 186, 194
    as site of wireless audition, 2, 11, 83–87, 243–259
    stately, 131, 136–137, 170, 172, 174, 181, 206–213
household, 7, 58, 83, 101, 117, 185
housekeeping, 2, 7, 16, 127, 141, 144, 162, 231
housewives, 11, 151, 186
housing, 31, 46, 51, 53–55, 72, 75–76, 90, 113–115, 139–149, 177, 185, 219, 237–238, 241, 247, 256, 264

"Housing and Social Conditions in Sweden," 75
Housing Centre, 147
Hughes, J. C. Pennethorne, 194
Hugo, Victor, 1
humanism, 20, 22, 27, 161, 164, 203, 210
humanitarian, 158
humanity, 10, 35, 91, 125, 127, 142, 247, 265

Ideal Home exhibition, 34, 66, 231
imagination, 7, 8, 10, 19, 22, 40, 53, 117, 128, 137, 167, 174, 211, 213, 226, 230
Independent Group, 265
individual freedom, 16, 237
individualism, 9, 138, 194, 229, 238, 242, 250
individuality, 144, 237, 250–251
industrial production, 18, 219
interwar period, 1, 16,18, 39, 77, 117, 127, 159, 177, 179, 220, 241
Ireland, 126, 175, 185, 231–237, 243

Jackson, Holbrook, 226, 229
Joad, Doreen, 55, 87
Jones, Inigo, 101
journalism, architectural, 46–50, 52, 68–70, 83, 151, 250

Keay, L. H., 53
Kentchurch Court, 208, 210
Keynes, John Maynard, 42
Knole, 131
knowledge, 2, 9, 39, 53, 58, 61, 65, 77, 90, 92, 109, 113, 116, 124–126, 130, 153, 160–162, 164, 175, 191, 201–202, 219, 223, 233, 257, 265

Labour Party, 16–17, 121, 127, 137, 147, 158, 179, 181–185, 211
ladies' clubs, 150
laissez-faire, 9, 12, 17
Lambert, Richard, 12, 116, 127, 130, 138, 151, 233
Lancaster, Osbert, 47
landscape, 4, 33, 92, 126, 136, 144, 149, 174, 179–181, 185, 189–190, 194–195, 200, 202, 235

Lane, Allen, 103
Langham Street, 25
Le Corbusier, 38, 47, 77, 96, 103–105, 144, 148, 200, 233, 240, 251, 253, 256–257
Leighton, Frederic, 1st Baron Leighton, 111
Lent, 101
Lethaby, William, 248
liberalism
   BBC executives and broadcasters and, 14, 55, 175, 181, 220, 223, 240, 264
   interwar Gladstonian, 9–10, 12, 16, 39, 77, 127, 139, 147, 159, 164, 181, 183
   Liberal Party, 16, 127, 180, 182, 223, 264
   radio as instrument of, 9, 12, 16–17, 31, 127, 163
   value of architectural and cultural programs to, 117, 163–164, 183
   Victorian, 131, 134, 137, 180
Lincoln, 189
Lindsay, Ian Gordon, 101
Listener, 12, 41, 51, 87, 95, 101, 127, 130, 134, 138, 151, 208, 233, 235, 265
listening-end work, 150
listening groups, formal, 31, 149–151, 233
listening in, 71
Liverpool, 53, 247
local county council, 4, 12, 59, 139, 149, 150–151, 162, 170, 223, 238
London Transport, 58, 95, 217, 220
Looking for the Town of Tomorrow, 148, 185
Lubetkin, Berthold, 72, 113
Ludwig, Margaret, 157, 265
Luker, Norman, 149
Lutyens, Sir Edwin Landseer, 4, 37, 84, 235
Lyon, Robert, 89

MacColl, Evan, 179
machine, 61, 72–73, 76, 136, 184, 237–238, 243, 251, 256–257
Manchester, 100, 139, 145, 170, 179
Mandler, Peter, 9, 182
manners, 9, 52, 138, 163–164, 188, 219, 248
Marble Arch, 65

market
   commercial (mass), 11, 17, 34, 50, 68, 70–72, 76–77, 79–80, 94–95, 147, 151, 158, 161, 167, 181–183, 219, 221, 223, 226, 229–230, 242
   of ideas, 10
   luxury, 4
   market towns, 191
   of symbolic goods, 34, 38, 40, 68, 70–72, 79–80, 267
Marshall, Howard, 100
Marxism, 210–211, 268
mass communication, 11, 86, 233
mass consumption, 34, 264
mass culture, 33, 37–38, 79, 198, 248
mass media, 1, 8, 37, 39, 94, 266–267
mass production, 29, 34, 38, 53, 137, 220, 225, 229, 247, 258, 264
Matheson, Hilda, 11–12, 14, 59, 91, 103, 153
Matless, David, 178
Maufe, Edward, 22, 25
McGrath, Raymond, 101
McKibbin, Ross, 44, 161
mechanical
   era, 18, 213, 221
   expression, 124, 126, 137, 240, 243, 253, 265
   fallacy, 124
   properties of radio, 22, 243, 253, 265
   reproduction, 113, 167, 213
   services, 238
memory, 1, 18, 71, 80, 168, 188, 207, 243
Mendelsohn, Erich, 77
Men Talking, 17
middle class. *See* social class
Midlands, 131, 174–175, 186, 208, 211
Mies van der Rohe, Ludwig, 77
Mill, John Stuart, 10, 14
misrepresentation, 160
modern architecture, 31, 65–67, 70, 111–116, 144, 226, 231
Modern Architecture Research Group (MARS Group), 91, 113, 178, 231, 240
modernism, 2, 7, 34, 38, 61, 66, 68, 76–77, 103–111, 109–116, 148, 175–177

modernity, 29, 33, 47, 111, 113, 116, 177, 178, 215, 248
monopoly, BBC's, 2, 11, 17, 119–121, 158, 164
morality, 9–10, 16, 47, 130, 142, 160–162, 189, 215, 223, 240, 253, 259, 268–269
Morris, William, 34, 179, 220, 226, 229
Morrison, Herbert, 101
Mowl, Timothy, 203
museum, 2, 34, 44, 46, 70, 77, 83–85, 89, 94–95, 181, 189, 195, 198, 210, 225, 254, 257
Muthesius, Hermann, 248, 250
mystification, 268

Nash, John, 25–27, 211
Nash, Paul, 92
"Nash's Terraces in Regent's Park," 211
nation, 2, 9, 10, 14, 16–17, 25, 33, 44–46, 49, 50, 52, 58, 67, 76, 87, 92, 95, 111, 124, 127, 130, 138, 144, 150, 164, 188, 213, 230, 233, 259
National Building Records, 58
National Council of Ramblers' Federations, 178
National Gallery of Ireland, 126
nationalization, 16, 181, 185
National Portrait Gallery, 126
National Programme, 161, 217
National Trust, 138, 179, 181
neo-Georgian tradition, 20, 240
New Statesman, 70
Newstead Abbey, 170–175, 181, 208, 211
Newton, Eric, 90, 94, 103
nineteenth century
  attitudes, 9, 14
  cultural institutions, 8
  industrialization, 18–19, 34, 46, 67, 83, 91, 101, 111, 127, 170, 179, 184, 200, 229, 237, 240
Northamptonshire, 206
Nottingham, 172

Office of Works, 185
Olmo, Carlo, 213–215
Ong, Walter, 71, 81
On the Map, 213

oral communication, 18, 22, 33–34, 44, 49, 71–72, 75, 81, 90–91, 148, 167, 191–192, 198, 201, 203, 265
oral travelogue, 33–34, 75, 148, 167, 191, 198, 201, 265
oratory, 38, 40, 49, 71, 86, 195, 263, 264
organicism, 14, 58, 137, 203, 220–221, 238, 240, 243, 253, 265, 266
Other People's Houses, 100
Owen, Thomas, 211
Ozenfant, Amédée, 47

Pakington, Humphrey, 62, 65, 105
pamphlets, BBC, 4, 44, 101, 103, 139, 142, 145, 149–151, 258, 265
Parker, Barry, 241
Parliament, 17, 127, 131, 139, 157–159, 177, 186
patriotism, 76, 131, 200
patronage, 16, 34, 39, 42–43, 49–50, 52, 162, 210, 220
Pedersen, Susan, 9
Penguin Books, 44, 62, 103
perception, 2, 16, 19, 29, 76–77, 80, 86–87, 91, 95, 109
  aesthetic, 87, 91
  ordinary, 86–87
Pevsner, Nikolaus, 7–8, 231
philistinism, 162
physical environment, 16, 81, 91, 96
Piccadilly Circus, 184
Pick, Frank, 34, 58, 72, 95, 101, 113, 217–231, 241, 254, 257–258, 265
picturesque, 27, 113, 131, 141, 168, 189, 196, 204, 207, 258, 264
Pitt, Percy, 91
planning, town, 4, 10, 16–17, 46–47, 51, 53, 58, 61, 72, 75, 115, 121, 125, 139, 144, 148, 178, 185, 189, 211, 213, 217, 221, 223, 231, 233, 235, 237–238, 240–243, 258–259, 264
Pleasures of Architecture, 119, 121, 124, 127
Plymouth, 58, 61, 194, 211
"Plymouth Rebuilding Plan," 211
Portland Place, 25

Portway, 185, 189
posthumanism, 27
Postmaster General, 11, 158
postwar period, 47, 76, 181, 182, 213, 241
prefabrication, 75–76
preservationism, 178–185
   activism for, 17, 33, 174, 177
   BBC and, 182–183, 194
   preservation societies, 34, 43, 178, 183
   radio and, 33, 58–59, 75, 130–131, 138, 144, 162, 178, 264
   strategies, 4, 115, 144, 178, 196
   travelogues and, 75, 101, 115, 121, 168, 175–177, 188, 196, 203–206
prewar period, 164, 241, 264
Price, Cedric, 265
print
   culture, 248
   medium of, 8, 18, 71, 73, 151, 167, 191, 203, 238
   printed material, 4, 127–128, 192, 230, 233
   prints, 38, 81, 101
privacy, 55, 142, 258, 261
private property, 16, 53, 100, 125, 127, 134, 136–137, 178, 180–181, 184, 189
Program Control Board, 41
proletarianization of culture, 17
propaganda, 12, 14, 42–43, 70–71, 185
public, 7–8, 10–11, 17, 33, 38, 40, 44, 49, 59, 71, 76–79, 80, 83–84, 86, 91, 93–94, 107, 109, 115, 130, 136, 138, 148–149, 151–153, 160, 162, 164, 172, 179–180, 183, 202, 213, 221, 261. *See also* education: public
   and art, 79–80, 95, 164, 188
   broadcasting and, 9, 11, 14, 40, 52, 71, 84, 86, 96, 157, 162
   opinion and behavior, 38, 40, 68, 75, 130, 139, 147–148, 153, 157–159, 161, 177, 181, 183, 261
   as patron, 4, 52, 101, 188
public art and buildings, 40, 80, 86, 94, 96, 100, 109, 115, 138, 142, 151, 164, 180–181, 219, 229
publications, 7, 12, 40–41, 44, 49, 70, 230
public finance, 4, 180, 182

Public Health Act of 1875, 223
public institutions, 14, 31, 153, 217, 244
public interest, 44, 59, 136–137, 162, 164
publicity, 2, 34, 37, 39, 44, 71, 151, 181, 221
   architecture and, 31, 43, 50, 58
public obligation, 9, 10, 68, 127, 136, 188
public service, 2, 8, 11–12, 34, 52, 68, 77, 79, 119, 121, 163–164, 178, 264
public space, 1, 75, 84, 96, 223, 248, 251, 258
Purpose and Admiration, 103

"Radiant City," 144, 148
Read, Herbert, 7, 58, 87, 94–95, 107, 126, 157, 231, 251–253, 256, 265
Reading (city), 62, 184
reading
   act of, 71, 81, 126, 153, 175, 189–191, 198, 206, 208, 225, 241, 248
   reading material, 151
   space of, 20, 31, 34, 58, 142, 150–151, 196, 201, 207
Registration Act, 42, 79
Reith, John, 9–12, 17, 20, 41–42, 50, 70, 79, 90, 116, 119, 126, 130, 153, 157–158, 160–162, 251, 259, 261
Religious Broadcasts, Department of, 101
representation, 19, 27, 33, 37–39, 46, 66, 79, 83, 183, 266–268
RIBA Journal, 121
Ricardo, Halsey, 126, 130, 163
Richards, James Maude, 4, 8, 68, 70, 101, 111
Richardson, Albert Edward, 4, 67, 96, 101
Rivera, Diego, 94
Robertson, Howard, 20, 22, 65, 72, 101
Robie House, 253
Rothenstein, Sir William, 125–126
Royal Academy of Art, 126
Royal Institute of British Architects (RIBA), 16, 18, 25, 37–39, 42–43, 50–51, 66, 68, 70, 84, 121, 207, 231
"Ruins and the Future," 211
rural electrification, 75
Rushton Hall, 206, 208
Ruskin, John, 179, 220, 229

Sadler, Michael, 126
Salmon, Christopher, 91, 121, 130, 149
Samson, Miles David, 202
Sapperton, 186
satellite town, 240–241
Savoy Hill, 119, 121, 157
Scannell, Paddy, 41, 158–160
Schirokauer, Arno, 84
Schoenberg, Arnold, 50
School Broadcasts, 11, 150–151
schoolchildren, 31, 61, 75, 100–101, 125–126, 131, 137–138, 141–142, 144, 150–151, 163, 167, 231, 244, 263
Scilly, Isles of, 201
self-display, 243, 247
self-governance, 10–11
sentimentalism, 76, 182–183
sentimentality, 73, 200–201, 256
Shand, Morton, 47, 77, 109
Shaw, Norman, 101, 248
Sheffield, 139, 184
Shell Guides, 168, 203
shopping, 7, 221, 224, 230
Shrewsbury, 168, 192
Siepmann, Charles, 12, 86, 92–93, 220
sight, 18, 89–90
Simon, Sir Ernest Darwin, 139–142, 147, 162, 164
simulacra, 263, 265, 266
simulations, 264, 265
slum, 100, 145, 240, 242
sociability, 248
social class, 9, 14, 111, 131, 149, 158, 164, 188, 198, 213, 244, 247, 261, 267–269
   aristocracy, 33, 37, 50, 86, 131–136, 157, 162, 164, 178–180, 182, 186, 242
   class interests, 10, 17
   class relations, 10, 127, 229, 259, 268
   educated and middle, 11, 17, 34, 37, 144, 147, 150–151, 157, 161, 164, 178, 180, 182, 200, 202, 210, 250, 269
   ruling, 14, 47
   working, 17, 55, 127, 131, 134, 139–147, 150, 157–158, 178, 182–183, 231, 240
socialism, 14, 17, 134–136, 147, 179–181, 183, 220, 242

social reform, 127, 150, 164, 180
Society for the Preservation of Ancient Buildings, 183
Somerville, Mary, 11
sound, 49, 121
   insulation of, 25
   qualities of, 18, 34, 72–73, 138, 153, 157, 203, 265
   sound bites and montages, 16, 18, 20, 43, 137, 196, 231
   sound effects, 79, 139, 157, 192
   sound factory, 20, 25, 167, 243
Spectator, 46, 119, 121, 139
speech, broadcast, 2, 9, 17, 29, 35–40, 46, 52, 62, 66, 72, 75, 77, 203, 208
Squire, J. C., 121
standardization, 70, 138, 148, 229, 251
Stobart, John Clarke, 11, 14, 130
Stocking Green Close, 188
storytelling, 2, 33, 75, 150, 167, 191, 264
Strachey, Amabel, 59, 62, 119–127, 162, 164
street, 11, 25, 47, 58, 66, 145, 184, 217, 223–225
suburb, 7, 61, 113, 139, 145–147, 179, 182, 185, 189, 194–196, 241
Summerson, John
   biography and thinking, 41, 51–52, 111, 170, 174, 177–179
   broadcasts on architecture, 4, 8, 33, 51, 53, 58, 76, 80, 96, 100–101, 105, 107, 153, 264
   oral travelogues, 75, 170, 172, 181, 183, 204–215, 265
   publications, 7
Swindon, 194
Sykes, Sir Frederick, 47, 101
symbolic, 7, 8, 11, 16, 18, 22–23, 26, 29, 31, 37, 39–40, 42, 52, 72, 80, 83, 91

Talks, Department of, 11, 12, 20, 43, 62, 70, 86, 91–92, 103, 105, 121, 127, 130, 149, 150–151, 153, 157, 160, 231, 240, 254
taste, 9, 76, 87, 90–95, 100–101, 109, 113, 123–124, 126, 130, 161–164, 177, 178, 183, 186, 192, 194, 198, 202, 210, 219, 231, 242, 247–248, 250–251, 253, 261, 263
taxation, 4, 136, 180–181

Index   329

technology
　of broadcasting, 1, 2, 14, 19–20, 25, 33–34, 66, 193, 243, 259, 265
　of building, 243
　modern, 184, 203, 233, 251, 257, 259, 265
Times, London, 46, 121, 181
To-day and To-morrow in Architecture, 62, 66
Tomlinson, Harold, 65
totalitarian regimes, 12
tourism, 4, 33, 38–39, 83, 168, 178, 183, 198, 202, 204, 208, 213
town, 4, 33, 47, 51, 53, 58–59, 61, 67, 72, 84, 90, 101, 115, 125, 131, 136, 139, 145–148, 168–170, 174–175, 179, 181, 184–186, 189–192, 194–204, 213–215, 221–223, 230, 242, 251, 264. *See also* planning, town
Town and Country Planning Act of 1932, 185, 223
Towndrow, Frederic, 53, 61–62, 67, 77, 101
Town Planning in Ireland, 231–235
Town Planning Review, 139
Town Tours, 170, 194–195, 202, 204
tradition, 240, 247–250
Travelers' Tales from Plymouth, 61
travel guides, 34, 167, 191
travelogues, oral, 33–34, 75, 101, 167–168, 174–177, 185, 188, 191–194, 198, 200–202, 204, 207–208, 263, 265
Tresham, Thomas, 206
Trotter, Dorothy, 20
twentieth century, 7, 8, 18–19, 34, 52, 76, 101, 111, 174, 179, 198, 225, 240, 242, 257, 261, 264, 267

"Ugliness Exhibition," 131, 134, 138, 162
Ulster, 185, 192, 237
"Ulster Holiday," 185
Underground Group, 220
underrepresentation, 160
unions, 17, 150, 157–159, 175
Unit One, 91
Unwin, Raymond, 4, 68, 101, 241
"Up to London," 195
urban space, 223
Urry, John, 202

utilitarianism, 27, 31, 87, 91, 109, 125, 254
utopianism, 241

Val Myer, George, 27
Vanbrugh, John, 207, 210
van Eck, Caroline, 210
Vernon Hill, 22
Victoria and Albert Museum, 18, 101
Victorian Society, 174
vision
　attributes of, 18, 265
　production of, 40, 46, 62, 71, 90, 202
voice
　in literature, 47
　radiophonic, 2, 4, 17, 19, 22, 25, 33, 38, 43, 71–72, 75, 103, 131, 137, 159, 163, 167, 170, 191–192, 203, 226, 230, 238, 240, 243, 258, 259, 263
Voysey, Charles, 248

Wacquant, Löic, 269
Warburg Institute, 210
Warschauer, Frank, 86
wartime, 1, 202
Waugh, Evelyn, 175
Webb, Phillip, 248
Weber, Samuel, 19, 39, 163
"Weekly Art Notes," 87
Weiss, Allen, 19
welfare, 182–183
　economy, 47
　housing, 264
　politics, 17, 33
　state, 16, 53, 75, 136
Welshpool, 168
West, Rebecca, 91, 175
West Country, 196
Western Men, 213
Whittaker, James, 254
"Why Bother about Art?," 93–94
Williams, Raymond, 9, 163
Williams, W. E., 61–62
Williams-Ellis, Clough, 53, 59, 62, 119–127, 131, 162, 164, 184
Wölfflin, Heinrich, 95

women
    audience and public, 10, 73, 100, 128, 131, 141, 144, 150, 153, 163, 202, 231, 241
    magazines for, 16, 34, 128
    middle-class, 157
    staff at BBC, 9, 11–12, 72, 119, 127, 161
    suffrage, 158
Women's Hour, 100
Wood, John, 213
Wood, Sinclair, 254
Worcester, 186, 192
word, spoken, 18, 41, 81, 151, 207
word, written, 17, 34, 43, 71
Workers Educational Association (WEA), 12, 46, 150
Working Men's Colleges, 34

work of art, 34, 38, 80, 83, 87, 92, 94, 96, 105–107, 126, 180, 220, 223, 226, 235, 258, 267–268
World War I, 2, 16, 50, 92, 93, 131, 179, 181, 240, 248
World War II, 17–18, 41, 44, 47, 58, 76, 81, 150, 153, 159, 189, 208, 211, 213
Wren, Christopher, 101, 207
Wright, Frank Lloyd, 253
Wythenshawe, 139, 142

Yerbury, F. S., 75, 76
Yorke, Francis Reginald Stevens, 4, 106, 111
Youth Hostels Association, 178

Zlín, 148, 185

women
    audience and public, 10, 73, 100, 128, 131, 141, 144, 150, 153, 163, 202, 231, 241
    magazines for, 16, 34, 128
    middle-class, 157
    staff at BBC, 9, 11–12, 72, 119, 127, 161
    suffrage, 158
Women's Hour, 100
Wood, John, 213
Wood, Sinclair, 254
Worcester, 186, 192
word, spoken, 18, 41, 81, 151, 207
word, written, 17, 34, 43, 71
Workers Educational Association (WEA), 12, 46, 150
Working Men's Colleges, 34

work of art, 34, 38, 80, 83, 87, 92, 94, 96, 105–107, 126, 180, 220, 223, 226, 235, 258, 267–268
World War I, 2, 16, 50, 92, 93, 131, 179, 181, 240, 248
World War II, 17–18, 41, 44, 47, 58, 76, 81, 150, 153, 159, 189, 208, 211, 213
Wren, Christopher, 101, 207
Wright, Frank Lloyd, 253
Wythenshawe, 139, 142

Yerbury, F. S., 75, 76
Yorke, Francis Reginald Stevens, 4, 106, 111
Youth Hostels Association, 178

Zlín, 148, 185